The Two Cultures Controversy

Ever since the scientist-turned-novelist C. P. Snow clashed with literary critic F. R. Leavis in the early 1960s, it has been a commonplace to lament that intellectual life is divided between "two cultures," the arts and the sciences. Yet why did a topic that had long been discussed inspire such ferocious controversy at this particular moment? This book answers that question by recasting the dispute as an *ideological* conflict between competing visions of Britain's past, present, and future. It then connects the controversy to simultaneous arguments about the mission of the university, the methodology of social history, the meaning of national "decline," and the fate of the former empire. By excavating the political stakes of the "two cultures" controversy, this book explains the workings of cultural politics during the 1960s more generally, while also revising the meaning of a term that continues to be evoked to this day.

GUY ORTOLANO is Assistant Professor of History at the University of Virginia.

C. P. Snow in 1963, the year of "The Two Cultures: A Second Look."
[Drawing by Juliet Pannett, reproduced with the kind permission of Denis Pannett.]

F. R. Leavis in 1961, the beginning of his retirement year. [Portrait by Peter Greenham, reproduced by permission of the Bridgeman Art Library, New York, and with the kind permission of the Master and Fellows of Downing College, Cambridge.]

The Two Cultures Controversy

Science, Literature and Cultural Politics in Postwar Britain

Guy Ortolano

University of Virginia

CAMBRIDGE
UNIVERSITY PRESS

CAMBRIDGE UNIVERSITY PRESS
Cambridge, New York, Melbourne, Madrid, Cape Town, Singapore,
São Paulo, Delhi

Cambridge University Press
The Edinburgh Building, Cambridge CB2 8RU, UK

Published in the United States of America by Cambridge University Press,
New York

www.cambridge.org
Information on this title: www.cambridge.org/9780521892049

First published 2009

Printed in the United Kingdom at the University Press, Cambridge

A catalogue record for this publication is available from the British Library

Library of Congress Cataloguing in Publication data
Ortolano, Guy.
  The two cultures controversy : science, literature and cultural politics
  in postwar Britain / Guy Ortolano.
     p.   cm.
  Includes bibliographical references and index.
  ISBN 978-0-521-89204-9 (hardback)
  1. Great Britain–Intellectual life–1945-   2. Snow, C. P. (Charles Percy),
  1905–1980. Two cultures and the scientific revolution.
  3. Leavis, F. R. (Frank Raymond), 1895–1978. Two cultures?
  4. Science and the humanities–Great Britain.
  5. Great Britain–Civilization–1945-   I. Title.
  DA566.4.O78 2008
  941.085′5–dc22   2008036974

ISBN 978-0-521-89204-9 hardback

Contents

Illustrations

Acknowledgments

If this book attends to the acrimony that occasionally characterizes intellectual life, I hope that it also attests to the importance of friends, colleagues, and institutions in making that life worthwhile. For their support of my own work I am grateful to the Department of History at Northwestern University; the Centre for the History of Science, Technology, and Medicine at Imperial College London; the Department of History at Washington University in St. Louis; the Society for the Humanities and the Department of Science & Technology Studies at Cornell University; and the Corcoran Department of History at the University of Virginia. Financial support has been generously provided by the Science in Human Culture Program, the British and Irish Studies Research Grant, the Evan Frankel Fellowship in the Humanities, and the Presidential Fellowship (all at Northwestern University), as well as the English Speaking Union, the Josephine De Kármán Foundation, the British Studies Program at the University of Texas, and the Society for the Humanities at Cornell University.

I have been assisted by archivists and librarians on both sides of the Atlantic, and am pleased to have the opportunity to thank them here: Pat Fox and the staff of the Harry Ransom Humanities Research Center at the University of Texas, Michael Bott at the Chatto and Windus archive at the University of Reading, Susan Knowles at the BBC Written Archives Centre in Caversham, Bill Noblett at the Cambridge University Library, and Teresa Sheppard at Cambridge University Press, as well as the staffs of the Houghton Library at Harvard University, the Royal Society in London, and the Gulbenkian Foundation in London. For providing access to papers in their possession, and for granting permission to publish the research that derives from those papers, I am grateful to the Master and Fellows of Churchill College, Cambridge; the Master and Fellows of Downing College, Cambridge; and the Master and Fellows of Emmanuel College, Cambridge. For their assistance in navigating these collections, I must particularly thank Joan Bullock-Anderson of Churchill College, Gemma Bentley (formerly) of Downing College, and the late

Janet Morris, who assisted me in my work at Emmanuel College in the autumn of 2001.

I have been assisted and encouraged by so many people who shared conversations, suggestions, insights, and hospitality that I cannot possibly thank them all here, but I do hope they know how appreciative I am. Each of these chapters, sometimes in article form, has benefited from readings by friends, colleagues, and scholars, some of whom might not even be fully aware of the roles they have played in shaping my thinking: T. H. Breen, John Brewer, John Bushnell, David Cannadine, Lorraine Daston, Dennis Dworkin, Jim Epstein, Mark Goldie, Richard Gooder, Derek Hirst, Rob Iliffe, William Lubenow, Marina MacKay, Peter Mandler, Jenny Mann, Anna-K. Mayer, Tim Parsons, Gayle Rogers, and Jeff Wallace. Various chapters have also been improved through discussions at the Centre for the History of Science, Technology, and Medicine at Imperial College London, the Public Affairs Residential College at Northwestern University, the Graduate Seminar at Northwestern University, the Klopsteg Lecture Series in Science and Human Culture at Northwestern University, the British Studies Seminar at the University of Texas, the History and Philosophy of Science Seminar at Washington University in St. Louis, the Society for the Humanities at Cornell University, the European History Colloquium at Cornell University, and the Science Studies Research Group at Cornell University. I am particularly grateful to those who have read the entire manuscript, in some cases more than once: Ken Alder, Howard Brick, David Edgerton, T. W. Heyck, Ahmet Karamustafa, Karen Mann, Alex Owen, Mark Pegg, and Kirk Willis. I hasten to add that the responsibility for any errors of fact, interpretation, or judgment is entirely my own.

An unanticipated pleasure in bringing this book to production has been my interactions with artists and estates regarding images for which they retain copyright. Thanks to John Partridge and the Churchill Archives Centre for permission to reprint the perspective of the Howell, Killick, and Partridge proposal for Churchill College, Cambridge; to Denis Pannett for permission to reprint the drawing of C. P. Snow by his mother, Juliet Pannett; and to the Bridgeman Art Library for permission to reprint Peter Greenham's portrait of F. R. Leavis. That portrait is also reproduced with the kind permission of the Master and Fellows of Downing College, Cambridge. I would also like to thank Ludmilla Jordanova of King's College London, Matthew Bailey of the National Portrait Gallery, and Mark Goldie and Barry Phipps of Churchill College for their assistance in locating these images. And finally, it has been a pleasure working with Cambridge University Press. The manuscript was much improved as a result of the scrutiny of the Press's reviewers, and I also want to thank Ethan Shagan for directing me to CUP, Linda Bree for her encouragement at a pivotal juncture, Paul Stevens and Jamie Hood for seeing the book through production, Sue Browning for editing the manuscript, and Michael Watson for his assistance at every step along the way.

A version of Chapter 4 appeared as "Human Science or a Human Face? Social History and the 'Two Cultures' Controversy," *Journal of British Studies* 43 (October 2004), pp. 484–505; I am grateful to the editors, and to the University of Chicago Press, for permission to reprint. Quotations from the papers of C. P. Snow are reproduced by permission of the Curtis Brown Group Ltd., London, on behalf of the Estate of C. P. Snow. Quotations from the correspondence of George Steiner are reproduced with his kind permission. References to papers at the Houghton Library are cited by permission of the Houghton Library, Harvard University. References to papers at the Harry Ransom Humanities Research Center are cited by permission of the HRHRC at the University of Texas. References to papers at the Cambridge University Library are cited by permission of the Syndics.

I would like to close by thanking five scholars in particular for their assistance and encouragement during the writing of this book. Kirk Willis introduced me to modern British history, and he generously read each of these chapters many times over. David Edgerton took an interest in this project at its inception, and his iconoclastic interpretations of twentieth-century history have shown me how seemingly familiar topics can be approached in innovative ways. Ken Alder helped me to see a book when I was still writing a paper, and nearly every idea in these pages has been turned over in conversation with him. Alex Owen led a seminar on historical theory and practice that indelibly shaped my thinking, and that informs these chapters in ways that neither of us would have expected. And my advisor, Bill Heyck: he will not necessarily agree with all of the interpretations in this book, but his generosity and guidance were essential to its development from beginning to end.

And lastly, to Jenny: portions of this book – those that don't deal with quarrelling, enmity, or recrimination – are dedicated to you, with love and thanks.

Introduction

History from the inside-out

"History . . . is made up of episodes," E. P. Thompson once wrote, "and if we cannot get inside these we cannot get inside history at all."[1] Thompson was emphasizing careful attention to particular episodes, attention that in turn has the potential to revise understandings of the larger histories into which those episodes fit. This book follows Thompson's injunction by attempting to "get inside" a notorious episode in British history: the "two cultures" controversy in the early 1960s. By examining the origins, content, and context of this controversy, I argue that what has previously been read as a *disciplinary* dispute about the arts and the sciences was actually an *ideological* conflict between competing visions of Britain's past, present, and future. This interpretation, in turn, revises our understandings of the other discussions that intersected with the controversy – and, from this perspective, the "two cultures" debate has the advantage of touching upon some of the most contentious issues in postwar British history. The expansion of the universities, the development of social history, anxieties about national decline, debates about the former empire, and the meaning of the 1960s all look different when their attendant claims for and against "science" are understood as parts of more ambitious arguments about the nature and direction of British – and human – society. On the broadest level, the "two cultures" controversy is a particular episode inside two larger histories: the relatively recent history of postwar Britain, and the longer tradition discussing the relationship between the arts and the sciences. Both of these histories, in fact, continue to be explained in terms that C. P. Snow employed in *The Two Cultures*: the history of postwar Britain as a story of decline, and discussions about the arts and the sciences as a conflict between two cultures. Rather than adopting these interpretations, this book revises them from the inside out – beginning with the "two cultures" controversy that was central to them both.

[1] E. P. Thompson, "The Peculiarities of the English," *Socialist Register, 1965*, ed. Ralph Miliband and John Saville (New York: Monthly Review Press, 1965), p. 338.

"So curious a storm"

The outline of the controversy is straightforward. On May 7, 1959, the scientist-turned-novelist C. P. Snow delivered the annual Rede Lecture at Cambridge University. Snow took as his subject the relationship between literary and scientific intellectuals, and his address was entitled *The Two Cultures and the Scientific Revolution.*[2] Snow argued that literary intellectuals had long harbored animus towards science, technology, industry, and progress, and that as a result they were obstructing economic development throughout Asia and Africa. His lecture generated widespread discussion until February 1962, when the literary critic F. R. Leavis challenged Snow's thesis in another Cambridge lecture, *Two Cultures? The Significance of C. P. Snow.*[3] Leavis did not engage with Snow's thesis so much as question his stature, depicting the esteem that Snow enjoyed as a telling indication of a misguided society. Leavis's broadside transformed the "two cultures debate" into the "Snow–Leavis controversy," but Snow refrained from replying for a year and a half. He eventually responded in the *Times Literary Supplement* (*TLS*) in October 1963, revisiting his thesis but only obliquely addressing Leavis.[4] During the next few years Leavis pressed his critique in a series of lectures at various universities: Harvard and Cornell in 1966, Wales in 1969, Bristol in 1970, and York in 1970 and 1971.[5] In 1970 Snow finally responded in another *TLS* essay, and shortly thereafter both Snow and Leavis collected and published their contributions to the "two cultures" debate.[6]

What this brisk outline does not convey is the polemical intensity that so charged the controversy. In his initial lecture, for instance, after expressing regret about the divisions between intellectuals, Snow swiftly proceeded to conflate Modernists with Nazis: he quoted a scientific

---

[2] C. P. Snow, *The Two Cultures and the Scientific Revolution* (Cambridge University Press, 1959).

[3] F. R. Leavis, "The Two Cultures? The Significance of C. P. Snow," *Spectator*, 9 March 1962, pp. 297–303, reprinted, with an essay by Michael Yudkin, as *Two Cultures? The Significance of C. P. Snow* (London: Chatto and Windus, 1962).

[4] C. P. Snow, "The Two Cultures: A Second Look," *Times Literary Supplement*, 25 October 1963, pp. 839–844, reprinted with the original lecture as *The Two Cultures: and A Second Look* (Cambridge University Press, 1964).

[5] F. R. Leavis, "Luddites? or, There Is Only One Culture"; " 'English', Unrest and Continuity"; " 'Literarism' versus 'Scientism': The Misconception and the Menace"; "Pluralism, Compassion and Social Hope"; "Elites, Oligarchies and an Educated Public"; all published, along with "Two Cultures? The Significance of Lord Snow," in *Nor Shall My Sword: Discourses on Pluralism, Compassion and Social Hope* (London: Chatto and Windus, 1972).

[6] C. P. Snow, "The Case of Leavis and the Serious Case," *Times Literary Supplement*, 9 July 1970, pp. 737–740, reprinted with related lectures and essays in *Public Affairs* (New York: Scribner's, 1971).

colleague with approval, "Didn't the influence of all they represent bring Auschwitz that much nearer?"[7] Leavis, for his part, began by questioning Snow's status as a novelist, and went on to express doubt as to whether he possessed a mind at all: "The intellectual nullity is what constitutes any difficulty there may be in dealing with Snow's panoptic pseudo-cogencies, his parade of a thesis: a mind to be argued with – that is not there."[8] The arguments that spiraled beyond Snow and Leavis were no less contentious, as charges and countercharges flooded the *Spectator*: "Leavis," declared one writer, "is the Himmler of Literature."[9] Small wonder that the American literary critic Lionel Trilling, observing the affair with dismay from New York, referred to it all as "so curious a storm."[10] Trilling was referring specifically to the uproar generated by Leavis's intervention, but he might well have said the same about the entire "two cultures" controversy.

From that day to this, commentators and historians have sought to explain the controversy. One approach has adopted the terms that Snow himself provided, depicting the argument as a clash between "two cultures," the arts and the sciences.[11] Snow argued that institutional positions combined with cultural prejudices to create a situation in which scientific and literary intellectuals would not – and increasingly could not – communicate with each other. He was speaking as a novelist, but had been trained as a scientist, and it became clear in his lecture that he favored the latter. Leavis declared this a slack formulation, but rather than demolishing Snow's argument, his polemic came to be read as its ultimate confirmation. This interpretation figured prominently in the *Spectator* after it published Leavis's text: for example, the physicist J. D. Bernal suggested, "If anything was needed to convince people of the truth and timeliness of the thesis of C. P. Snow's *Two Cultures*, it would be Dr. Leavis's lecture."[12] Aldous Huxley expressed this characterization clearly (if inelegantly) when he posited symmetry between the "scientism" of Snow and the "literarism" of Leavis.[13]

---

[7] Snow, *The Two Cultures*, p. 7.   [8] Leavis, *Two Cultures?*, p. 12.

[9] William Gerhardi, "Sir Charles Snow, Dr. F. R. Leavis, and the Two Cultures," *Spectator*, 16 March 1962, p. 329. The debate carried on for the remainder of March: see Paul Boytinck, *C. P. Snow: A Reference Guide* (Boston: Hall, 1980).

[10] Lionel Trilling, "Science, Literature, and Culture: A Comment on the Leavis-Snow Controversy," *Commentary*, June 1962, p. 461.

[11] Aldous Huxley, *Literature and Science* (London: Harper and Row, 1963); David K. Cornelius and Edwin St. Vincent, eds., *Cultures in Conflict: Perspectives on the Snow–Leavis Controversy* (Chicago: Scott Foresman and Co., 1964). See also many of the contributions catalogued in Boytinck, *C. P. Snow: A Reference Guide*.

[12] J. D. Bernal, "Letters," *Spectator*, 23 March 1962, p. 365.

[13] Huxley, *Literature and Science*, p. 1.

Upon closer examination, however, the arguments and participants in the controversy refuse to align along disciplinary lines. Snow, after all, had not practiced science for nearly a quarter of a century, and when he delivered the Rede Lecture his stature rested upon his work as a novelist. His lecture called for a revolution in scientific education – not as an end in itself, but as part of an ambitious program of domestic modernization and global industrialization. Leavis, for his part, spent his career attacking not physicists and biologists but writers and critics, and his Richmond Lecture directed its fire not against Snow's proposals for science but at his stature as a novelist. The arts-versus-sciences dichotomy similarly fails to explain the positions in the wider debate: two of Snow's most trenchant critics were the physical chemist Michael Polanyi and the biochemist Michael Yudkin, while his defenders included the novelist William Gerhardi and the poet Edith Sitwell.[14] Leavis received support from scientists who were eager to distance themselves from Snow, but the literary establishment generally welcomed Snow's argument: *Encounter* ran the Rede Lecture in two parts, the BBC broadcast a version that summer, and the *TLS* endorsed Snow over Leavis.[15] Similar examples could be multiplied many times over, and together they suggest that these arguments amounted to more than routine defenses of disciplinary interests. Or, to put the point more sharply, the arts-versus-sciences dichotomy does not begin to bear the explanatory burden that has been placed upon it.

A second, and more productive, approach has situated the controversy in a longer tradition discussing the relationship between the arts and the sciences.[16] The exchange between Thomas Huxley and Matthew Arnold in the 1880s figures as a touchstone in these accounts. Huxley endorsed scientific education in an address in Birmingham in 1880, to

---

[14] Michael Polanyi, "The Two Cultures," *Encounter*, September 1959, pp. 61–64; Michael Yudkin, "Sir Charles Snow's Rede Lecture," originally published in the *Cambridge Review* and reprinted in Leavis, *Two Cultures?*, pp. 33–45; Gerhardi, "Sir Charles Snow, Dr. F. R. Leavis, and the Two Cultures," pp. 329–331; Edith Sitwell, *ibid.*, p. 331.

[15] *Encounter* carried discussion of Snow's lecture in six of nine consecutive issues: June, July, August, September 1959, and January, February 1960. C. P. Snow, "The Imperatives of Educational Strategy," recorded 3 June 1959 and broadcast 8 September 1959, BBC WAC: MF T491; "A Question of Brains," *Times Literary Supplement*, 23 March 1962, p. 201.

[16] Trilling, "Science, Literature, and Culture;" Wolf Lepenies, *Between Literature and Science: The Rise of Sociology* (Cambridge University Press, 1988); Stefan Collini, "Introduction," in C. P. Snow, *The Two Cultures* (Cambridge University Press, 1993). On this tradition more generally, see David Hollinger, "The Knower and the Artificer," *American Quarterly* 39 (Spring 1987), pp. 37–55; Frank Miller Turner, *Contesting Cultural Authority: Essays in Victorian Intellectual Life* (Cambridge University Press, 1993).

which Arnold responded in defense of humane letters in the Rede Lecture of 1882.[17] The route between Arnold's Rede Lecture of 1882 and Snow's Rede Lecture of 1959 is marked by a series of landmarks: in 1928 the Cambridge Union debated the proposition that "the sciences are destroying the arts"; in 1946 the BBC called the division between scientific and humanistic thought "the challenge of our time"; and by 1956 the polymath Jacob Bronowski had repeatedly addressed the subject in lectures and in print.[18] These prominent discussions were connected by less celebrated commentaries, and in the years preceding Snow's Rede Lecture the subject was ubiquitous. Consider this pastiche of quotations from the *Listener* between 1953 and 1959:

If there is almost no contact between science and philosophy, there is naturally still less between science and the other faculties of arts. We all live in our watertight compartments . . . [W]e must as a first and necessary step do what we can to establish a two-way traffic between the scientists on the one hand and the non-scientists on the other . . . The scientist needs to know more of general culture and the historian requires a better grounding in science . . . But the dichotomy between science and humanities is a false one . . . A 'scientist' without any knowledge of the various arts, history, philosophy, etc., is as much an incomplete personality as a 'humanist' without knowledge of the basic ideas, concepts, and methods of science . . . Let us help to provide a force that will overcome any inertia that is delaying our scientists and students of the arts from going forward together into the untravelled world.[19]

From this perspective, the exchange between Snow and Leavis figures as another contribution in a long-running conversation.

Yet this explanation has limitations as well. After all, the very existence of this tradition begs the question of how so familiar a subject could have ignited so contentious a debate. Stefan Collini offers one answer to that question: "[I]n this kind of cultural civil war," he explains, "each fresh engagement is freighted with the weight of past defeats, past

---

[17] T. H. Huxley, "Science and Culture," *Science and Education: Essays* (New York: D. Appleton, 1896), pp. 134–159; Matthew Arnold, "Literature and Science," *The Complete Prose Works of Matthew Arnold*, ed. R. H. Super (Ann Arbor: University of Michigan Press, 1974), vol. X, pp. 53–73.

[18] Grace Wyndham-Goldie, *et al.*, *The Challenge of Our Time* (London: P. Marshall, 1948); Jacob Bronowski, *The Common Sense of Science* (Cambridge, Mass.: Harvard University Press, 1951); Bronowski, "Architecture as a Science and Architecture as an Art," *Royal Institute of British Architects Journal* 62 (March 1955), pp. 183–189; Bronowski, *Science and Human Values* (New York: Harper and Row, 1956). *The Common Sense of Science* was originally presented on the BBC's Third Programme in 1948, and *Science and Human Values* derived from a lecture series of 1953.

[19] All quotations derive from the *Listener* (in the order cited): 1 November 1956, p. 697; 19 November 1953, p. 846; 10 November 1955, p. 778; 21 November 1957, p. 845 (two quotations); 29 January 1959, p. 215.

atrocities; for this reason there is always more at stake than the ostensible cause of the current dispute."[20] But if the historian or commentator is not sufficiently attentive to this dynamic, and fails to attend to the differences as well as the similarities between iterations in this tradition, they risk imposing a common interpretation upon very different episodes: Huxley and Arnold argued about the relative position of science and literature in education, so Snow and Leavis must have argued about the relative position of science and literature in education – despite that awkward bit when Snow implicated Modernists with Auschwitz.[21] Moreover, once Snow and Leavis are understood to have been re-enacting an earlier performance, their exchange can be dismissed as little more than an unfortunate departure from the script. The historian Dominic Sandbrook, for instance, suggests that their argument "really only amounted to a rehash of [the] much more genteel debate conducted between Matthew Arnold and T. H. Huxley in the 1880s," while the literary scholar Alvin Kernan concludes, "Neither Snow nor Leavis . . . offered anything new to the long-standing and often-rehearsed argument between the poets and the philosophers."[22] As a result of their efforts to identify the longer tradition into which Snow and Leavis fit, such accounts neglect the content and context of their particular exchange. It is necessary, therefore, not only to situate the controversy within a longer tradition, but also to dislodge it where appropriate from the confines of that tradition.[23]

So the controversy was charged by disciplinary tensions, and it somehow fits into a longer tradition, yet neither explanation sufficiently accounts for the arguments and energies of this particular episode. The fact of personal differences between Snow and Leavis is similarly unhelpful: after all, they had coexisted peacefully in and around Cambridge for more than three decades, and they both later denied the

---

[20] Collini, "Introduction," p. xxxv.

[21] Thompson noted the "danger . . . that a model, even when flexibly employed, disposes one to look only at *certain* phenomena, to examine history for *conformities*, whereas it may be that the discarded evidence conceals new significances." "The Peculiarities of the English," p. 350. For further development of this point, see D. N. McCloskey, *If You're So Smart: The Narrative of Economic Expertise* (University of Chicago Press, 1990).

[22] Dominic Sandbrook, *White Heat: A History of Britain in the Swinging Sixties* (London: Little, Brown, 2006), p. 50; Alvin Kernan, *In Plato's Cave* (New Haven: Yale University Press, 1999), p. 110.

[23] For a forceful articulation of the case against the presumption of intellectual continuity over time, see Mark Gregory Pegg, *The Corruption of Angels: The Great Inquisition of 1245–1246* (Princeton University Press, 2001), especially Chapter 3, "Wedged between Catha and Cathay," pp. 15–19.

existence of any enmity between them prior to the debate.[24] Why, then, did this familiar topic inspire such ferocious controversy in the early 1960s? The answer to that question leads beyond personal antipathies or disciplinary rivalries, and into the cultural politics of postwar Britain.

Playing the stranger

This book offers a cultural history of the "two cultures" controversy. While it is informed by the work of social and intellectual historians, it resists the social historian's inclination to read the debate as an expression of conflict between social classes or institutional interests, as well as the intellectual historian's desire to identify genealogies of thinkers who grappled with related issues in different times or places.[25] Instead, by using the controversy to explore society and culture in postwar Britain, this book follows the approaches of cultural historians who seek to enter past cultures through those aspects that today seem unusual. In a classic account, for example, Robert Darnton takes the supposedly "hilarious" slaughter of a house full of cats as an opportunity to recover aspects of artisanal culture in Old Regime France. "When you realize that you are not getting something – a joke, a proverb, a ceremony – that is particularly meaningful to the natives," he explains, "you can see where to grasp a foreign system of meaning in order to unravel it."[26] Darnton might have added "a controversy" to his list, as Natalie Zemon Davis does when she suggests that "a remarkable dispute can sometimes uncover motivations and values that are lost in the welter of the everyday."[27] The exchange between Snow and Leavis was one such dispute, one that was charged by – and is revealing of – the context and culture in which it took place.[28]

---

[24] John Halperin, *C. P. Snow: An Oral Biography* (New York: St. Martin's Press, 1983), pp. 185–186; Ivar Alastair Watson, " 'The Distance Runner's Perfect Heart': Dr. Leavis in Spain," *Cambridge Review*, November 1995, p. 72.

[25] Roy Porter, "The Two Cultures Revisited," *Cambridge Review*, November 1994, pp. 74–80; Guy Ortolano, "Two Cultures, One University: The Institutional Origins of the 'Two Cultures' Controversy," *Albion* 34 (Winter 2002), pp. 606–624; Lepenies, *Between Literature and Science*.

[26] Robert Darnton, *The Great Cat Massacre, and Other Episodes in French Cultural History* (New York: Vintage, 1985), pp. 77–78; this example derives from Chapter 2, "Workers Revolt: The Great Cat Massacre of the Rue Saint-Séverin," pp. 75–104.

[27] Natalie Zemon Davis, *The Return of Martin Guerre* (Cambridge, Mass.: Harvard University Press, 1983), p. 4.

[28] This approach follows the influential example of the anthropologist Clifford Geertz: "Deep Play: Notes on the Balinese Cockfight," *Daedalus* (Winter 1971), pp. 1–38; Geertz, *The Interpretation of Cultures: Selected Essays* (New York: Basic Books, 1973). Geertz's impact across various fields, including anthropology, literary studies, and history, is the subject of "The Fate of 'Culture': Geertz and Beyond," ed. Sherry B. Ortner,

Darnton and Davis are early modern historians, but their emphasis upon the unfamiliar is particularly instructive for the historian of the recent past. The historical method is a matter of approach as much as subject, and key to that approach is the perspective afforded by distance. It is difficult enough for historians to establish interpretive distance from the Protestant Reformation or the French Revolution, but that problem is compounded when the object of study is less obviously remote – as in the case of postwar Britain.[29] In order to analyze this period historically, then, it is essential to register its distance – that is, its *difference* – from the present. Steven Shapin and Simon Schaffer refer to this challenge as the need for the historian to "play the stranger," and they suggest that moments of controversy offer an ideal opportunity to achieve this perspective: "[H]istorical actors frequently play a role analogous to that of our pretend-stranger," they explain, because "in the course of controversy they attempt to deconstruct the taken-for-granted quality of their antagonists' preferred beliefs and practices."[30] That is, in the course of public debate, assumptions and values that might otherwise remain hidden are exposed and articulated, making a moment of controversy a fresh point of entry into a world that initially seemed familiar.

Another problem in writing recent history arises when the historian's interpretive categories are inherited from the very actors being studied. As Lionel Trilling cautioned, "We cannot think modernly in ancient words; we betray either the one time or the other."[31] In the history of postwar Britain, such inherited (if not ancient) categories include "decline" and the "two cultures." This state of affairs would hardly be tolerated in histories of the Reformation or slavery, and it is equally problematic (if less readily apparent) when the subject is more

Representations 59 (Summer 1997). Dominick LaCapra criticizes this approach as applied to cultural history in "Is Everyone a *Mentalité* Case? Transference and the 'Culture' Concept," *History and Criticism* (Ithaca: Cornell University Press, 1985), pp. 71–94.

[29] In this way, recent history lends itself to a problem identified by Collini, "the deeply entrenched cultural prejudice that we already know the answer and know that it is not very interesting," *Absent Minds: Intellectuals in Britain* (Oxford University Press, 2006), p. 502. On the problem of contemporary history, see Peter Catterall, "What (if Anything) is Distinctive about Contemporary History?" *Journal of Contemporary History* 32 (4) (October 1997), pp. 441–452.

[30] Steven Shapin and Simon Schaffer, *Leviathan and the Air-Pump: Hobbes, Boyle, and the Experimental Life* (Princeton University Press, 1985), p. 7. On the analysis of controversy in science and technology studies, see Trevor Pinch, "Scientific Controversies," *International Encyclopedia of the Social and Behavioral Sciences*, ed. N. J. Smelser and P. B. Baltes (Oxford: Elsevier, 2001), pp. 13719–13724.

[31] Lionel Trilling, *Matthew Arnold* (London: George Allen and Unwin, 1955), p. 333.

immediately familiar. To explain the "two cultures" controversy by referring to a conflict between two disciplinary cultures would be akin to explaining that witches were persecuted in early modern Europe because they were witches, or that fugitive slaves were returned to their owners because they were property. Adopting these categories as our terms of explanation ("witch," "property," "two cultures") merely repeats them in the present as they were used in the past, when it is the development and deployment of the categories themselves that requires historical explanation. It is the "two cultures" *controversy*, not the *two cultures*, that must be the object of study in order to apprehend this episode's meaning and significance.

In the extensive literature about Snow, Leavis, and the "two cultures" controversy, the most insightful accounts have adopted this critical perspective upon the "two cultures" categories. Leavis's biographer, Ian MacKillop, achieved this perspective by placing Leavis, rather than Snow, at the center of the narrative. From that point of view, the argument between them appeared less like a contest between science and literature, and more like a conflict between competing interpretations of the past. "It was wrong to depict the conflict between Snow and Leavis as one between the scientific and the literary," MacKillop concluded. "It was a conflict over history, in which Leavis was increasingly interested in the 1960s."[32] Stefan Collini's introduction to the reprint of *The Two Cultures* similarly applies pressure upon the disciplinary categories. "It is fatally easy," he warns, "in discussing this theme, to slip into dealing with 'science' and 'literature' as stable entities, frozen at one moment in time (usually the moment when our own views were first formed)."[33] Collini instead registers the shifting associations of those domains, while identifying the contemporary concerns that charged this particular episode – including, among others, Sputnik, social class, the meritocracy, university expansion, and Harold Wilson's "white heat." And David Hollinger, writing about another tradition entirely, discusses the deployment by American liberals of "scientific" values – such as honesty, tolerance, democracy, and secularism – in episodes of cultural politics from the 1940s to the 1960s. Snow then appears, rather unexpectedly, towards the end of this story, wielding the values associated with "science" against rivals of his own.[34] Despite their differences of emphasis, these accounts by MacKillop,

---

[32] Ian MacKillop, *F. R. Leavis: A Life in Criticism* (London: Allen Lane, 1995), p. 325.
[33] Collini, "Introduction," p. lxv.
[34] Hollinger, "Science as a Weapon in *Kulturkampfe* in the United States During and After World War II," *Isis* 86 (September 1995), pp. 440–454.

Collini, and Hollinger each attend to the ways that the "two cultures" controversy provided an outlet for broader concerns.

A historical perspective also requires that, even as Snow's categories are unpacked, his significance is acknowledged. This sympathy can be difficult to achieve, since Snow's reputation today is not what it was during his lifetime. Yet the cultural historian's reason for studying Snow is not his status today as a novelist or thinker, but his past significance as, in David Cannadine's phrase, "a man who mattered in his day."[35] Cannadine explains, "His novels no longer command a broad or appreciative audience, but for anyone interested in certain aspects of British life between the 1920s and the 1960s, they will always remain essential reading."[36] That is, Snow matters to historians today because he mattered to contemporaries then, and the rise and fall of his reputation provides one way of tracking the broader social attitudes to which it had been tied. David Edgerton, in a critical analysis of *The Two Cultures* and its historiographical impact, similarly insists upon Snow's historical significance. Of the many British writers with scientific backgrounds during the twentieth century, Edgerton notes, "Snow was and is easily the most famous and certainly the most influential as an ideologue."[37] Rather than denying or debunking Snow's stature, Edgerton instead *reads* that stature for what it reveals about British society and culture. He depicts Snow as an exemplary exponent of a technocratic critique of modern Britain. That critique lamented the supposedly marginalized status of science, technology, and expertise, even as it (paradoxically) flourished due to a widespread commitment to all three – as illustrated, in part, by the hostile reception that greeted Leavis's rejoinder.[38] Edgerton then takes Leavis's critique as seriously as Snow's stature, reading them both so as to force reconsiderations of the debate, its context, and its legacy. Cannadine thus acknowledges Snow's deflated reputation as a novelist, while Edgerton refutes Snow's account

---

[35] David Cannadine, "C. P. Snow, 'The Two Cultures,' and the 'Corridors of Power' Revisited," in *Yet More Adventures with Britannia*, ed. Wm. Roger Louis (London: I. B. Tauris, 2005), p. 113.

[36] *Ibid.*

[37] David Edgerton, *Warfare State: Britain, 1920–1970* (Cambridge University Press, 2006), p. 197. The other writers Edgerton cites in this context include Eric Ambler, William Cooper, Nigel Balchin, and Nevil Shute (H. G. Wells, of course, was the most important such writer of the previous generation). For further elaboration on Edgerton's revisionist arguments regarding Snow and *The Two Cultures*, see his *Warfare State*, pp. 191–210; Edgerton, "C. P. Snow as Anti-Historian of British Science: Revisiting the Technocratic Moment, 1959–1964," *History of Science* 43 (June 2005), pp. 187–208.

[38] On a similar dynamic in an earlier period, see Frank Miller Turner, "Public Science in Britain, 1880–1919," *Isis* 71 (December 1980), pp. 589–608.

of science, culture, and the British state, but they both acknowledge and emphasize Snow's historical significance.[39]

Instead of adding yet another commentary to the vast journalistic literature about the "two cultures," this book develops the approaches and insights of this more select historiography. Rather than assuming that this episode and its context are already familiar, it takes the furore as an opportunity to enter its world with the eyes of a stranger; rather than adopting the actors' own categories as its terms of analysis, it explains the origins and content of those categories themselves; and rather than dismissing the significance of figures who have fallen out of favor, it recovers the context in which their arguments and reputations thrived. We will see that Snow and Leavis differed in their assessments of what they thought of as "modern civilization." For Snow modern civilization was *industrial civilization*: it had its origins in the eighteenth and nineteenth centuries, and it delivered material prosperity and social opportunity to the majority of the population. For Leavis, by contrast, modern civilization led to *mass civilization*: it had its origins in the seventeenth century, and it displaced a unified culture that had previously flourished.[40] In response to these developments, and by contrast with socialism on the left and conservatism on the right, Snow and Leavis both placed their faith in the talented individual. But while Snow believed that the individual should work through existing institutions to extend the benefits of modern civilization (a position I label "technocratic liberalism"), Leavis hoped that intelligent individuals might sustain the capacity for creative thought that modern civilization threatened (a position I label "radical liberalism").[41]

---

[39] Leavis adopted a similar approach in his Richmond Lecture: "[Snow] has become for a vast public on both sides of the Atlantic a mastermind and a sage. His significance is that he has been accepted [as an] authoritative intellect by the cultural conditions manifested in his acceptance." Leavis, *Two Cultures?*, p. 10. For further discussion of this historiography, see Guy Ortolano, "The Literature and the Science of 'Two Cultures' Historiography," *Studies in History and Philosophy of Science* 39 (March 2008), pp. 143–150.

[40] In this context, the term "modern civilization," however problematic as a historical category, has certain advantages over the more anodyne "modernity." The analytical, detached connotation of "modernity" would imply that Snow and Leavis were responding to the actual onset of a distinct epoch – one that has been identified by scholars, and about which they differed. "Modern civilization," by contrast, should be read to refer to their own, in many ways contradictory, understandings of history and society, the contents of which are examined in Chapters 1 and 2. For a survey of the emergence and critiques of the categories "modern" and "civilization," see Barbara Weinstein, "Developing Inequality," *American Historical Review* 113 (February 2008), pp. 1–18.

[41] The fate of liberalism in twentieth-century Britain is a vexed issue; in seeing it persisting after the demise of the Liberal Party – especially among intellectuals – I follow Peter

These worldviews collided in the "two cultures" controversy, but the arguments did not stop at the conclusions of their lectures or the gates of their colleges. What can we learn if we follow Snow and Leavis as they moved away from their lecterns and through widening disputes – from turf battles within Cambridge, to arguments over British history, to disputes about the former empire? In each of these cases, at approximately the same time, claims on behalf of "science" were being pressed to the fore, so that – however improbably – these seemingly disparate discussions all intersected with the "two cultures" controversy. Like that controversy, they, too, were animated by more than the topics at hand, so that uncovering the stakes of the argument between Snow and Leavis helps to explain the workings of cultural politics in Britain during the 1960s more generally.

From economic "decline" to post-declinism

Revising our understanding of the "two cultures" controversy in turn revises our understanding of the context into which it fits. This book challenges accounts of postwar Britain that focus upon social stagnation, cultural ossification, and economic decline. This has certainly been a prominent reading of postwar British history – indeed, it was the interpretation offered by Snow in *The Two Cultures* (1959), endorsed by Arthur Koestler in *Suicide of a Nation?* (1963), and extended by Martin Wiener in *English Culture and the Decline of the Industrial Spirit* (1981).[42] However commonsensical it might seem to characterize decolonizing Britain as a nation in "decline," this influential interpretation of postwar British history actually emphasized *economic* decline (rather than imperial retreat), which it explained as a result of *British* actions (rather than international developments).[43] Snow, Koestler, and others argued

Clarke, *Liberals and Social Democrats* (Cambridge University Press, 1978). James Cronin disconnects the fate of a social group from the political party that ostensibly represents it in *Labour and Society* (New York: Schocken, 1984).

[42] Arthur Koestler, ed., *Suicide of a Nation? An Enquiry into the State of Britain Today* (London: Hutchinson, 1963), originally a special issue of *Encounter*, July 1963; Martin Wiener, *English Culture and the Decline of the Industrial Spirit, 1850–1980* (Cambridge University Press, 1981; 2nd edn., 2004). The genre also includes, along with many other important works: Michael Shanks, *The Stagnant Society: A Warning* (Baltimore: Penguin, 1961), and Perry Anderson, "Origins of the Present Crisis," *New Left Review* 23 (January–February 1964), pp. 26–53. This literature is discussed in Edgerton, *Warfare State*, Chapter 5, and Jim Tomlinson, *The Politics of Decline: Understanding Postwar Britain* (Harlow: Longman, 2001).

[43] On the latter point, see David Edgerton, "The Prophet Militant and Industrial: The Peculiarities of Correlli Barnett," *Twentieth Century British History* 2 (1991), pp. 360–379; Edgerton, *Science, Technology, and the British Industrial 'Decline', 1870–1970*

that British society marginalized professionals and experts, that it fostered a "mediocracy" rather than a meritocracy, and that it exhibited pervasive hostility towards science and technology. These arguments then informed historical explanations of Britain's supposed economic decline: Wiener, for instance, stated that the central problem of modern British history was the explanation of economic decline, and he sought to explain that phenomenon by reading this account of British culture backward into the nineteenth century.[44] Wiener's book captured the attention of Margaret Thatcher's cabinet, and it was part of a historiography that flourished from the 1980s.[45] Today, even in works that explicitly disavow "decline" as an interpretive framework, these underlying assumptions about science, technology, and expertise continue to figure in accounts of postwar British history.[46]

(Cambridge University Press, 1996); Jim Tomlinson, "Inventing 'Decline': The Falling Behind of the British Economy in the Postwar Years," *Economic History Review* 49 (1996), pp. 731–757.

[44] In the preface to the reprinted edition of *English Culture and the Decline of the Industrial Spirit* (2004), Wiener relates his book to Koestler and *Suicide of a Nation?*, and to the work of Tom Nairn, Perry Anderson, and the *New Left Review* (pp. xiii–xv). Edgerton refers to the period 1959–1964, which included Snow's lecture, Koestler's volume, and Anderson's "Origins of the Present Crisis," as the "technocratic moment" in British history, by which he means that in this period a technocratic critique of British institutions flourished (*Warfare State*, Chapter 5). This critique propelled anxieties about, and remedies for, economic decline to the center of political debate, for reasons that Tomlinson explains in *The Politics of Decline*. Wiener conceived of his book during the 1970s, and, when he acknowledges the influence of Koestler, Nairn, and Anderson upon his thinking at the time, he confirms that his arguments were informed by the discussions that flourished during the technocratic moment. *English Culture and the Decline of the Industrial Spirit* thus remains a landmark of modern British historiography, but today its significance is as an example of, rather than an explanation for, a major theme in modern British history.

[45] See, in addition to Wiener, Correlli Barnett, *The Audit of War: The Illusion and Reality of Britain as a Great Nation* (London: Macmillan, 1986); Barnett, *The Lost Victory: British Dreams, British Realities, 1945–1950* (London: Macmillan, 1995); S. N. Broadberry and N. F. R. Crafts, "British Economic Policy and Industrial Performance in the Early Post-war Period," *Business History* 38 (1996), pp. 65–91; Broadberry and Crafts, "The Post-war Settlement: Not Such a Good Bargain after All," *Business History* 40 (1998), pp. 73–79; Sidney Pollard, *The Wasting of the British Economy: British Economic Policy from 1945 to the Present* (London: Croom Helm, 1982); David Coates, *The Question of UK Decline: State, Society, and Economy* (London: Harvester Wheatsheaf, 1994). Although they have been classed alongside each other here, it is important to note that there are substantial differences among these works: see Tomlinson's discussion of this literature in "Economic 'Decline' in Post-war Britain," in *A Companion to Contemporary Britain, 1939–2000*, ed. Paul Addison and Harriet Jones (Oxford: Blackwell, 2005), pp. 164–179.

[46] For instance, Andrew Marr, *A History of Modern Britain* (London: Macmillan, 2007). Marr's book is too eclectic and optimistic to be classed as a strictly "declinist" account, and he sympathetically cites the revisionist George Bernstein, *The Myth of Decline: The Rise of Britain since 1945* (London: Pimlico, 2004). But in his second and third sections, covering 1951–1979, Marr frequently channels the "Suicide of a Nation?" critique – for

Recently, however, historians have challenged the concept of economic decline on a number of fronts, from its material reality to its
historiographical centrality.[47] It is important to begin by recognizing that
the British economy grew substantially during the postwar era, and that
the phenomenon under consideration consists of relative, not absolute,
economic decline. But even if Britain's rate of growth did not always
match that of selected national comparators, economic historians have
shown that such discrepancies are generally attributable to a combination of statistical anomalies (such as the selection of the dates being
compared) and prior European differences (such as their later shifts
from agriculture).[48] Indeed, surveying these arguments regarding relative rates of growth, Jim Tomlinson concludes, "These various
reassessments of economic performance leave the idea of a failure in
growth highly qualified, as at most relatively small deviations around
trends which are broadly European in scope."[49] The European context
is crucial: in that international frame, even the challenges of the 1970s

instance, when he writes, "It was the same vague, cheerful, fairies-in-the-garden faith in
science and professionalism articulated by the wartime planner Harold Wilson. *Yet
professionalism, never mind science, was sadly lacking*," p. 243 (emphasis mine).

[47] Two early accounts to analyze declinism historically were McCloskey, *If You're So
Smart*, pp. 40–55, and David Edgerton, *England and the Aeroplane: An Essay on a
Militant and Technological Nation* (Basingstoke: Macmillan, 1991). Edgerton also
challenges ideas about the marginalization of science and technology in British culture
in *Science, Technology, and the British Industrial 'Decline', 1870–1970*, and he advances
what he terms a "post-declinist" account of twentieth-century Britain in *Warfare State*.
Tomlinson historicizes the emergence of ideas about economic decline in "Inventing
'Decline'"; he discusses the historical origins of, and historiographical debates about,
the concept in "Economic 'Decline' in Post-War Britain"; and he examines the political
uses to which "decline" has been (and continues to be) put in *The Politics of Decline*. See
also Peter Clarke and Clive Trebilcock, eds., *Understanding Decline: Perceptions and
Realities of British Economic Performance* (Cambridge University Press, 1997); Richard
English and Michael Kenny, eds., *Rethinking British Decline* (London: Macmillan,
2000); W. D. Rubinstein, *Capitalism, Culture, and Economic Decline in Britain, 1750–
1990* (London: Routledge, 1993); Barry Supple, "Fear of Failing: Economic History
and the Decline of Britain," *Economic History Review* 47 (1994), pp. 441–458. The
historiographical centrality of the concept is questioned by McCloskey in *If You're So
Smart*, and by Lawrence Black and Hugh Pemberton in "Introduction: The Uses (and
Abuses) of Affluence," in *An Affluent Society? Britain's Post-war "Golden Age" Revisited*
(Aldershot: Ashgate, 2004), pp. 1–13.
[48] C. Feinstein, "Benefits of Backwardness and Costs of Continuity," in *Government and
Economies in the Post-war World: Economic Policies and Comparative Performance*,
ed. Andrew Graham and Anthony Seldon (London: Routledge, 1990), pp. 288, 291;
N. F. R. Crafts, "The Golden Age of Economic Growth in Western Europe, 1950–
1973, *Economic History Review* 48 (1995), pp. 429–447; Alan Booth, "The Manufacturing Failure Hypothesis and the Performance of British Industry during the Long
Boom," *Economic History Review* 56 (2004), pp. 1–33; C. Feinstein, "Structural Change
in the Developed Countries during the Twentieth Century," *Oxford Review of Economic
Policy* 15 (1999), pp. 35–55.
[49] Tomlinson, "Economic 'Decline' in Post-war Britain," p. 175.

appear not as the consequences of British decisions, much less as evidence of a British "disease," so much as local variations on the transnational developments of inflation, energy crises, and the shift from heavy industry. And in a global perspective, any relative economic decline amounts at most to a minor rearrangement among the world's wealthiest nations – a development that might warrant explanation, but that hardly constitutes one of the most important themes of modern British history.[50] Today, after a generation of such critiques, maintaining economic decline as a framework for postwar British history would require something approaching Ptolemaic levels of intricacy.

Yet problematizing "decline" as an economic fact nevertheless begs the question of how it came to occupy so prominent a position in the culture and historiography of postwar Britain. After all, many politicians and commentators certainly *believed* Britain to be enduring a painful economic decline. The consequence of the revisionist historiography discussed above is that, in order to account for this conviction, it becomes necessary to shift attention from the dubious matter of economic decline, to the indisputable phenomenon of cultural *declinism* – that is, to the emergence, workings, and manipulation of anxieties about decline. If not the direct reflection of economic experience, why did declinism flourish after the war, especially from the late 1950s? In fact, declinism emerged not as a disinterested characterization of economic developments, but rather as part of a technocratic critique of society and the state: it was an ideological argument, deployed for political purposes.[51] This insight returns us once again to key declinist texts, such as those by Snow and Koestler, but with a historical perspective upon their key claims: Koestler's insistence that concerns about decline had nothing to do with the end of the empire, or Snow's lament that British society marginalized scientific experts.[52] Instead, as Tomlinson shows,

---

50 A point made by Edgerton in *England and the Aeroplane*, McCloskey in *If You're So Smart*, and Tomlinson in a review of Booth, *British Economic Development since 1945*, in *Contemporary British History* 10 (Summer 1996), p. 250. For further development of this point, see Chapter 5.

51 In addition to the works by Edgerton and Tomlinson, see Ian Budge, "Relative Decline as a Political Issue: Ideological Motivations of the Politico-Economic Debate in Postwar Britain," *Contemporary Record* 7 (Summer 1993), pp. 1–23; Guy Ortolano, "'Decline' as a Weapon in Cultural Politics," in *Penultimate Adventures with Britannia*, ed. Wm. Roger Louis (London: I. B. Tauris, 2008), pp. 201–214. For a critical perspective upon the assumptions of "decline," and the premises of declinism, during an earlier period, see Martin Daunton and Bernhard Rieger, eds., *Meanings of Modernity: Britain from the Late-Victorian Era to World War* II (Oxford: Berg, 2001).

52 Koestler insisted in the introduction to "Suicide of a Nation?": "We hold . . . that psychological factors and cultural attitudes are at the root of the economic evils – *not* the loss of Empire . . . What ails Britain is not the loss of Empire but the loss of incentive."

the end of the empire contributed to a climate in which economic declinism could flourish; and, as Edgerton shows, the enthusiastic receptions that greeted Snow's argument signal a society and culture that were *already* convinced of the importance of scientific expertise.[53]

This book, then, should be read as part of an emerging *post-declinist* historiography: a historiography that departs not only from the presumption of economic decline, but also – and more importantly – from the underlying assumptions about science and technology, society and culture, and experts and the state that structured declinism. The result is a very different picture of postwar Britain.[54]

The meritocratic moment, c. 1945–c. 1975

The three decades after the Second World War have emerged as a coherent period in twentieth-century history. The years between the Education Act of 1944 and the election of Margaret Thatcher as Conservative leader in 1975 included a quarter-century of domestic consensus and international prosperity.[55] Amid this political and economic stability, and between the welfare state, the defense establishment,

"Introduction: The Lion and the Ostrich," *Encounter*, July 1963, p. 8 (emphasis in original). Snow argued in *The Two Cultures*, "It is the traditional culture, to an extent remarkably little diminished by the emergence of the scientific one, which manages the western world," and he went on to assert that "this cultural divide . . . probably seems at its sharpest in England." Snow, *The Two Cultures*, pp. 11, 16.

[53] Jim Tomlinson, "The Decline of the Empire and the Economic 'Decline' of Britain," *Twentieth Century British History* 14 (2003), pp. 201–221; Edgerton, *Warfare State*, Chapter 5.

[54] Edgerton: "[T]he undermining of declinism involves a radical reconsideration of many aspects of twentieth-century British history . . . It is very much about understanding the assumptions made in the analysis of modern British history." Review of Clarke and Trebilcock, eds., *Understanding Decline*, in *Historical Journal* 42 (March 1999), pp. 313–314. For reconsiderations of declinist characterizations of English culture, see Peter Mandler, "Against 'Englishness': English Culture and the Limits to Rural Nostalgia, 1850–1940," *Transactions of the Royal Historical Society*, 6th series, 7 (1997), pp. 155–175; Mandler, "The Consciousness of Modernity? Liberalism and the English National Character, 1870–1940," in *Meanings of Modernity*, ed. Martin Daunton and Bernhard Rieger (Oxford: Berg, 2001), pp. 119–144; Mandler, *The English National Character: The History of an Idea from Edmund Burke to Tony Blair* (New Haven: Yale, 2006). For an example of a self-consciously "post-declinist" analysis, one that attends in particular to declinist arguments regarding science and technology, see (in addition to Edgerton's *Warfare State*) S. Waqar H. Zaidi, "Barnes Wallis and the 'Strength of England'," *Technology and Culture* 49 (2008), pp. 62–88.

[55] E. J. Hobsbawm, *The Age of Extremes: A History of the World, 1914–1991* (New York: Pantheon, 1994). Paul Addison locates a political consensus "from about 1950 to about 1975" in "The Impact of the Second World War," in *A Companion to Contemporary Britain, 1939–2000*, ed. Paul Addison and Harriet Jones (Oxford: Blackwell, 2005), p. 15. For reconsideration of the concept, see Harriet Jones and Michael Kandiah,

and the mixed economy, British society came to be dominated as never before by complex institutions managed by specialized professionals.[56] In a phrase that aptly conveys the distinctiveness of these decades, while also acknowledging the fact of its longer history on either end, Harold Perkin referred to this period as the "plateau" of the professional society – that is, of a society organized around "career hierarchies of specialized occupations, selected by merit and based on trained expertise."[57] Complex institutions, specialized occupations, expert professionals: it is this social context – rather than the "traditional culture" excoriated by Snow, the "cult of amateurishness" bemoaned by Koestler, or the "gentlemanly ideal" emphasized by Wiener – that provides the setting for the arguments and developments examined in this book.[58] After all, although they are not always discussed in this way, Snow and Leavis – with their grammar school educations, PhD degrees, and respective careers in the civil service and the university – were themselves prominent exemplars of these broader developments.[59]

This period constituted the "meritocratic moment" in modern British history. As Perkin emphasized, by way of contrast with previous eras that valorized pedigree or entrepreneurship, during the third quarter of the twentieth century "ability and expertise were the only respectable justification for recruitment to positions of authority and responsibility."[60]

---

eds., *The Myth of Consensus: New Views on British History, 1945–1964* (New York: St. Martin's, 1996).

[56] These trends only continued: between 1950 and 1971 the share of the workforce employed by the state increased from 8% to 17% (and if nationalized industries are included, that figure rises to 27%), while from 1957 to 1969 the share of manufacturing production enjoyed by the largest 200 firms increased from 73% to 86%. H. Perkin, *The Rise of Professional Society: England since 1880* (London: Routledge, 1989), p. 437.

[57] Perkin, *The Rise of Professional Society*, p. 2. On the professions before this period, see Penelope J. Corfield, *Power and the Professions in Britain, 1700–1850* (London: Routledge, 1995). The term "professional society" in Perkin's sense refers not to a society in which professions exist, but more precisely to a society organized around the professions in a particular way. On the origins of this society, see Perkin, *The Origins of Modern English Society, 1780–1880* (London: Routledge, 1969); for an international perspective, one that follows the story after the postwar "plateau," see Perkin, *The Third Revolution: Professional Elites in the Modern World* (London: Routledge, 1996).

[58] Snow, *The Two Cultures*, p. 11; Koestler, "The Lion and the Ostrich," p. 8; Wiener, *English Culture and the Decline of the Industrial Spirit*, p. 139.

[59] On Snow's bureaucratic career, and his status as "an exemplary new man" and "the new technical middle classes' spokesman," see Edgerton, *Warfare State*, p. 197. On Leavis's importance to the development of the literary critic's claims to professional expertise, see Carolyn Steedman, "State-Sponsored Autobiography," in *Moments of Modernity: Reconstructing Britain, 1945–1964*, ed. Becky Conekin, Frank Mort and Chris Waters (London: Rivers Oram, 1999), pp. 41–54.

[60] Perkin, *The Rise of Professional Society*, p 405.

Justification is the key term: the meritocratic ideal was never fully realized in practice, but it was widely accepted in principle – as illustrated when the House of Lords was re-imagined as a repository of experts.[61] In 1962 the journalist Anthony Sampson thought he detected signs of "changing people" and a "meritocracy" in *Anatomy of Britain*, and just three years later the transformation seemed complete: "The ancient debate between amateurs and professionals, or gentleman and players, has lost much of its point," he wrote in 1965, "for only a few top people . . . would now dare admit to amateur attitudes."[62] In this new meritocracy – a word itself coined in 1958, in a warning of the stratification such a society might engender – expertise, rather than property or capital, would be the coin of the realm, and expertise was a set of skills transmitted through education to the capable individual.[63] The promise was equality of opportunity rather than result, and the bargain was that experts would employ their talent and training to benefit the nation as a whole. The most glaring discrepancy between this ideal and the reality lay in the relative lack of opportunities that this society made available to women – one of several contradictions that, as we shall see, generated social and political movements challenging the meritocracy to deliver on its promises.

The expert represented the meritocracy's ideal citizen. To be sure, experts long predated 1945, but the meritocratic moment witnessed an increase in their numbers and an extension of their authority.[64] "By the 1950s," write Becky Conekin, Frank Mort, and Chris Waters, "the authority of experts had become central not only to economic management and social policy, but also to the areas of cultural taste, the urban and rural environments, consumer behaviour and the psychological

---

[61] In adopting this approach, I agree with Wiener about the value of Raymond Williams's insight that "it is with the discovery of patterns of a characteristic kind that any useful cultural analysis begins, and it is with the relationship between these patterns, which sometimes reveals unexpected identities and correspondences in hitherto separately considered activities, sometimes again reveals discontinuities of an unexpected kind, that general cultural analysis is concerned." Raymond Williams, *The Long Revolution* (London: Chatto and Windus, 1961), p. 47, quoted in Wiener, *English Culture and the Decline of the Industrial Spirit*, p. x.

[62] Anthony Sampson, *Anatomy of Britain* (London: Hodder and Stoughton, 1962), p. xii; Sampson, *Anatomy of Britain Today* (London: Hodder and Stoughton, 1965), p. 669 and *passim*.

[63] Michael Young, *The Rise of the Meritocracy, 1870–2033: An Essay on Education and Equality* (London: Thames and Hudson, 1958).

[64] "[T]he period from the middle of the war to the mid-1960s [was] one that witnessed a quantitative expansion of experts and their forms of knowledge." Conekin, Mort and Waters, *Moments of Modernity* (London, Rivers Oram, 1999), pp. 14–15. On the rise of the expert, professional middle classes between 1939 and 1970, see Edgerton, *Warfare State*, pp. 145–190; the precursors and trajectory of this trend are strikingly illustrated on p. 173.

well-being of communities."[65] Professional politicians thus employed expert economists to manage the economy and maintain full employment. But the authority of experts extended beyond matters of governance. Architects, designers, and scientists were depicted as capable experts at the Festival of Britain in 1951, and the promise of expert "planning" came to be applied to townscapes no less than the economy.[66] Expert authority even extended to the domain of literary criticism: when in 1960 the Crown brought an obscenity suit against Penguin for publishing *Lady Chatterley's Lover*, literary critics filed into the Old Bailey to offer their testimony as to the novel's "literary merit" – the standard established by the Obscene Publications Act of 1959. Experts were also securing their authority in the theater: Baz Kershaw argues that, before the Second World War, theater audiences had been accepted as active arbiters of taste, but from 1956 the founder of the English Stage Company at the Royal Court Theatre worked to shift that authority to the artist – as registered in the proposal that "Judge Not" be included in the audience's programs.[67] And in 1950s fiction, and then the following decade's films, crimes were being solved not by Dorothy Sayers's amateur aristocrat Peter Wimsey (who had been retired in 1937), but by Ian Fleming's James Bond (who emerged in 1953). Whatever Fleming's authorial intentions, Agent 007 can be read as embodying several postwar ideals: professionally trained, technologically proficient, and deployed by the state, James Bond was a superhero for the welfare state.[68]

Nothing represented the promise of professional expertise better than science and the scientist. In colonial affairs, for instance, Joseph Morgan Hodge identifies a "triumph of the expert" in the fifteen years after the war, when authority shifted "from the fabled district administrator who

---

[65] Conekin, Mort, and Waters, *Moments of Modernity*, pp. 14–15. Conekin discusses "the new post-war public sphere, dominated by experts and professionals" in *The Autobiography of a Nation: The 1951 Festival of Britain* (Manchester University Press, 2003), p. 34.

[66] Conekin, *The Autobiography of a Nation*; Conekin, " 'Here is the Modern World Itself': The Festival of Britain's Representations of the Future," in *Moments of Modernity*, ed. Becky Conekin, Frank Mort and Chris Waters (London: Rivers Oram, 1999), pp. 228–246.

[67] Baz Kershaw, "Oh for Unruly Audiences! Or, Patterns of Participation in Twentieth-Century Theatre," *Modern Drama* 44 (Summer 2001), pp. 133–154; Dan Rebellato, *1956 and All That: The Making of Modern British Drama* (London: Routledge, 1999).

[68] The significance of the transition from Wimsey to Bond is noted by Peter Clarke, *Hope and Glory: Britain, 1900–1990* (London: Allen Lane, 1996), p. 274. For further discussion of Bond, see Dominic Sandbrook, *Never Had It So Good: A History of Britain from Suez to the Beatles* (London: Little, Brown, 2005), Chapter 16. For a different interpretation of Bond's significance, one that depicts him as the product of Fleming's "revulsion from socialist Britain" (p. 108), see Simon Winder, *The Man Who Saved Britain: A Personal Journey into the Disturbing World of James Bond* (New York: Farrar, Straus and Giroux, 2006).

'knew his natives' to the specialist who 'knew his science'."[69] Scientists emerged from the war keen to capitalize on their prestige, and the expanding postwar state was eager to oblige. In 1946 the Barlow Report on Scientific Manpower declared, "Never before has the importance of science been more widely recognized or so many hopes of future progress and welfare founded upon the scientist."[70] These hopes were matched by institutional commitments and sterling investments: from 1945, for instance, the University Grants Committee encouraged two students in science and technology for every student from all other fields combined.[71] This commitment to science and technology was publicized by "scientific correspondents" on newspaper staffs, such as Ritchie Calder of the *News Chronicle*, John Langdon-Davies of the *Daily Mail*, and Chapman Pincher of the *Daily Express*. In newspaper reports and radio broadcasts, no less than in government reports and political committees, scientists were cast as the nation's best hope in a competitive world, and this faith in the scientist contributed to the widespread appeal of "scientific modernization" more generally. In 1951 – a dozen years before anyone would hear of Harold Wilson's "white heat" – the Festival of Britain displayed little nostalgia in its depiction of a modern nation embracing a scientific and technological future. Five years later, Anthony Crosland sought to modernize the Labour Party through *The Future of Socialism*.[72] Crosland's bracing manifesto anticipated the scientific and modernizing drive that characterized Labour politics in the early 1960s, but the simultaneous attempt by the Conservative government to harness its own modernizing program testified to the appeal of this movement across the political spectrum.[73]

---

[69] Joseph Morgan Hodge, *Triumph of the Expert: Agrarian Doctrines of Development and the Legacies of British Colonialism* (Athens: Ohio University Press, 2007), p. 12. See also Frederick Cooper and Randall Packard, Introduction to *International Development and the Social Sciences: Essays on the History and Politics of Knowledge*, ed. Cooper and Packard (Berkeley: University of California Press, 1997), p. 13; Monica van Beusekom and Dorothy Hodgson, "Lessons Learned? Development Experiences in the Late Colonial Period," *Journal of African History* 41 (2000), p. 31.

[70] *Scientific Manpower: Report of a Committee Appointed by the Lord President of the Council* (London: HMSO, 1946; cmnd. 6824), p. 631.

[71] H. Perkin, *Key Profession: The History of the Association of University Teachers* (New York: A. M. Kelley, 1969), p. 218.

[72] Anthony Crosland, *The Future of Socialism* (London: Jonathan Cape, 1956). On the difficulties the modernizers met, see Lawrence Black, *The Political Culture of the Left in Affluent Britain, 1951–64: Old Labour, New Britain?* (Basingstoke: Palgrave Macmillan, 2003). On the appeal of science and modernization in the early 1950s, see Conekin, *The Autobiography of a Nation*; in the early 1960s, see Sandbrook, *White Heat*, especially Chapter 3.

[73] Jim Tomlinson, "Conservative Modernisation, 1960–64: Too Little, Too Late?" *Contemporary British History* 11 (Autumn 1997), pp. 18–38.

Education was the domain where these advances were to be secured and extended. The postwar decades witnessed the expansion and restructuring of education at every level. The Education Act of 1944 extended educational opportunity to all, particularly through the secondary level following examination at age eleven. The resulting "eleven-plus" was intended to stream students into the education that suited their abilities, a progressive ambition that managed to identify and develop talent (even as it had the unintended consequence of reinforcing, rather than eliminating, class boundaries). The progressive response to the shortcomings of the eleven-plus was the comprehensive school for students of all levels. Two hundred comprehensive schools existed by 1964, the Labour government of 1964–70 increased that figure tenfold, and by 1970 one-third of British children were in comprehensives.[74] Numbers were increasing in the universities as well, driven by massive state investment after the war. These investments targeted science and technology: government grants to universities increased by a factor of ten between 1945 and 1952, and two-thirds of these grants went to students in scientific and technological subjects.[75] University expansion continued throughout the 1950s, and it accelerated with the implementation of the Robbins Report in the next decade.

In short, despite obstacles to reform and the persistence of tradition, from 1945 – and especially during the 1950s and 1960s – the "modern" seemed to promise liberation from the past and a preferable future.[76] Economic prosperity, full employment, and educational opportunity were applying pressure upon barriers of class to create a society more open to talent, a society in which scientists and other experts would deploy their training to benefit the nation. But this vision of a brave new Britain was not without critics, as skeptics launched their attacks from two opposed camps: those who believed that these developments were advancing too rapidly, and those who believed they were not advancing rapidly enough. These positions collided in the cultural politics of the period, and in these arguments "science," "technology," and "modernization" connoted a future that either beckoned or threatened, a future that might be tempered – for better or worse – by competing values that were loosely associated with "literature," "humanism," or the

---

[74] Perkin, *The Rise of Professional Society*, p. 449; Marr, *A History of Modern Britain*, p. 248. See also Roy Lowe, "Education," in *A Companion to Contemporary Britain, 1939–2000*, ed. Paul Addison and Harriet Jones (Oxford: Blackwell, 2005), pp. 281–296.

[75] Perkin, *Key Profession*, pp. 132, 218.

[76] On the reality, and tenacity, of the past that this position opposed, see David Kynaston, *Austerity Britain: 1945–1951* (London: Bloomsbury, 2007); Ferdinand Mount, "Ration Book," *Times Literary Supplement*, 15 June 2007, pp. 7–8.

"arts."[77] It was amid these discussions, and in this context, that the "two cultures" controversy provided an opportunity for broader debates about Britain's past, present, and future.

Overview and arguments

This book begins by situating the Rede and Richmond lectures in the context of Snow's and Leavis's worldviews more generally. The first two chapters offer sympathetic accounts of these men and their ideas: not because they address continuing problems, but to accomplish the historian's goal of explaining their arguments and styles in the "two cultures" controversy. The approach in these chapters follows the example of *Leviathan and the Air-Pump*, which recovers the science of a political theorist (Hobbes) and the political theories of a scientist (Boyle). So rather than emphasizing Snow's ideas about science and Leavis's ideas about literature, Chapter 1 presents Snow as a writer and critic of contemporary *literature*, while Chapter 2 attends to Leavis's attitudes towards *science*.[78] The goal is not to deny the disciplinary dimensions of their argument by simply substituting political commitments for disciplinary loyalties, but rather to recover the complicated positions in which ideas about science and literature, individuals and society, and the past and the present all had a place.

The next four chapters follow Snow and Leavis as they worked to advance these positions in various contexts. Chapter 3 focuses on their efforts to realize their ideals within their own Cambridge colleges, first recovering Snow's efforts to mould the arts side of the new Churchill College, and then examining Leavis's failure to secure his succession at Downing; this chapter argues that, in the course of these excursions into college micropolitics, the contrasting approaches of Snow and Leavis were shaped by their contrary conceptions of "politics" itself. Chapter 4 identifies a network of alliances between the actors in the "two cultures" controversy and the academics who advocated a more scientific style of

---

[77] Snow alternated among referring to the non-scientific half of his dichotomy as "the arts," "literary intellectuals," and the "traditional culture" (and when he spoke of "science" and "scientists," he generally took physics and physicists to be representative). None of these categories should be read as an exact set of fields, so much as a general term of reference for non-scientific things. While the elasticity of these terms frustrated Snow's critics, it raises the productive historical question of how this ostensibly singular field came to be defined and invoked differently according to time, context, and purpose. At the time of these arguments, the field from which Snow and Leavis both derived their authority was literature (Snow as a practitioner, Leavis as a critic), so that is the term employed in the title of this book.

[78] Shapin and Schaffer, *Leviathan and the Air-Pump*.

history in the early 1960s; it argues that this familiar episode in the development of historiography was at root a *political* one, in which the language of science was adopted (or resisted) in the hope of realizing (or frustrating) ideological goals. Chapter 5 situates Snow's entry into what he called "the corridors of power" in the context of the emergence of a new anxiety in British political discourse, economic decline; this chapter argues that "decline" is just one possible – and by no means the best – interpretation of postwar British history, and that it emerged in this period for political (rather than economic) reasons. Chapter 6 turns to the global dimensions of the controversy, which raged simultaneously with the retreat of the British Empire and the peak of the Cold War. In this context, the "two cultures" debate provided an opportunity to work through questions about the future of the former empire, and in these discussions "Asia" and "Africa" could function as imagined locations where arguments about Britain's past and the world's future were joined in one place. Yet by comparing the different forms these arguments took in the United States and Britain, this chapter also argues that, despite these global pretensions, even this international dimension was in its own way as local as a dispute within Cambridge.

Snow, Leavis, and their respective allies engaged in a ferocious argument, one that points to fundamental differences, yet it is also the case that such dichotomies threaten to impose a beguiling sense of clarity upon complicated positions. Chapter 7 thus considers the many *similarities* between Snow and Leavis, so as to characterize the historical moment that contained them both. For example, they were both married to talented women, Pamela Hansford Johnson and Queenie Dorothy Leavis, who managed to pursue intellectual careers of their own despite their restricted access to professional society. As Snow and Leavis engaged in their argument, however, various social movements, including second-wave feminism, challenged the meritocracy to fulfill its own promises of ensuring equal opportunity. Despite their many differences, Snow and Leavis experienced mutual discomfort with such egalitarian demands, and this discomfort forced them to rearrange their priorities by the 1970s. By examining this process, Chapter 7 offers an explanation as to why one dimension of the politics of the left shifted in this period from materialist analysis to cultural critique. And finally, the conclusion considers how British history and other episodes of disciplinary conflict look different as a result of this analysis.

The book's most general arguments address three objects of study: the "two cultures" controversy, the postwar British context, and the historical tradition discussing the arts and the sciences. First, beginning with Snow's initial comments on the "two cultures" in 1956, and concluding with the final exchange of unpleasantries in 1970, the "two cultures" controversy overlapped with the "long" 1960s, from 1956 to 1970.[79] The controversy thus provides a unique vantage point from which to view the agendas and rivalries that simmered beneath – and occasionally boiled over – a seemingly placid postwar consensus. When the arguments of Snow and Leavis are situated within their more general worldviews, it becomes clear that the Rede and Richmond lectures provided the *occasion*, and "arts-versus-sciences" the *language*, for a dispute that was *political*. Their argument reveals tensions between advocates and critics of "modern civilization," tensions that repeatedly surfaced in the many disputes that intersected with the controversy. Excavating the political positions in the "two cultures" controversy, then, sheds light not only on the argument between Snow and Leavis, but also upon cultural politics in Britain during the 1960s more generally.

Second, and despite their undeniable differences, Snow and Leavis shared a common set of assumptions. They believed that social hierarchy was inevitable and desirable, but they differed from previous generations by assuming that the qualification for ascent within that hierarchy should be merit (rather than, say, property or capital). Snow and Leavis were thus committed to a *fluid social hierarchy*, and together they testify to a "meritocratic moment" in British society and culture during the three decades after the Second World War. This term refers to a period when a meritocratic ideal predominated: that is, British society did not necessarily function along meritocratic lines, but the meritocratic principle nevertheless organized ideas and discussions of various social practices. The origins and meanings of the meritocracy are discussed above; Chapters 1 and 2 explain its importance to the positions of Snow and Leavis; Chapters 3 and 5 examine its impact upon education and politics; and Chapter 7 identifies the social and intellectual pressures that eventually contributed to its eclipse. The meritocratic promise negotiated a long-standing tension between liberty and equality in liberal thought.[80] The opposition to inherited privilege led to policies against social inequality (such as the eleven-plus examination), yet the commitment to hierarchies of merit generated resistance to policies aimed at social equality (such as comprehensive schools). The resulting

---

[79] Sandbrook similarly locates the 1960s in Britain from 1956–1970 in *Never Had It So Good* and *White Heat*. Arthur Marwick's preference for 1958–1974 is a product of his admirably international perspective: *The Sixties: Cultural Revolution in Britain, France, Italy, and the United States, c.1958-c.1974* (Oxford University Press, 1998).

[80] See David Wootton, "Liberalism," *The Oxford Companion to Twentieth-Century British Politics*, ed. John Ramsden (Oxford University Press, 2002), pp. 380–381.

political program – the pursuit of equal opportunity, alongside the acceptance of social inequality – was more or less workable, unless the meritocracy was pressed to realize its promise of providing truly equal opportunity.

Towards the end of the third quarter of the twentieth century – that is, from the late 1960s into the 1970s – advocates of economic, educational, and gender equality applied pressure upon the meritocratic edifice at precisely this point. In response to this challenge, either true equality of opportunity would be introduced (requiring massive financial investment and extensive social engineering), or a new rationale would be required to explain the persistence of social inequality. In the final quarter of the century, such a rationale emerged in the ideal of the *market*. By contrast with the meritocratic ideal, marketplace thinking explains the existence of hierarchies as the collective result of countless individual choices. This explanation transfers responsibility for structural inequality away from society (for having failed to provide equal opportunity), and to the individual (for having made unfortunate choices). As marketplace thinking displaced meritocratic commitments, the agenda of national politics shifted from ensuring institutional equality to liberating individual enterprise; and, with the ascendance of the marketplace ideal, the meritocratic moment was eclipsed (which is not to say eliminated: meritocratic ideals persisted, and they still persist, but their predominance as a cultural ideal is diminished). This is an abstract way of explaining complicated developments, and neither Snow nor Leavis ever spoke in these terms. Yet in their robust meritocratic visions of the 1950s, their hostility to egalitarian demands during the 1960s, and their frustration with the marginalization of their assumptions in the 1970s, their personal journeys enable us to identify this ideological shift during the late twentieth century.

Third, the encounter between Snow and Leavis is part of a longer tradition discussing the relationship between the arts and the sciences – a tradition that also includes the exchange between Arnold and Huxley in the 1880s, and the so-called "science wars" of the 1990s.[81] My challenge to a disciplinary interpretation of the "two cultures" controversy does not deny that it was somehow situated within this tradition – a tradition that is undoubtedly recurrent, and an object of study in its own right. Connecting the dots between various installments in this tradition

---

[81] Paul White, *Thomas Huxley: Making the "Man of Science"* (Cambridge University Press, 2003); John Guillory, "The Sokal Affair and the History of Criticism," *Critical Inquiry* 28 (Winter 2002), pp. 470–508. See also the special "Two Cultures?" issue of *History of Science* 43 (2005).

were further iterations of the same conversation, frequently imbued with tones of novelty and urgency, suggesting that the tradition remained obscure even to many of its participants. Snow's achievement was to provide a label for this dialogue, the "two cultures" – a phrase that has come to define the terms not only of the argument between Snow and Leavis, but also of that longer discussion that continues to this day.

Within the terms of that discussion, "science" is frequently figured as a dynamic force *vis-à-vis* the more static fields of classics, literature, or the arts. Huxley, for instance, aimed to reform education with an injection of science, and in order to do so he challenged the position of classics, while Snow envisioned the prosperity that awaited the developing world, if only scientists could displace literary intellectuals from positions of political authority. In both cases, "science" was depicted as a progressive force against a static – and even reactionary – literary establishment. However, closer examination of the Snow–Leavis debate complicates this picture at every turn: the discipline of English only emerged in Cambridge after the First World War; literary fiction figured as a site of conflict between competing schools and styles after the Second World War; social history promised to transform historiography from the early 1960s; and the history and sociology of science has recast conceptions of the emergence and workings of science since the 1970s. Despite influential formulations to the contrary, then, these examples reveal the ways in which humanistic knowledge, no less than scientific knowledge, is forged and contested in a dynamic social context.

Yet this book aims to achieve more than complicating the images of "science" and "literature" in this or that controversy: it seeks to dislodge the "two cultures" as a category of analysis. If the "two cultures" dichotomy is misleading in attempting to explain even the argument from which it emerged, its applicability to other arguments at other times is no less problematic. Indeed, to analyze any episode through the lens of "two cultures" imposes categories born of a unique historical moment upon very different circumstances, and those categories then shape the interpretation of that episode by situating it within a narrative of disciplinary conflict. Such a narrative obscures the ways in which participants might have failed to align along disciplinary lines, while diverting attention from the other issues and loyalties that might have structured their arguments. Therefore, a first step towards understanding the argument between Snow and Leavis must be to adopt a critical stance towards the categories that would reduce complicated positions to a conflict between "two cultures."

What, then, is the significance of the "two cultures" controversy to the historical tradition discussing the arts and the sciences? We shall see that, for reasons that Snow and Leavis did not create, their argument in the 1960s reveals a reshuffling of the ideological terrain in that tradition during the late twentieth century. From Huxley in the 1880s to Snow in the 1960s, figures who associated their positions with science frequently challenged their rivals from the left, branding them conservatives or reactionaries standing in the way of progress and reform. From the late 1960s, however, these positions came to be reversed, and the subsequent post-modern and post-colonial turns in literary studies fostered leftist critiques of scientific objectivity and Western hegemony. Snow and Leavis did not cause this transformation, but their shifting alliances and antipathies did reflect it; and, from that perspective, the "two cultures" controversy figures as a transformative moment in the historical tradition discussing the arts and the sciences.

1   C. P. Snow and the technocratic liberalism

Beyond the two cultures

C. P. Snow's Rede Lecture of 1959, *The Two Cultures and the Scientific Revolution*, met an enthusiastic reception. The text ran in back-to-back issues of *Encounter*, where it was followed by a laudatory roundtable featuring prominent intellectuals.[1] The novelist and critic Walter Allen expressed complete agreement with the division between the arts and the sciences that "C. P. Snow so brilliantly describes"; the scientist A. C. B. Lovell declared that Snow had "beautifully exposed the basic crisis of our existence"; and even Bertrand Russell extended his approval in an open letter to Snow: "All that you say as to what ought to be done commands my assent."[2]

One contributor to the forum, however, dissented from the consensus. J. H. Plumb, the Cambridge historian, rejected the premise of *The Two Cultures*: "I do not think that the division is between a literary culture and a scientific one," he explained. "Such an analysis is both too superficial and too unhistorical."[3] Plumb granted that Snow had stumbled across a division in British society, but he argued that Snow misinterpreted that division as a conflict between *cultures* when it was actually between *classes* – that is, between an established upper-middle class, and an assertive lower-middle and upper-working class. Snow responded sharply, dismissing Plumb's essay as "a baffling piece of . . . 'psychologising' " and reiterating his thesis about the gap between cultures.[4] On its surface their dispute might not seem surprising: Snow, trained as a scientist, had challenged the humanities in his call for more scientists and engineers,

---

[1] C. P. Snow, "The Two Cultures and the Scientific Revolution," *Encounter*, June 1959, pp. 17–24; July 1959, pp. 22–27; Walter Allen, *et al.*, "A Discussion of C. P. Snow's Views," *Encounter*, August 1959, pp. 67–73.

[2] Allen, "A Discussion of C. P. Snow's Views," pp. 67–68, p. 67; A. C. B. Lovell, "A Unified Culture," *Encounter*, August 1959, p. 68; Bertrand Russell, "Snobbery," *Encounter*, August 1959, p. 71.

[3] J. H. Plumb, "Welfare or Release," *Encounter*, August 1959, p. 68.

[4] C. P. Snow, "The 'Two-Cultures' Controversy: Afterthoughts," *Encounter*, February 1960, p. 65.

so Plumb, a practitioner of the humanities, responded to Snow's claims by disputing his premise.

Yet that interpretation of the exchange – and of the "two cultures" debate more generally – fails to capture the whole of the story. In fact, Snow and Plumb were close friends, both having made their way from Alderman Newton's Grammar School in Leicester to Christ's College in Cambridge. For nearly half a century they remained in frequent correspondence, sharing a love of good wines and exchanging gossip about the worlds of literature, politics, and academia.[5] Indeed, it was Snow who had suggested that the editors of *Encounter* invite Plumb to contribute to their forum; and when Plumb sent Snow a copy of his critique, which dismissed the importance of disciplines in favor of other social divisions, Snow expressed his thanks.[6] And this was no mere courtesy: Snow's correspondence from the period bristles with hostility against what he thought of as a reactionary establishment. In short, Plumb's public argument was not very different from Snow's private position – one that had something to do with disciplines, but everything to do with politics.

This chapter examines the ideological position that Snow advanced in *The Two Cultures*. It does so by following the development of that position from the time of Snow's scientific work in the 1930s to his literary success in the 1950s. Its aim is not to rehabilitate Snow's reputation or to endorse his interpretations, but rather to explain why he was speaking and what he was saying when he stepped onto that stage in 1959. We will see that, as Snow made his way from Leicester to London, he accumulated allies who shared his hostility to literary Modernism, and in the fifteen years following the war this group secured significant positions in the metropolitan literary world. But Snow's aims were never solely artistic: his campaign against Modernism was directed against what he viewed as its hostility to modern society, whereas he wanted to praise that society for the progress and opportunity he believed it afforded. This liberal worldview reached its most complete expression in his *Strangers and Brothers* series, a sympathetic exploration of bureaucracies and the men who made them work. After nearly fifteen years of

---

[5] Plumb's half of this correspondence is held with Snow's papers at the Harry Ransom Humanities Research Center (HRC): Snow 166.1–166.18; Snow's letters are with Plumb's papers at the Cambridge University Library (CUL).

[6] Snow's suggestion of Plumb is inferred from his handwritten note on a letter from the co-editor of *Encounter*, Melvin Lasky: Lasky to Snow, 8 May 1959, HRC: Snow 94.17; Snow's grateful receipt of Plumb's essay is recorded in a letter to Plumb, 7 July 1959, CUL: Plumb papers, File "Snow 1946 to 1968," Box "C. P. Snow + Pam, 1946 to 1968."

struggle, having finally secured his position as a novelist and commentator, Snow was positioned to deliver the sharpest version of these views to date in the Rede Lecture in Cambridge.

A traveler in this world

The initial title for the eleven-volume novel sequence that Snow published between 1940 and 1970 was "A Traveler in this World."[7] The eventual title, *Strangers and Brothers*, expressed what Snow took to be the dual (and dueling) facts of human existence – as he explained, "The phrase . . . is supposed to represent the fact that in part of our lives each person is alone . . . and in part of our lives . . . we can and should feel for each other like brothers."[8] "A Traveler in this World" referred more specifically to the novel's narrator, Lewis Eliot. Eliot was Snow's thinly veiled alter-ego (as his wife confirmed, "[H]e *is* Lewis Eliot, there's no doubt about that"), and by identifying him as a "traveler" Snow was highlighting the social mobility that was central to the experience of them both.[9] A life such as Snow's, which wound its way from Leicester to Cambridge to Westminster, cannot be offered as a representative story of the twentieth century, but in its range of experiences, occupations, and acquaintances it is a revealing one.

Charles Percy Snow – "Percy," "CP," or just plain "Snow," he was not known as Charles until middle age – was born into a lower-middle-class home in Leicester in 1905.[10] His father was a clerk in a boot and shoe factory, as well as a church organist, and his mother was the strong domestic figure later portrayed in *Time of Hope* (1949).[11] Percy was affable and ambitious, a natural leader with a remarkable memory, thick glasses, and a passion for cricket and games of all sorts (his brother

---

[7] Snow to Charles E. Cuningham, 11 August 1948, Harry Ransom Humanities Research Center (HRC): Snow 144.10.

[8] Philip A. Snow, *Stranger and Brother: A Portrait of C. P. Snow* (London: Macmillan, 1982), p. xiii.

[9] Pamela Hansford Johnson, as quoted in John Halperin, *C. P. Snow: An Oral Biography, Together with a Conversation with Lady Snow (Pamela Hansford Johnson)* (New York: St. Martin's Press, 1983), p. 252.

[10] This material draws from William Cooper, "C. P. Snow," in *British Writers*, ed. Ian Scott-Kilvert (New York: Scribner's, 1984), vol. VII, pp. 321–341, as well as Stanley Weintraub, "Snow, Charles Percy, Baron Snow (1905–1980)," *Oxford Dictionary of National Biography* (Oxford University Press, 2004). See also David Cannadine, "C. P. Snow, 'The Two Cultures,' and the 'Corridors of Power' Revisited," in *Yet More Adventures with Britannia*, ed. Wm. Roger Louis (London: I. B. Tauris, 2005), pp. 101–118; David Shusterman, "C. P. Snow," *Dictionary of Literary Biography, Vol. 15: British Novelists, 1930–1959; Part 2: M-Z*, ed. Bernard Oldsey (Detroit: Gale, 1983), pp. 472–490, in addition to Halperin, *C. P. Snow* and Philip A. Snow, *Stranger and Brother*.

[11] Snow, *Time of Hope* (London: Faber and Faber, 1949).

estimated that they played nearly 3,400 games of table tennis over four years in Cambridge).[12] At Alderman Newton's Grammar School he was taken under the wing of Herbert Edmund ("Bert") Howard, an iconoclastic young history teacher who provided the model for George Passant in the initial installment of the Lewis Eliot series.[13] Since Alderman Newton's had no arts course in the sixth form, Snow – a voracious reader and talented student – specialized in science. He earned a scholarship to Leicester University College, where he took a First in chemistry and then an MSc, but already his horizons extended well beyond Leicester.

Snow arrived in Cambridge on a scholarship in 1928. He completed a doctorate in chemistry two years later, and was promptly elected a fellow of Christ's College – no mean achievement, as it was unusual for colleges to take fellows from among their own students.[14] At Christ's Snow began navigating between literature and science, living first in Milton's rooms before moving to Darwin's, and during breaks from his scientific work he began to write novels.[15] Before the age of thirty, though, he devoted most of his energy to scientific research. His work lay in the domain where chemistry and physics overlapped – Snow's PhD was in chemistry, but he was fascinated by physics. Between 1928 and 1935 he published twenty-two papers, all of them dealing with the interactions of molecules and radiation.[16] This research was distinguished: in the judgment of one historian of science, "In spite of difficulties, [Snow's] analyses were landmarks in the early development of infrared spectroscopy: these were papers of which anyone could have felt proud."[17] Snow was off to a fast start in his research, but not all of his work would prove so successful.

Snow next turned to work on photochemistry with his friend Philip Bowden. On Friday, May 13, 1932, the *Times* carried news of a significant breakthrough: Snow and Bowden appeared to have created vitamin A through irradiation.[18] Frederick Gowland Hopkins – Nobel Laureate, President of the Royal Society, and Cambridge professor – personally notified the *Times*, and a preliminary report appeared in *Nature*. "If the results of these experiments are in harmony with the

---

[12] Philip A. Snow, *Stranger and Brother*, p. 52.
[13] Snow, *Strangers and Brothers* (London: Faber and Faber, 1940), later retitled *George Passant*.
[14] J. C. D. Brand, "The Scientific Papers of C. P. Snow," *History of Science* 26 (June 1988), p. 112. The following account of Snow's scientific work derives from Brand's article.
[15] Halperin, *C. P. Snow*, p. 19.
[16] Brand, "The Scientific Papers of C. P. Snow," pp. 124–125.   [17] *Ibid.*, p. 115.
[18] "Birth of a Vitamin," *Times*, 13 May 1932, p. 11.

spectroscopic evidence," Snow and Bowden wrote, "it will appear that a photochemical transformation of carotene into vitamin A has been effected."[19] The newspaper back home was less inhibited (and less accurate): "Triumph of Young Scientist," proclaimed the *Leicester Mercury*, "Leicester Man Isolates New Vitamin."[20] Their procedures and interpretations were called into question in *Nature*, however, and within weeks Snow and Bowden had to retract their conclusion.[21] The setback was devastating: as Snow later recalled, "I was extremely miserable. Everything, personal and creative, seemed to be going wrong."[22] The episode did not end Snow's scientific career – he still had three years of productive work before him, in which he would publish nearly as many papers again as he already had – but it did help turn his attention towards the literary life he had long imagined.

These literary inclinations were encouraged when Snow published a novel, *Death under Sail*, to favorable notice in 1932.[23] The reviewer in *John O'London's* predicted, "If I am not mistaken (and if he finds time to writer other books) Dr. C. P. Snow . . . is going to take high rank among modern writers of the detective story."[24] Two more books soon followed: *New Lives for Old* (1933) and *The Search* (1934), the latter figuring as a subject of intellectual conversation in Dorothy Sayers's *Gaudy Night*.[25] In 1935 Snow turned away from research to focus on writing, while remaining a tutor at Christ's and serving as editor of the Cambridge Library of Modern Science. In 1937 he became editor of the popular science magazine *Discovery*, staying on the following year when Cambridge University Press took over publication.[26] By 1940 Snow had achieved enough notoriety to be included on the Gestapo's list of writers to be eliminated upon the occupation of Britain, along with Noël Coward, Virginia Woolf, Sigmund Freud, and Lytton Strachey (the

[19] F. P. Bowden and C. P. Snow, "Photochemistry of Vitamins A, B, C, D," *Nature*, 14 May 1932, p. 720.
[20] "Triumph of Young Scientist," *Leicester Mercury*, 12 May 1932, p. 9.
[21] I. M. Heilbron and R. A. Morton, "Photochemistry of Vitamins A, B, C, D," *Nature*, 11 June 1932, pp. 866–867; F. P. Bowden and C. P. Snow, "Photochemistry of Vitamins A, B, C, D," *Nature*, 25 June 1932, p. 943.
[22] Quoted in Brand, "The Scientific Papers of C. P. Snow," p. 119.
[23] C. P. Snow, *Death under Sail* (London: Heinemann, 1932).
[24] "A New Detective," *John O'London's Weekly*, 30 July 1932, HRC: Snow, Addition to His Papers, 7.5.
[25] C. P. Snow (anonymously), *New Lives for Old* (London: Victor Gollancz, 1933); Snow, *The Search* (Victor Gollancz, 1934); Dorothy Sayers, *Gaudy Night* (London: Victor Gollancz, 1935).
[26] Philip A. Snow, *Stranger and Brother*, p. 50. On *Discovery*, see Nicola M. R. Perrin, "Discovery: A Monthly Journal of Popular Knowledge," unpublished MSc thesis, University of London (1999).

document was not a highpoint of Nazi intelligence, as Strachey and Freud were already dead).[27]

In 1940 Snow began a long, if more obscure, career as a bureaucrat and administrator. He began by recruiting scientists to work on radar for the Ministry of Labour, and within two years became its director of technical personnel. This work sent him traveling between universities throughout Britain, and he later surmised that in this period he came to know as many scientists as anyone in the world.[28] Snow was good at this work, and was recognized in 1943 with the CBE – the first of several honors to come. At the end of the war he moved to London to pursue his writing full time, but he kept one foot in Whitehall (as a Civil Service Commissioner from 1945) and another in industry (as a director of English Electric from 1947). Indeed, in this period Snow was as much a bureaucrat as a novelist, which helps to explain his belief that bureaucracies were at the center of modern life, and that meaningful political change occurred entirely within them.

In 1950 Snow married the novelist and critic Pamela Hansford Johnson. It was at this time that, following Johnson's preference, "Percy" became Charles, and the couple soon became a fixture on the London literary scene. At the same time Snow was finding new audiences in politics and in punditry: he was awarded a Knighthood in 1957, followed the Rede Lecture of 1959 with the Godkin Lectures at Harvard in 1960, and privately advised the Labour Party before their victory in 1964. That election brought Snow into national politics as spokesman for the new Ministry of Technology in the House of Lords, a position that saw this son of a clerk become Baron Snow of Leicester. Snow's term in government was rocky, however, and he stepped down after less than two years. He completed *Strangers and Brothers* in 1970, and continued to write, review, and lecture until his death in 1980.

Bureaucratic realism

Snow's views on science, literature, and society were forged in Cambridge during the 1930s.[29] The Cavendish was an international hub

[27] *Times Literary Supplement*, 14 November 2003, p. 16.
[28] C. P. Snow, *Public Affairs* (New York: Scribner's, 1971), p. 187.
[29] See Stefan Collini's introduction to Snow, *The Two Cultures* (Cambridge University Press, 1993), pp. xxii–xxv. On science and politics in 1930s Cambridge, see Gary Werskey, *The Visible College: The Collective Biography of British Scientific Socialists of the 1930s* (London: Allen Lane, 1978); for the broader context, see William McGuckcn, *Scientists, Society, and State: The Social Relations of Science Movement in Great Britain, 1931–1947* (Columbus: Ohio State University Press, 1984).

for physics, its director Ernest Rutherford stalking the labs while bellowing "Onward Christian Soldiers," and Hopkins's Dunn Laboratory was a leading center for biochemistry. Snow came to know scientists such as J. D. Bernal, P. M. S. Blackett, J. B. S. Haldane, and Peter Kapitza, as well as the grand figures of Rutherford and Hopkins, and he was particularly inspired by their confidence and optimism. Later recalling Rutherford's exuberant refrain, "This is the heroic age of science! This is the Elizabethan age!", Snow added only that "he was absolutely right."[30] Snow came to believe that scientific practice, because of its inclination towards discovering and telling the truth, was inherently moral, and that science even offered a model of the ideal society. When a new generation of scientists entered the worlds of policy and politics after the Second World War, Snow believed they did so as "new men" – bringing new hope for old problems by instinct and action.[31]

To Snow, the contrast between these scientific instincts and more literary attitudes could not have been more stark than in the Cambridge that greeted him upon his arrival from Leicester. In addition to Rutherford and Hopkins, Cambridge in the 1930s was also home to the literary critic F. R. Leavis. Working in a new field (the English Tripos dated from 1917) and editing a new journal (he and his wife Q. D. Leavis helped found *Scrutiny* in 1932), Leavis was developing the ideas that would influence literary studies throughout the English-speaking world. Literary criticism in general, and Cambridge English in particular, could thus hardly be branded static domains of inherited ideas – after all, Leavis and his colleagues were more likely to be challenging orthodoxies than defending them – but that was not the way things looked to Snow. Leavis's style of criticism struck him as deeply conservative, even reactionary, because it seemed more interested in lamenting the disappearance of the past than in bringing about a new and better future. In private he took to mocking Leavis, deriding him as a "wheel-monger" for his sympathetic discussion of George Sturt's *The Wheelwright's Shop*.[32] To Snow, such

---

[30] C. P. Snow, *The Two Cultures and the Scientific Revolution* (Cambridge University Press, 1959), pp. 4–5.

[31] For Snow's ideas on science and scientists, see the essays in *Public Affairs*, especially "Science and Government," and "The Moral Un-neutrality of Science" (in addition to "The Two Cultures"). See also "The Men of Fission," *Holiday*, April 1958, pp. 95, 108–115, and "The Age of Rutherford," *Atlantic Monthly*, November 1958, pp. 76–81. Scientists also figured prominently in his novels, especially *The Search*, *The New Men* (London: Macmillan, 1954), and *The Affair* (London: Macmillan, 1960).

[32] Snow to S. Gorley Putt, 10 April 1934, HRC: Snow 134.7. Leavis had discussed Sturt sympathetically, if not so straightforwardly, in *Culture and Environment*, co-written with Denys Thompson (London: Chatto and Windus, 1933).

nostalgia was typical among literary intellectuals who failed to acknowledge the misery that had characterized most people's lives in the past.
He thought this attitude especially engrained in the English Tripos,
where the exclusion of H. G. Wells, for instance, signaled to Snow a
hostility to progress itself.[33] Already we can discern the broad associations that Snow was later to pack into his explosive remarks about
"scientific" and "literary" intellectuals.

In this Cambridge, dominated by Rutherford on one hand and Leavis
on the other, Snow developed the stance that informed his thinking for
decades to come.[34] Today that stance might appear eccentric, even
wrongheaded, but the aim here is to understand rather than criticize it.
Snow believed that literature took a disastrous turn between 1914 and
1950 (the precise dates varied, depending on the time he was writing,
but generally the crisis coincided with the previous generation of
writers). In that period, Snow argued, writers such as James Joyce,
Virginia Woolf, and William Faulkner had abandoned the effort to
produce narratives about society – in Snow's shorthand, "realism" – in
favor of the celebration of technical experimentation and social alienation – what Snow meant by "Modernism." He referred to the work
produced by the latter as the "anti-novel," which was represented above
all by *Finnegans Wake*. The anti-novel seemed to Snow to reject the
effort to depict the social world and speak to a wide audience, and as
such he believed that it rejected society itself. Instead, Snow continued,
Modernist writers glorified the alienated individual, a tendency that led
them to embrace reactionary attitudes – and here Snow pointed to
figures such as Joyce, Wyndham Lewis, Ezra Pound, T. E. Hulme, and
D. H. Lawrence. This reaction derived from hostility to what Snow
called the "scientific revolution," the ongoing phase of industrialization
in which productive capacity increased through the application of science
and technology.[35] This development, in Snow's view, had increased the
complexity of social organization, and it had done so at the moment that
the social sciences began to fill roles that had previously belonged to

---

[33] Snow to Putt, 23 December 1934, HRC: Snow 134.4. On Snow's identification with
Wells, and his resentment of the reception of Wells in Cambridge English, see Collini's
introduction to Snow, *The Two Cultures* (1993), pp. xxiii–xxv.

[34] Snow frequently rehearsed versions of this argument, for example, "Valedictory,"
Sunday Times, 28 December 1952, p. 7, and "Challenge to the Intellect," *Times Literary
Supplement*, 15 August 1958, p. 2946, in addition to *The Two Cultures*. One of its earliest
expressions was in the proposal for *The Mermaid*, written in 1948 and discussed below.

[35] David Landes later provided what has become the more familiar term (the "second
industrial revolution") and periodization (the late nineteenth century) in *The Unbound
Prometheus: Technological Change and Industrial Development in Western Europe from 1750
to the Present* (Cambridge University Press, 1969).

writers. Rather than accepting these developments and exploring them through fiction, Snow believed that the Modernist generation had withdrawn from a society they could neither understand nor influence.

Towards the end of the 1940s, however, Snow detected renewed hope for literature. The writers who attracted his attention included Pamela Hansford Johnson, William Cooper, and William Gerhardi, all of whom – like Snow himself – were interested in exploring the changing relationship between the individual and society. In Snow's optimistic reading of history, the scientific revolution had created vast new bureaucracies, along with a new class of professionals and managers to staff them. The society that resulted promised material comfort, educational opportunity, and social status to a greater share of the population than ever before, but in order to realize this promise these professionals – managers, technicians, scientists, civil servants, and others – needed to understand their institutions, their society, and themselves. Snow was attracted to writers who confronted this challenge, and who attempted to explain (rather than repudiate) the emerging society. These writers rejected the recent and regrettable Modernist detour, and drew inspiration instead from nineteenth-century realism – and it was that heritage, and this movement, that Snow was committed to promoting through his fiction and criticism.

Snow's every effort in this regard was conditioned by his conception of how politics worked. His sense of politics was consistent with a faith in bureaucracies and managers: Snow believed that change was effected through existing institutions rather than radical protests. He referred to this process as "closed politics," which he took to function similarly in the Vatican, Kremlin, British Cabinet, medieval monasteries, or – as in his most famous novel, *The Masters* – Oxbridge colleges. There was little place here for ideology or rebellion; instead, Snow's model of politics required the cultivation and management of tactical alliances. So in *The Masters*, as two fellows plot their candidate's campaign to become master, Eliot observes, "They knew how men in a college behaved, and the different places in which each man was weak, ignorant, indifferent, obstinate, or strong. They never overplayed their hand [and] knew how to give way. [As a result] little of importance happened in the college which they did not support."[36] The resulting coalitions had little to do with labels such as "left" or "right" – as Eliot explains, "College politics often cut right across national ones. Thus Winslow, an upper class radical, became in the college extremely reactionary, and Francis Getliffe and I, both men of the left, found ourselves in the college supporting the

[36] C. P. Snow, *The Masters* (London: Macmillan, 1951), p. 34.

'government'."[37] And although Snow primarily thought of politics as a matter of rational choices between reasonable people, he allowed that it could be complicated by the vagaries of psychology – as on the occasion when Eliot notices Chrystal taking steps that Chrystal himself did not understand.[38] Incremental, managerial, tactical, and clandestine: this is how Snow believed politics worked, and it was this conception of politics that guided his efforts to influence literature upon moving to London in 1945.

The campaign

As November turned into December in 1947, a sense of despair pervaded Snow's letters to his old friend from Christ's, Gorley Putt. The second novel in the Lewis Eliot sequence, *The Light and the Dark*, had recently come out, and the early reviews were disheartening. "So far, failure," Snow wrote, "and I do not expect anything but abuse from the *New Statesman* and the *Listener*." Snow felt himself to be "writing dead in the teeth against the fashion," and he saw little chance that the literary establishment would ever come around.[39] He decided that they needed to take the initiative: "We've got to be more active and less proud," he exhorted Putt.[40] Putt had read English with Leavis in Cambridge, and Snow hoped that he would attain a position that would enable him to intervene in literary debates.[41] Their subsequent "campaign" (as they called it) may not have altered the course of literary history, but it does reveal the intimate connections among Snow's ideas about history, fiction, and politics.[42]

Snow first set about courting the reclusive writer William Gerhardi.[43] Born to British subjects in St. Petersburg in 1895, Gerhardi had been educated in London; he then served in the British embassy in Petrograd,

---

[37] *Ibid.*   [38] Halperin, *C. P. Snow*, p. 149.
[39] Snow to Putt, 29 [24?] November 1947, HRC: Snow 134.5.
[40] Snow to Putt, 17 February 1948, HRC: Snow 134.5.
[41] Snow to Putt, 29 [24?] November 1947, HRC: Snow 134.5.
[42] Snow's campaign was one strand of many calling for a "return to realism" after the war; on the problems with that narrative, see Marina MacKay, "'Doing Business with Totalitaria': British Late Modernism and the Politics of Reputation," *ELH* 73 (2006), pp. 729–753. See also her *Modernism and World War II* (Cambridge University Press, 2007).
[43] On Gerhardi, see Bo Gunnarsson, *The Novels of William Gerhardie* (Abo Akademi University Press, 1995); Michael Holroyd, "Gerhardie, William Alexander (1895– 1977)," *Oxford Dictionary of National Biography* (Oxford University Press, 2004); Donna Olendorf, "Gerhardie, William Alexander," *Contemporary Authors*, ed. Linda Metzger and Deborah A. Straub, New Revision Series (Detroit: Gale, 1986), vol. XVIII, pp. 179–181. Gerhardi added the "e" to his surname in 1967.

until the Bolshevik Revolution ruined his father. He served as member of the Scots Guards in the anti-Bolshevik campaign of 1918–1920, and returned to England to read Russian at Oxford. He settled in London and began to write a series of plays, stories, critical studies, and novels, earning praise for his ironic sensibility from such figures as Katherine Mansfield, Edith Wharton, and Evelyn Waugh. Then, during the 1930s, he fell out of favor among the literary left, who criticized him for not engaging with Marxism when writing about the Russian Revolution. In 1948, though, Gerhardi was an ideal candidate for the job of "grand old man" of Snow's movement: his interest in Chekhov rendered him an ally in the effort to revive realism, his clear prose offered an alternative to experimental Modernism, and his ironic political comedy was consistent with a vision of politics as managerial rather than ideological.[44]

Snow wrote to inform Gerhardi that he intended to discuss his work in an upcoming broadcast. "The occasion is comic, and I thought might amuse you," Snow said, but he added that he had other ambitions: "[I]t is also the first blow in a campaign. A number of my literary associates and I are angry at the imbecile treatment you have received from the 30-ish generation of critics."[45] Snow hoped to persuade the critic Desmond MacCarthy, who had endorsed *Strangers and Brothers* in 1940, to review Gerhardi's collected works. "I don't know him well, but his values are our own," he told Gerhardi. "I think his advice is worth taking about how to begin a literary war."[46] But Snow failed to secure MacCarthy's agreement over dinner, and so decided to write the review himself. In the *Sunday Times* Snow praised Gerhardi for having escaped the "literary ice age" that had descended upon English letters around 1930.[47] Putt, meanwhile, had reported from Exeter that *Time and Tide* had accepted his proposal for a piece on Gerhardi.[48] In just the first five months of 1948, then, Snow's campaign had scored some victories: he had forged a relationship with Gerhardi, placed two favorable reviews on

[44] As early as 1935 Snow recommended Gerhardi's work to Putt, alongside Chekhov and Wells: Snow to Putt, 1 September 1935, in Caroline Nobile Gryta, "Selected Letters of C. P. Snow: A Critical Edition," unpublished PhD dissertation, Pennsylvania State University (1988), p. 84.

[45] Snow to Gerhardi, 27 January 1948, Cambridge University Library (CUL): Snow–Gerhardie correspondence, File 8292/23/1.

[46] Snow to Gerhardi, 12 February 1948, CUL: Snow–Gerhardie correspondence, File 8292/23/2; 27 February 1948, File 8292/23/4.

[47] *Sunday Times*, 23 May 1948, included in CUL: Snow–Gerhardie correspondence, File 8292/23/7. Gerhardi actually protested this characterization of his writing, but Snow immediately smoothed things over: Snow to Gerhardi, 25 May 1948, CUL: Snow–Gerhardie correspondence, File 8292/23/9.

[48] Putt to Snow, 20 February 1948, CUL: Snow–Gerhardie correspondence, File 8292/23/3.

his behalf, and – most importantly – inserted his own critique of literary history into public circulation.

As Snow was establishing his relationship with Gerhardi, his campaign caught its first break. Pamela Johnson reported that she had been approached with an offer to establish a new journal. With *Horizon* and *The Windmill* struggling, there seemed to be room for a lively new periodical. "This, I think, is really it at last," she wrote. "I am anxious that you and Harry and I should meet at the earliest moment and flog out a scheme."[49] Along with Jack Plumb (then engaged in his own battles in Cambridge, examined in Chapter 4), Pamela Johnson and Harry Hoff were two of Snow's closest confidantes.

Johnson came to Snow's attention when she favorably reviewed *Strangers and Brothers* in 1940.[50] The daughter of a colonial administrator in west Africa, she was born in London in 1912 and educated in Clapham.[51] She left school at sixteen to work in a bank, but kept up her reading and also began writing. In 1934 she won a poetry prize, and around the same time she began a relationship with Dylan Thomas.[52] After two years they decided against marriage, and at the end of 1936 she wed an Australian journalist, Gordon Neil Stewart. Her first novel, *This Bed Thy Centre* (1935), met considerable success, and – encouraged by Cyril Connolly – Johnson left her job to focus on her writing.[53] She established herself as a novelist and reviewer, and later as an authority on Proust and a BBC regular. Her review of *Strangers and Brothers* instigated a correspondence with Snow, and the following year the two met in London.[54] Over tea in Piccadilly they learned that they shared similar attitudes about writing, especially in their mutual hope for a revival of narrative.[55] Johnson's marriage to Stewart ended in 1949, and she and Snow married in a ceremony at Christ's the following year. In 1948, though, when this meeting was called to plan a new journal, the nuptials were still two years away.

---

[49] Johnson to Snow, 11 March 1948, HRC: Snow 111.4.
[50] Snow to Harry Hoff, 26 March [?] 1940, in Gryta, "Selected Letters of C. P. Snow," pp. 112–113.
[51] This material on Johnson draws from Alan Maclean, "Johnson, Pamela Helen Hansford [*married name* Pamela Helen Hansford Snow, Lady Snow] (1912–1981)," *Oxford Dictionary of National Biography* (Oxford University Press, 2004), as well as from Johnson's memoir, *Important to Me* (New York: Scribner's, 1974).
[52] Pamela Hansford Johnson, *Important to Me*, pp. 140–149.
[53] Pamela Hansford Johnson, *This Bed Thy Centre* (London: Chapman and Hall, 1935).
[54] Halperin, *C. P. Snow*, p. 248.
[55] Johnson discussed the state of the novel in "The Sickroom Hush over the English Novel," *List*, 11 August 1949, quoted in Rubin Rabinovitz, *The Reaction against Experiment in the English Novel, 1950–1960* (New York: Columbia University Press, 1967), pp. 5–6.

Like Snow and Plumb, Harry Hoff had gone from provincial origins to Christ's College in Cambridge. When he arrived at Christ's in 1931 to read natural sciences, Snow became his tutor.[56] The two struck up a friendship, especially when they realized that they both wanted to write novels that eschewed technical experiment. Hoff echoed Snow in linking Modernism with reactionary politics, and – in what could have been Snow's own words – he later asserted that experimental novelists were driven by their hatred of industrial society.[57] Writing under the pseudonym William Cooper, Hoff came to be admired for his "Scenes from Life" novels, beginning with *Scenes from Provincial Life* in 1950.[58] These novels were characterized by their understated wit in following Hoff's alter-ego, Joe Lunn. "I am a realistic novelist," Hoff later said. "My aim is to tell the truth, laughing."[59]

Hoff, Johnson, and Snow gathered for what they called a "council of war" to discuss their prospective journal, *The Mermaid*.[60] Snow reported that MacCarthy and Gerhardi were going to figure as distinguished ornaments, that Putt would join them as central to the working group, and that Johnson was "the Fuhrerin of the new movement."[61] The campaign was up and running, but they needed to identify additional writers who might prove sympathetic to the cause. Snow contacted the young novelist Francis King, telling him that he considered King the most promising male writer under the age of thirty. Might King know of others dissatisfied with recent literature and criticism? "There's going to be some fun," he promised, "now the recent Ice Age of English Literature (1930–1947) is ebbing away."[62]

The "Ice Age of English Literature" was a characteristic concept in the group's diagnosis of the novel, which they set out in detail in a polemical manifesto.[63] That manifesto followed Snow's characteristic interpretation of literary history, depicting Modernism as a detour from

[56] Cooper, "C. P. Snow," p. 339.
[57] William Cooper, "Reflections on Some Aspects of the Experimental Novel," in *International Literary Annual*, ed. John Wain (London: John Calder, 1959), discussed in Rabinovitz, *The Reaction against Experiment in the English Novel*, pp. 6–7.
[58] William Cooper, *Scenes from Provincial Life* (London: Jonathan Cape, 1950).
[59] Quoted in "Hoff, Harry S(ummerfield)," *Contemporary Authors*, ed. Linda Metzger and Deborah A. Straub, New Revision Series (Detroit: Gale, 1987), vol. XX, p. 232.
[60] Snow to Putt, 25 March 1948, HRC: Snow 169.10; Johnson to Snow, 11 March 1948, HRC: Snow 111.4.
[61] Snow to Putt, 25 March 1948, HRC: Snow 169.10.
[62] Snow to Francis King, 18 & 22 April, 27 October 1948, HRC: Snow 134.10.
[63] "The MERMAID Proposal," HRC: Snow 111.4. When she submitted the final version to her editor, Johnson made clear that Snow had written the document (in consultation with the group): Johnson to Robert Lusty, n.d., HRC: Snow 111.4.

the realist tradition in which they (rather grandiosely) imagined themselves:

> We have expressed our belief in the literature of human truth: in the line of Homer, Petronius, and the Latin novelists, the sagas, Lady Murasaki, Chaucer, down to the great nineteenth-century novelists, Dostoevsky, Tolstoy, Dickens, and Balzac: the succession is clear down to the present day in the fine, though minor stream of the French novelists, Roger Martin du Gard and Mauriac: and to the service of this belief we offer *The Mermaid*.[64]

Johnson enthusiastically submitted the credo to Michael Joseph's publishing firm. The planning moved forward through April, but hit a roadblock in May. "The only development is dismal and apparently conclusive," she despondently told Plumb. " '[F]or the time being', they've shelved the whole scheme."[65] *The Mermaid* had been canceled due to a paper shortage; deterred but determined, the campaign carried on.

Rather than starting a new journal, Snow redirected his efforts towards securing positions at established publications. During the war he had hoped to see Johnson hired by the *New Statesman* or *Tribune*, and in 1948 she was finally meeting success on that front.[66] Putt continued to circulate their credo around Exeter, and he reported interest from *The Wind and the Rain*, a quarterly magazine edited by the young poet Neville Braybrooke. At the same time, he was angling for a position as a director at the Phoenix Press, where he hoped to bring Snow onboard: "Once inside the citadel of an established quarterly, I shall open the gates to you all. At a suitable stage, when you personally are entrenched too, you can then open the financial floodgates and expand the paper in size, circulation and power."[67] He donated £100 to *The Wind and the Rain*, enough to secure a position on its advisory board.[68] Snow accepted an offer to lecture at Exeter's summer school, where he addressed a new generation on two of his favorite themes: "The Credo of a Novelist" and "The Novel: Recent Trends."[69] Putt later recalled the "conspiratorial area of Snow's imagination," which he linked to his "mania for launching a critical movement favourable to the reception of his own fiction."[70] At the time, however, Putt was enjoying the action:

---

[64] "The MERMAID Proposal," HRC: Snow 111.4.

[65] Johnson to Plumb, 15 May 1948, CUL: Plumb papers, Box "C. P. Snow + Pam: 1946 to 1968," File "Snow 1946 to 1968."

[66] Snow to Johnson, 23 November 1944, in Gryta, "Selected Letters of C. P. Snow," p. 129.

[67] Putt to Snow, 20 May 1948, HRC: Snow 169.10.

[68] Putt to Snow, 19 June 1948, HRC: Snow 169.10.

[69] Putt to Snow, 16 July 1948, HRC: Snow 169.11.

[70] Putt's annotation on a letter from Snow, 24 February 1948, HRC: Snow 134.5.

"Oh, Snow my boy, you *have* stirred up the old Exeter tortoise to some purpose!" he wrote. "I can't tell you with what pleasure I find myself taking an active part in this campaign!"[71] Gerhardi, too, was throwing himself into things, publishing a fawning letter about his own work under the name of a woman.[72]

Snow, meanwhile, urged Alan Pryce-Jones, editor of the *Times Literary Supplement*, to hire Putt as a reviewer.[73] He was also becoming friendly with Leonard Russell of the *Sunday Times*, and was well aware of the opportunity that beckoned there: "If I do secure this," he told his publisher, "I should guarantee to make a difference within quite a short time."[74] Snow and Russell would occasionally meet in an old billiards hall, where Russell learned to his surprise that this novel-writing scientist was a formidable critic. Snow held forth on the disaster of the Modernist novel and plotted its demise, until one evening when he thrust a copy of his credo into Russell's hands. Russell read it that night and wired Snow immediately to offer him a column.[75] Just eight months after their plans for *The Mermaid* had folded, with Snow at the *Sunday Times*, Johnson at the *Observer*, and Putt at the *Times Literary Supplement* and *Time and Tide*, Snow and his allies were positioned amid the heights of metropolitan reviewing. "If we survive ten years," he predicted, "we shall have some literary power."[76]

Snow had found an ideal position from which to promote his ideas. "I am fighting the hardest battles of my writing life," he told his brother. "[The *Sunday Times*] is, of course, a most valuable strategic position, and I don't want to give it up until I have secured the major objectives."[77] In his fortnightly reviews of new fiction, Snow praised novels that rejected experiment, addressed a wide audience, or featured respectable classes (or at least someone striving for that status). He sought writers to endorse, a goal that he contrasted with Leavis and *Scrutiny*: "It *is* important to praise where we can," Snow told Putt. "Remember that Leavis as a Victorian critic would almost certainly have despised the books which he now studies with loving attention [, and]

[71] Putt to Snow, 20 May 1948, 19 June 1948, HRC: Snow 169.10.
[72] Putt's annotation on a letter to Snow, 25 June 1948, HRC: Snow 134.8.
[73] Snow to Putt, 13 June 1948, HRC: Snow 134.6. In his own annotation to this letter, Putt explained that he and Pryce-Jones had been colleagues during the war.
[74] Snow to Peter du Sautoy, 25 January 1949, HRC: Snow 85.1.
[75] Leonard Russell, "Billiard-Room Talks," *Sunday Times*, 6 March 1960, p. 18.
[76] Snow to Philip A. Snow, 22 December 1948, quoted in Philip A. Snow, *Stranger and Brother*, p. 100.
[77] Snow to Philip A. Snow, 19 August 1949, quoted in Philip A. Snow, *Stranger and Brother*, p. 101.

that you and I would have had to rescue them."[78] But when the books that landed on his desk explored darker themes – such as, on one occasion, rape, murder, disease, lynching, and suicide – Snow registered dismay. He rebuked William Faulkner, for instance, for his grim subject matter, unreadable style, and hostility to punctuation: "[A] genuine, but very limited, artist," ran Snow's verdict, "and artists of his kind have been rather excessively praised in the last twenty years."[79] At the *Sunday Times* Snow used his position to direct attention away from those trends, and towards a more accessible and optimistic style of literature instead.

After four years of reviewing, Snow felt cause for satisfaction. "[H]as the gap between the reading public's opinion and 'literary' opinion been tending to get larger or smaller?" he asked in his farewell column. "I think the answer is, if anything: very slightly smaller."[80] The stream-of-consciousness (or as Snow called it, "moment-by-moment") technique appeared to have run its course, and he predicted that the coming decade would see a turn "to novels in form more traditional, in substance less specialised, in intention more wide-ranging, in total effect both more investigatory and more human."[81] He thought that his critical analysis of literary trends had made an impact, and the moment seemed right to press the movement forward on other fronts. In 1952 Snow ended his association with the *Sunday Times*, and turned his attention to his own fiction in earnest.

Strangers and Brothers

In the 1930s Snow endured humiliation as a scientist, and in the 1940s he faced a critical reception as a novelist, but in the 1950s he achieved success so rapidly that even he was caught by surprise. The decade got off to a fast start when the British Annual of Literature named *Time of Hope* the best novel of 1949.[82] Snow was soon finding himself placed among exclusive (if contradictory) company: one critic compared him to Stendhal, another went with Trollope, still another thought Proust.[83] "[W]e can speak of 'a Snow situation' as we speak of 'a Proustian

---

[78] Snow to Putt, 19 January 1949, HRC: Snow 134.6. For further discussion of Snow's reviewing practices in the *Sunday Times*, see Rabinovitz, *The Reaction Against Experiment in the English Novel*.

[79] C. P. Snow, "Cult of the Atrocious," *Sunday Times*, 16 October 1949 (typescript in HRC: Snow 34.2).

[80] Snow, "Valedictory," p. 7.   [81] *Ibid.*

[82] Snow to Spencer Curtis Brown, 2 January 1950, HRC: Snow 85.2.

[83] "New Novels," *Spectator*, 14 May 1954, p. 600; "Snow: Major Road Ahead!" *New Statesman and Nation*, 22 September 1956, pp. 350–352; Helen Gardner, "The World of C. P. Snow," *New Statesman*, 29 March 1958, pp. 409–410.

experience'," Helen Gardner wrote in the *New Statesman*. "[T]he whole enterprise seems to me the most impressive attempt in our generation to explore through fiction the moral nature of man."[84] *The Masters* and *The New Men* won the James Tait Black Memorial Prize of 1954, and the Readers' Subscription Book Club, with a board consisting of W. H. Auden, Jacques Barzun, and Lionel Trilling, named *The New Men* its selection for February 1955. Trilling wrote that Snow renewed his hope for the novel, and he praised *The Masters* in particular as "a paradigm of the political life."[85] 1958 was an especially exciting year: Snow received red-carpet treatment on a visit to Harvard, he was offered a visiting chair at the University of California at Berkeley, and he returned from America with the news that Trilling, Alfred Kazin, and Norman Podhoretz were singing his praises.[86] He began to think himself a candidate for the Nobel Prize.[87]

Confident that *Strangers and Brothers* had secured its place in literary history, Snow became fond of relating the tale of its origin. On 1 January 1935, the story went, he was alone and depressed in Marseilles when inspiration struck: "Suddenly I saw, or felt, or experienced, or whatever you like to call it, both the outline of the entire *Strangers and Brothers* sequence and its inner organization."[88] There is no reason to doubt that he planned the series that evening, but its organization actually developed over time: in September 1935 Snow expected it to consist of three novels; by 1939 that number had grown to four; and it was not until the end of the war that it definitively assumed its eleven-volume structure.[89] The first installment, *Strangers and Brothers*, was published in 1940, and it was later retitled *George Passant* when "Strangers and Brothers" became the name of the sequence as a whole.

Strangers and Brothers examined the workers and workings of bureaucratic Britain.[90] The narrator, Lewis Eliot, hails from the lower-middle

---

[84] Gardner, "The World of C. P. Snow," p. 410.
[85] Lionel Trilling, "The Novel Alive or Dead," *Griffin*, February 1955, p. 9. *The Griffin* was the publication of the Readers' Subscription Book Club; a copy of this issue is included with Snow's personal library, HRC: PN 3354 T754 HRC.
[86] Snow to Harvey Curtis Webster, 4 March 1958, HRC: Snow 205.4; Snow reported the news about the Berkeley chair in a letter to Hoff, 19 September 1958, HRC: Snow 118.3.
[87] Philip A. Snow, *Stranger and Brother*, p. 130.
[88] Snow to Michael Millgate, 1 March 1961, in Gryta, "Selected Letters of C. P. Snow," p. 214.
[89] Snow to Putt, 1 September 1935, in Gryta, "Selected Letters of C. P. Snow," p. 81; Philip A. Snow, *Stranger and Brother*, p. 60.
[90] The first three books were published by Faber and Faber; Snow switched to Macmillan beginning with *The Masters*. The omnibus edition, which included revised versions of all

class of a provincial town, and the novels follow Lewis's journey through the labyrinthine establishments of society and state. Along the way readers become acquainted with aristocrats and bureaucrats, barristers and dons, writers and scientists, and ministers and civil servants. These lives intersect in the meritocracies and bureaucracies of modern Britain: bureaucratic meritocracies such as Cambridge colleges and the scientific establishment, and meritocratic bureaucracies such as Parliament and Whitehall. Each installment could be read individually, but Snow intended for the work to be judged as a whole.

The series opens with *George Passant*, which depicts the impact of a charismatic, but flawed, idealist upon a provincial town in the 1920s. *The Light and the Dark* (1947) follows, its brilliant hero Roy Calvert struggling with depression to the point of being driven to the most dangerous missions of the Second World War. *Time of Hope* (1949) recounts Eliot's personal story, a tale of ambition and self-discovery which sees him recover from the bankruptcy of his father to achieve success at the bar. *The Masters* (1951), the book that made Snow's career and established him as an analyst of politics, was an early entry into the genre of postwar academic fiction. Snow went on to develop the theme of politics from the perspective of scientists in *The New Men* (1954), which follows Britain's atomic scientists as they work to build an atomic bomb, and then to prevent its use.

By the mid 1950s Snow's sails were taking wind: the *New Statesman* called *The New Men* an "exceptional novel," and the *Spectator* compared Snow to Stendhal.[91] *Homecomings* (1956) resumes Eliot's personal story, following his progress through university, industry, and the civil service. *The Conscience of the Rich* (1958) moves back to the interwar period, as Eliot witnesses the conflict between privilege and obligation in a wealthy Jewish family. That was followed by another Cambridge thriller, *The Affair* (1960), in which an unpopular fellow – and fellow-traveler – is wrongly accused of scientific fraud. *Corridors of Power* (1964) takes Snow's interest in politics directly into Parliament, where Eliot watches the plotting of a Conservative MP to divest Britain of the bomb. Four years later, and now writing deliberately against the spirit of the 1960s, *The Sleep of Reason* (1968) criticizes the permissive society through the story of the trial of a pair of homicidal lesbians. And finally, *Last Things*

---

eleven novels in the order the author intended (rather than the order of publication), was published in three volumes by Macmillan in 1972.

[91] "New Novels," *New Statesman and Nation*, 1 May 1954, p. 573; "New Novels," *Spectator*, 14 May 1954, p. 600.

(1970): Eliot's hopeful look at the next generation, and Snow's answer to more romantic accounts of radical rebellion.

These novels conveyed a characteristic mood – a restrained, ponderous sobriety that has aptly been called "dreamy."[92] Their appeal lay partly in the sense they conveyed of providing access to sayings and doings that normally unfolded behind closed doors. For our purposes, however, they provide access of another kind: not to the way the world worked, but to the way Snow thought it did. Snow was forthright about the fact that all of his writings, both fiction and non-fiction, were variations on a theme; for instance, he explained that he deliberately intertwined the arguments of his Godkin Lectures, *Science and Government*, and his political novel, *Corridors of Power*.[93] Indeed, since they mutually developed his ideas about society, Snow wanted his novels to be read alongside *The Two Cultures*: "In the Rede Lecture I gave an explicit account of what my social thinking is like. Ideally I should like my novels to be read with that as a kind of explicit gloss or social commentary at the side."[94] While they should not be read as direct reflections of British society, Snow's novels do provide a rich body of evidence into how he believed that society worked.

The world that Snow created was very much a man's world. Despite his ambition to depict the whole of social experience, the actors (which is not to say the characters) were overwhelmingly men – indeed, not for nothing was the sequence entitled *Strangers and* Brothers. Trilling observed, by way of contrast with Cyril Connolly's remarks on the feminization of the English novel, that Snow's work exhibited a decidedly masculine emphasis: "[Snow] and his characters treat women very fairly, sometimes with admiration, often with tenderness," he explained. "But women are the honored guests in a masculine world – the communication is all between men."[95] This emphasis resulted from Snow's interest in the public lives of the professional classes, since in his view both the public and the professional remained the preserves of men (as revealed on the occasion that he suggested that scientists made unusually good "husbands and fathers").[96] To be sure, Snow regretted that Britain halved its talent pool by not training more women as

---

[92] Ian MacKillop, *F. R. Leavis: A Life in Criticism* (London: Allen Lane, 1995), p. 315.
[93] Snow to Podhoretz, 9 March 1960, HRC: Snow 165.10.
[94] "Interview with C. P. Snow," *English Literature* 3 (July 1962), pp. 106–107.
[95] Trilling, "The Novel Alive or Dead," p. 11.
[96] Snow, "The Moral Un-neutrality of Science," delivered in 1960 and reprinted in *Public Affairs*, p. 187. Collini observes, "All the pieces collected in *Public Affairs* reflect the tone of this wholly male world of briskly competent meritocrats, conscious of access to power and flushed with a pride in their own shrewdness." Collini, Introduction to Snow, *The Two Cultures*, p. lxx, n. 47.

scientists, and he consistently advocated the education of women in the name of national survival.[97] But in Snow's work the language of gender was more than simply a claim about, or a reflection of, social realities: it also conveyed broader associations, such as in his depictions of the "scientific" (progressive, masculine, and generally positive) and "literary" (reactionary, effeminate, and generally negative) cultures.

Snow was especially interested in exploring the relationships between individuals and institutions. As he explained to his publisher when he first conceived the sequence, "How much of what we are is due to accidents of our class and time, and how much is due to something innate and unalterable within ourselves?"[98] He wanted to tackle that question in a more sympathetic light than had the previous generation, and he situated his characters within organizations that both constrained and enabled their efforts: *constrained* because they were always contained within existing institutions, but *enabled* because those institutions made meaningful change possible. Snow believed that the novelist's duty was to explore the organizations upon which society depended, and to educate the people within them about the world in which they lived. In the course of that effort emerged his ultimate theme, power: "All my novels are part of one complicated theme, which is power in the modern state," he explained. "And in writing about power I have been trying to show how it is really exerted in Britain."[99] Anthony Sampson, whose *Anatomy of Britain* appeared in 1962, could not have said it better himself.[100]

In style and in content, *Strangers and Brothers* extended a campaign that began before *The Mermaid* and carried on through the *Sunday Times*. That campaign rejected what Snow understood as the Modernist disdain for contemporary society, and it advocated instead sympathetic consideration of the relationship between individuals and institutions. Whatever the judgment of posterity, in their time Snow's novels achieved many of the goals that he set: they created a world in which individuals were optimistic, society was functional, and politics were pragmatic. In other words, *Strangers and Brothers* represented the realization of the worldview that Snow developed and advocated over the course of his life.

---

[97] Snow, *The Two Cultures*, p. 51, n. 20. David Edgerton discusses the "masculinization" of British science after the Second World War in *Warfare State: Britain, 1920–1970* (Cambridge University Press, 2006), pp. 172–180.

[98] Quoted in Cooper, "C. P. Snow," p. 333.

[99] Quoted in Shusterman, "C. P. Snow," p. 489.

[100] Anthony Sampson, *Anatomy of Britain* (London: Hodder and Stoughton, 1962).

Technocratic liberalism

Snow's worldview may be understood as a "technocratic liberalism." *Liberal* because predicated upon the individual, embracing neither the egalitarianism of socialism nor the fixed hierarchies of conservatism; *technocratic* because the individual was always embedded within organizations, bureaucracies, and institutions that required the art of management. Snow approved of modern society because he was convinced that it had improved living conditions and increased social mobility for the majority of the population. He believed that the task at hand now was to extend these benefits still further, opening institutions of academia, industry, and the state to talented individuals at home while fostering industrialization abroad. This work would be accomplished not by protest or revolution, but by replacing the conflicts of politics with the management of experts – that is, through technocracy. In short, Snow advocated working through existing organizations, incrementally but progressively, to extend prosperity and opportunity.[101]

Although he occasionally followed the parlance of the day by expressing adherence to "socialism," Snow was not a socialist and his commitment was not to equality. He was, however, pragmatic in his politics, and he viewed the Labour Party as the best available vehicle for the realization of his ideals. When Putt stood for Parliament as a Liberal in 1945, Snow complimented him for the effort but scorned his naiveté: "You ought to have been standing as a Labour candidate."[102] Putt found this admonition odd, since he thought of Snow as a liberal, but Snow explained that any political party needed a broad social base. In the context of his approach to politics, this position made sense: Snow may have been liberal, and he may even have been *a* liberal, but in politics he was pragmatic and he always voted Labour.

Snow's position was based upon his progressive reading of history. He thought of history as a sequence through the agricultural, industrial, and scientific revolutions. This linear reading, unfolding along axes of "time" and "development," shaped Snow's reading of international politics: Britain and the West had advanced the furthest, the Soviet Union stood where the West had a century before, and the states of Asia and Africa lined up after them. Snow believed that Britain industrialized first by a stroke of luck, amassing wealth and power as a consequence, but that its elite remained committed to economic and educational structures that

---

[101] For another perspective on Snow's politics, see John de la Mothe, *C. P. Snow and the Struggle of Modernity* (Austin: University of Texas, 1992), Chapter 6.
[102] Snow to Putt, 5 August 1945, HRC: 134.8.

were appropriate to an earlier stage. These outmoded structures were retarding Britain's embrace of the scientific revolution, in which science and technology promised further advance. Fortunately, the sheer complexity of an industrial society had generated the organizations essential to its management, so the necessary structures were already in place. These structures were not a necessary evil, but a historical achievement – a good thing in and of themselves: "Trade unions, collective dealing, the entire apparatus of modern industry – they may be maddening to those who have never had the experience of the poor, but they stand like barbed wire against the immediate assertion of the individual will."[103] Britain's elites simply needed to understand this history, embrace these institutions, and propel the nation along the path of development.

Snow was the bureaucracy's intrepid explorer, and the organization man's ethnographer. The problems he identified were complex, but the new class of managers were up to the job: "Disciplined, unexhibitionistic, capable of subduing their egos . . . these men are coming forward everywhere to answer the social need," he said. "They are the 'new men' of our time."[104] Popular conceptions of politics as the deeds of great men failed to recognize the complex forces at work in a modern society – forces that were neither so romantic, nor so sinister, as was often supposed. The actual picture of power in Britain, Snow suggested, was a man with a briefcase, striding briskly through an office: "I am thinking of the higher officials, the factory managers, the upper bureaucrats, the cost accountants, the personnel officers, the chief designers, the people who are springing up because our societies cannot get on without them," he explained. "So far as anyone possesses power in the modern world, these do."[105] These chaps, in Snow's account, were competent, practical, sensible, and loyal, not to mention vigorous, powerful, muscular, and active (if also, less flatteringly, "short and thick").[106] If someone must possess power, these managers were better than any previous ruling class: "That is why the managerial society is in the long run men's best source of social hope."[107] Snow's faith in managerial man was not shared universally: as *Private Eye* put it in 1963, "The face of power is a grey man, walking down a grey corridor, and murmuring 'we'll fix it later'."[108] But Snow's confidence never wavered, and in his view the

---

[103] C. P. Snow, *The Two Cultures: and A Second Look* (Cambridge University Press, 1964), p. 89.
[104] C. P. Snow, "New Men for a New Era," *Sunday Times*, 24 August 1958, p. 12.
[105] C. P. Snow, "The Corridors of Power," *Listener*, 18 April 1957, p. 620.
[106] *Ibid.*   [107] *Ibid.*
[108] Christopher Booker, *et al.*, *Private Eye's Romantic England* (London: Weidenfeld & Nicolson, 1963), p. 30.

question facing Britain was whether these admirable foot soldiers in the war against want were to be trusted to carry out their good work.

Such capable managers represented the promise of the meritocratic society. The meritocracy might be understood as the characteristic ideal of the middle class: opposed to the privilege of those above, and eager to put distance between themselves and those below. In principle it is neither egalitarian nor privileged, but instead an open hierarchy of diligence and talent. Indeed (apart from the reference to God), Snow would likely have agreed with Trollope – with whom he was often compared, and about whom he later wrote a biography – when he said, "Make all men equal today, and God has so created them that they shall be unequal tomorrow."[109] Since inequality was inherent, and therefore inevitable, society should be structured so as to identify, educate, and deploy talented individuals, putting them to work on the problems that confronted economies, governments, and states. In the early 1960s Snow's prolific output was one locus among many of the meritocratic ideal, and its broader story has been told by Harold Perkin in *The Rise of Professional Society*.[110]

This meritocratic commitment was related to Snow's own biography. Snow believed in social mobility because he had lived it – in his journey from Leicester to Cambridge, into the civil service, private industry, and literary London, and (eventually) all the way to the House of Lords. Of course there is often a gap between ideal and practice, and the meritocratic ideal was dimmed somewhat by the fact that, at the age of fifty-six, Snow had only applied for one job in his life (the position was Master of Birkbeck College, and he was turned down).[111] Nevertheless, Snow *believed* in the meritocracy, in its magnificence and its existence, to the extent that when the soon-to-be Baron Snow visited the College of Heralds he took as his motto *Aut Inveniam Viam Aut Faciam*, "I will either find a way or make one."[112] It was the perfect liberal motto, equally

---

[109] Quoted in Asa Briggs, *Victorian People: A Reassessment of Persons and Themes, 1851–1867*, rev. edn. (University of Chicago Press, 1972), p. 12; Snow's book was *Trollope* (London: Macmillan, 1975).

[110] See also Arthur Koestler ed., "Suicide of a Nation?" *Encounter*, July 1963 (discussed in Chapter 5), revised and published as *Suicide of a Nation? An Enquiry into the State of Britain Today* (London: Hutchinson, 1963); Sampson, *Anatomy of Britain*; Harold Perkin, *The Rise of Professional Society* (London: Routledge, 1989). For echoes of this ideology in the United States, see Paul Forman, "The Primacy of Science in Modernity, of Technology in Postmodernity, and of Ideology in the History of Technology," *History and Technology* 23 (March/June 2007), pp. 1–152, especially the discussion of Daniel Bell on pp. 50–51.

[111] C. P. Snow, "Recent Thoughts on the Two Cultures," Foundation Oration, Birkbeck College, London, 12 December 1961, British Library: WP 8944/39.

[112] Philip A. Snow, *Stranger and Brother*, p. 161.

confident in the capacity of the individual and the perfectibility of the system.

Snow's technocratic liberalism is thrown into sharper relief by contrast with the positions it opposed. We have already discussed Snow's opposition to Modernism for what he thought to be its hostility to contemporary society, contempt for popular taste, and resistance to lower-middle-class ambition. He was also suspicious of political radicalism for its hostility to the state and embrace of social protest (a position that, as we shall see in Chapter 4, explains his hostility to the New Left). Snow's reading of history as a continuum, his analysis of bureaucracies as functionally similar, and his suspicion of ideological claims – in short, his ideology – led him to dismiss the significance of ideological differences. So just as he denounced radicalism on the left, Snow also opposed Cold Warriors on the right. He was no crypto-communist, as that label would imply sympathy for an ideology that he simply did not think relevant to understanding what was merely another version of the modern bureaucratic state.[113] Snow acknowledged that the Soviet system differed from Western ones in some ways, but he thought that Western leaders should evaluate and, where appropriate, address these differences, rather than dismiss them in an irrational spasm. He was, therefore, endlessly frustrated by Western fascination with protest writers such as Boris Pasternak and Aleksandr Solzhenitsyn, whom he thought of as the marginal equivalents of Western radicals.[114] Instead, Snow celebrated Gerhardi, who omitted discussion of Marxism in writing about the Bolshevik Revolution, and Mikhail Sholokhov, the Soviet hero, Nobel laureate, and defender of socialist realism, who attracted international ire by denouncing Pasternak and Solzhenitsyn.

Snow was equally quick to denounce dissident writers at home, and as the 1950s unfolded he increasingly turned against the "Angry Young Men." Snow had initially been receptive to this new generation of writers, especially for their rejection of technical innovation in favor of traditional forms, and he even provided one of the earliest endorsements of Kingsley Amis's *Lucky Jim* (1954).[115] He was also impressed by John Wain, John Braine, and Angus Wilson, whose work he endorsed in the

---

[113] Robert Conquest offers a critical assessment of Snow's position in *The Dragons of Expectations: Reality and Delusion in the Course of History* (New York: Norton, 2005), pp. 145–148.

[114] C. P. Snow, "Liberal Communism: The Basic Dogma, the Scope for Freedom, the Danger in Optimism," *Nation*, 9 December 1968, pp. 617–623.

[115] Kingsley Amis, *Lucky Jim* (London: Gollancz, 1954). Amis thanked Snow for the "puff" in a letter of 8 February 1954, HRC: Snow 51.14.

Sunday Times.[116] Before long, however, Snow's attitude soured, and he explained this growing hostility in political terms: in 1960 he told Hoff that Amis represented "trivial protest – contracting out – the final and most elaborate reactionary disguise."[117] The next month Snow developed this point further, insisting that an ostensibly apolitical stance was in fact reactionary, and contrasting "lower-class manners" and "upper-class politics" with his own preference for "upper-class manners" and "progressive politics."[118] He then took this case public, dismissing the Angry Young Men in an interview: "You don't make yourself a rebel by being rude or even by taking off your tie. You make yourself a rebel by doing something to protest seriously against the society in which you're living. The angry young men have never done that."[119] The key word there is "seriously," which functioned to exclude anyone who differed from Snow's own conception of political action.

Snow's opposition to Modernism, radicalism, Cold Warriors, and Angry Young Men was all of a piece. His worldview rested upon the embrace of modern society and its meritocratic promise, and his politics consisted of pragmatic efforts to advance the fortunes of both. Together these tenets amounted to a meritocracy of experts, a managerial individualism, a technocratic liberalism – the worldview of which Snow was both embodiment and advocate. This position informed his celebration of science and his hostility to criticism in interwar Cambridge; it drove his efforts to shape literature and criticism in postwar London; and it saturated the corridors of power in *Strangers and Brothers*. By the mid 1950s Snow's novels were enjoying widespread success, and that success, in turn, was providing more opportunities to promote the position behind them.

Making *The Two Cultures*

Snow initially floated the idea of the "two cultures" in the *New Statesman* in 1956.[120] Adopting the tone of a disinterested ethnographer, Snow

---

[116] Rabinovitz, *The Reaction against Experiment in the English Novel*, p. 117.

[117] Snow to Hoff, 14 October 1960, in Gryta, "Selected Letters of C. P. Snow," p. 198.

[118] Snow to Hoff, 1 November 1960, HRC: Snow 118.3.

[119] Snow, quoted in Roy Newquist, *Counterpoint* (New York: Rand McNally, 1964), p. 555. Snow made a related point when he recalled an exchange with Russian friends: "It puzzled them that some of the writers of the fifties, who seemed to be making protests, were, in practical social terms, doing no such thing. It was then that some of them invented the term – 'literature of trivial protest'." Snow, *Variety of Men* (London: Macmillan, 1967), p. 233.

[120] C. P. Snow, "The Two Cultures," *New Statesman and Nation*, 6 October 1956, pp. 413–414.

sketched a series of differences between scientists and literary intellectuals. On one side was the confident scientific culture, situated in universities and research establishments that felt like frontier towns on the cusp of the future. Their culture was optimistic, honest, rigorous, and – by contrast with their effete literary counterparts – heterosexual.[121] It was not necessarily uniformly on the left in politics (engineers, physicians, and chemists were said to tend towards the right), but in their orientation towards the future scientists were intuitively progressive. They took little interest in the "traditional" culture: they were most interested in music and social history, but in literature their tastes lay with the engineer-turned-novelist Nevil Shute. Shute had not garnered attention from the New Critics, Snow noted, but these scientists had no patience for the myopic New Criticism: their culture was living the epic of the age. By contrast, the traditional culture ("mainly literary," Snow explained) was declining in status and significance. There were no frontier towns here, only a few besieged camps painfully aware that their day had passed. Instead of recognizing the improvements that science had made possible, Snow noted, Dostoevsky, Pound, and Faulkner had embraced reactionary attitudes. The scientific culture was insulated from those attitudes, which made the gap between cultures a loss not only for literary intellectuals, but also – given their monopoly on positions of power – for society.

Snow had thus established the contours of his argument, but there were notable absences in this version as well. This sketch lacked the most ambitious claims of later iterations: the characterization of literary intellectuals as Luddites, the observation that the world was divided between the rich and the poor, and the call to confront these crises by reforming education.[122] It took less than six months for Snow to introduce this last point in his next major statement, which came in a two-part series in the *Sunday Times*.[123] His shift in emphasis was clear from the headlines: "A Study of Education in a Scientific Age," and "A Revolution in Education." The stakes were now higher than they had

---

[121] On the associations between homosexuality and the arts, see David Edgerton, "Science and the Nation: Towards New Histories of Twentieth-Century Britain," *Historical Research* 78 (February 2005), pp. 96–112, especially pp. 97, 103.

[122] Although they were absent in this installment of the argument, Collini observes that Snow's references to literary intellectuals as "natural Luddites," as well as his conceptions of the scientific and literary cultures more generally, dated from Snow's experience in Cambridge in the 1930s: Collini's introduction to Snow, *The Two Cultures* (1993), pp. xxii–xxv.

[123] C. P. Snow, "Britain's Two Cultures: A Study of Education in a Scientific Age," *Sunday Times*, 10 March 1957, p. 12; "A Revolution in Education," *Sunday Times*, 17 March 1957, p. 5.

previously been, as Snow suggested that the "two cultures" raised the question of whether Britain would "keep going as a modern state." He introduced the dual specters of the Soviet Union (with its prodigious output of scientists) and imperial Spain (with its painful history of eclipse), and the alternatives were clear: either Britain would summon the courage to restructure its education, or it would meet the fate of the bygone Spanish empire. And in a crucial revision, Snow revivified the traditional culture that he had previously cast as moribund, propping it up here as the "prevailing" culture instead. The effect of these changes was to transform his argument, from a cocksure dismissal of the literary culture to an urgent diagnosis of the crisis it had brought about.

Snow continued to hone his argument in an extraordinary series of statements the following year. When *The Search* was reissued in 1958, he took the opportunity to situate that early novel in terms of the "two cultures" thesis.[124] In April he wrote an admiring article on "The Men of Fission," the scientists in whose hands Britain's future lay. Oblivious to trivialities of race and class, aloof from party politics, and indifferent to financial concerns, these middle-class scientists had come up on scholarships through grammar schools and provincial universities, and now populated frontier towns such as the nuclear establishment at Harwell. There they worked tirelessly to keep Britain even with its competitors, despite the decline being threatened by its educational system. "It is the Doctor Bradleys," Snow wrote, referring to the scientist he was profiling, "not the people in the traditional culture, who represent intellectual creativeness, moral strength, social hope."[125] Three months later he introduced a difference between the *individual* condition (tragic, because every individual is doomed to a solitary death) and the *social* condition (for which there is the hope of material betterment) – a distinction that was central to the Rede Lecture, and that featured prominently in the dispute with Leavis.[126] Later that summer, writing in the *Times Literary Supplement*, Snow connected literary sensibility with "extreme social reaction" – a phenomenon that he hoped to say more about in the future.[127]

That opportunity came in November's *Atlantic Monthly*. Snow insisted that scientists such as Rutherford were instinctively on the side of their fellow human beings: in another phrase that would become

---

[124] Snow, "A Note," *The Search*, rev. edn. (New York: Scribner's, 1958), pp. v–vi.
[125] Snow, "The Men of Fission," p. 115.
[126] C. P. Snow, "Man in Society," *Observer*, 13 July 1958, p. 12.
[127] Snow, "Challenge to the Intellect," p. 2946.

famous, he declared that Rutherford had "the future in his bones."[128] Scientific society was free from prejudices of race, class, and nation, an admirable contrast with "the ambiguous relations with Fascism into which Yeats and T. S. Eliot found themselves entering."[129] Indeed, Snow observed, scientists were well aware of those associations, which contributed to the gap between cultures. And in a review of J. D. Bernal's *World Without War* that same month, Snow introduced a concern for the developing world that would be central to the Rede Lecture: "Industrialization is now, as it always has been, the one hope of the poor," he wrote, and he implored Raymond Williams and Richard Hoggart to reconsider their ideas about culture in light of that fact.[130] Delusions of a lost golden age, sustained in the face of all facts by influential intellectuals, were preventing the West from extending the industrialization that Asia and Africa desperately needed – and that they were certain to get, one way or another.

The lecture Snow delivered in 1959, then, did not emerge as a bolt from the blue, but rather advanced a position that he had been developing for years. The bemused sociological account of 1956 grew to include issues of education and national survival in 1957, and the following year it incorporated ideas about the scientists in charge of Britain's future, the dubious politics of their literary rivals, and the benefits of industrialization. This development, in turn, was itself situated within a longer history in which Snow had forged these positions. The former chemist and civil servant urging his audience to embrace the scientific revolution was also the literary critic plotting to overthrow Modernism, the novelist exploring bureaucracy, and the pundit celebrating the manager. These were diverse positions, but they were not unrelated, and, rather than reducing them to an endorsement of "science," it makes sense to view them as parts of Snow's worldview more generally.

While Snow was assembling his case, others had had enough. *Nature* insisted towards the end of 1958, "[T]he division between the scientist and the student of the humanities must end."[131] But instead of bridging that division, Snow had something else in mind. He remarked upon the curious complacency of the nation's intellectuals, which he suspected resulted from Britain's transition to a welfare state without social rupture. Snow, for his part, hoped that society and culture might yet be shaken up: "I am looking for a cruder sign of returning health," he

---

[128] Snow, "The Age of Rutherford," p. 80.   [129] *Ibid.*
[130] C. P. Snow, "Act in Hope," *New Statesman*, 15 November 1958, p. 699.
[131] C. P. Snow, "Technological Humanism," *Nature*, 8 February 1958, p. 370.

wrote. "The one I should welcome most is a serious intellectual row."[132]
In the debates that followed, Snow frequently adopted an ameliorative
pose – but that should not obscure the fact that he was leveling a polemic
that he had been honing for decades.

The Rede Lecture

On May 7, 1959, C. P. Snow delivered the Rede Lecture in Cambridge.
He took as his subject the relationship between scientific and literary
intellectuals – a topic with a long history already, but one that Snow's
dual careers as a scientist and a novelist qualified him to address anew.
The themes in his lecture would have been familiar to anyone
acquainted with his prior pronouncements: writers who resented the
course of history, scientists who were intuitively on the side of the poor,
and an establishment that favored literary intellectuals to the detriment
of everyone else. He situated these themes amid some of the most
pressing issues of the day, including educational reform, national
decline, Cold War tensions, and the vanishing empire. Snow had been
developing these various ideas for nearly three decades, and in the Rede
Lecture he stitched them together into a single polemic. He argued that
industrial society generated material prosperity and social opportunity,
and that the task facing Britain and the West was to secure that society at
home while extending it abroad. The trick of the Rede Lecture was to
insert this charged ideological vision into a familiar observation about
disciplinary specialization.

While *The Two Cultures* is often remembered as a lecture about two
groups of intellectuals, that was merely the starting point for Snow's
argument. His case hinged on its optimistic interpretation of the
Industrial Revolution: "[W]ith singular unanimity," he declared, "in any
country where they have had the chance, the poor have walked off the
land into the factories as fast as the factories could take them."[133]
Literary intellectuals had failed to recognize the benefits of industrialization in the past, and they remained hostile to the scientific revolution in the present. Yet these Luddites (as Snow branded them)
continued to occupy positions of power in Britain, freezing out the
scientists and technologists who alone possessed the know-how of
economic advance. Snow then raised the stakes still further, casting his

---

[132] C. P. Snow, "The Irregular Right: Britain Without Rebels," *Nation*, 24 March 1956,
pp. 238–239.
[133] Snow, *The Two Cultures*, p. 25.

argument on a global scale: the secret to industrial development was out, and the poor nations of the world were not going to remain poor much longer. They would develop their economies one way or another, and if Britain and the West failed to act, then the Soviet Union would. Snow's conclusion: it was imperative that Britain overcome the obstacles posed by its dominant literary culture, and overhaul its system of education to produce – and export – more scientists and engineers.

Snow laced his argument with explosive claims, the most arresting of which were his characterizations of the politics and moralities of the two cultures. In the nineteenth century, he said, the literary culture – and by this Snow referred variously (and problematically) to creative writers, literary intellectuals, and political elites – had reacted with horror to the Industrial Revolution, even as they skimmed its wealth to secure their positions. Then, at the beginning of the twentieth century, the writers who dominated literary sensibility – such as Yeats, Pound, and Lewis – inherited this hostility to the modern world, retreating from society and celebrating the alienated individual instead. This attitude, Snow claimed, was complicit with the worst crimes of the age – indeed, he confessed that he could not disagree with the scientist who had asked, with regard to Modernist writers, "Didn't the influence of all they represent bring Auschwitz that much nearer?"[134] Today, though, the traditional culture itself sensed that its days were numbered – as Snow put it, the disaffection of *Lucky Jim* was partly the anxiety of the marginalized arts graduate.

By contrast, scientific intellectuals – of whom Snow took physical scientists to be representative – were optimistic both about the future and about their place in it. Unlike their literary peers, scientists recognized the material progress that resulted from industrialization, and they were eager to help spread that progress throughout the world. With their aversions to the prejudices of race and nation, scientists saw themselves as the agents of liberation for millions of people. Snow did not insist that scientists shared common social origins, religious beliefs, or political stances: he reported that a majority came from poorer homes, rejected religion, and voted for the left, but acknowledged that those traits did not necessarily hold among chemists and engineers. The important point was not that scientists voted Labour, but that even conservative scientists were progressive in their disposition towards the future and their embrace of humankind. Although it is Leavis who is usually cast as the moralist between the two, Snow insisted that scientific practice itself

[134] Snow, *The Two Cultures*, p. 7.

fostered virtuous morality: "In the moral [life], they are by and large the soundest group of intellectuals we have," he said. "[T]here is a moral component right in the grain of science itself."[135]

Snow moved confidently from observations about the reading habits of scientists and cocktail conversation among writers, to the issues of international development, the Cold War, and national decline. He explained that the capital, manpower, and education necessary for the task of international development had to come from somewhere – was the West going to let Communist countries take the lead? He compared the education systems of Britain, the United States, and the Soviet Union, especially their respective outputs of scientists and engineers, and where they differed he concluded that somebody had it wrong. That "somebody" generally turned out to be Britain, and here Snow played his trump card by appealing to anxieties about national decline. He confessed that he often found himself thinking about the Venetian Republic in its final days: like Britain, the Venetians had become rich largely through luck, developed considerable political skills, and thought of themselves as patriots and realists. They had recognized that history was turning against them, yet proved unwilling or unable to alter their habits and arrest their decline. The implicit question lingered: would Britain meet the same fate, or might its leaders still embrace the reforms necessary to maintain its position?

Snow confessed that he had his doubts. He explained that structures in Britain had a tendency to "crystallize" – that is, to harden to a point at which reform became impossible. The crystallization of Britain's education system dated from the nineteenth century, and its economic base was crystallizing at present. Snow worried that the separation between the two cultures was similarly on the verge of becoming permanent. This intensification of the disciplinary crisis points to a curious aspect of the rhetoric of the Rede Lecture, namely its contention that the separation between literary and scientific intellectuals was a *recent* phenomenon. Snow reminded his audience that prime ministers at the turn of the century had taken a serious interest in science, and that even the wartime minister John Anderson had done research in chemistry. "None of that degree of interchange at the top of the Establishment is likely, or indeed thinkable, now."[136] Interactions between the two cultures had, in Snow's account, only recently become impossible, but the emerging chasm between them threatened to keep it that way. Snow stepped into a long tradition lamenting divisions between the arts and sciences and

[135] *Ibid.*, p. 13.   [136] *Ibid.*, p. 17.

promptly erased its history, thereby capitalizing on the familiarity of the theme while improbably managing to lend it a sense of urgency.

The two cultures debate

The Two Cultures caused an immediate sensation. The earliest discussions took place in the periodical press, where specialized knowledge and disciplinary distinctions tend to give way before the less inhibited claims of intellectual polemic.[137] Snow had already arranged for publication of his lecture in *Encounter*, and the day after the lecture the editor wrote Snow to solicit the names of scientists and humanists who could keep the conversation going in the following issue.[138] The accolades poured forth: the *New Statesman* declared that "Snow's thesis is not likely to be easily controverted," John Beer wrote in the *Cambridge Review* that "Sir Charles Snow's Rede Lecture is the sort of lecture which justifies the endowment of lectureships," and the *Listener* called the gap Snow had discussed "a central problem of our time."[139] Asa Briggs chaired a BBC discussion on art and science in schools, and by that autumn *The Two Cultures* had made its way into Britain's secondary schools.[140] In 1960 Jacob Bronowski and Bruce Mazlish began their influential *The Western Intellectual Tradition* by citing Snow, and they explained that the relationship between the humanities and sciences constituted the central problem of contemporary culture.[141] *The Two Cultures* was also receiving international attention: the physicist Abdus Salam presented its arguments to the All Pakistan Science Conference in 1961, and Snow's dichotomy inspired discussions of "lyrics" and "physics"

---

[137] To follow the debate, see Paul Boytinck, *C. P. Snow: A Reference Guide* (Boston: Hall, 1980); D. Graham Burnett provides a nice overview of the stages of the debate in "A View from the Bridge: The Two Cultures Debate, Its Legacy, and the History of Science," *Daedalus* 128 (Spring 1999), pp. 193–218, especially pp. 200–205.

[138] Snow's prior publishing arrangements are inferred from R. J. L. Kingsford to Snow, 30 December 1959, HRC: Snow 75.1; the forum, by Walter Allen, *et al.* and titled "A Discussion of C. P. Snow's Views," is discussed in a letter from Lasky to Snow, 8 May 1959, HRC: Snow 94.17.

[139] *New Statesman*, 6 June 1959, p. 806; John Beer, "Pools of Light in Darkness," *Cambridge Review*, 7 November 1959, p. 106; "A Great Debate," *Listener*, 3 September 1959, p. 344.

[140] Asa Briggs "Matters of Moment: Art and Sciences in the Schools," 22 October 1959, BBC Written Archives Center (BBC WAC): MF "MAT," T331; de la Mothe, *C. P. Snow and the Struggle of Modernity*, p. 62.

[141] Jacob Bronowski and Bruce Mazlish, *The Western Intellectual Tradition: From Leonardo to Hegel* (London: Harper and Row, 1960), pp. vii–viii.

among Soviet intellectuals.[142] The American reaction was particularly enthusiastic: Snow's lecture was assigned reading for all freshmen at Columbia University in 1960; it persuaded the editors at Basic Books to include non-fiction writing in their book club; and Senator John F. Kennedy declared *The Two Cultures* "one of the most provocative discussions that I have ever read of this intellectual dilemma."[143]

The Two Cultures faced criticism as well.[144] Michael Yudkin, a Cambridge biochemist, published one of the most thorough of these critiques in the *Cambridge Review*.[145] Yudkin disputed each element of Snow's argument, from its assumptions to its assertions to its conclusions, and he particularly challenged its utilitarian thrust. Snow had suggested that science and technology were marginalized in Britain, leading Yudkin to protest: "It is barely possible to read a newspaper without seeing an appeal by a politician, or an industrialist, or a university teacher, for more scientists, larger sums of money for technical research, or an expansion of the universities."[146] While Snow had depicted his appeal on behalf of science and technology as a desperate plea to a hostile establishment, Yudkin pointed out that his argument was situated amid a widespread consensus on the importance of both. The scientist and philosopher Michael Polanyi registered a similar objection in the pages of *Encounter*, but it was Leavis who would eventually emerge as the most prominent critic along these lines – only for his argument to be obscured by the tone of his lecture.[147]

Generally, though, when Snow surveyed the discussion he concluded that his thesis had been accepted – and so he continued to sharpen his argument.[148] In a broadcast in the summer of 1959, he dispensed with the ameliorative introduction in order to launch straight into the charge

---

[142] Abdus Salam, "Technology and Pakistan's Attack on Poverty," HRC: Snow 177.8. Snow reported the success of *The Two Cultures* in the Soviet Union to Jacques Barzun, 16 June 1960, HRC: Snow 56.1; thanks to Yohanan Petrovsky-Shtern for bringing the specific discussion of the "physics" and the "lyrics" to my attention.

[143] Academic Afternoon and Freshman Week Coordinator to the Faculty of Columbia University, 25 May 1960, HRC: Snow 56.1; Irving Kristol to Snow, 4 April 1960, HRC: Snow 56.9; John F. Kennedy quoted in Philip A. Snow, *Stranger and Brother*, p. 117.

[144] See Burnett, "A View from the Bridge," pp. 193–218, especially pp. 200–205.

[145] Michael Yudkin, "Sir Charles Snow's Rede Lecture," originally published in the *Cambridge Review* and reprinted in F. R. Leavis, *Two Cultures? The Significance of C. P. Snow* (London: Chatto and Windus, 1962), pp. 33–45.

[146] *Ibid.*, p. 43.

[147] Michael Polanyi, "The Two Cultures," *Encounter*, September 1959, pp. 61–64. See Chapter 5 for further discussion of Polanyi.

[148] Snow, "The 'Two-Cultures' Controversy: Afterthoughts."

that literary intellectuals were Luddites.[149] The following year he explained that he intended his lecture to inspire action: at least to improve education in Britain and America, but also to spur industrialization throughout the world.[150] He then reiterated his contention that the writers who dominated literary sensibility in the twentieth century must be considered reactionary, since they did not embrace the progress afforded by industrialization. To illustrate these tendencies he cited a handful of unsavory lines from D. H. Lawrence in *Women in Love* ("I abhor humanity, I wish it was swept away") and *Sea and Sardinia* ("If I were dictator, I should order the old one to be hanged at once"), and from there it was a small step to conflating Lawrence with Hitler (a step Snow took briskly).[151] At Birkbeck College in 1961, Snow acknowledged three criticisms of his argument, two of which he was willing to accept: he had perhaps cast too wide a net by conflating all literary intellectuals with a few dominant figures, and he had not sufficiently acknowledged the role of the social sciences. He refused, however, to brook any criticism regarding his optimistic reading of industrialization: "This seems to me intellectually and emotionally half-baked to an almost insane degree."[152] Whenever he revisited the issue, Snow made clear that his political strictures against Modernists and his optimistic assessment of industrialization were not incidental to *The Two Cultures* – indeed, they were its very heart.[153]

Snow remained astonished and delighted by the reception his argument met. "It is all extremely unreal," he remarked, mentioning invitations to drinks with Nehru, as well as his expectation that he would be offered (and turn down) a position in a future Labour government.[154] There are several reasons for this reception. First, there is the fact of

[149] C. P. Snow, "The Imperatives of Educational Strategy," recorded 3 June 1959, broadcast 8 September 1959, BBC WAC: MF T491.
[150] Snow, "The 'Two-Cultures' Controversy: Afterthoughts," p. 64.
[151] *Ibid.*, pp. 66–67. These quotations came in response to G. H. Bantock, a former contributor to *Scrutiny* who invoked Lawrence against Snow; Leavis had not yet had his say, but the fact that Snow was already taking aim squarely at Lawrence – widely known as a Leavisian favorite – suggests that he was already figuring prominently in Snow's mind.
[152] Snow, "Recent Thoughts on the Two Cultures."
[153] In a subsequent discussion with his publisher, while preparing *The Two Cultures: and a Second Look* (Cambridge University Press, 1964), Snow promised to "devote much more attention to *what is really right at the core of the whole argument: the scientific and industrial revolution* and what this means in terms of human life" (emphasis mine): "Interview with Sir Charles Snow," 29 May 1963, Cambridge University Press: "Agreements," 5184.
[154] Snow to Plumb, 1 November 1960 & 15 September 1959, CUL: Plumb papers, Box "C. P. Snow and Pam, 1946–1968," File "Snow 1946–1968."

Snow's stature at that moment, when he was approaching the zenith of his prominence as a writer and a commentator. Second, his unusual biography, especially his career path from scientist to novelist, positioned him to pronounce with authority on both science and literature. Snow deliberately cultivated this authority, referring to days spent interviewing scientists followed by evenings at literary parties. Third, *The Two Cultures* was in many ways an excellent lecture: quotable and peppered with anecdotes, it commanded the right tone for the occasion, while offering a thesis both familiar and ambitious. Fourth, and less visibly, Snow benefited from an aggressive marketing push. The month before delivery, he reported heavy interest from the major Sunday newspapers, and Cambridge University Press duly sent advance copies to the *Times, Sunday Times, Observer, New Statesman, New Scientist, Nature,* and *Economist.*[155] When the American edition was published later that year, the press alerted 1,600 college presidents, and they also mailed review copies to more than fifty magazines, journals, and newspapers.[156] Requests for foreign translations poured into the office, leading Cambridge University Press to express interest in a larger volume by Snow exploring the same theme.[157] In short, *The Two Cultures* may have caught fire, but Snow had considerable help stoking the flames.

A fifth explanation – easily the most important, from that day to this – concerns the relationship between the tradition that preceded the Rede Lecture and the debate it inaugurated. Snow himself recognized the significance of this factor: one of the two reasons he cited for the sensation was that the ideas were already "in the air."[158] Commentators had, of course, long discussed various aspects of the relationship between the arts and the sciences, occasionally in concert but frequently in isolation. Snow's Rede Lecture forever changed that fact, turning countless disparate discussions into a single conversation with a common point of reference. That is, after May 1959 it became impossible to discuss the arts and the sciences except through the prism of the "two cultures" – and not only impossible but also undesirable, because to

---

[155] Memoranda, 20 & 22 April 1959, Cambridge University Press: Snow, 1959, 5184.
[156] The American publicity of 1959 is recounted in the promotional materials for *The Two Cultures: and a Second Look* five years later: Ronald Mansbridge, March 1964, Cambridge University Press: Snow 1964, 5184; the details of the review copies mailed to American publications are taken from Mansbridge's publicity letter of 12 November 1959, Cambridge University Press: Snow, 1959, 5184; the persons and publications receiving complimentary copies in Britain are listed in a memorandum of 22 April 1959, Cambridge University Press: Snow, 1959, 5184.
[157] Peter E. T. Davies to Snow, 4 December 1959, and R. J. L. Kingsford to Snow, 30 December 1959, HRC: Snow 75.1.
[158] Snow, *The Two Cultures: and A Second Look,* p. 54.

frame an issue in terms of the "two cultures" was immediately to enter a larger conversation, garnering wider attention for whatever it was that one wanted to say.

And so conversations proliferated under the generous rubric of the "two cultures," a subject that came to include discussions not only of the arts and sciences and education but also British history, national decline, the Cold War, non-Western economies – and, one is tempted to add, pretty much anything else. Commentators seized the opportunity to press their own concerns to the fore, a pattern that was already apparent in that initial discussion in *Encounter*. The contributors to that forum addressed many of the issues that Snow had raised, such as the separation between the two cultures, the importance of education, and worldwide industrialization, but from those familiar touchstones they moved towards matters closer to their own hearts – such as the university scientist's frustration with the resistance to science within universities, and the future Master of Churchill College's call for higher salaries for Cambridge professors. The discussions then branched out still further, coming to include a warning of crisis in the plastic arts, the denunciation of patriarchy, and a plea to enter the space race.[159]

The same dynamic characterized critical responses as well. Snow's critics targeted his reading of history, his claims about the morality of creative writers, his prescriptions for the developing world, his proposals for education – in short, nearly every facet of his argument. These critiques may be divided into two general (but not mutually exclusive) categories: those that objected to its premises, and those that objected to its proposals. In the first category fell Plumb's contention that the "two cultures" were better understood as two classes, G. H. Bantock's defense of creative writers against Snow's slanders, Polanyi's rejection of the view that science was marginalized in modern society, and Yudkin's challenge to Snow's every premise.[160] In the second category fell Herbert Read's denunciation of the "technologism" that threatened human sensibility, and Kathleen Nott's discomfort with Snow's apparent valuation of material advance over culture and morality.[161] Corralling

---

[159] Allen, *et al.*, "A Discussion of C. P. Snow's Views," pp. 67–73.

[160] Plumb, "Welfare or Release," pp. 68–70; G. H. Bantock, "A Scream of Horror," *Listener*, 17 September 1959, pp. 427–428; Polanyi, "The Two Cultures"; Yudkin, "Sir Charles Snow's Rede Lecture."

[161] Herbert Read, "Mood of the Month – X," *London Magazine*, August 1959, pp. 39–43 (Snow responded in October, to which Read replied in November); Kathleen Nott, "The Type to Which the Whole Creation Moves? Further Thoughts on the Snow Saga," *Encounter*, February 1962, pp. 87–88, pp. 94–97.

these various arguments in this way does not adequately convey their complexity, but the sheer impracticality of discussing each in full itself makes the point: *The Two Cultures* provided an opening for critics and admirers alike to advance a staggering array of concerns.

Conclusion

This chapter opened with Snow's gracious reception of a critique of *The Two Cultures* by his friend J. H. Plumb. Plumb had dismissed the significance of the division between literary and scientific intellectuals, and Snow's reaction would be puzzling had he thought of his lecture primarily as a claim about disciplines or cultures. In fact, although Snow believed there were differences between scientists and writers, that was merely part of the more ambitious argument that he developed as a commentator and novelist after the war. This argument found its widest audience in the Rede Lecture of 1959, *The Two Cultures and the Scientific Revolution*.

Snow believed that modern society, as it existed in Britain, generated wealth and opportunity for the majority of the population, and he wanted to see that society celebrated at home and extended abroad. He thought that this program would best be realized through the fluid hierarchy of the meritocratic society, and he challenged those groups who stood in its way: Modernist writers behind him, a hidebound establishment on his right, and radical critics on his left. Snow's ideology was, by contrast, a *technocratic liberalism*: an optimistic faith in progress and reform, in which talented individuals worked through existing institutions to benefit society.

In *The Two Cultures* Snow audaciously projected this argument against a global backdrop, even as he packaged it within a seemingly unobjectionable lament about disciplinary specialization. The lecture's achievement was, therefore, considerable: it invested a familiar conversation with his ideological position; it instigated discussions of the past, present, and future on terrain that he established; and it popularized a term that soon emerged as a touchstone in subsequent debate. In little more than an hour's work, Snow at once entered, deployed, and transformed the long-standing discussion of the arts and the sciences.

At this point Snow's pose remained that of a man with a foot in both cultures. He had cast himself as a scientist-by-day and novelist-by-night, with the unique authority to assess the attributes of both – as John Beer put it in the *Cambridge Review*, "Sir Charles Snow writes as a scientist with pronounced artistic leanings. When he defines his theme . . . it is as a man who has seen a good deal of both cultures and is familiar with the arguments used by exponents of each."[162] The intervention of a literary rival, however, would transform Snow's position, inserting him squarely into the side of the dichotomy that he obviously preferred. In 1962 just such a rival emerged in the figure of F. R. Leavis.

[162] Beer, "Pools of Light in Darkness," p. 106.

2   F. R. Leavis and the radical liberalism

Against science?

On February 28, 1962, in the Richmond Lecture at his own Downing College, F. R. Leavis set out to demolish *The Two Cultures* once and for all.[1] He concluded his lecture by expressing the hope that it would never again be necessary to pay such attention to C. P. Snow. Leavis was dismayed, then, when his polemic came to be interpreted as another example of a literary intellectual's hostility towards science – and thus as further confirmation of the "two cultures" dichotomy that Snow had identified. In this sense, and despite his disinterested pose, Snow's greatest success in the Rede Lecture was to establish the terms through which their argument would be understood: Snow was read as an advocate of science, Leavis as a defender of literature, and together they took their places in a seemingly familiar conversation.[2]

Yet just as Snow cannot be understood as an opponent of "literature" exactly, Leavis's argument was not directed against "science" as such. "My concern for 'English literature'," he later insisted, "implies no slighting of the sciences."[3] Leavis maintained that he respected science and scientists, and he rejected Aldous Huxley's characterization of the controversy as a clash between "literarism" and "scientism."[4] Certainly science, as a defining feature of the modern world, figured centrally in Leavis's historical vision, but the impulse to reduce it to something that he could be "for" or "against" tacitly accepts the "two cultures" framework. Instead of adopting Snow's terms in that way, this chapter takes Leavis's ideas about science as a point of entry into his worldview more generally.

---

[1] F. R. Leavis, *Two Cultures? The Significance of C. P. Snow* (London: Chatto and Windus, 1962).

[2] See, for example, Aldous Huxley, *Literature and Science* (London: Harper and Row, 1963); David K. Cornelius and Edwin St. Vincent, eds., *Cultures in Conflict: Perspectives on the Snow–Leavis Controversy* (Chicago: Scott Foresman and Co., 1964); and many of the citations in Paul Boytinck, *C. P. Snow: A Reference Guide* (Boston: Hall, 1980).

[3] F. R. Leavis, *English Literature in Our Time and the University* (London: Chatto and Windus, 1969), p. 3.

[4] *Ibid.*, pp. 28, 40, 64–65.

Its goal is neither to endorse his interpretations nor to excuse his denunciations, but rather to explain an intellectual position, a critical practice, and a polemical intensity that has startled observers from that day to this.

Leavis believed that contemporary Britain confronted a terrifying crisis. That crisis had its origins in the seventeenth century, when a series of developments – including, but not limited to, the Civil War and Restoration, the development of capitalism, and the emergence of science – together signaled the arrival of a new civilization. Of the alternatives available for confronting that crisis, including conservatism on the right and Marxism on the left, Leavis embraced a defiant individualism – an ideological position that I characterize as *radical liberalism*. This position was related to the liberalism advocated by Snow, but it differed from Snow's position in its critical assessment of modern civilization. This stance informed Leavis's criticism throughout his career, and the literary criticism of the 1930s was of a piece with the social criticism of the 1960s. Yet Leavis was no more a detached critic than a conventional academic: in response to this crisis he advocated a positive program and a politics to effect it, and this argument found its largest audience yet in the Richmond Lecture of 1962.

Career and context

The English Tripos is a relatively recent innovation in Cambridge.[5] English literature became increasingly prevalent in English universities during the late nineteenth century, ironically (given Leavis's later program) for its utility in educating a broad public: English offered a less exclusive option than classics for the growing numbers of adults, women, and prospective civil servants in higher education.[6] During the First World War this pragmatic function was fortified by an ideological dimension, as propagandists and educationalists cast the study of the national literature as a unifying social force.[7]

In Cambridge, English literature remained part of the Modern Languages Tripos, until three dons – the King Edward VII Professor of English Literature, Arthur Quiller-Couch ("Q"), the Anglo-Saxonist H. M. Chadwick, and the romanticist Mansfield Forbes – carved out a

---

[5] On the establishment of Cambridge English, see Ian MacKillop, *F. R. Leavis: A Life in Criticism* (London: Allen Lane, 1995), pp. 51–68. On the development of literary studies in Britain more generally, see Chris Baldick, *The Social Mission of English Criticism, 1848–1932* (New York: Oxford University Press, 1983); Anne Samson, *F. R. Leavis* (University of Toronto Press, 1992). For the American story, see Gerald Graff, *Professing Literature: An Institutional History* (University of Chicago Press, 1987).

[6] Baldick, *The Social Mission of English Criticism*, Chapter 3.   [7] *Ibid.*, Chapter 4.

distinct English Tripos in 1917.[8] They recruited teaching faculty from various disciplines, and the first examinations took place in 1919. The students who returned from the war and joined the new course combined an invigorating sense of purpose with the desire to break from the past – as Basil Willey later recalled, "Many of us were just back from the 1914–18 war, and we were unsatisfied with the woolly generalities and the vague mysticism of the accepted schools of criticism."[9] Cambridge English was free from the historical scholarship and linguistic requirements that characterized the subject elsewhere, but these innovations made it all the more pressing that the course establish its methods and credentials.

I. A. Richards emerged as a key figure in that project.[10] Richards had taken a BA in moral sciences in 1915, and four years later Forbes and Chadwick persuaded him to lecture for the English Tripos. During the next two decades, when resident in Cambridge, Richards lectured on such topics as modern novels, modern poetry, and theories of criticism. He brought rigor to the subject through his insistence on close reading and criticism, and he imbued it with intellectual respectability through his interest in the psychological (and thus scientific) basis of literary response. Richards developed these ideas in *Principles of Literary Criticism* (1924), which employed psychology to establish grounds for literary evaluation, and he extended his arguments in *Science and Poetry* (1926).[11] He also began to deliver what would become a famous set of lectures on "Practical Criticism," in which he invited his audience to comment upon poems without any information about the authors' biographies or their historical context. The responses that he collected served as the basis for his analysis of the problems of criticism, which provided the core of his influential book, *Practical Criticism: A Study of Literary Judgment* (1929).[12] One member of the audience who participated

---

[8] MacKillop, *F. R. Leavis*, p. 56. Forbes began his career as a historian, before moving into English; MacKillop characterized his field as "idiosyncratic: roughly, romanticism and literary criticism, when not Scottish baronial architecture." MacKillop, *F. R. Leavis*, pp. 49, 158.

[9] Baldick, *The Social Mission of English Criticism*, p. 134.

[10] This paragraph primarily draws from Richard Storer, "Richards, Ivor Armstrong (1893–1979)," *Oxford Dictionary of National Biography* (Oxford University Press, 2004). See also Stefan Collini, "On Highest Authority: The Literary Critic and Other Aviators in Early Twentieth-Century Britain," in *Modernist Impulses in the Human Sciences, 1870–1930*, ed. Dorothy Ross (Baltimore: Johns Hopkins University Press, 1994), pp. 152–170; John Paul Russo, *I. A. Richards: His Life and Work* (Baltimore: Johns Hopkins University Press, 1989).

[11] I. A. Richards, *Principles of Literary Criticism* (London: Kegan Paul, 1924); Richards, *Science and Poetry* (London: Kegan Paul, 1926).

[12] I. A. Richards, *Practical Criticism: A Study of Literary Judgment* (London: Harcourt Brace, 1929).

in these exercises was a popular young lecturer, Frank Raymond Leavis. During the 1930s, as Richards's attention and his person were pulled in other directions, Leavis was part of a second generation of teachers and critics who together developed Cambridge English.[13]

Leavis had been born in Cambridge in 1895, and – apart from a period of service in France during the First World War – he lived there until his death in 1978. He remembered his father as a "Victorian radical," with "a fierce, Protestant conscience . . . divorced from any religious outlet."[14] Harry Leavis owned a piano shop on Regent Street, directly across from Downing College – the college that his son would establish as one of the leading schools of criticism in the English-speaking world. Leavis's pianos have held up better than Leavis Pianos: the intellectual historian Quentin Skinner owned one of the former as recently as 1979, whereas the space occupied by the latter today houses a Pizza Hut.[15] F. R. Leavis went to state schools until, at the age of sixteen, a scholarship enabled him to enroll in the nearby Perse Grammar School. After service bearing stretchers in France during the war, he entered Emmanuel College to read history in 1919. The following year he switched to the new tripos in English, taking first-class honors in 1921 and completing a PhD in 1924.[16] For the remainder of the decade Leavis lectured and taught in Cambridge, stringing together a series of probationary posts while working to secure a permanent position.

In 1929 he married Queenie Dorothy Roth. Roth had arrived at Girton College on a scholarship in 1925.[17] She came from an observant Jewish home in north London, where the family lived above her father's hosiery shop. Roth was an intense, well-read, and spectacularly suc- cessful student, earning a starred First in English, as well as enough

---

[13] On the subsequent trajectory of Richards's career, see Rodney Koeneke, *Empires of the Mind: I. A. Richards and Basic English in China, 1929–1979* (Stanford University Press, 2004). On the distinctive attributes of Cambridge English, and the part Leavis played in its development, see Stefan Collini, "Cambridge and the Study of English," *Cambridge Contributions*, ed. Sarah J. Omrod (Cambridge University Press, 1998), pp. 42–64.

[14] MacKillop, *F. R. Leavis*, p. 29. This paragraph draws from MacKillop's biography.

[15] Personal communication with the author, October 30, 2006. The piano was purchased by Susan James in 1972. Skinner recalls it as a small German instrument with a good tone; the name "Leavis" was affixed in brass letters on the keyboard cover. They sold it in 1979.

[16] F. R. Leavis, "The Relationship of Journalism to Literature: Studied in the Rise and Earlier Development of the Press in England," unpublished PhD thesis, University of Cambridge (1924).

[17] This material on Q. D. Leavis derives from MacKillop, *F. R. Leavis*, pp. 85–87, 100–101, 104–108.

prizes to enable her to pursue a doctorate. Upon her engagement to Leavis in February 1929, her orthodox parents cut most of their ties; it was a searing experience, but the couple wed on September 16, 1929. Her PhD thesis, supervised by Richards and examined by E. M. Forster, was published as *Fiction and the Reading Public* (1932) – an influential book that took a sociological approach in its analysis of the relationship between literature and its environment.[18] During the subsequent decades Q. D. Leavis supported her husband's career, raised their three children, and persevered through illness, while also managing to pursue a remarkable career of her own: she co-edited *Scrutiny*, supervised undergraduates, and established herself as an authority on the novel. The Leavises soon became a formidable duo in Cambridge, their home at Chesterton Hall Crescent serving as a gathering place for research students on Friday afternoons. There they enjoyed tea, cakes, and hard-boiled eggs, while discussing their intentions to upend the conventions of the literary and academic worlds.[19]

From these early years in Cambridge, Leavis thought of himself as an outsider amid the academic establishment. His career overlapped with several generations of critics in Cambridge, against whom he defined his ideas and his style. These rivals included E. M. W. Tillyard and, later, Graham Hough, but Leavis was never at a loss to identify additional foils. In his correspondence, "Tillyard" and "Hough" figured the way that "Wells" and "Snow" did in his published writing: less as actual people than as symbolic menaces. It is important to bear this aspect of his identity in mind, since for at least a generation – especially in the United States – Leavis's name has been associated with traditional criticism and outmoded orthodoxies. Yet he was neither traditional nor orthodox – as testified to by the Home Office's investigation when he sought to import a copy of the banned book *Ulysses*.[20] Leavis was, after all, a member of the first generation of students to read English in Cambridge, and he took the unusual option of writing a PhD. The PhD itself was a recent innovation, introduced partly to satisfy the credentialing needs of scientists, and Leavis was one of the first postgraduates in Cambridge to pursue it – indeed, among the thousands of theses in the University Library today, his is number sixty-six. He was innovative as a scholar and a teacher, publishing his first book on contemporary poetry, and analyzing the verse of the undergraduate William

---

[18] Q. D. Leavis, *Fiction and the Reading Public* (London: Chatto and Windus, 1932).
[19] For more on the Leavises and their circle in this period, see Denys Thompson, ed., *The Leavises: Recollections and Impressions* (Cambridge University Press, 1984).
[20] MacKillop, *F. R. Leavis*, pp. 88–91.

Empson in his lectures.[21] In short, Leavis figured as an oppositional force against inherited orthodoxies and the academic establishment, and he always remained convinced that he had been denied recognition as a direct result.

Despite these obstacles, during the 1930s Leavis secured his position in Cambridge. In 1932 he left Emmanuel to become Director of Studies in English at Downing, and that same year he and his collaborators launched *Scrutiny*. *Scrutiny* became one of the most influential literary journals of its time, and the Leavises ran it from its founding in 1932 to its demise in 1953. The quarterly never missed an issue, even during the war, and it pioneered iconoclastic readings of literary history while advocating radical reforms in education.[22] In 1935 Leavis became College Lecturer at Downing, and the next year – at the age of 41 – he finally secured a permanent position in Cambridge as Assistant Lecturer and Fellow of Downing. Not until 1954, however, did he become a member of the Faculty Board in English, and it was only in 1959 – just three years before his retirement – that he was named Reader. Upon retirement in 1962 Leavis was appointed an Honorary Fellow at Downing College, a position he held for two years before resigning in a terrible row over his successor. From 1965 he continued to lecture and write, while commuting to a series of honorary and visiting positions at other universities. Leavis died in 1978 – the year that he was named a Companion of Honour, "for services to the study of English Literature."[23]

Leavis's prolific output of books may be organized into five (overlapping) areas. He first established himself as a critic of poetry, analyzing contemporary verse in *New Bearings in English Poetry* (1932) and the poetic tradition in *Revaluation* (1936). During the second decade of *Scrutiny* his interests turned towards the novel, leading to *The Great Tradition* (1948), *D. H. Lawrence: Novelist* (1955), *Dickens the Novelist* (with Q. D. Leavis, 1970), and *Thought, Words, and Creativity: Art and Thought in Lawrence* (1976). His literary criticism was never far from his social criticism, initially in *Mass Civilisation and Minority Culture* (1930) and *Culture and Environment* (with Denys Thompson, 1933), and later in *Two Cultures? The Significance of C. P. Snow* (1962) and *Nor Shall My Sword: Discourses on Pluralism, Compassion and Social Hope* (1972). Towards the end of his life Leavis ventured the most philosophical statement of his critical suppositions in *The Living Principle: "English" as*

---

[21] F. R. Leavis, *New Bearings in English Poetry* (London: Chatto and Windus, 1932).

[22] On *Scrutiny*, see Francis Mulhern, *The Moment of "Scrutiny"* (London: New Left Books, 1979).

[23] Quoted in MacKillop, *F. R. Leavis*, p. 409.

a Discipline of Thought (1975). And throughout each of these phases he maintained a commitment to pedagogy and the university, the subjects of *Culture and Environment* (1933), *Education and the University: A Sketch for an "English School"* (1943), and *English Literature in Our Time and the University* (delivered 1967, published 1969).[24]

This body of work ranged widely across topics and periods, but as a whole it testifies to a worldview capable of accounting for everything from the literary canon to the market economy. This worldview consisted of a dense web of assumptions, perspectives, and interpretations, through which Leavis apprehended any evidence put before him – it was, in short, his ideology. Placing this worldview on a political spectrum can be a frustrating task, but it was undoubtedly structured by a deep conservatism: after all, as we shall see, Leavis's criticism was predicated upon an idealized past that had never existed, the very definition of political reaction. But before his worldview can be "placed," it must first be unpacked, and to that end his literary criticism provides the essential point of departure.

Life, language, and thought

Leavis tended to import concepts from previous work with little or no explanation, introducing them to clinch a line of argument – or, in the eyes of his critics, to avoid argument altogether.[25] The result could be frustrating in its assurance that the mere invocation of a name (Babbitt, Wells, Snow) or term (creation, standards, life) effectively functioned as an irrefutable argument. Moreover, Leavis's strictures against writers and critics were notorious, and they were often couched in a style that seemed to implicate the reader in the author's own sneer – as when he inquired, "How is it that [Arnold Bennett] can go on exposing

---

[24] With the exception of *Mass Civilisation and Minority Culture*, which was published by the Minority Press in Cambridge, these books were all published by Chatto and Windus in London. Leavis also published four additional collections of essays during his lifetime: *For Continuity* (Cambridge: Minority Press, 1933), *The Common Pursuit* (London: Chatto and Windus, 1952), *"Anna Karenina" and Other Essays* (London: Chatto and Windus, 1967), and, with Q. D. Leavis, *Lectures in America* (London: Chatto and Windus, 1969). G. Singh edited two posthumous collections of Leavis's essays: *The Critic as Anti-Philosopher: Essays and Papers* (Athens: University of Georgia Press, 1983); *Valuation in Criticism and Other Essays* (Cambridge University Press, 1986).

[25] On Leavis's intellectual development and critical positions, see Michael Bell, *F. R. Leavis* (London: Routledge, 1988); Bell, "F. R. Leavis," *The Cambridge History of Literary Criticism: Volume 7, Modernism and the New Criticism*, ed. A. Walton Litz, *et al.* (Cambridge University Press, 2000), pp. 389–422; Gary Day, *Re-reading Leavis: Culture and Literary Criticism* (New York: St. Martin's Press, 1996); in addition to Collini, "Cambridge and the Study of English"; MacKillop, *F. R. Leavis*; Mulhern, *The Moment of "Scrutiny."*

himself in this way without becoming a by-word and a laughing-stock?"[26] Three decades later, in the lecture about Snow that posed essentially the same question, Leavis began by acknowledging, "The commentary I have to make on [Snow] is necessarily drastic and dismissive," before unloading a ferocious denunciation.[27] The point here is not to excuse these tendencies, merely to acknowledge that they were indeed central to Leavis's practice. But, in order to understand Leavis's position, it is necessary to move past the polemics and approach the criticism on its own terms.

The essential concept in Leavis's thought was "life." Like any theoretical shorthand, "life" was intended not to confuse but to clarify – and, in light of subsequent developments in literary theory, it is curious to recall that "life" was once derided as jargon. To Leavis, life was the creative act at the core of what it meant to be human. He employed the term more often than he defined it, but late in his career – after his intervention against Snow – he ventured the occasional explanation: "To be spontaneous, and in its spontaneity creative, is of the essence of life," he wrote in 1972.[28] Three years earlier he offered another, slightly different definition: "Life is growth and change in response to changing conditions."[29] A sense of what this meant is conveyed in a passage Leavis often quoted to his students, from a letter by D. H. Lawrence upon the death of the poet Rupert Brooke:

The death of Rupert Brooke fills me more and more with the sense of the fatuity of it all. He was slain by bright Phoebus' shaft – it was in keeping with his general sunniness – it was the real climax of his pose. I first heard of him as a Greek god under a Japanese sunshade, reading poetry in his pyjamas, at Grantchester, – at Grantchester upon the lawns where the river goes. Bright Phoebus smote him down. It is all in the saga.

O God, O God it is all too much of a piece: it is like madness.

Leavis appreciatively remarked, "The passage really *belongs* in its epistolary context – it has been thrown off with an unstudied spontaneity; but how marvellous is the living precision with which the delicate complexity of the reaction, the wholeness of the characteristic Laurentian response, is conveyed!"[30] To Leavis, Lawrence's reaction upon

[26] F. R. Leavis, *Mass Civilisation and Minority Culture* (Cambridge: Minority Press, 1930), p. 17.
[27] Leavis, *Two Cultures?*, p. 11.
[28] F. R. Leavis, *Nor Shall My Sword* (London: Chatto and Windus, 1972), p. 15.
[29] Leavis, *English Literature in Our Time and the University*, p. 2.
[30] F. R. Leavis, *"Anna Karenina" and Other Essays*, p. 175, reprinted from " 'Lawrence Scholarship' and Lawrence," *Sewanee Review* 71 (January–March 1963), pp. 25–35.

learning of Brooke's death was spontaneous and genuine. He drew upon the resources of language to convey – rather than merely "express" – his emotion, and as such this passage testifies to a mind in touch with life.[31]

This sense of life served as the concept through which Leavis evaluated everything from Sunday papers to human history. Since change was inevitable, he maintained, it was imperative not to arrest it, but rather to respond to it. The ideal response took the form of creation, and the supremely creative act of which humans were capable was thought. From there the reasoning glided smoothly along the path that established literary criticism as *the* essential pursuit: thought was only possible through language, and the most advanced use of language was that of great writers. Literature thus figured for Leavis as much more than a body of wisdom or a source of refinement: it was the most telling index of the state of life in a culture. The literary critic's expertise in assessing literary creation thus became the surest way to diagnose the health of a culture past or present, and for this reason the critic had an essential role to play outside the university and in society at large.[32]

The particular object of the critic's attention was language. Language, to Leavis, was more than a means of communication: it was the tissue that connected the entire culture, and it was itself textured by generations of judgments and adjustments. "[Language] is a vehicle of collective wisdom and basic assumptions," he explained, "a currency of criteria and valuations collaboratively determined."[33] It was language that enabled thought, which Leavis understood as the amending and extending of inherited assumptions and evaluations. Thought, in this sense, was not a matter of finding words to communicate ideas that already existed, but rather of working through language to forge new ideas entirely. To put it another way, to Leavis thought was an act of

The late Ian MacKillop discussed this passage in a wonderful essay posted to his website; unfortunately, the link is no longer active.

[31] On the German tradition of *Lebensphilosophie*, with its similarities to Leavis's sense of "life," see Paul Forman, "The Primacy of Science in Modernity, of Technology in Postmodernity, and of Ideology in the History of Technology," *History and Technology* 23 (March/June 2007), pp. 1–152, especially pp. 45–47; on the relationship between Leavis and Heidegger, as well as his entry on Leavis in *The Cambridge History of Literary Criticism*.

[32] Terry Eagleton states the Leavisian case well: "The quality of a society's language was the most telling index of the quality of its personal and social life: a society which had ceased to value literature was one lethally closed to the impulses which had created and sustained the best of human civilization." Eagleton, *Literary Theory: An Introduction* (Minneapolis: University of Minnesota Press, 1983), p. 32.

[33] F. R. Leavis, "The Pilgrim's Progress," in *"Anna Karenina" and Other Essays*, p. 41, originally published as an afterword to John Bunyan, *The Pilgrim's Progress* (New York: New American Library, 1964).

creation rather than *discovery*: it was the extension of the shared human consciousness through language.

Leavis's sense of the relationship between language, thought, and reality is best illustrated through his ideas on the creation of literary meaning. For Leavis, meaning was not something apart from – and thus conveyed by – language; rather, meaning was created *through* language. A poem, for example, succeeded not by describing something that already existed, but by enacting an experience in the mind of the reader: "Words in poetry invite us, not to 'think about' and judge but to 'feel into' or 'become' – to realize a complex experience that is given in the words."[34] The same was true of prose, as Leavis explained after a discussion of a novel by Lawrence: "I have not been offering to define any thought that is *behind* the novel-long tale. The tale itself *is* the thought."[35] The critic's task, then, was to "realize" (or re-create) as fully as possible the work at hand, and in the process to assess its creative success or failure – not in terms of how it measured up to an independent standard, but by the degree to which it created an experience in the mind of the reader. At its core, then, Leavisian criticism was *evaluative* rather than *interpretive*, entailing arguments about how and why literary works succeeded or failed rather than what they said or meant. When Leavis set about this task as a critic of poetry and prose, the results were alarming for what they revealed about the fate of language – and thus of life – since the seventeenth century.

Paradise lost

An early engagement with science in Leavis's work came in the 1930s, as he developed the historical narrative that structured his ideas about the fate of language and life since the seventeenth century. This narrative depicted a relentless assault upon a once-vibrant culture, but Leavis's vision had not always been quite so dark: his PhD thesis of 1924, "The Relationship of Journalism to Literature" (which greets the reader today with a note from the author disavowing its contents), praised the function of journalism for maintaining lines of communication between writers and the public.[36] But as the 1920s proceeded, his assessment of the role played by journalism became considerably less sanguine, so that

---

[34] Leavis, *The Common Pursuit*, pp. 212–213; originally published as "Literary Criticism and Philosophy: A Reply," *Scrutiny* 6 (June 1937), pp. 59–70.

[35] F. R. Leavis, *Thought, Words and Creativity: Art and Thought in Lawrence* (New York: Oxford University Press, 1976), p. 121 (emphasis in original).

[36] See the discussion in John Ferns, *F. R. Leavis* (New York: Twayne, 2000), pp. 20–25.

by 1930 his prognosis was dire.[37] And while his judgments about particular writers changed over time, this pessimistic assessment of the relationship between journalism and literature informed Leavis's criticism throughout his career.

As discussed in Chapter 1, the 1930s were exciting times for science in Cambridge, a period when its laboratories were at the center of developments in physics and biochemistry. The decade also witnessed a brief hiatus in the long-term trend towards increasing numbers of university places, and with their institutional positions relatively stable, discussions of the arts and sciences flourished.[38] In this context, while willing to take a swipe at what he saw as naive scientific utopianism (as in a review of H. G. Wells in the debut of *Scrutiny*), Leavis focused his attention upon his own area of study: the fate of language and sensibility since the seventeenth century.[39] He had switched from History to English as an undergraduate, but Leavis's thinking on these matters remained deeply historical. Indeed, the historical narrative that informed his literary criticism helps to make sense not only of his views on science, but also of other innumerable judgments that can appear eccentric on their own: from the devaluation of Milton, to the elevation of Gerard Manley Hopkins, to the dogged championing of Lawrence. Each of these judgments had their place in a drama that began with that familiar epic trope, the Fall.

Leavis's historical narrative opened at a time brimming with life, the age of Shakespeare. Shakespeare was a genius, to be sure, but the expression of his genius was only possible through the language that he inherited: "By the time Shakespeare was discovering his genius there was ready to his hand a vernacular that was marvellously receptive, adventurous and flexible."[40] This language was part of a community in which work and leisure, song and dance, custom and habit were united as parts of a common culture – an organic community.[41] In such a community and culture Shakespeare could write plays that were at once popular

---

[37] For further discussion of this pessimism, and the reasons for it, see Mulhern, *The Moment of "Scrutiny."*

[38] See Roy Porter, "The Two Cultures Revisited," *Cambridge Review*, November 1994, pp. 74–80.

[39] Collini discusses Leavis's dismissal of Wells in his introduction to Snow, *The Two Cultures* (Cambridge University Press, 1993), pp. xxiii–xxv.

[40] Leavis, *Nor Shall My Sword*, p. 129.

[41] On the organic community, see Leavis and Denys Thompson, *Culture and Environment: The Training of Critical Awareness* (London: Chatto and Windus, 1933), especially the (unnumbered) chapters "The Organic Community" and "The Loss of the Organic Community." See also Leavis's discussion of Cecil Sharp's recovery of Appalachian culture in "Literature and Society," *Scrutiny* 12 (Winter 1943), pp. 2–11.

entertainment and the highest creative expression, and in this way Shakespeare's works were a product of – and a testament to – the vitality of life in Tudor England.[42]

Then, during the seventeenth century, disaster struck. Influenced by T. S. Eliot's critical work in the 1920s, Leavis believed that the seventeenth century was pivotal in the emergence of a new civilization. That period was characterized by the shift in thought and feeling that Eliot famously labeled the "dissociation of sensibility": "It is something which had happened to the mind of England between the time of Donne or Lord Herbert of Cherbury and the time of Tennyson and Browning," Eliot explained. "[I]t is the difference between the intellectual poet and the reflective poet."[43] Leavis followed Eliot in identifying a breach during this period, and he directed particular attention to the factors that caused it.[44] The seventeenth century was the age of the Civil War and the Commonwealth, Puritanism and Nonconformism, the rise of capitalism and the emergence of science. Together, Leavis explained, these developments severed the connections within a previously unified culture to usher in an entirely new civilization – the one that, in his view, persisted into the present. By the time of the Restoration, the unified community that had made Shakespeare's work possible was being marginalized by a fashionable society in London and the Court. "As a result of the social and economic changes speeded up by the Civil War," Leavis explained, "a metropolitan fashionable Society, compact and politically in the ascendant, found itself in charge of standards."[45] This coterie deliberately differentiated itself from society at large, adopting standards of taste, refinement, and politeness that exacerbated the breach.[46]

---

[42] Leavis, *Mass Civilisation and Minority Culture*, p. 25.

[43] T. S. Eliot, "The Metaphysical Poets," *Selected Essays* (New York: Harcourt Brace, 1932), p. 247; the essay dates from 1921. On the "dissociation of sensibility," see Frank Kermode, *Romantic Image* (London: Routledge and Paul, 1957); F. W. Bateson, "Dissociation of Sensibility," *Essays in Critical Dissent* (London: Longman, 1972), pp. 142–152.

[44] For Leavis on the dissociation of sensibility, see "English Poetry in the Seventeenth Century," *Scrutiny* 4 (December 1935), pp. 236–256, reprinted as "The Line of Wit," in *Revaluation: Tradition and Development in English Poetry* (London: Chatto and Windus, 1936), Chapter 1; as well as "Eliot's 'Axe to Grind' and the Nature of Great Criticism," in *English Literature in Our Time and the University*, Chapter 3. See also Bell, *F. R. Leavis*, pp. 57–61, where he notes that "Eliot came to revise, indeed effectively to reverse, his view of Donne and to dissociate himself from the phrase 'dissociation of sensibility' " (p. 59), while also discussing Leavis's engagement with the concept (pp. 60–61).

[45] F. R. Leavis, "English Poetry in the Eighteenth Century," *Scrutiny* 5 (June 1936), pp. 13–31, reprinted as "The Augustan Tradition," *Revaluation*, Chapter 4, quotation p. 96.

[46] For Leavis on the seventeenth century, see *Education and the University: A Sketch for an English School* (London: Chatto and Windus, 1943), Chapter 2; *English Literature in Our*

The triumph of the new civilization registered throughout the sensibility of the age. In Leavis's view, since sensibility was manifest in language, poetry and prose provided the surest access to these wider developments. Instead of being recognized as the shared medium through which consciousness was created, language was reconceived as a tool to describe a reality that existed independently. In other words, as the age of Shakespeare gave way to the age of Newton, language became associated with *description* rather than *creation*. Indeed, Leavis continued, language actually came to be cast as a barrier between the observer and the observed. That is, language – which, in Leavis's view, enabled thought – became conceived of as an impediment to thought, something to be circumvented as much as possible through abstraction, mathematics, and plain prose.[47] When the Court returned to London in 1660, it endorsed these new ideals of "logic" and "clarity" by patronizing the Royal Society. The Royal Society occupied an important place in Leavis's history, because it testified to the changed ethos of a new civilization. In 1667 Bishop Sprat endorsed its "close, naked, natural way of speaking – positive expression, clear senses, a native easiness, bringing all things as near the mathematical plainness as they can, and preferring the language of artisans, countrymen and merchants before that of wits and scholars."[48] The prior unity between language and thought had been disrupted by a philosophy that cast language as an obstacle to thought, and the victory of that philosophy was so decisive that the arid language of "mathematical plainness" had inexplicably been equated with the vibrant tongue of "artisans, countrymen and merchants."

Yet before Leavis is read as hostile to science *as such*, it is imperative to recognize that his analysis of the Royal Society was exactly paralleled by his critique of John Milton. Again, as with the "dissociation of sensibility," Leavis's ideas about Milton were forged through his engagement with Eliot's criticism.[49] No less than the plain prose endorsed by the

---

Time and the University, Chapter 3; *Nor Shall My Sword*, Chapter 4; *The Living Principle: 'English' as a Discipline of Thought* (London: Chatto and Windus, 1975), Chapter 1.

[47] Leavis particularly developed these ideas in the first chapter of *The Living Principle*, where he referred to the division between language and reality as the "Cartesian duality." Despite the clarity the term offers, I have refrained from adopting it so as not to organize a lifetime of thought by a label introduced only at its end.

[48] Thomas Sprat, *History of the Royal Society* (1667), quoted in Leavis, *English Literature in Our Time and the University*, p. 94. Leavis also discusses the Royal Society in "The Relationship of Journalism to Literature," pp. 89–90, *Revaluation*, pp. 35, 96, and *Nor Shall My Sword*, p. 172.

[49] For Leavis on Milton, see "Milton's Verse," *Scrutiny* 2 (September 1933), pp. 123–136, reprinted in *Revaluation*; and "In Defence of Milton," *Scrutiny* 7 (June 1938), pp. 104–114 and "Mr. Eliot and Milton," *Sewanee Review* 57 (Winter 1949), pp. 1–30, both reprinted in *The Common Pursuit*.

Royal Society, Milton's verse represented for Leavis the rejection of the language of daily life.[50] But whereas the Royal Society advocated a transparent style, Milton's language called attention to its own inventiveness and lyricism. To Leavis, this language exhibited "a feeling *for* words rather than a capacity for thinking *through* words."[51] The result was poetry that astonished the intellect, yet proved incapable of producing corresponding emotion: "Milton seems . . . to be focusing rather upon words than upon perceptions, sensations, or things."[52] There was no doubt in Leavis's mind that Milton was a writer of genius, but by contrast with Shakespeare this genius did not draw upon – and was not expressed through – a vibrant English idiom. "The ethos of his stylistic invention," Leavis explained, "denies his verse anything like a Shakespearean relation to the living language."[53] Indeed, Milton's verse actually exhibited the "consistent rejection of English idiom," to the point that it seemed that Milton had, in his Latinate verse, "forgotten the English language."[54] By rejecting that idiom, Milton cut himself off from the living language, with the result that his verse remained "remote from speech."[55] To Leavis, Milton was typical as a product of his society, but his undeniable literary achievement was most atypical – and that achievement influenced the lesser poets who followed the path of his unfortunate detour.

These parallel critiques of Milton and the Royal Society bring Leavis's reading of the seventeenth century into sharper focus. First, his criticism of the literary Milton and the scientific Royal Society dissolves opposition to "science" and sympathy to "literature" as a primary axis of antagonism in his thought – that is, since Leavis was critical of both, for similar reasons, an interpretive framework other than the disciplinary is required to make sense of his position. Second, his criticism of both the revolutionary Milton and the royally patronized new science dissolves high politics as an axis of antagonism – that is, these positions cannot at once be explained as a conservative's hostility to radicals (hence the assault upon Milton) and a radical's hostility to the Court (hence the assault upon the Royal Society). In fact, to read Leavis as directing his critique against Milton, or the Royal Society, is to grasp the wrong end of the stick. Although the genius of Milton and the power of science undoubtedly exacerbated the situation, in Leavis's eyes neither was the

---

[50] Bell explains Leavis's position: "The Miltonic manner pulled away from the genius of the spoken tongue and thereby helped to consolidate linguistically the special realm of the 'poetic'." *F. R. Leavis*, p. 59.

[51] Leavis, *Revaluation*, p. 48 (emphasis in original).   [52] *Ibid.*

[53] Leavis, *English Literature in Our Time and the University*, p. 98.

[54] Leavis, *Revaluation*, p. 50.   [55] *Ibid.*, p. 53.

problem in and of itself: they were both part of something still more comprehensive, and as such they pointed towards the total transformation that was the actual target of Leavis's critique. For Leavis, the seventeenth century inaugurated the terrible course of modern civilization – terrible not because of this or that development, but because of the assault it unleashed upon the unified culture that had once sustained life.

Leavis pursued the consequences of this history in his revisionist readings of the literary tradition. By the time of John Bunyan's death in 1688, he argued, the age of Shakespeare had given way to the age of Newton in science (with his investigations of laws of nature that were thought to exist outside of the human mind), Locke in philosophy (with his belief in the mind as a recipient of external sense impressions), and Dryden in poetry (with his blank verse and mannered style that bore no relation to a living language).[56] The following Augustan Age testified to a new ethos in society and literature: this was the era of decorum and manners, correctness and elegance, order and consistency, wit and good form.[57] William Blake was aware of the new idiom's limits, and in striving to break free he forged his own words and technique. Blake thus figured as the antithesis of his age, and he even went some way towards reversing the ideals that derived from the Restoration – as in his attacks upon the world of Newton and Locke (attacks that Leavis adopted in the decade after his Richmond Lecture). Yet Blake remained isolated in his time: he had no public to write for, Leavis continued, and as a result he became careless in his late prophetic works.[58] By the time of Wordsworth's death in 1850, Leavis believed that the advance of modern civilization had been fatally accelerated by the Industrial Revolution.[59] The remnants of the embattled culture persisted only in language – and two of Leavis's major books, *New Bearings in English Poetry* and *The Great Tradition*, identified the writers who worked through that language to sustain what was left of the living tradition.

Leavis's historical interpretation and literary criticism were inextricably connected, and they both derived from his pessimistic assessment of the fate of language and life since the seventeenth century. That century had seen a wedge driven between language and thought in the human

---

[56] For Leavis on Newton (although more often invoked than analyzed), see *English Literature in Our Time and the University*, Chapter 1; *Nor Shall My Sword*, Chapter 4; *The Living Principle*, Chapter 1. For Leavis on Locke, see *Nor Shall My Sword*, p. 127. For Leavis on Dryden, see *English Literature in Our Time and the University*, Chapter 3.

[57] For Leavis on the Augustan Age, see *Revaluation*, especially Chapter 4.

[58] For Leavis on Blake, see *Revaluation*, pp. 103–105; *The Common Pursuit*, pp. 186–188; *Nor Shall My Sword*, pp. 11–37.

[59] Leavis, "Literature and Society," in *The Common Pursuit*, p. 192.

mind, between popular culture and polite society in human relations, and between the old and the new in human civilization, and the course of history ever since had been dominated by that civilization's advance. Leavis's vision was bleak, but not entirely so – after all, it also affirmed the possibility of determined resistance to the onslaught of history. It was a vision in which the literary critic had an essential role to play.

The crisis and the critic

Surveying the international scene in 1930, Leavis depicted a desperate situation. The year after the stock market crash in New York, he observed that "currency has been debased and inflated."[60] It no longer corresponded to the small amount of gold that guaranteed its value, and the resulting inflation threatened the possibility of fine living. Neither the United States nor the Soviet Union offered answers to the crisis, and in fact their relationship only entrenched the conditions that had brought it about. Leavis might have been discussing the crisis of international finance, but *Mass Civilisation and Minority Culture* actually addressed the state of language and criticism. The "inflated currency" was a surfeit of endorsements of art and literature, and the small quantity of "gold" to which those endorsements bore little relation was the judgment of the minority that was actually capable of aesthetic discrimination. The ultimate cause of these developments, Leavis argued, was the elevation of material prosperity as a paramount concern, so that, in its determination to achieve parity with the United States, the Soviet Union was worshipping the very idol that created the crisis.

This seemingly idiosyncratic diagnosis of the "crisis" in the 1930s must be set in the context of broad transformations in publishing and broadcasting during the first third of the century. The BBC had been established in 1922, and by 1938 the number of wireless sets had increased from 36,000 to almost 9,000,000. Between 1907 and 1935 the publication of newspapers increased 162.6 percent; from 1891 to 1931 the number of authors, editors, and journalists more than trebled; and during the same period advertising emerged as the financial basis of the newspaper industry.[61] In Leavis's perspective, these transformations were working together to shift cultural authority from the critic to the market. His alarm at this development need not be reduced to a narrow lament about the marginalization of his own expertise: from Leavis's point of view, after three difficult centuries, the displacement of the

[60] Leavis, *Mass Civilisation and Minority Culture*, p. 12.
[61] Mulhern, *The Moment of "Scrutiny,"* pp. 7–9.

critic's authority threatened the possibility of sustaining the living language. But only the literary critic possessed the sensitivity and training required to identify that language, and only that language offered the possibility of the continued creation that was life.

The critic, in this view, represented the last defense against forces that had been on the march since the seventeenth century. "Upon this minority depends our power of profiting by the finest human experience of the past," Leavis insisted. "[T]hey keep alive the subtlest and most perishable parts of tradition."[62] It had long been the case that those capable of discriminating judgment were a minority of the population, he argued, but until recently the authority of that minority had at least been acknowledged. Recent developments in publishing, broadcasting, and marketing were replacing the authority of the critic with the demands of the market. The pursuit of sales diluted quality, creating a downward spiral that threatened the existence of standards altogether. Leavis anxiously observed that anyone who protested these developments was labeled "high brow" – a term of derision wielded against the minority who were engaged in the work of maintaining standards. The animus against standards was obvious in the abominable reviewing in newspapers and periodicals, which left little room for serious publications such as the *Calendar of Modern Letters*. Yet without publications such as the *Calendar*, there would be no forum to sustain creative work; and without continued creation, after three centuries of struggle, the language would run dry.

Needless to say, Leavis was alarmed. He encapsulated the crisis by identifying an opposition between "mass civilization" and "minority culture": the *mass civilization* of marketing, standardization, and leveling-down, versus the defenders of a *minority culture* that recognized a responsibility to sustain literature, language, and life in the face of these developments. But once the minority became conscious of the crisis, how should it respond? That question led Leavis from diagnosis to prescription.

Ideological alternatives

Leavis's ideology resists being placed on a linear spectrum. Even in his voluminous correspondence, he rarely addressed matters of politics. Contemporaries classified him as everything from a Nazi to a Stalinist, and scholarly assessments range from suggesting that he moved rightward during his career, to downplaying the significance of politics to his

---

[62] Leavis, *Mass Civilisation and Minority Culture*, p. 5.

criticism, to reading his criticism as a retreat from politics.[63] Yet Leavis's intellectual position may be understood as a coherent ideology if its various elements – the epistemology, history, literary criticism, and social analysis – are considered in relation. At this point the discussion turns from the workings of his worldview to consider its place in British political thought more generally – and, as is often the case, that place becomes apparent through contrast with the positions that Leavis was *against*.

The first decade of *Scrutiny*, during the 1930s, was marked by its engagement with English Marxism.[64] Leavis claimed victory in that battle, and a generation later Perry Anderson affirmed the victory of *Scrutiny* over the "modish literary leftism" in Britain at the time.[65] "This was the heyday of the Marxizing intellectual," Leavis recalled of the *Scrutiny* days. "We were anti-Marxist – necessarily so."[66] By "anti-Marxist" Leavis meant three things: *Scrutiny* opposed the reductionism that would deny autonomy to literature; it opposed the tendency towards abstraction that would attempt to systematize "thought"; and it opposed the materialism that Leavis believed characteristic of Marxism and modernity alike. This last point was particularly important: by treating Marxism as a product of modern civilization, Leavis believed that his position criticized them both. That is, like capitalism, science, or advertising, Marxism was yet another product of the process that had its origins in the seventeenth century – the process that was itself the object of Leavis's critique. Since Marxism was a product of the civilization that it sought to critique, its shortcoming was not that it was too revolutionary,

---

[63] William Gerhardi, "Sir Charles Snow, Dr. F. R. Leavis, and the Two Cultures," *Spectator*, 16 March 1962, pp. 329–331; John Wain, "21 Years with Dr. Leavis," *Observer*, 27 October 1963. Eagleton, *Literary Theory*, pp. 30–43 and Samson, *F. R. Leavis*; G. Singh, *F. R. Leavis: A Literary Biography* (London: Duckworth, 1995); Mulhern, *The Moment of "Scrutiny."*

[64] For Leavis and *Scrutiny* on Marxism, the key texts are (in chronological order): " 'Under Which King, Bezonian?' " *Scrutiny* 1 (December 1932), pp. 205–215; "Restatements for Critics," *Scrutiny* 1 (March 1933), pp. 315–323; "Marxism and Cultural Continuity," *For Continuity* (Cambridge: Minority Press, 1933), pp. 1–12; " 'The Marxian Analysis,' " *Scrutiny* 6 (September 1937), pp. 201–204; "Retrospect of a Decade," *Scrutiny* 9 (June 1940), pp. 70–72; "Literature and Society," *Scrutiny* 12 (Winter 1943), pp. 2–11; "Critic and Leviathan: Literary Criticism and Politics," *Politics and Letters* 1 (Winter-Spring 1948), pp. 58–61; " '*Scrutiny*': A Retrospect," first published in the Cambridge University Press's reprint of *Scrutiny* in 1963, then reprinted in *Valuation in Criticism and Other Essays*. On Leavis and Marxism, see especially Mulhern, *The Moment of "Scrutiny."*

[65] Perry Anderson, "Components of the National Culture," *New Left Review* 50 (July-August 1968), pp. 3–57, reprinted in *English Questions* (London: Verso, 1992), pp. 48–104, quotation p. 100.

[66] Leavis, *Valuation in Criticism*, p. 221.

but that it could not be revolutionary enough.[67] Of course, the kind of revolution that Leavis and *Scrutiny* advocated differed from that of the Marxists: Leavis sought a revolution not of society but of mind, and its battleground would be not in the streets but in the curriculum.

In his desire to effect this revolution, Leavis was skeptical of both socialists on the left and conservatives on the right. It is no exaggeration to say that he loathed socialism, viscerally and intellectually, because of its goals of social equality and material betterment. He believed that the pursuit of equality denied the need for cultural leadership, and that the quest for prosperity revealed the misplaced priorities of a sick civilization. Leavis was more in sync with the Conservative grassroots during the 1950s and 1960: he shared their hostility towards socialism and planning, as well as their commitment to the individual rather than abstractions such as "society."[68] But he nevertheless kept his distance from the Tories, associating them with a conservatism for which he had little sympathy. He maintained that his conception of literature as a response to its times was antithetical to such notions as "traditional wisdom" or "literary values" – as he put it in his Richmond Lecture, "I haven't chosen to say that mankind will need all its traditional wisdom; that might suggest a kind of conservatism that, so far as I am concerned, is the enemy."[69] Leavis insisted that the most salient fact about the past was that it could not be recovered, and since change was inevitable he sought not to arrest it but to respond to it. The pragmatic response that Leavis had in mind included a radical overhaul of education: he hoped that it would be centered around a discipline that had only recently emerged in Cambridge, and that had engaged in modernizing battles against entrenched disciplines such as classics.

Further evidence that Leavis was no traditional conservative lies in his attitude towards religion. The familiar image of Leavis as a Puritan derives from the strenuous tone of his criticism, his apparent indifference to worldly matters, and the devotion he inspired from his students – but not from any religious commitment on his part. In the landmark essay that distanced *Scrutiny* from Marxism, Eliot's conservatism and religiosity came in for rough treatment as well: "[A]s for Anglo-Catholicism and Royalism, those who may find these . . . convincing do not convince us that they are taking up an effective attitude towards the

---

[67] For a critique of this position, see Anderson, "Components of the National Culture," in *English Questions*, pp. 96–103.
[68] On these sympathies among the grassroots of the Conservative Party, see E. H. H. Green, *Thatcher* (London: Hodder Arnold, 2006), pp. 45, 192, and *passim*.
[69] Leavis, *Two Cultures?*, pp. 26–27.

problems."[70] As had been the case with his father, religion did not sing to Leavis, and this stance informed his sustained reading of Eliot's *Four Quartets*.[71] He read *Four Quartets* as a series of meditations by a poet striving towards, yet failing to reach, a transcendent reality – a striving that Leavis identified as the religious impulse. He believed that Eliot's verse represented an extraordinary achievement, one that was far more real than anything divine or transcendent would ever be, yet Eliot's religious cast of mind prevented him from recognizing his creative achievement. Leavis was too much of a humanist to endorse that impulse, and he was too secular to sympathize with it.

After the war Leavis felt increasingly out of step with the age. The watchwords of the establishment – planning, progress, modernization, standard of living, and so on – became like fingernails on a chalkboard, mindlessly repeated without any thought to where they came from or where they would lead. The feeling was mutual: Noel Annan deemed Leavis a "deviant" from his generation, a figure who "gloried in his contempt for its pieties."[72] Leavis expressed that contempt in the title of the book that contained his Richmond Lecture: *Nor Shall My Sword: Discourses on Pluralism, Compassion and Social Hope*. "Nor Shall My Sword," of course, quoted Blake, and Leavis meant for it to signal both his militant commitment to his ideals, and his sympathy for the isolated genius who had been so out of step with his age. The subtitle was even more revealing, its ironic reference to "pluralism, compassion and social hope" intended to skewer pretensions that Leavis viewed as pernicious clichés.

Radical liberalism

But to adopt a Leavisian formulation, "What for – what ultimately for?"[73] We have seen that Leavis rejected the priorities of the British establishment, and that he denounced the materialism that he thought equally characteristic of Britain, the United States, and the Soviet Union. He opposed socialism on the left and conservatism on the right, as well as their more rigorous incarnations in the forms of Marxism and religion. Against these paired oppositions, his positive position begins to emerge. The former stance, in its root-and-branch rejection of the parameters of conventional discourse, is best understood as *radicalism*;

---

[70] Leavis, " 'Under Which King, Bezonian?' " p. 213.
[71] Leavis, *The Living Principle*, pp. 155–264.
[72] Noel Annan, *Our Age: English Intellectuals between the World Wars – a Group Portrait* (New York: Random House, 1990), p. 315.
[73] Leavis, *Two Cultures?*, p. 22.

the latter, in its mutual hostility towards Marxism and conservatism, is best understood as *liberalism*. Leavis's ideology may thus be understood as "radical liberalism": *radical* in its antagonism towards contemporary society, *liberal* in its commitment to the individual.[74]

When pressed, Leavis characterized himself as a liberal. Q. D. Leavis could be blunt about her hostility to the left, as when she refused to support an embattled lecturer on political grounds.[75] She also indicated that she was more comfortable than her husband with the idea of being a conservative, and even of voting Conservative: an undergraduate later recalled her saying that she was a paternalist rather than a democrat, and as early as 1974 she expressed confidence that Margaret Thatcher would make a good Prime Minister.[76] Such explicit declarations were rare from Leavis, but as the 1964 election approached he did declare his intention to vote Liberal. "[A] Labour Government will be a deadly and callous enemy," he explained. "And who can find respectable reasons for supposing that a Conservative Government will be any better? It's still possible to hope that a Liberal or two will have the insight, courage, and disinterestedness to say . . . the right things."[77] He even went so far as to sponsor the Liberal candidate in Cambridge, only to become dismayed when that candidate endorsed comprehensive education – a cowardly bow to the egalitarian impulse, one that Leavis thought was implicated with the general assault upon standards.

While he had little patience for high politics, intellectually Leavis situated himself within a liberal tradition. When Chatto and Windus agreed to publish John Stuart Mill's essays on Jeremy Bentham and Samuel Taylor Coleridge, he undertook to write the introduction himself.[78] In his analysis of those two representative Victorian minds, Leavis followed Mill in distancing himself from the utilitarianism of Bentham – half of the "technologico-Benthamism" against which he railed throughout the 1960s. Leavis read Bentham's ambition to systematize human society as the successor to Newton's achievement in astronomy

---

[74] Roy Fuller referred to Leavis as a "liberal," before discussing the apolitical trajectory of his career, in "The Critic and the Weekly," *New Statesman*, 14 July 1972, p. 56. Eagleton discusses the liberal humanism of Leavis, differentiating it from Eliot's conservatism, in *Literary Theory*, pp. 42–43.

[75] Raymond Williams, "Seeing a Man Running," in Denys Thompson, ed., *The Leavises*, p. 115.

[76] Rupert Christiansen, "Footsteps from the Floor Above," *Spectator*, 8 July 1995, p. 33; Q. D. Leavis to David Holbrook, 9 November 1974, Downing College: DCPP/LEA/4 Leavis, F. R. (7).

[77] Unidentified newspaper clipping in the possession of Richard and Jean Gooder in Cambridge (with thanks to Richard and Jean Gooder).

[78] John Stuart Mill, *Mill on Bentham and Coleridge*, introduction by F. R. Leavis (London: Chatto and Windus, 1950).

(a proposition with which Bentham would have agreed), and he identified that impulse running from Newton to Adam Smith to Bentham,
and from Bentham to Herbert Spencer to I. A. Richards (with whom
the Leavises had fallen out). Despite his hostility towards that tradition,
the individual figured no less at the center of Leavis's worldview: he
applauded Mill's recognition of "the need to safeguard, not only the
rights, but the individuality, of the individual against the pressure of a
democratic civilization," and he believed the individual needed protec-
tion from "that endless growth in the range and complexity of state
organization and bureaucratic control which makes the individual feel
so helpless in the modern world."[79] This suspicion of bureaucracy and
the state should not be read as an endorsement of "unchastened individualism," which Leavis thought Dickens had rightly sent up in the
figure of Josiah Bounderby in *Hard Times*.[80] Instead, Leavis's sense of
the relationship between the individual and society might be understood as "liberalism with a human face": a conception of the individual
neither collapsed within society (as in socialism), nor completely
detached from it (as in Benthamism).

Further indications of the tradition into which Leavis fit emerge
through other sympathies that he expressed. He admired Matthew
Arnold for exhibiting "the flexibility, the sensitiveness, the constant
delicacy of touch for the concrete in all its complexity, the intelligence
that is inseparably one with an alert and fine sense of value," and he
directed interested students to Lionel Trilling's *Matthew Arnold*
(1939).[81] Trilling was the doyen of a triumphant American liberalism,
having recently declared, "In the United States at this time liberalism is
not only the dominant but even the sole intellectual tradition."[82] In
1951 Leavis favorably reviewed *John Stuart Mill and Harriet Taylor: Their
Friendship and Subsequent Marriage*. The review affirmed his profound
respect for Mill, and it especially praised his independence from con-
vention: Mill, Leavis wrote, "reminds us how defiant of propriety,
conventional morality and accepted standards of decent behavior Great
Victorians could be."[83] The author of the book was Friedrich von
Hayek, scourge of socialists and champion of the individual; Leavis said

---

[79] F. R. Leavis, introduction to Mill, *Mill on Bentham and Coleridge* (London: Chatto and
Windus, 1950), pp. 16, 27.

[80] *Ibid.*, p. 35.

[81] *Ibid.*, p. 38; Lionel Trilling, *Matthew Arnold* (New York: Norton, 1939). Arnold can be
no less difficult to place, as Collini discusses in *Arnold* (Oxford University Press, 1988),
pp. 88–92.

[82] Trilling, *The Liberal Imagination* (New York: Viking, 1950), p. ix.

[83] F. R. Leavis, "Saints of Rationalism," *Listener*, 26 April 1951, p. 672.

nothing of Hayek's politics, and would have rejected his economism, but the sympathy is nevertheless suggestive. On other occasions Leavis endorsed John Kenneth Galbraith, the liberal economist who called attention to spiritual poverty amid material affluence, and Michael Polanyi, the Hungarian scientist-turned-philosopher who championed individualism against Marxism during the Cold War.[84] Mill, Arnold, Trilling, Hayek, Galbraith, and Polanyi: they had their differences, but it is surely not insignificant that Leavis – never one to be shy about stating his dislikes – expressed admiration for each of them. The fact that he respected these figures, ranged as they were across centuries, continents, and disciplines, suggests that he shared with them unacknowledged sympathies. Intellectual sympathy points towards ideological compatibility, and that compatibility helps locate Leavis's worldview within the liberal tradition.

These liberal inclinations led Leavis to favor the meritocratic society. He may have written fondly of Tudor England, but in the circumstances of the moment Leavis's ideal society was not one in which individuals *knew* their place, but rather one in which they *took* their place – and once in place, took their cues. He did not use the word (nobody did before 1958), but this commitment is the essence of the meritocratic vision. As previously discussed, the meritocracy is the ideal of the ambitious middle class – the segment of society that is equally hostile to the demands of those below and the privileges of those above. Leavis's father was a shop owner, while Snow's father was a factory clerk, but Leavis and Snow were both grammar school products and professional intellectuals. They exuded hostility against inherited privilege no less than egalitarian leveling, and they wanted to see society reformed so as to cultivate talent. For Leavis, talent – or, in his idiom, intelligence – was not the preserve of a traditional elite: after all, as Neil Roberts writes, the tradition that Leavis admired included "the tinker's son who wrote *The Pilgrim's Progress*, the clerk's son who wrote *Great Expectations*, the steward's daughter who wrote *Middlemarch* and above all the miner's son who wrote *The Rainbow* and said that the other Cambridge made him dream of beetles."[85] That "other Cambridge" was the Cambridge of

---

[84] John Kenneth Galbraith, *The Affluent Society* (Boston: Houghton Mifflin, 1958); Leavis wrote appreciatively of Galbraith in *English Literature in Our Time and the University*, pp. 31–32. On Michael Polanyi, I am indebted to Jessica Reinisch, "The Society for Freedom in Science, 1940–1963," unpublished MSc thesis, University of London (2000); for discussion of Leavis's interest in Polanyi, see Chapter 5.

[85] Neil Roberts, " 'Leavisite' Cambridge in the 1960s," in *F. R. Leavis: Essays and Documents*, ed. Ian MacKillop and Richard Storer (Sheffield Academic Press, 1995), p. 266.

public school graduates, Bloomsbury intellectuals, and an elite leisured class, whereas at Downing Leavis ran an English School that functioned as a center for an alternative ethos. The meritocracy was, in short, a liberal program of reform, directed against privilege and in favor of talent. But while Snow thought that the meritocracy would work through existing institutions to extend material prosperity, Leavis intended for it to foster a critical minority capable of exposing – and opposing – the values embedded within precisely those goals.

"To stand out and be isolated"

Over the course of his career Leavis worked to translate this worldview into various forms – that is, into reading lists, curricula, examinations, disciplines, colleges, and universities. Once institutionalized, these ideas would be in a position to influence students and teachers, private reading and public debate, ideas within the university and ideas about the university. Leavis himself understood this to be a form of politics, which is why in the 1930s he claimed that his program was more revolutionary than anything the Marxists had dreamed up; why in the 1940s he argued that the English School must stand at the center of the university so that all students would pass through it; and why in the 1960s he opposed the democratization of the university as an assault upon standards.

Within the terms of this project, literary criticism was not a retreat from politics: it was its essential front. Recall that the immediate crisis was the assault upon standards, that without standards there would be no way to recognize the creative use of language, and that without recognition the language could not be sustained. This threat to language resulted from developments unleashed during the seventeenth century, developments that together amounted to the emergence of modern civilization. The characteristic attribute of this civilization was that *feeling* was conceived as something different from *thinking*, and that words were conceived as obstacles to thought. Lost was the awareness that language *enabled* thought, and that thought was the creative act that was *life*. Through a complicated chain of reasoning, one that entailed particular notions of history and language, an assault upon intellectual standards became a threat to humanity. The literary critic thus bore the dual burdens of maintaining standards and fostering a public, so as to sustain the possibility of continued creation. In this endeavor, ranged against three centuries of history and beset on all sides by a hostile establishment, the price of failure was too terrible to contemplate.

In the day-to-day matters that constituted these efforts – the committee meetings, letters to editors, public lectures, and so forth – Leavis's tactics were shaped by his conception of how politics worked. Recall that Snow's idea of politics entailed diplomatic maneuvering and the building of coalitions, structured by temperament rather than ideology, and in which unintended slights or unexpected sympathies might tip the scales. Leavis's sense of politics was entirely different: since he viewed himself, his cause, and his values as besieged, working constructively within existing institutions was not a viable option. Leavis instead pursued a politics of defiance, of the dramatic gesture that might startle and provoke otherwise somnambulant colleagues, critics, or politicians. He was well aware of his reputation for being difficult, of his intimidating presence, and of the prestige conveyed by awards and honors, and he employed each of these attributes as weapons in his battles. He may have overplayed his hand in this regard: Clive James suggests that the brutality of Leavis's attacks left little to distinguish his colleagues from Hitler, and others have wondered whether the Leavises' intellectual arguments could really have been worth the friendships they left behind.[86] But if that is the question, whatever the verdict of others, the Leavises knew their answer: yes, they *were* that important.

A recollection by Raymond Williams provides a revealing glimpse into Leavis's conception of politics. Williams had joined the faculty of Cambridge English in 1961, and he was serving as secretary when a paper on the novel was proposed. He convened a committee, and later recalled that Leavis's contribution was helpful. On one occasion, though, Leavis differed from the majority as to whether novels in languages other than English should be included in the paper. He expressed his position forcefully, but failed to carry the table, at which point he turned to Williams directly: "I put it directly to you, Mr. Secretary. The coherent course would be the English novel from Dickens to Lawrence." It was a canny move, since Leavis knew this was the course that Williams offered, but Williams deferred to the majority. Leavis pressed the point again: "No, I am putting it to you, directly"; again Williams deferred, and again Leavis repeated: "To you." Leavis failed to carry the meeting, but he later made clear how he thought a majority could have been found: "If you had voted for Dickens to Lawrence," he insisted to Williams, "it would have turned the committee." Williams remarked that the majority were against them, but Leavis insisted that a decisive stand would have shifted the balance: "You could have turned it," he said. "You were not prepared to stand out and be isolated." *To stand out*

---

[86] Clive James, *May Week Was in June* (London: Cape, 1990), pp. 63–68; James Wood, "Don't Mess with the Don," *Guardian*, 21 July 1995.

and be isolated: in Leavis's mind, dissent from consensus was itself a form of politics.[87]

Leavis approached these contests with considerable self-awareness. As the above example suggests, he employed his posture as an outsider and his willingness to endure conflict to his tactical advantage.[88] This sense of politics shaped his behavior beyond the university as well. In the early 1970s, for example, he and his neighbors were concerned about the traffic, noise, and rubbish emanating from a local pub. There were community meetings, and a letter was drafted, but Leavis behaved abruptly towards his neighbors and confrontationally towards the pub. He later wrote to his neighbor to explain his behavior, and defended his preference for a confrontational approach by insisting that nothing would be gained by seeking to remain on good terms with either the brewer or the landlord.[89] The politics of confrontation was not merely something that Leavis was driven to during exasperating faculty meetings: it was his way of approaching problems and accomplishing goals more generally.

This account of Leavis's political style has attempted to round out perceptions of him as difficult, uncollegial, or paranoid (which is not to say that he could not be all three). The goal has not been to endorse his tactics or excuse his polemics, but to demystify the tone of his argument against Snow. In Leavis's thinking judgments about literature were judgments about life, and the advocacy of those judgments often needed to be belligerent. Through the Richmond Lecture Snow became acquainted with the seriousness with which Leavis approached his role as a critic, and with the strenuousness of his conception of political action.

The Richmond Lecture

During their many years in Cambridge, Snow's and Leavis's paths crossed occasionally. One evening in 1935, for instance, Leavis dined at Christ's College and sat next to Snow. The evening got off to a rocky start when Leavis accused Snow of being a bad influence on a former student, S. Gorley Putt. Snow changed the subject, trying out a favorite argument that it was Proust's integrity rather than his prose that pulled the reader through his narrative. The gambit worked: when Leavis

---

[87] Williams, "Seeing a Man Running," pp. 116–119.
[88] Leavis to Holbrook, 12 December 1968, Downing College: DCPP/LEA/4 Leavis, F. R. (5).
[89] Leavis to Shire [?], 15 January 1973, Emmanuel: ECA COL 9.59a.108.

objected, Snow pointed out that Leavis's wife Q. D. Leavis, and his collaborator Denys Harding, were on his side of the argument. Leavis relented, and proceeded to complain in what Snow called "superb persecuted form" that he was swamped with work and besieged by enemies. Snow suggested a grant that would relieve him of some teaching, knowing as he did that Leavis would never follow his advice.[90] Even in this early meeting, when Snow and Leavis were younger men nearer the beginnings than the ends of their careers, the characteristics that would fuel later antagonisms were evident. Snow had a foot in two fields, as a tutor to science students and the author of three novels; he was an able conversationalist, pronouncing confidently on French literature; and he was a proficient academic, dispensing advice about funding. Leavis, for his part, was willing to be abrasive, and he could not sit silently while others promulgated errors in judgment. He felt overworked and embattled, yet soldiered on because of the importance of his calling.

In the decades that followed, Snow regarded Leavis with a wary combination of respect and disdain. He knew the value of remaining on good terms with so eminent a critic: "It's my conviction," he advised a friend, "that if you are in touch with people, *even if they wish you ill* they are less likely to do you harm."[91] Twice in the 1950s he wrote supportive letters to Leavis, and both times he received gracious replies.[92] A favorable notice might lead Snow to hope for a connection between the reviewer and Leavis, but for the most part he expected hostility from Leavisian quarters.[93] He thought of Leavis's criticism as contrary to his own views on writing, history, and politics – Leavis's apolitical pretensions, Snow privately maintained, were actually reactionary.[94] As he secured his standing during the 1950s, Snow became increasingly inclined

---

[90] Snow to Putt, 1 February 1935, 27 February 1935, Harry Ransom Humanities Research Center (HRC): Snow 134.4. Caroline Nobile Gryta dates the second of these letters to November, reading "ii" to refer to the eleventh month: "Selected Letters of C. P. Snow: A Critical Edition," unpublished PhD dissertation, Pennsylvania State University (1988), pp. 78, 94.

[91] Snow to Harry Hoff, 15 November 1951, HRC: Snow 118.2 (emphasis in original).

[92] The first letter concerned a feud between Leavis and the *Times Literary Supplement*, and the second conveyed Snow's regrets upon the end of *Scrutiny*; Leavis's replies are held with Snow's papers: Leavis to Snow, 31 March 1950, 6 January 1954, HRC: Snow 132.10.

[93] Snow surmised that a favorable reviewer had a connection to Leavis in a letter to Plumb, 22 October 1951, Cambridge University Library (CUL): Box "C. P. Snow and Pam: 1946 to 1968," File "Snow 1946 to 1968." Two years before Leavis's lecture, Snow wrote, "That kind of hostility, plus the Leavisite hostility, I shall live with [?] as long as I live. Some of them would cheerfully assassinate me." Snow to Plumb, 22 April 1960, CUL: Box "C. P. Snow and Pam: 1946 to 1968," File "Snow 1946 to 1968."

[94] Snow to Hoff, 1 November 1960, HRC: Snow 118.3.

to articulate this opinion: in 1958 he contrasted the optimism of Rutherford in the 1930s with the dire tones of Eliot and Leavis; and in 1960 he explained that Raymond Williams and Richard Hoggart were irrelevant to politics because they had arrived at their socialism through Leavis.[95] Yet Snow could not entirely suppress a begrudging admiration, for instance on the occasion that he was delighted with a review by the American intellectual Norman Podhoretz: "Trilling's star pupil, also Leavis-trained. Very good background provided one escapes."[96] In fact, just weeks before the Richmond Lecture, Snow recommended somebody for a position by noting that he had studied with Leavis.[97] That training, Snow noted, was not without its faults, but on balance an association with Leavis was an endorsement that Snow (like any other writer) would have welcomed.

Snow did not figure so prominently in Leavis's mind. On at least one occasion Leavis remarked that they got along well, so long as they avoided discussion of Snow's novels, and he later insisted that no enmity existed between them before the 1960s.[98] Cambridge's most recognizable critic generally paid little attention to Snow, waiting almost three years before discussing *The Two Cultures*. But, as Ian MacKillop showed, in the early 1960s Leavis had increasing reason to take note of Snow. Himself an undergraduate at Downing during this period, MacKillop recalled an exchange in the undergraduate magazine *Delta* in which Morris Shapira, Leavis's "lieutenant" at Downing, challenged the association between the realism admired by Leavis and that practiced by Snow.[99] Other critics had taken to associating Leavis's stringent criticism with Snow's unadorned prose: Putt remarked to the English Association that "[t]he scientist in Snow [and] the critic in Leavis . . . have for us the same lesson," and Angus Wilson linked the two together as advocates of realism in fiction.[100] Leavis himself began to notice references to *The Two Cultures* in scholarship essays, which suggested

---

[95] C. P. Snow, "The Age of Rutherford," *Atlantic Monthly*, November 1958, pp. 76–81; Snow to Norman Podhoretz, 2 February 1960, HRC: Snow 165.10.

[96] Snow to Plumb, 13 May 1958, CUL: Box "C. P. Snow and Pam: 1946 to 1968," File "Snow 1946 to 1968."

[97] Snow to the Principal of Kingston upon Hull, 12 February 1962, HRC: Snow 109.1.

[98] Leo Salingar, *Cambridge Quarterly* 25 (1996), p. 401; Ivar Alastair Watson, " 'The Distance Runner's Perfect Heart': Dr. Leavis in Spain," *Cambridge Review*, November 1995, p. 72.

[99] MacKillop, *F. R. Leavis*, pp. 312–314.

[100] *Ibid.*, pp. 316–317. S. Gorley Putt, "Technique and Culture: Three Cambridge Portraits," *Essays and Studies* 14 (1961), p. 34; Angus Wilson, "If It's New and Modish, Is It Good?" *New York Times Book Review*, 2 July 1961, p. 1, reprinted as "A Plea Against Fashion in Writing," *Moderna Sprak* 55 (1961), pp. 345–350. Wilson repeated his claim in "Fourteen Points," *Encounter*, January 1962, pp. 10–12.

that the text had made its way into secondary education. He finally purchased a copy of *The Two Cultures* in the summer of 1961, and around the same time he was heard muttering about Snow while sitting for a portrait.[101] Leavis's students noticed him referring mischievously to Snow's novels, a tendency that crept into his correspondence as well.[102]

Then, in the fall of 1961, the undergraduates of Downing selected Leavis to deliver the annual Richmond Lecture.[103] Leavis was set to retire at the end of the academic year, bringing a close to an era in which his name had been synonymous with unforgiving criticism, and he decided to devote his Richmond Lecture to a critical appraisal of Snow and *The Two Cultures*. He reported that he was investing as much time, thought, and energy into the lecture as into anything he had previously written, and by January the writing was coming quickly.[104] Leavis had earned his reputation as a polemicist, and the Richmond Lecture soon became anticipated even beyond Cambridge: the BBC requested permission to record it, and the *Evening Standard* noted that the question mark in the title – "Two Cultures? The Significance of C. P. Snow" – promised "one of [Leavis's] most skilful and provocative acts of critical surgery."[105] When Leavis rose to speak in Downing's hall on February 28, 1962, he met a crowded audience that included Snow's friends J. H. Plumb and George Steiner. The seats were all taken, many were left standing, and some were perched in the sills of the hall's deep-set windows, waiting for the don to begin.[106]

Leavis proceeded to release a torrent of contempt. He declared that Snow was "intellectually as undistinguished as it is possible to be" and "portentously ignorant," an ignorance manifested in the fact that Snow "doesn't know what he means, and doesn't know he doesn't know."[107]

---

[101] Peter Greenham, quoted in MacKillop, *F. R. Leavis*, p. 5.

[102] In July 1961 Leavis lamented his exclusion from the "corridors of power" in the Cambridge English Faculty; Snow, with his knack for such turns of phrase, had introduced that one as early as 1957, and later adopted it as the title of a novel. Leavis to D. F. Pocock, 25 July 1961, Emmanuel College: ECA COL 9.59a.121.20; C. P. Snow, "The Corridors of Power," *Listener*, 18 April 1957, pp. 619–620.

[103] Downing College: Governing Body Minutes, 27 October 1961, 106. For a narrative of the lecture, see MacKillop, *F. R. Leavis*, Chapter 9.

[104] G. Singh, *F. R. Leavis: A Literary Biography*, p. 288; MacKillop, *F. R. Leavis*, p. 317.

[105] R. E. Keen to Leavis, 23 February 1962, BBC Written Archives Centre (BBC WAC), Caversham: F. R. Leavis, File I, 1940–1962; Leavis denied permission in his reply of 27 February 1962. "Stormy Don's Swan Song Should Be a Fiery One," *Evening Standard*, 28 February 1962.

[106] MacKillop, *F. R. Leavis*, p. 318. I am grateful to David Holbrook for sharing his recollections of the occasion.

[107] Leavis, *Two Cultures?*, pp. 9–10. The text originally appeared as "The Two Cultures? The Significance of C. P. Snow," *Spectator*, 9 March 1962, pp. 297–303. Leavis's original manuscript is held at Harvard University: Houghton Library, MS Eng 1218.

The Rede Lecture displayed "an embarrassing vulgarity of style," posing a curious problem for the critic: "The intellectual nullity is what constitutes any difficulty there may be in dealing with Snow's panoptic pseudo-cogencies, his parade of a thesis: a mind to be argued with – that is not there."[108] Leavis then took aim at Snow's reputation as a novelist: "Snow is, of course, a – no, I can't say that; he isn't: Snow thinks of himself as a novelist."[109] But in fact, "as a novelist he doesn't exist; he doesn't begin to exist. He can't be said to know what a novel is."[110] He dismissed Snow's most recent novel, *The Affair* – a bestseller in Britain, the Soviet Union, and the United States, and a hit on the London stage – as a "feeble exercise," before rounding again on *The Two Cultures*: "Snow's argument proceeds with so extreme a naïveté of unconsciousness and irresponsibility that to call it a movement of thought is to flatter it."[111] After just five minutes, a contingent from Churchill College departed; they were followed by Jack Plumb, slamming the door behind him.[112]

It is not surprising that the lecture was read as little more than a vicious attack upon Snow. This was a predominant criticism of Leavis in the *Spectator* after it published his lecture, and it was certainly Snow's reading of the matter: "The thing which irritates most is that the text . . . consists almost entirely of unsupported personal abuse."[113] Even Lionel Trilling, who was normally reluctant to criticize Leavis, chastised him for his "impermissible tone."[114] A reading of the Richmond Lecture as merely an attack upon Snow misinterprets its argument, but it is a misinterpretation for which Leavis bears responsibility. It is true that the occasion was a public event, and thus meant to engage as it instructed, and the Richmond Lecture in particular was delivered at the invitation of Downing's undergraduates, among whom Leavis's strictures against canonical figures and contemporary icons were legendary. Moreover, the critique of Snow's intellectual pretensions and public standing was central to Leavis's argument, which was that Snow's prominence itself required explanation. But that said, Leavis allowed – indeed, he encouraged – his argument to be lost amid the rhetorical display that astonished his audience. He later insisted that his performance had been

---

[108] Leavis, *Two Cultures?*, pp. 11–12.   [109] *Ibid.*, p. 12.   [110] *Ibid.*, p. 13.
[111] *Ibid.*, pp. 14–15.   [112] Plumb to Snow, 5 March 1962, HRC: Snow 226.12.
[113] See especially Gerhardi, "Sir Charles Snow, Dr. F. R. Leavis, and the Two Cultures," pp. 329–333; Snow to Plumb, 7 March 1962, HRC: Snow 226.12.
[114] Lionel Trilling, "Science, Literature, and Culture: A Comment on the Leavis–Snow Controversy," *Commentary*, June 1962, pp. 463–464. Trilling's reluctance to criticize Leavis was apparent in his refusal to review the reprint of *Scrutiny* for the BBC unless he found himself able to take a favorable view: Memorandum, 8 April 1963, BBC WAC: F. R. Leavis, File II, 1963–1964.

a "classic," but part of him knew that the attacks upon Snow had obscured his larger purpose.[115] During the next decade Leavis continued to denounce the orthodoxy of which he took Snow to be representative, but he took care to do so in terms that would not allow his argument to be so misunderstood again.[116]

That argument unfolded as follows: Snow was ignorant, yet taken to be a sage; his novels were lifeless, yet hailed as profound literature; *The Two Cultures* was hollow, yet widely influential. The significance of C. P. Snow lay not in his thought, but in the fact that despite his absence of thought he was hailed and admired – he was significant as testimony to the state of the civilization that produced him. In his easy recourse to clichés such as "social hope," the poor walking into the factories "as fast as the factories could take them," and the prospect of "jam tomorrow" for the developing world, Snow expressed the assumptions of a civilization that esteemed material advance but failed to recognize its own emptiness. That emptiness was apparent in the boredom and alcoholism existing alongside the technological marvels of America today, which was itself the civilization being promised to Asia and Africa tomorrow. Great writers, such as Joseph Conrad and D. H. Lawrence, had been the enemies of such complacency, questioning the assumptions that drove civilization forward without thought to the costs they entailed. Since that development was inexorable, however, it was essential that the creative response to change – *life*, in Leavis's parlance – be preserved. That response was realized through language and transmitted through literature, and the place where it might be sustained was the university. Because of the centrality of language to thought, the English School would stand at the center of the ideal university, in close touch with other fronts of creative thought (including the sciences). In such a university the claptrap in the Sunday papers would not be taken as the best that was thought and said, and in such a university it would have been unnecessary to have paid this attention to Snow.

The Snow–Leavis controversy

The following day the BBC reported that "when Cambridge men argue, it is generally best for Oxford men to stay out of the ring," but what

---

[115] Leavis to J. Schwartz, 19 March 1964, Harvard University: Houghton Library, Autograph File L.

[116] After preparing a subsequent lecture on similar themes, Leavis explained that he had deliberately minimized the references to Snow so as not to obscure his substantive argument. Leavis to A. I. Doyle, 9 September 1965, Downing College: DCPP/LEA/2 Leavis, F. R.

followed in the press was nothing less than a melee.[117] The *Times* ran a story so garbled and incomplete that Leavis decided to allow the full text to be published.[118] The *Spectator* decided to commission a libel report before moving forward, and their caution was well founded: the report concluded that "the work contains serious professional libels on Sir Charles Snow," meaning that the text could not be published without Snow's permission.[119] Cyril Ray – an assistant editor at the magazine, whom Snow had sponsored for the Athenaeum – visited the Snows at their home in London to seek their permission. Snow was suffering from a detached retina, so his wife read the lecture aloud; she was furious, but Snow agreed to allow publication.[120]

Its cover emblazoned with an unflattering cartoon of Snow, the *Spectator* ran the complete text of Leavis's lecture on March 9. The following issue featured a section devoted entirely to correspondence, beginning with a blistering attack on Leavis from William Gerhardi. "Flushed with rising bile, spluttering, the doctor becomes irresponsible and silly," Gerhardi charged. "Seven times seventy devils splatter their spleen through one loud orifice."[121] In the ensuing controversy, aptly characterized as a "miasma of personality-mongering" by Trilling, Snow and Leavis both found their partisans.[122] The physicist J. D. Bernal defended Snow's scientific credentials, while Leavis's publisher Ian Parsons noted that Cambridge would be reprinting the entire run of *Scrutiny*.[123] They each had their detractors as well: the poet Edith Sitwell surmised that Leavis was jealous of Snow's fame, while the historian Robert Conquest faulted the "journalistic crudity" of Snow's thesis.[124]

---

[117] Ten O'clock News, BBC Home Service, 1 March 1962, BBC WAC: Microfilm "Ten": T539–540.

[118] MacKillop, *F. R. Leavis*, p. 321; Graham Chainey, *A Literary History of Cambridge* (Cambridge: Pevensey, 1985), p. 216. Chainey disputes Philip A. Snow's claim that Leavis sold the rights to the *Spectator* ahead of time in a letter to the *Cambridge Review*, March 1988, p. 48. MacKillop doubted that Leavis publicized the lecture ahead of time (p. 321), which is consistent with Leavis's refusal to allow the BBC to record the lecture.

[119] The Spectator Limited, "Proposed Publication in the Spectator of the Text of a Lecture Delivered by F. R. Leavis at Downing College Cambridge on or about the 28th February 1962: Libel Report," p. 6, University of Reading: Chatto and Windus.

[120] MacKillop, *F. R. Leavis*, p. 321.

[121] Gerhardi, "Sir Charles Snow, Dr. F. R. Leavis, and the Two Cultures," p. 329.

[122] In addition to the special section of 16 March (cited above), the *Spectator* ran letters on 23 March 1962, pp. 365–367; 30 March 1962, pp. 395–396; and 6 April 1962, p. 442. Trilling, "Science, Literature, and Culture," p. 463.

[123] J. D. Bernal, "Letters," *Spectator*, 23 March 1962, p. 365; Ian Parsons, "Letters," *Spectator*, 23 March 1962, p. 365.

[124] Edith Sitwell, "Sir Charles Snow, Dr. F. R. Leavis, and the Two Cultures," *Spectator*, 16 March 1962, p. 331; Robert Conquest, "Letters," *Spectator*, 30 March 1962, pp. 395–396.

In a span of four weeks, the *Spectator* printed forty-two letters in all – a majority of these supported Snow, but that advantage was partly offset when the *Spectator* itself challenged *The Two Cultures*.[125]

As this debate raged around him, Snow responded in two ways. Publicly, he refused to be drawn into an argument with Leavis. He said that he could not envision a reasoned response to such an attack, parading his credentials as if he were applying for a job.[126] Instead, he explained, there were only two courses of action: either sue Leavis for libel, or do nothing. He could not contemplate the first, and so he would remain above the fray.[127] Snow's next public statement, his Rector's address at St. Andrews in April, did not mention Leavis at all – but then again, it did not have to: the address was entitled, "On Magnanimity."[128] Magnanimity had its place, but Snow knew that it was important to hit back, and so privately he was mounting a vigorous counterattack. Plumb suggested a well-placed satire, and wondered whether Leavis's personal life might provide any fodder.[129] Snow paid close attention to the unfolding debate, eager to seize upon any opportunities that might emerge. When a backer of Leavis confessed to not actually having read Snow's novels, he detected a chance to flay Leavis's qualifications as a teacher. Snow contacted A. Norman Jeffares, Professor of English at Leeds University, and suggested that he write a letter observing that Leavis trained his students to comment on novels they had not read.[130] As we shall see in Chapter 3, Snow was similarly leaning on friends in other fields to defend his arguments and affirm his credentials.

At Downing, meanwhile, Leavis felt triumphant. His assurance was aided by the impregnable logic of an argument that rendered all defenses of Snow further evidence of the degeneracy of civilization, and all attacks upon himself affirmations that he had diagnosed the situation correctly. Anthony Storr judged the situation astutely when he surmised, in a letter to the *Spectator* defending Snow, that "Dr. Leavis's outburst . . . will surely evoke almost as many counter-attacks upon himself as would gratify him."[131] As the counterattacks continued, Leavis refused to relent, working his argument against Snow into the introductory essay to

---

[125] "The Two Cultures," *Spectator*, 30 March 1962, pp. 387–388.
[126] Snow to Plumb, 7 March 1962, HRC: Snow 226.12.
[127] Snow to Levin, 13 March 1962, Harvard University: Houghton Library, Levin papers, MS Am 2461 (918), Storage 342, Box 18, "Snow, C. P."
[128] C. P. Snow, "On Magnanimity," *Harper's*, July 1962, pp. 37–41.
[129] Plumb to Snow, 5 March 1962, HRC: Snow 226.12.
[130] Snow to Jeffares, 30 March 1962, HRC: Snow 226.13.
[131] Anthony Storr, "Sir Charles Snow, Dr. F. R. Leavis, and the Two Cultures," *Spectator*, 16 March 1962, p. 332.

the reprint of *Scrutiny*.[132] The Richmond Lecture introduced Leavis to a wider public than he had previously known, and it was merely the first shot in his campaign against the "orthodoxy of enlightenment" during the coming decade.

Snow, for his part, began to reconsider his decision to refrain from replying.[133] When Steiner visited the Snows in London, he found his hosts obsessed with Leavis.[134] More than four months after Leavis's lecture appeared in the *Spectator*, when Leavis's editor at Chatto and Windus wrote to procure permission to publish the text as a book, Snow and Johnson attempted to shame him into letting the affair rest.[135] When those appeals failed, Snow reminded him that he retained the right to pursue action on any alterations or additions – an implicit threat, but one that failed to derail publication.[136] Snow was grasping for ways to limit the damage that, he was convinced, was jeopardizing his chances for the Nobel Prize.[137] Every year thereafter he anticipated the announcement of the prize, which he came to view as the only way to repair the damage Leavis had wrought. Snow was disappointed each year as it was awarded to somebody else, but at the same time he was working in other ways to undermine Leavis and what he stood for.[138]

Conclusion

Leavis was frustrated whenever his Richmond Lecture was read as an attack upon Snow or an assault upon science. Instead of adopting those interpretations, this chapter has situated its argument in the context of Leavis's worldview more generally. Leavis believed that history had gone badly off track when a new civilization emerged during the seventeenth century, so that all that remained of a once-vibrant culture was transmitted through the language of great novelists and poets. In the twentieth century, however, the authority of the critic to recognize that language was challenged by the tastes of the market, and this development

---

[132] F. R. Leavis, "A Retrospect," *Scrutiny* 20 (Cambridge University Press, 1963), pp. 1–24 (written in August 1962).

[133] Snow to Burroughs Mitchell, 9 May 1963, HRC: Snow 1.5.

[134] Steiner, 21 September 1962, Churchill College: Steiner papers, GSNR 1/5.

[135] Snow to Parsons, 27 July 1962; Pamela Johnson to Parsons, 4 August 1962, University of Reading: Chatto and Windus.

[136] Snow to Parsons, 7 August 1962, University of Reading: Chatto and Windus.

[137] Snow to Plumb, 7 March 1962, HRC: Snow 226.12; Snow to Mitchell, 19 March 1962, HRC: Snow 226.13. See also Philip A. Snow, *Stranger and Brother: A Portrait of C. P. Snow* (London: Macmillan, 1982), p. 130.

[138] Philip A. Snow, *A Time of Renewal: Clusters of Characters, C. P. Snow, and Coups* (London: Radcliffe Press, 1998), p. 171.

threatened the possibility of the continued creation that was *life*. In response to this crisis, and by contrast with Snow's technocratic optimism, Leavis embraced a radical liberalism: a belief in the capacity of certain individuals to resist the historical forces, social conventions, and institutional constraints that mass civilization relentlessly advanced. This position informed his Richmond Lecture of 1962, which began by drawing the audience's attention to the crisis represented by Snow's stature. At the dawn of the 1960s, in their Rede and Richmond lectures, Snow and Leavis advanced competing readings of the past and visions for the future, and in the following years they worked publicly and privately to translate their visions into institutional realities.

3   A tale of two colleges

Ideas of a university

Snow and Leavis, Rede and Richmond, technocrat and radical: the "two cultures" controversy derived not merely from a conflict between personalities or disciplines, but from contrary ways of viewing the world. Both Snow and Leavis opposed Marxists on the left and Tories on the right, believed in a fluid social hierarchy instead, and situated themselves within a liberal tradition. Yet their liberalisms stood at odds with one another, distinguished by their contrary attitudes towards "modern civilization." The crux of their disagreement was whether that civilization enabled or stifled the realization of the individual's capacities.

As a site where ideals are translated into practice, education emerged as central to the conflict. Indeed, both Snow's Rede Lecture and Leavis's Richmond Lecture advocated revolutions in British education. Snow argued that Britain's universities must produce more scientists and engineers, filling pubic ministries and private companies with minds at ease in modern civilization and at home in its bureaucracies. As he pleaded in the peroration to *The Two Cultures*, "For the sake of the intellectual life, for the sake of this country's special danger, for the sake of the western society living precariously rich among the poor, for the sake of the poor who needn't be poor if there is intelligence in the world, it is obligatory for us and the Americans and the whole West to look at our education with fresh eyes."[1] Education was central to Leavis's argument as well, which contrasted Snow's model of the university as a site of scientific and technical training with his preferred vision of an elite institution sustaining the capacity for creative thought: "Like Snow I look to the university," Leavis noted towards the conclusion of his lecture. "Unlike Snow, I am concerned to make it really a university, something . . . more than a collocation of specialist departments – to

---

[1] C. P. Snow, *The Two Cultures and the Scientific Revolution* (Cambridge University Press, 1959), p. 48.

make it a centre of human consciousness."[2] To Leavis, human consciousness itself was threatened by the civilization busily attending to the prescriptions for education in *The Two Cultures*.

Snow and Leavis were two voices in a dissonant chorus clamoring to define the mission of the university in the early 1960s. Britain's university system was coming under strain from two sources: demographic change initiated by the postwar surge in the birthrate, and political change initiated by the Education Act of 1944. Together these developments produced a record number of students of university age, a higher percentage of whom were prepared to benefit from higher education. Anticipating these pressures, postwar governments established a series of commissions to guide university development. The most important of these commissions was established by Harold Macmillan in 1961, and two years later the Robbins Report called for the dramatic expansion of the British university system. These reports on higher education were the products of a state committed to rational planning and professional expertise. The assumption shared in these reports – indeed, the assumption embedded in the commissioning of these reports – was that change could be managed by the right people to the right ends. In the postwar decades, however, the inherited assumption that there were "right" people who could identify "right" ends overlapped with new notions as to who those people, and what those ends, might be. That is, amid a continuity of ideas as to the reality of social and intellectual hierarchies, there emerged competing claims regarding the qualifications for ascent within them.[3] As the site both of existing arrangements and of their perpetuation, the university occupied essential terrain in this struggle to recast inherited hierarchies of class as fluid meritocracies of talent.

Snow's and Leavis's lectures represented two contributions in this discussion. Yet the function of the university, and its place in society, would ultimately be decided not on grand public occasions, but in the more mundane work of college committees, faculty boards, and governing bodies. The Rede and Richmond lectures offered public expressions of priorities and ambitions, but it was away from the lecterns, and in their own colleges, that Snow and Leavis sought to translate social priorities into institutional realities.

---

[2] F. R. Leavis, *Two Cultures? The Significance of C. P. Snow* (London: Chatto and Windus, 1962), p. 29.
[3] Michael Bell makes a related point with regard to literary studies in "F. R. Leavis," in *The Cambridge History of Literary Criticism, Vol. 7: Modernism and the New Criticism*, ed. A. Walton Litz, Louis Menand, and Lawrence Rainey (Cambridge University Press, 2000), p. 392.

University expansion

The British university system expanded slowly before the Second World War, and the majority of the growth had occurred before 1914. Five provincial redbrick institutions became universities between 1900 and 1910, doubling the number of English universities at a stroke.[4] During the same period, Oxford and Cambridge grew slightly, from 6,000 students in 1900 to 7,000 by 1914.[5] The percentage of people of university age enrolled in universities rose from 0.83 percent in 1910 to 1.1 percent in 1921.[6] These increases accelerated following the First World War, encouraged and managed by the state through the new University Grants Committee (established in 1919). Altogether the number of students in England's civic universities rose from 10,000 in 1910 to 22,000 in 1939.[7] By the eve of the Second World War, including Oxbridge and the civic redbricks, in addition to institutions in London and Scotland, there were 63,420 students in 21 British universities.[8] Much of this growth took place during the 1920s, and the depression of the 1930s saw the end of the period of university expansion that had begun in the late-Victorian period.

The end of the Second World War ushered in a second period of expansion. Nothing demonstrates the driving force behind this growth better than the Barlow Report of 1946.[9] In 1945 the government appointed a commission to recommend policies on the development of the nation's scientific personnel. The commission was led by the Treasury official Alan Barlow, and it also included the Ministry of Labour's wartime director of technical personnel, C. P. Snow. Barlow concluded that only one in five students who were capable of higher education attended university, and that the sciences offered the best opportunity for developing this underutilized talent. The report presented an ambitious program of expansion and democratization, funded by the state and directed towards science, and its major recommendation was printed in boldface: "We are satisfied that the immediate aim should be to double the present output, giving us roughly 5,000 newly qualified scientists per annum at the earliest possible moment."[10] The

---

[4] T. W. Heyck, "The Idea of a University in Britain, 1870–1970," *History of European Ideas* 8 (1987), p. 210.

[5] *Ibid.*, p. 207. [6] *Ibid.* [7] *Ibid.*, p. 210.

[8] David Edgerton, *Science, Technology, and the British Industrial "Decline,"* 1870–1970 (Cambridge University Press, 1996), p. 22.

[9] *Scientific Manpower: Report of a Committee Appointed by the Lord President of the Council* (London: HMSO, 1946; cmnd. 6824).

[10] *Ibid.*, p. 636.

eminent scientist P. M. S. Blackett, President of the Association of Scientific Workers, enthusiastically welcomed Barlow, hailing it as "one of the major achievements of the Labour Government" and "a decisive step forward in the task of fitting the higher education of Britain to our future national tasks."[11] To Blackett, and to like-minded observers, university expansion represented a victory for science and progress alike.

The next fifteen years saw dramatic increases in university enrollments, resources, and facilities. Undergraduate enrollments increased 144 percent between 1945 and 1963.[12] Civic universities absorbed half of that increase, and five provincial colleges gained university status: Nottingham (1948), Southampton (1952), Hull (1954), Exeter (1955), and Leicester (1957).[13] Enrollments at Oxford and Cambridge rose throughout most of the 1950s, and toward the end of the decade university expansion accelerated.[14] In the late 1950s the University Grants Committee (UGC) decided to establish seven new universities, the first of which – Sussex – opened its doors in 1961.[15] The majority of these increases, in terms of resources and personnel, were directed toward science and technology: the UGC encouraged two students in science and technology for each student in every other field combined.[16] As a result, between 1938 and 1963 the number of undergraduates in scientific subjects increased 331 percent, in technological fields 267 percent.[17] Denizens of Cambridge, where natural science students outnumbered those in English by a ratio of three to one, were following these developments closely.[18] The *Cambridge Review* was filled with commentary on issues relating to the future of the university: the forthcoming Bridges Report on the relationship between the colleges and the university, the need for increased UGC oversight of funding, a proposed graduate school for the arts, and so on. After all, the transformation of higher education meant not just the establishment of new institutions, but the overhaul of existing ones as well.

---

[11] P. M. S. Blackett, "Summary of Presidential Address to Association of Scientific Workers," 24 May 1947, held with Blackett's papers at the Royal Society, London: Blackett E.22.

[12] *Higher Education, Appendix Two (A): Students and Their Education* (London: HMSO, 1963; cmnd. 2154-II), p. 17. Academic years are referred to by the year they commence – for instance, "1945" refers to the academic year 1945–1946.

[13] I am grateful to T. W. Heyck for sharing his notes on university development.

[14] *Higher Education, Appendix Two (A)*, pp. 20, 18.

[15] Stefan Collini, "HiEdBiz," *London Review of Books*, 6 November 2003, p. 5.

[16] Harold Perkin, *Key Profession: The History of the Association of University Teachers* (New York: A. M. Kelley, 1969), p. 218.

[17] *Higher Education, Appendix Two (A)*, p. 22.

[18] The exact figures, for the year 1961, were 937 science students to 369 in English. Robert Dean, "The Tripos of 1961," *Cambridge Review*, 28 October 1961, p. 57.

The increased numbers of women undergraduates into the universities was one of the most important social changes of the postwar era, but the fortunes of women in the immediate postwar years tell a less familiar story. While a significant share of the increases in student numbers reflect the increased numbers of women in the system, the percentage of women in universities actually remained steady between 1938 and 1961 (at about 25 percent).[19] In fact, between 1954 and 1959 – the period of the most dramatic expansion to date – the proportion of women among university students actually declined.[20] This decline resulted from the emphasis on science and technology, at the expense of the arts: at a quarter of the student population, women were over-represented in the arts (42 percent of students in 1961), but under-represented in the sciences (22 percent). The numbers for applied science were even more dramatic: in 1961 women accounted for 3 percent of the students in applied science, a field that had increased its places 267 percent since 1938.[21] In other words, growth was happening, but it was happening in areas in which women were under-represented, so that, despite increasing numbers of female students, their percentage among the student population remained steady. The numbers broken down by class tell an even more exclusive story.[22] So while Snow maintained that science tended to be dismissed in British education, and that social status remained the preserve of the arts, his claims were belied by the emphasis of policymakers on science and technology.

The expansion of the universities and their re-orientation toward science and technology were being driven not by the realization of democratic ideals, but by the needs of an expanding state. David Edgerton refers to the "warfare state" to direct attention to the intimate relations between science and technology, universities and industry, and the government and military in this period. Challenging historio-graphical emphases on the welfare state after 1945, Edgerton shows that the growth in the state occurred in supply ministries, rather than social services.[23] These expanding ministries required increasing

---

[19] *Higher Education, Appendix Two (A)*, p. 24. The figures for students from the working class were similar, at about a quarter of student enrollment: Peter Clarke, *Hope and Glory: Britain 1900–1990* (London: Allen Lane, 1996), p. 288.

[20] David Edgerton, *Warfare State: Britain, 1920–1970* (Cambridge University Press, 2006), pp. 175–180. See also Edgerton, *Science, Technology, and the British Industrial "Decline,"* p. 22.

[21] *Higher Education, Appendix Two (A)*, p. 26.

[22] Fewer than 1 percent of children whose fathers were manual laborers attended university. Clarke, *Hope and Glory*, p. 288.

[23] Edgerton, *Warfare State*.

numbers of scientific and technological experts, trained in universities and managed by the new Scientific Civil Service – a branch of the civil service that had been established in 1945, on the recommendation of the ubiquitous Alan Barlow.[24] Indeed, Barlow's centrality to both civil service re-organization and university expansion illustrates the identity of interests between the state and universities in this period. It is only after 1945 that the Treasury came to supply half of the universities' funding, but from that point forward its investments increased dramatically: in 1956 the UGC provided £3.8 million for capital projects, and just seven years later that figure had increased nearly tenfold.[25]

In the 1950s it became a commonplace to claim that, in order for Britain to remain internationally competitive, it must emphasize science, technology, and industry, and Snow's Rede Lecture represented a particularly forceful expression of such techno-nationalist assumptions. Snow depicted an education system geared to produce a superfluity of arts graduates and narrow specialists, whereas the nation actually required scientists, researchers, and engineers. As a result of these misplaced priorities, he argued, Britain was on the verge of international eclipse, and the West faced the prospect of standing by idly while the Soviet Union won the race to industrialize the developing world. In the Rede Lecture Snow demanded that Britain refashion its universities to produce four tiers of scientifically trained professionals: (1) as many first-rate scientists as possible, (2) a larger stratum engaged in research and development, (3) an even larger group – "thousands upon thousands" – with some education in science to fill administrative, management, and technical positions, and (4) politicians and adminis-trators capable of understanding scientific recommendations.[26] He argued that these personnel represented the minimum that was neces-sary to keep Britain afloat – and the Soviets at bay – in a competitive world. He assured his audience that if Britain failed to reform its edu-cation along these lines the results would be "disastrous," even "fatal."[27] The success of the Rede Lecture was to package this ambitious program of economic, social, and educational reform into a seemingly unobjec-tionable lament about disciplinary specialization.

---

[24] *The Scientific Civil Service: Reorganisation and Recruitment during the Reconstruction Period* (London: HMSO, 1945; cmnd. 6679), which includes the annex, "Report of the Barlow Committee on Scientific Staff," April 1943. See also Edgerton, *Warfare State*, Chapter 3, especially p. 116.
[25] Collini, "HiEdBiz," p. 5.   [26] Snow, *The Two Cultures*, pp. 35–36.
[27] *Ibid.*, p. 19.

The Robbins Report

The Two Cultures and the Scientific Revolution found influence at the highest levels of policy formation, not least in the deliberations of Lionel Robbins's committee on higher education. The Prime Minister had personally invited Snow to serve on the committee, but Snow politely declined (at that moment – the peak of his fame – he was besieged by invitations from Berkeley to Moscow).[28] When Robbins heard the news, he wrote to request Snow's informal guidance – after all, he explained, it was his desire to redress the "two cultures" problem that led him to accept the commission in the first place.[29] After two years of interviews, analyses, and consultations, during which the "two cultures" problem frequently arose, Robbins's committee reported in October 1963.[30] They recommended the dramatic expansion of enrollments and facilities, and emphasized investment in science and technology in particular. The vision was of a more inclusive, expansive system of higher education, one that would be tied to industrial needs and serve the national interest. They aimed to more than treble the number of university students by 1990 (from 120,000 to 370,000), and to double the number of students in higher education generally by 1980 (from 216,000 to 560,000).[31] Science students were to comprise the new majority – a goal that came within sight when the Colleges of Advanced Technology were awarded university status. At the same time, in an attempt to reconcile the competing goals of maintaining standards while expanding access, Robbins institutionalized a controversial "binary" system, establishing more comprehensive "polytechnics" alongside the universities.

The Robbins Report has been called "one of the great state papers of the century."[32] Within days the government embraced many of its most

---

[28] Harold Macmillan to Snow, 26 January 1961, HRC: Snow 142.9.
[29] Lionel Robbins to Snow, 31 January 1961, HRC: Snow 172.8.
[30] Testimony of the National Union of Students, 11 October 1961, pp. 240–241; the National Froebel Foundation, 27 September 1961, p. 259; and J. D. Cockcroft, 13 October 1961, pp. 287–288, all in *Higher Education: Evidence, Part I, Vol. A* (London: HMSO, 1963; cmnd. 2154); also the testimony of Alexander Todd and Solly Zuckerman on behalf of the Advisory Council on Scientific Policy, 5 January 1962, pp. 437–439; and the National Association of Head Teachers, 2 October 1961, p. 508, in *Higher Education: Evidence, Part I, Vol. B* (London: HMSO, 1963; cmnd. 2154).
[31] Clarke, *Hope and Glory*, p. 288; *Higher Education: Report of the Committee Appointed by the Prime Minister under the Chairmanship of Lord Robbins, 1961–1963* (London: HMSO, 1963; cmnd. 2154), p. 268.
[32] The accolade is that of John Carswell, Treasury official and assessor to the committee, quoted in Noel Annan, *Our Age: English Intellectuals between the World Wars – a Group Portrait* (New York: Random House, 1990), p. 371.

ambitious recommendations, including the acceleration of university expansion, the establishment of university places for all qualified students, and the conversion of Colleges of Advanced Technology into universities. The Chancellor matched these promises by committing an additional £3.5 billion during the next decade, doubling the state's investment at a stroke.[33] Within five years, the number of British universities reached fifty-six, and thirty new polytechnics had been commissioned as well.[34] But despite its central place in the history of education during the twentieth century, historians disagree about the ultimate significance of the Robbins Report. After all, universities had been expanding since the nineteenth century, and the sciences had been growing rapidly since 1945. From this perspective, the seminal statement on university development appears as confirmation of trends already underway: as Sheldon Rothblatt explains, "Robbins has . . . been variously interpreted as the kindling of the torch of a new era or as the dying embers of an old. The latter seems more plausible, for the Robbins Report followed time-honoured assumptions about universities."[35] Indeed, nobody is more aware of the dangers of upsetting tradition than a committee of academics seeking to gain their colleagues' approval. The report thus sought to guide expansion while promising autonomy, to open access while maintaining standards, and to increase funding while keeping the state at bay.[36] The result was a Janus-faced report, looking backward to late-nineteenth-century traditions and forward to late-twentieth-century needs. Historians interpret it accordingly: to some Robbins represented "the last expression of Victorian expansionism," while to others "the rationale for universities in Britain shifted decisively in the 1960s."[37]

However contradictory such analyses might appear, they share one element in common: the Robbins Report figures as a pivotal moment in both. Whether as the last gasp of nineteenth-century ideals, or the moment when the university became imagined as an engine of economic advance, Robbins represented a transition from one set of priorities to

---

[33] "Press Notice: Government Statement," issued from Downing Street, 24 October 1963, a copy of which is held with the supplementary papers of the Governing Body, Downing College, Cambridge, October 1962 – October 1964, D/M/P/9.

[34] Clarke, *Hope and Glory*, p. 289.

[35] Sheldon Rothblatt, *The Modern University and Its Discontents: The Fate of Newman's Legacies in Britain and America* (Cambridge University Press, 1997), p. 273.

[36] Annan, *Our Age*, p. 373.

[37] A. H. Halsey, *Decline of Donnish Dominion: The British Academic Professions in the Twentieth Century* (Oxford: Clarendon, 1992), p. 5; Desmond King and Victoria Nash, "Continuity of Ideas and the Politics of Higher Education Expansion in Britain from Robbins to Dearing," *Twentieth Century British History* 12 (2001), p. 188.

another – and to the exclusion of still others. While the siren song of teleology might make expansion, scientization, and democratization the "obvious" course of university development in a postwar market democracy, it is essential to bear in mind the multiplicity of possibilities available to reformers in the early 1960s. This was the time of "waiting for Robbins," a window of opportunity when the function of the university itself seemed open to redefinition, and when possibilities seemed limited only by the intersection between tradition and imagination. It was in this context that Snow and Leavis advanced their competing visions, and, from this perspective, they were both modernizers. After all, they had arrived at Cambridge through local grammar schools, they studied subjects that benefited from the relatively recent shift away from classics, and they opted to pursue the recent innovation of a doctorate.[38] Late in their careers, after lifetimes spent working in and around universities, Snow and Leavis offered proposals for the mission of the university and its place in society. The differences in their prescriptions were not a simple matter of a "progressive" versus a "reactionary"; rather, at a juncture characterized by flux and possibility, Snow and Leavis offered competing notions of "progress" itself.

Churchill College

In his novel *Memoirs of a New Man* (1966), William Cooper depicts a struggle over staffing in a fictional Oxford college.[39] Established as a college dedicated to science, Clarendon is Oxford's answer to the new Churchill College in Cambridge. Like Churchill, Clarendon's modern mission is reflected in its architectural style – as Cooper put it, "The Gibbs building at King's College in Cambridge elevated one's spirit with a style, elegant and formal, to live up to. The first quad at Clarendon College tended to let one's spirit alone."[40] The undergraduates at Clarendon are scientists, but the Governing Body includes Fellows from other fields so that the students will become conversant across "The Two Cultures."[41] Clarendon houses a sociologist, a political scientist, a philosopher, and even a novelist – this last the result of an unsuccessful attempt to forestall the hiring of a Fellow in English Literature, an abysmal colleague, wretched human being, and obvious send-up of Leavis. At one point the Fellows divide along "two cultures" lines

---

[38] Zouyue Wang, "The First World War, Academic Science, and the 'Two Cultures': Educational Reforms at the University of Cambridge," *Minerva* 33 (1995), pp. 107–127.
[39] William Cooper, *Memoirs of a New Man* (London: Macmillan, 1966).
[40] *Ibid.*, p. 60.   [41] *Ibid.*, p. 59 and *passim*.

regarding the hiring of a new Fellow, when the sociologist detects something more at work: " 'After all,' he added, his sharp little eyes sparkling with sarcasm, 'a college is a microcosm. Here we see being fought out some of the major issues that preoccupy society in general.' "[42] Cooper might have gleaned that perspective from his friend C. P. Snow, who in the early 1960s was engaged in just such fights as a founding Fellow of Churchill College.

Over brandy one night in Sicily in 1955, a fortnight after his resignation as Prime Minister, Winston Churchill lamented not having done more to promote science, technology, and engineering in Britain. He was expressing the sentiments of his longtime science advisor, Lord Cherwell; both Cherwell and Churchill admired the Massachusetts Institute of Technology (MIT), and regretted that Britain had nothing comparable. One of Churchill's dinner companions that night was his wartime secretary, John Colville, who volunteered to raise the funds for such an institution. Churchill agreed, and Colville began enlisting a formidable Board of Trustees, including the Master of Trinity College, Lord Adrian; the Provost of King's College, Noel Annan; the brilliant chemist, Alex Todd; the director of Britain's nuclear research establishment, John Cockcroft; and the Vice-Chancellor of Cambridge, Brian Downs. Joined by the chairmen of Shell, ICI, Vickers, and Associated Electrical Industries, the board began to meet regularly at Churchill's home in London. Funds poured in from British industry and American benefactors, but it soon became clear that it would be impossible to establish a university on the scale of MIT.

The Cambridge men suggested the establishment of a new Cambridge college instead, one devoted to science and technology and named after Churchill. Churchill hesitated, but then agreed: "After all," he remarked with satisfaction, "it will put me alongside the Trinity."[43] After a flurry of fund-raising, memoranda, false starts, and appointments, they launched the plan for Churchill College in 1958. The press announced it on May 15, 1958, and Cockcroft was selected the first Master in October. Doors opened to twenty-six postgraduate students two years later, and the first cohort of undergraduates arrived in 1961. Churchill was the first completely new college in Cambridge since the 1880s, and it boasted statutes as innovative as its architecture: seventy percent of its students and staff would be scientists and engineers; one third would be postgraduates; and its fellowship would include a large number of international visitors. However deliberately modern, though, Churchill

---

[42] *Ibid.*, p. 74.
[43] John Colville, *Footprints in Time* (London: Collins, 1976), pp. 256–258.

College was of – rather than ahead of – its time: the historian (and Churchill Fellow) Mark Goldie notes that the first men's college in Cambridge to admit women was also the last to be established for men, and he speculates that the Master's lodge may have been the last home in England to be built with bells to call the servants.[44]

Established as a memorial to Britain's great wartime Prime Minister, Churchill College stands as a reminder of postwar techno-nationalism. The scheme was a cooperative venture between industry, government, and university, and it was designed to meet the need for the scientists and engineers necessary to maintain Britain as a great power. Churchill made these ambitions explicit when he informed potential donors, "The future of Britain depends on the skill and craftsmanship with which we can meet the challenge of the new technological age."[45] That future required – almost literally – an army of technologists, "for our country stands in need of them as its first and principal line of defence for the future years."[46] Colville went even further, casting Churchill College in the context of another struggle for national survival: "There is a new Battle of Britain to be fought and won in our workshops and laboratories."[47] The newspapers adopted the line accordingly: the *Daily Herald* noted with approval that Churchill planned the college "to keep Britain great"; the *Liverpool Daily Post* agreed that "if Britain is to hold her own in the world she must be able to do so through her science and technology"; and the *Birmingham Post and Gazette* called the plan "essential to the survival of this country as a great and self-sustaining power."[48] Even the Church of England offered its benediction, the archbishop of York insisting that Christian culture must embrace science.[49] Churchill College – named for a statesman, established by a team of academics and industrialists, welcomed by the national press, and blessed by the Church of England – testifies to a state and a culture thoroughly committed to harnessing science, technology, and industry to the goal of national advance.[50]

---

[44] On the origins, founding, and ironies of Churchill College, I am indebted to an unpublished paper by Mark Goldie, "Churchill College: Origins and Contexts."

[45] Quoted in "A 'Churchill' College," *Times*, 15 May 1958.

[46] Quoted in "Churchill College: Churchill's Appeal," *New York Herald Tribune*, 15 May 1958.

[47] John Colville, "A Battle of Britain Still to Win," *Daily Telegraph*, 26 June 1958.

[48] "Churchill Plan for Atom Age," *Daily Herald*, 15 May 1958; "Churchill College," *Liverpool Daily Post*, 15 May 1958; "Churchill College," *Birmingham Post and Gazette*, 15 May 1958.

[49] Goldie, "Churchill College: Origins and Contexts," p. 7.

[50] Churchill College was not an isolated case, as commentators frequently linked its fortunes to those of St. Catherine's, and Nuffield, in Oxford: "Nuffield College," *Manchester Guardian Weekly*, 29 May 1958; "More Oxford," *Times Education Supplement*, 11 July 1958.

The proposals for the new college did come under criticism. The Council of the Senate in Cambridge approved the scheme in December 1957, but objections were raised once the plans were made public.[51] E. M. W. Tillyard – Shakespeare scholar, Master of Jesus College, and Leavis's arch-nemesis on the English Faculty – resented that the university had been presented with a *fait accompli* on an issue so important as the establishment of a new college.[52] The Senate debated the issue in November. Critics and skeptics included the professors of Anglo-Saxon and of History, as well as a classics don who was soon to become headmaster of Eton. The main point of contention centered upon the statutory requirement that 70 percent of Churchill's students and staff come from the sciences: such a stipulation struck the plan's opponents as contrary to the ideals of liberal education.[53] Churchill had influential partisans of its own, however, and they responded vigorously. Noel Annan answered Tillyard in the *Cambridge Review*, pointing out that the alternative to a "*fait accompli*" was a half-baked scheme.[54] In the Senate Alex Todd and Brian Downs insisted that the arts would be well represented at Churchill, and Annan forcefully argued that the real breach of tradition would be for the university to dictate to colleges the fields of its members.[55] In the end, after the objections had been aired, Churchill carried the day: the Senate approved the proposal without a division.[56]

Despite institutional support from Cambridge, financial support from industry, political support from both major political parties, and an enthusiastic reception by the press, a mythology soon emerged casting Churchill as a necessary imposition upon an ungrateful establishment. "Cinderella Science Goes to the Ball . . . at Last," declared the *Evening News*, depicting science as an unwanted stepchild finally being given its chance.[57] Another paper claimed that the ratio of science students to those in other subjects in British higher education was one in six, despite the fact that UGC policy encouraged two students in science and technology for one in all other fields combined. The same article objected to the notion that a college with more science than arts students was "barbarian," although it is not clear who, if anyone, ever expressed such a position.[58] Yet these dubious interpretations caught on, so that, when

---

[51] Churchill College Governing Body (CCGB) Archives: CCGB 310/1.
[52] E. M. W. Tillyard, Letter, *Cambridge Review*, 24 May 1958, p. 585.
[53] Goldie, "Churchill College: Origins and Contexts," p. 19; a transcript of the Senate debate of 18 November 1958 is held in the Churchill College Archives: CCGB 316/1.
[54] Noel Annan, Letter, *Cambridge Review*, 31 May 1958, pp. 607–608.
[55] Churchill College: CCGB 316/1.
[56] Goldie, "Churchill College: Origins and Contexts," p. 9.
[57] "Cinderella Science Goes to the Ball . . . at Last," *Evening News*, 15 May 1958.
[58] "Churchill College," *Cherwell*, 17 May 1958.

Churchill opened its doors to much acclaim two years later, a writer in
New York recalled "a great deal of early opposition to the plan. . . . King's
College and Trinity supplied their masters [*sic*] to the new college's board
of trustees, [while] the rest of the colleges supplied ammunition against
it."[59] As we have seen, there was some opposition to the plan, but that
opposition paled by comparison with the support that it received. Indeed,
the proposal, establishment, and reception of Churchill College all
evidence a deep technocratic commitment in postwar Britain.

As such misleading accounts proliferated, more telling criticisms
failed to gain traction. "[I]t is plain that what is contemplated is a college
that is to be the home of an elite," objected one don in the Senate, who
worried that "the likely result . . . would be to set up a college whose
undergraduates in science and technology would feel themselves distinguished above their like in other colleges."[60] He was right to detect
more than a whiff of elitism in the plans for the new college: indeed,
Churchill College's initial appeal openly declared its ambition to cultivate a technological "*corps d'elite*."[61] The ambition was not simply to
produce more scientists and engineers – after all, the Colleges of
Advanced Technology could accomplish that goal, and even a relatively
large Oxbridge college would not add much in quantitative terms. But
because it carried powerful imprimaturs, both of Cambridge and of
Britain's greatest statesman, Churchill College was designed to produce
leaders in the field of science and technology. Rather than hiding this
aim, the founders publicized it – and press coverage followed suit.[62] In
the Senate, meanwhile, Annan confidently dismissed the charges of
elitism: "On [the] question that this college will set up an undesirable
elite, I wonder . . . whether elites are quite so wicked and undesirable."[63]
Churchill College was the construction of a technocratic – not a
democratic – consensus, one that gave new meaning to the stirring
words of its patron, "Never in the field of human conflict was so much
owed by so many *to so few*."

Snow in Churchill

Snow had long taken an interest in Britain's university system. While
recruiting scientists for the Ministry of Labour during the war, he

[59] Richard C. Wald, "New Churchill College Slated to Open at Cambridge Oct. 1,"
New York Herald Tribune, 25 August 1960.
[60] Churchill College: CCGB 316/1, p. 6.   [61] Churchill College: CCGB 310/1.
[62] See, for instance, Kenneth Rose, "Choosing Technology's Few," *Daily Telegraph*,
10 September 1958.
[63] Churchill College: CCGB 316/1, p. 8.

relished the opportunity to compare universities from Aberdeen to Exeter.[64] After the war, as we have seen, he served on the Barlow Commission that recommended the expansion of student numbers and an emphasis upon the sciences. Privately, he continued to advance his ideas: he told a friend in 1955, "With three or four scientifically-inclined universities of about 4,000–5,000 students each, we could somewhere double our existing production of scientists."[65] Snow consistently favored expanded student numbers, increased opportunities for women, and the shifting of resources toward science and technology.[66]

Snow frequently invoked the language of democracy to advance these goals, but his actual motivations were more complicated than that.[67] Like John Stuart Mill a century earlier, Snow believed that national progress depended upon the identification and development of all available talent.[68] "I think we're drawing on far too few people for our top jobs," he explained in 1961. "We've not gone anything like deeply enough into the population, [although] there are great reservoirs of ability in this population which are just not being touched for effective purposes."[69] These ideas partly resulted from Snow's own biography as a scholarship student from Leicester, and they were also informed by his familiarity with the obscure social backgrounds of a number of Britain's leading scientists (including, among others, Churchill's own Master, J. D. Cockcroft). Such a view could find itself aligned with a democratic impulse, but Snow's actual ambition was to staff the nation's administrative, political, and industrial organizations with competent workers and intelligent managers. These people – the ones, he believed, who made society work – must be familiar with science and technology, partly so that they could understand these important facets of the modern world, but also so that they would internalize the optimism and

---

[64] Snow to S. Gorley Putt, 16 March 1941, in Caroline Nobile Gryta, "Selected Letters of C. P. Snow: A Critical Edition," unpublished PhD dissertation, Pennsylvania State University (1988), p. 124.

[65] Snow to Maurice Cranston, 9 December 1955, in Gryta, "Selected Letters of C. P. Snow," p. 166.

[66] The possibility of admitting women as postgraduates into Churchill arose in the Educational Policy Sub-Committee (of which Snow was a member) on 21 and 28 June 1958. In a rare intervention, Winston Churchill personally endorsed the idea, but it was rejected as too radical by founding fellows keen to garner the approval of their colleagues and donors. "Churchill College: Admission of Women," CCGB 210/2.

[67] C. P. Snow, "Miasma, Darkness, and Torpidity," New Statesman, 11 August 1961, pp. 186–187.

[68] John Stuart Mill, "The Subjection of Women," in Three Essays (Oxford University Press, 1975).

[69] Snow to Muggeridge, "Appointment with Sir Charles Snow," 18 August 1961; transcript held in the Harry Ransom Humanities Research Center (HRC): Snow 8.1 (quotation p. 7).

progressivism that characterized science and scientists. For Snow, university reform was one component in a more ambitious program of social reform.

Snow believed that developments within Oxbridge colleges reflected broader social trends. The origins and effects of these trends feature in his two academic novels, *The Masters* (set in 1937) and *The Affair* (set in 1953–1954).[70] Both stories unfold inside the same Cambridge college, but in nearly two decades the college changes fundamentally. *The Masters* conveys the suffocating claustrophobia among a group of thirteen fellows living at close quarters. The college itself seems a holdover from another era, a time when colleges were smaller, conviviality was valued, and research was suspect; it offers "physical contact with past time," a continuity so striking that "a sixteenth-century member of the college, dropped in the first court now, would be instantaneously at home."[71] Despite these connections with the past, the college has actually been recast continually over time; the current incarnation dates from the 1880s, when the dual revolutions of science and industry forced the university to incorporate science and the middle class. In *The Masters*, as in the real Cambridge, experimental science required facilities too large for any single college to provide, and as a result power was shifting from the colleges to the university. When Lewis Eliot returns nearly two decades later, he finds his college wholly transformed. "I got pleasure out of being there, but no sense of the past," he muses. "I could even think of the Baron de Charlus's roll-call of his friends, and say to myself, 'Despard-Smith, *dead*, Eustace Pilbrow, *dead*, Chrystal, *dead*: Roy Calvert, *dead*.'"[72] The eccentric Gay remains, but – by repeatedly forgetting who Eliot is – even his presence testifies to a severed connection with the past. The college's members are younger and more numerous, and intimate bonds between fellows are replaced by professional relations among colleagues. While *The Masters* feels as though it is set in a gentleman's club, *The Affair* seems to unfold in a research institute.

Believing that Oxbridge colleges represented sites of broader social change, Snow seized the opportunity to help shape Churchill College. Free from the history that stifled innovation, yet benefiting from its relationship to an ancient university, Churchill offered the unbeatable combination of a fresh start with instant pedigree. Between 1958 and 1960, as the college evolved from statutes to reality, Snow served on the

---

[70] C. P. Snow, *The Masters* (London: Macmillan, 1951); *The Affair* (London: Macmillan, 1960).
[71] Snow, *The Masters*, pp. 301, 300.   [72] Snow, *The Affair*, p. 17.

Executive Committee, the Appointments Committee, and the Educational Policy Sub-Committee, and he remained a member of the Fellowship Electors when it replaced the Appointments Committee in 1960.[73] In 1960 he was elected an "Extraordinary Fellow," a title that had been created so that persons of exceptional distinction could maintain an affiliation even when not resident in Cambridge; just Churchill's third fellow, Snow was continually re-elected for the remainder of his life.[74] The *Cambridge Review* had called his Rede Lecture a "ready-made manifesto for the promoters of Churchill College," and, pursuing a mandate to "crystalise [sic] into practical forms the objects of the College as laid down in the Trust Deed," Snow was involved in the establishment, structure, and staffing of the college from its inception.[75]

Snow's efforts on these committees reflected two major priorities. His experience had taught him that reputation mattered to professional success, so he hoped to associate eminent names with Churchill, however minimal their participation in college life. As he negotiated between eminent American academics and the Governing Body, the expected time in residence for these scholars steadily retreated from one term, to three weeks, to a fortnight – until, at one point, Snow suggested that even the rumor of a prominent visitor would raise the status of the college.[76] Such maneuverings were not altogether cosmetic: after all, personal associations can build institutional reputations, and even a brief visit from a critic such as Lionel Trilling would benefit students and fellows alike. However, brief visits by famous figures had little to do with the particulars of undergraduate education, and when Snow turned his attention to matters of pedagogy his efforts reflected a second priority. Recall that Snow believed that large organizations were inevitable and necessary to a modern economy, and that these institutions secured social opportunity and material prosperity for the majority of the population. But rather than training young people to prosper in such a society, Snow believed that the humanistic disciplines – especially

---

[73] The papers of each committee are held in the archives of Churchill College: CCGB 202, CCGB 205, CCGB 204, CCGB 315.

[74] Thanks to Mark Goldie for sharing his list of the Masters and Fellows of Churchill College.

[75] John Beer, "Pools of Light in Darkness," *Cambridge Review*, 7 November 1959, p. 106; Standing Executive Committee, 9 June 1958, Churchill College: CCGB 316/2. Snow was present at this meeting that established the Educational Policy Sub-Committee, and – given his tendency to use the word "crystallize" – the formulation of the committee's duties was likely his.

[76] Snow to Harry Levin, 1 January 1960, Harvard University: Houghton Library, Levin papers, MS Am 2461 (918), Storage 342, Box 18, "Snow, C. P."

literary criticism – inculcated contempt for it. He therefore sought to secure places within Churchill for retired civil servants, military officers, and other professionals, so that their example and experience could serve as a model for the college's undergraduates.[77]

Snow did not take comparable interest in the two issues with which he was publicly associated: establishing Churchill as a center of excellence in science and technology, and bridging the gap between the "two cultures."[78] Snow had not been a practicing scientist for more than two decades, and he had focused on his literary career since the Second World War, so it should not be surprising that his contribution to the college fell on the literary side. While there was much talk in the press about Churchill College serving to mend the breach between the arts and the sciences, Snow focused on securing the standing of the arts *vis-à-vis* the sciences. He attempted to lure J. H. Plumb away from Christ's College; when Plumb declined, Snow expressed worry that the arts would remain second-class citizens in Churchill.[79] He explained to Harry Levin, Professor of Comparative Literature at Harvard, "I am passionately anxious to get an English scholar at Churchill College who is as clever as the scientists."[80] These efforts are only surprising if *The Two Cultures* is read apart from Snow's broader social vision – but it was that vision, rather than any balance of power between disciplines, that informed both his Rede Lecture and his work at Churchill.

Snow's greatest ambition was to establish Churchill as a counterweight to Cambridge English. Recall that, in Snow's worldview, the problems in literature, criticism, and society were related: the arid analysis of the New Criticism, and the stream-of-consciousness style of Modernism, both testified to a retreat by writers and critics from their audience, a retreat that was symptomatic of the reactionary tendencies of intellectual culture in the first half of the century. In his own writing, therefore, Snow aimed to reconnect writers and readers, but his style met hostility from the literary establishment, so – as Chapter 1 showed – he

---

[77] Snow to J. C. R. Hamilton (Bursar), 3 July 1967, 5 July 1967, HRC: Snow 74.8; the Fellowship Electors approved the idea on 12 July 1967: CCGB 130/1, Paragraph 335.

[78] Interest in the "two cultures" surfaced in newspaper coverage, committee work, and college life: for instance, "Humaner Science," *Sunday Times*, 18 May 1958; the minutes of the Educational Policy Sub-Committee of 21 June 1958, Churchill College: CCGB 204; and the schoolmasters' conference on the place of the arts in a science college, 12 March 1966, Churchill College: CCAC 140/2/1. Snow was occasionally present at the Educational Policy Sub-Committee, and was an obvious choice to speak at the conference, but in his day-to-day concerns he expressed relatively little interest in the issue.

[79] Snow to Plumb, 21 September 1959, Cambridge University Library: Plumb Papers, File "Snow 1946 to 1968," Box "C. P. Snow + Pam, 1946 to 1968."

[80] Snow to Levin, 23 December 1959, Harvard University: Houghton Library, Levin papers, MS Am 2461 (918), Storage 342, Box 18, "Snow, C. P."

worked to nurture an alternative critical establishment. By the end of the 1950s Snow was even making inroads at the heart of the New Criticism: he had already befriended John Crowe Ransom, and he was soon to receive an honorary degree from Kenyon College.[81] Churchill English represented another front in the same battle, and within the college Snow's intentions were no secret: when Annan suggested a fellow in English, he quickly noted that it "may gladden the heart of Sir Charles Snow that this is not a typical piece of English Faculty criticism."[82] Snow's priorities were influencing appointments that promised to define Churchill English.

Snow wielded the most influence in the appointment of overseas fellows in the arts. One of Churchill's most distinctive features was its generous proportion of Title E and Title F members: "Extraordinary Fellows" not resident in Cambridge, and "Overseas Fellows" visiting from abroad. As the sole elector of external fellows in the arts, Snow used the Title E and Title F fellowships to secure the affiliation of his closest American friends and allies.[83] In February 1960 he suggested five illustrious names to Cockcroft, including Harry Levin ("perhaps the most highly reputed American authority on comparative literature"), Jacques Barzun, Provost of Columbia ("capable of holding his own even among hungry and argumentative scientists"), and Lionel Trilling ("I owe a lot to him personally").[84] But the quarters for visiting fellows remained under construction, and a year later the appointments still needed to be made. Snow suggested five names again, and again Levin, Barzun, and Trilling headed the list.[85] He assured the Governing Body, "These names would carry considerable weight in all American literary academic circles," and in April 1961 the Fellowship Electors agreed to offer an Extraordinary Fellowship to Barzun.[86] The Master dispatched Snow to secure Barzun's agreement, and Barzun accepted the honor later that month.[87]

Harry Levin proved a more reluctant recruit. Snow broached the idea of a fellowship in December 1959, initiating a prolonged effort that

---

[81] Snow to Plumb, 20 March 1961, HRC: Snow 166.8.
[82] Minutes of the Fellowship Electors, 4 February 1960, Churchill College: CCGB 205/2.
[83] Snow to Levin, 23 December 1959, Harvard University: Houghton Library, Levin papers, MS Am 2461 (918), Storage 342, Box 18, "Snow, C. P."
[84] Snow to Cockcroft, 3 February 1960, HRC: Snow 79.9. The remark about Barzun is from a similar document written a year later: Snow to Cockcroft, 3 March 1961, HRC: Snow 79.10.
[85] Snow to Cockcroft, 3 March 1961, HRC: Snow 79.10.
[86] Snow to Cockcroft, 3 March 1961, HRC: Snow 79.10; Churchill College Fellowship Electors, 18 April 1961, Churchill College: CCGB 130/1.75.
[87] Cockcroft to Fellowship Electors, 26 May 1961, Churchill College: CCGB 130/1.

ultimately resulted in Levin accepting a Title F fellowship for 1966–1967.[88] Initially, though, Levin rebuffed Snow, explaining that he shared Snow's concern about the "two cultures," but that he was just about to accept a chair in Comparative Literature at Harvard.[89] Snow glided swiftly past Levin's "two cultures" reference, but he applauded the news of the new position: "More and more I think this is the only way to teach literature," he wrote. "English teaching as practised at Cambridge, England has done a finite amount of harm." Levin had not said "no" outright, so Snow promised to ask the electors to offer a fellowship after 1962.[90] But Levin demurred again, and now explained that the barrier was actually Cambridge English itself: "I believe in science," he remarked, sticking with the "two cultures" concern that he assumed was motivating Snow. "What I don't believe in are the theological dogmas promulgated by such men as C. S. Lewis and F. R. Leavis, and I am afraid I should not fit in at all with the people on your English Faculty."[91]

Levin could not have known that confessing to a hostility to Cambridge English, far from putting the matter to rest, would instantly transform his candidacy into Snow's top priority. "I entirely agree that the dominant opinions in this Faculty are repellent almost beyond belief," Snow wrote. "[But] there are a great many youngish men, now attaining positions of influence, who are determined to stop the rot." If Cambridge English was the problem, Churchill English could be the answer: "I do not want humane studies in this country to fritter away into triviality," said Snow, "and I believe Churchill College might become an important rallying ground."[92] Snow pleaded and cajoled, until Levin finally agreed; then Levin withdrew, but then he agreed; and then he withdrew again.[93] Now, however, the problem was not Cambridge English in general, but Churchill English in particular: Levin did not relish the prospect of being a colleague of Snow's most important recruit, a brilliant young critic named George Steiner.

---

[88] Snow to Levin, 23 December 1959, Harvard University: Houghton Library, Levin papers, MS Am 2461 (918), Storage 342, Box 18, "Snow, C. P."
[89] Levin to Snow, 28 December 1959, Harvard University: Houghton Library, Levin papers, MS Am 2461 (918), Storage 342, Box 18, "Snow, C. P."
[90] Snow to Levin, 1 January 1960, Harvard University: Houghton Library, Levin papers, MS Am 2461 (918), Storage 342, Box 18, "Snow, C. P."
[91] Levin to Snow, 6 January 1960, Harvard University: Houghton Library, Levin papers, MS Am 2461 (918), Storage 342, Box 18, "Snow, C. P."
[92] Snow to Levin, 14 January 1960, HRC: Snow 133.15.
[93] Levin to Snow, 21 January 1960, 15 November 1960, HRC: Snow 133.15. Levin was elected for 1964–1965 in the meeting of Fellowship Electors of 14 February 1963, Churchill College: CCGB 130/1; he took up residence in the spring of 1967.

Churchill English

Steiner occupies a towering position among literary and cultural critics. He has held positions at Princeton, Cambridge, Geneva, Oxford, and Harvard; received at least eight honorary doctorates; and is both a Fellow of the British Academy and an honorary member of the American Academy of Arts and Sciences – indeed, a complete list of Steiner's awards, honors, and publications would easily fill numerous pages.[94] Snow, by contrast, today lingers on the margins of literary history, remembered chiefly for a one-hour lecture delivered in 1959. In the late 1950s and early 1960s, though, the roles were reversed: Snow (born 1905) was an eminent man of letters from Cambridge to Harvard to Berkeley, his novels commanded international attention, and his commentaries appeared regularly in the *Times Literary Supplement*, *Nation*, *New Statesman*, and *Spectator*. Steiner was Snow's junior by a generation. Born in Paris in 1929, his family fled for New York in 1940; equally comfortable in French, English, and German, he attended Chicago and Harvard. Between 1952 and 1956 he wrote for the *Economist*, before spending two years at the Institute for Advanced Study in Princeton. After a year as Fulbright professor in Austria, Steiner returned to Princeton in 1959. It was in December of that year that Snow contacted Steiner regarding the possibility of a fellowship at a new Cambridge college.

Steiner's first book, *Tolstoy or Dostoevsky*, was subtitled "An Essay in the Old Criticism," and its international scope and hostility to New Criticism appealed to Snow's desire to transcend the provincialisms of contemporary criticism.[95] The provincialisms Snow loathed were geographical (which literatures should be studied in English departments) and methodological (which modes of analysis should flourish in those departments). In 1961, in the *Kenyon Review*, Snow attacked these orthodoxies in a manifesto for a new style of criticism.[96] He argued that the novel was international in form, so that even comic novels (such as *Lucky Jim*) represented the latest installments in a tradition that derived from Chekhov, arrived in English through William Gerhardi, and flowed to the present through Evelyn Waugh, Anthony Powell, and William Cooper. But instead of recognizing this tradition, Snow thought that

---

[94] Christopher J. Knight, *Uncommon Readers: Denis Donoghue, Frank Kermode, George Steiner and the Tradition of the Common Reader* (University of Toronto Press, 2003).

[95] George Steiner, *Tolstoy or Dostoevsky: An Essay in the Old Criticism* (New York: Knopf, 1959).

[96] C. P. Snow, "Science, Politics, and the Novelist, or, The Fish and the Net," *Kenyon Review* 23 (Winter 1961), pp. 1–17.

contemporary fiction and criticism engaged in a conspiracy of denial, each narrowing their range to what little could be communicated through stream-of-consciousness prose. As a result, he suggested, entire realms of experience – such as modern science, and closed politics – remained unexamined. Snow sought to explore these facets of modern society through his own fiction, and doing so required that he employ a style that derived from Trollope rather than Joyce. But the critical denigration of such efforts resulted from a mode of criticism that had developed alongside the Modernist detour, making it imperative that that critical mode itself be displaced.

Steiner figured as the hero of this manifesto. Snow acknowledged Harry Levin at Harvard, whose comparative approach, he suggested, offered hope for American criticism, but Steiner took top honors. "George Steiner's *Tolstoy or Dostoevsky* is one of the important critical events of recent years," Snow declared, applauding its "colossal nerve and daring."[97] He said that he might quibble with particular arguments, but that any such complaints paled by comparison to what Steiner represented. "If Steiner is followed by some critics as dashing and imaginative as himself," Snow promised, "then we may get a new approach to novel criticism."[98] This approach promised to stimulate a necessary literary revival, one that would produce valuable exploratory fiction, rather than the "trivial protest" of Angry Young Men.[99] Snow concluded with a hopeful glimpse of the approaching critical shake-up: "[O]ften I get an intimation, more perhaps in the United States than in my own country, that that is just the occasion, the discontinuity, the flash of liberation, which our best talents are waiting for."[100]

The admiration was mutual. Reviewing *The Affair* in 1960, Steiner compared Snow to Balzac, Trollope, Proust, and Stendhal.[101] "This is, of course, to compare Snow's work with the very finest in the art of the novel," he allowed. "But throughout *The Affair* the comparison with Proust is openly invoked, and it is a mark of Snow's excellence that it can justly be made."[102] Steiner did register an objection to Snow's style, suggesting that the precision of his prose curtailed its ability to convey the full chaos of feeling and music of experience, but on balance the review was highly favorable. Steiner praised the "majestic ease" of *The Affair*, and the "superb structure" of the *Strangers and Brothers* sequence.[103] The plot was "relentlessly exciting," featuring a touch of "high comedy," and Snow pulled off a scene that was "a classic in the art

[97] *Ibid.*, p. 6.   [98] *Ibid.*, p. 7.   [99] *Ibid.*, pp. 4, 16.   [100] *Ibid.*, p. 17.
[101] George Steiner, "The Master Builder," *Reporter*, 9 June 1960, pp. 41–43.
[102] *Ibid.*, p. 43.   [103] *Ibid.*, pp. 42, 43.

of narrative."[104] Steiner's tone was respectful, not effusive, but he left no doubt that Snow was a novelist of the first order – an endorsement that Snow was later to crave, but that Steiner would refuse to repeat.

Snow and Steiner forged a fast friendship as the walls were going up at Churchill. In the summer of 1959 H. Sykes Davies of St. John's declined the college's offer to become Director of Studies in English, and in December the Fellowship Electors agreed to permit Snow to approach Steiner.[105] Initially Steiner would hold an overseas fellowship, but Snow hoped that his appointment might prove permanent – as he told the Master, "He may be a real flyer."[106] Steiner soon determined that he wanted to make a home in England, and Snow replied that, if he liked the college, and the college liked him, Steiner could become Director of Studies in English.[107] "I believe this is the most adventurous appointment that a Cambridge college has made for some time," he wrote.[108] After the initial flush of enthusiasm, however, doubts began to emerge, as Steiner worried that he might not fit into college life.[109] Snow reassured him that Churchill would be nothing like the claustrophobic societies of *The Masters*, but Steiner's anxiety proved only too prescient: despite Churchill's steadfast support, Steiner was never accepted by the Cambridge English Faculty. Barred from lecturing, and repeatedly denied a university post, he eventually left Cambridge for a position in Geneva. But even in exile Steiner retained his Fellowship at Churchill, a reminder of happier days when Snow's friend and ally was poised to take charge of English in a Cambridge college.

From Snow's perspective, Steiner's appointment was a coup in several respects. First, Steiner was an influential and prominent critic who endorsed Snow's literary approach, and now his support would be situated alongside (if not quite inside) Cambridge English. Second, with his interests in comparative literature, the history of science, and new technologies, Steiner promised an alternative to Cambridge English. For instance, while Snow was recruiting Steiner, Steiner reported that he had recently delivered a talk on the "retreat from language" since the seventeenth century, exploring the advance of symbolic and mathematical logic and the consequent restriction of the scope of literary

---

[104] *Ibid.*, p. 42.
[105] Appointments Committee, 30 May 1959, 14 July 1959, Churchill College: CCGB 130/1; Fellowship Electors, 14 December 1959, Churchill College: CCGB 130/1.19.
[106] Snow to Cockcroft, 16 March 1960, HRC: Snow 79.9.
[107] Steiner to Snow, 11 February 1960, HRC: Snow 191.3; Snow to Steiner, 4 March 1960, HRC: Snow 191.3.
[108] Snow to Steiner, 4 March 1960, HRC: Snow 191.3.
[109] Snow to Steiner, 27 April 1960, HRC: Snow 191.3.

representation. He cast the talk as an extension of Snow's own ideas, and even incorporated Snow's depiction of Joyce as a blind alley in literary history (despite his own comparative admiration for Joyce).[110] Third, and most importantly, Steiner declared his ambition to open Cambridge English to disciplines such as sociology, anthropology, and psychology. "Something must be done to open the windows on to the world in Cambridge English Studies!" he proclaimed.[111] Of course, a challenge to Cambridge English would entail a confrontation with Leavis, and Steiner confessed to precisely these intentions: "I sometimes have a malicious dream about posting on the gates of Downing College notice of a lecture entitled 'The Small Tradition'," he wrote, adding that Leavis's dismissal of certain writers "verges on the grotesque."[112] Pro-Snow, anti-Leavis: with Steiner soon to begin his fellowship, Snow no doubt felt satisfied with his success in shaping Churchill English.

Steiner garnered his share of successes as Churchill's Director of Studies in English. By the autumn of 1964, with fifteen students, English was the largest arts subject in the college.[113] In the English Tripos of 1965, a Churchill student won the prestigious Rylands Prize, and, at a time when it meant more than it would today, only one student of fourteen received a Third.[114] Steiner had positioned Churchill English to reach beyond traditional literary studies, including comparative literature, linguistics, sociology, and communication theory, and he and Snow compiled an impressive list of overseas fellows, including Barzun, Levin, and John Hollander.[115] By 1965, Steiner was so impressed with Churchill English that he worried about the standing of science in the college![116] "When I came here," he later recalled, "there was a muddy field, a wooden hut, three frightened students (rejects of all other colleges). As I look out my window tonight, a great complex is in operation, some twenty men are taking the English Tripos, two men are here doing Ph.D. work in English, John Hollander is billowing across the lawn etc. This has been a marvellous adventure, the best in my life."[117] However,

---

[110] Steiner to Snow, 29 February 1960, HRC: Snow 191.3. Steiner reiterated the connection between the essay and Snow's ideas in a letter of 21 January 1961, HRC: Snow 191.3. The essay appeared as "The Retreat from the Word," *Kenyon Review* 23 (Spring 1961), pp. 187–216.
[111] Steiner to Snow, 5 September 1962, HRC: Snow 191.3.
[112] Steiner to Snow, 21 January 1961, HRC: Snow 191.3.
[113] Steiner to Snow, 15 September 1964, Churchill College: GSNR 1/5.
[114] Steiner to Snow, 25 June 1965, HRC: Snow 191.5.
[115] Steiner to J. R. (Jack) Pole, 20 February 1966, Churchill College: CCAC 140/2/1. Barzun was a Title F fellow in 1963–1964; Levin and Hollander were in residence in 1967.
[116] Steiner to Snow, 23 May 1966, HRC: Snow 191.6.
[117] Steiner to Snow, 27 May 1968, HRC: Snow 191.7.

while Snow might have shared Steiner's satisfaction with the progress of Churchill College, he felt painfully betrayed by Churchill English at the moment he needed it most.

"What a trap!"

Snow's efforts on behalf of Levin, Steiner, and Barzun might be interpreted as routine advocacy on behalf of friends, but from Snow's perspective it was significant that he had these friends and not others. As Chapter 1 showed, Snow conceived of his novels and criticism as parts of an ambitious project, one dedicated to exploring and celebrating the workings of modern society. He understood his work as a corrective to the social criticism he thought had been embedded in literature since 1914, and he devoted his criticism to countering that criticism's modes of analysis and interpretation. When Snow's creative work met critical resistance, he read that resistance as an objection not of taste but of conviction, and set out to discredit it accordingly. And when his work met critical praise, he read that praise as an appreciation not of plot but of worldview, and he set out to befriend the critic accordingly. To Snow, critical sympathy pointed to political compatibility, and "friend" was synonymous with "ally."

Upon learning of Leavis's Richmond Lecture, and confronting the greatest crisis of his professional life, Snow summoned the support of all his friends and allies. Publicly he refused to reply to Leavis's personal assault, but privately he orchestrated an assiduous counterattack. "I think I have got to ask my friends to do some of the fighting for me," he told Plumb two days before the *Spectator* printed Leavis's lecture.[118] Leavis had challenged not Snow's thesis, so much as his right to advance a thesis – indeed, the Richmond Lecture questioned Snow's credentials to speak at all. Snow anticipated the poverty of a response that would lamely reiterate his qualifications, so he asked proxies to affirm his standing instead.[119] He asked Plumb to support his interpretation of history, and J. D. Bernal to endorse his achievement as a scientist. Plumb and Bernal duly sprang into action, sending authoritative letters to the *Spectator*.[120] But Snow had never claimed to be a historian, and he had not practiced science for decades. Since the thrust of Leavis's criticism targeted his standing as a novelist, the burden of the counterattack would fall to Steiner.

---

[118] Snow to Plumb, 7 March 1962, HRC: Snow 226.12.   [119] *Ibid.*
[120] *Ibid.*; Snow to Bernal, 7 March 1962, HRC: Snow 226.13; Plumb, "Letters," *Spectator*, 30 March 1962, p. 396; Bernal, "Letters," *Spectator*, 23 March 1962, p. 365.

To Snow's dismay, however, Steiner proved a reluctant ally. By early 1962 their relationship had been strained for about six months, perhaps because Steiner had declared T. F. Powys (rather than Snow) the best writer in English since Lawrence.[121] Then, as fate would have it, shortly before the Richmond Lecture Steiner had proposed a critical appreciation of Leavis to *Encounter*.[122] As events overtook him, a comment on the "two cultures" controversy became unavoidable. Steiner edited his piece to depict the Richmond Lecture as an unfortunate – yet ultimately insignificant – result of Leavis's excessive identification with Lawrence. He showed a draft to Snow, who declared such an oblique rebuke insufficient.[123] The master of personal politics had spent years positioning his pieces on the board for precisely this moment, and the time had come for him to realize the benefits of having maneuvered a friend into a Cambridge college. By post and by phone, then, Snow leaned on Steiner heavily. "The most friendly thing you could do would be not to minimize this last lecture, but to make something of it, and to wind into your essay as spirited a defense of me – not as pundit, but as writer – as you feel you honestly can," he insisted. "I believe this might undo a little of the harm. But, more important, it would mean that I did not feel deserted."[124]

Steiner felt himself to be in an impossible position. "What a trap!" he wrote to his parents. "Whatever I say will offend."[125] He remained grateful to Snow, personally and professionally, but could not bring himself to produce the endorsement that his patron demanded. "Why is [Snow's] skin so thin?" he wrote to his parents, "Because he knows Leavis is, *au fond*, right! That is the terrible thing."[126] The *Encounter* article appeared in May; it chastized Leavis, but did not endorse Snow. When Steiner visited the Snows in London later that year, his hosts remained hopeful that he might yet intervene. "[T]hey want one thing from me," he said after this meeting, "an essay saying C. P. is a great novelist."[127] Their hope was not unwarranted: two years before Steiner had discussed Snow – "the master builder" who assembled "a classic in the art of narrative" – alongside Proust, Balzac, Trollope, and

---

[121] Steiner, 12 March 1962, Churchill College: GSNR 1/5.
[122] News of the planned article is from Steiner's letter to his parents, 18 February 1962, Churchill College: GSNR 1/5; the essay was published as "F. R. Leavis," *Encounter*, May 1962, pp. 37–45, and reprinted in *Language and Silence: Essays on Language, Literature, and the Inhuman* (New York: Athenaeum, 1967).
[123] Snow to Steiner, 13 March 1962, HRC: Snow 226.12.   [124] *Ibid.*
[125] Steiner, 5 March 1962, Churchill College: GSNR 1/5.
[126] Steiner, 17 March 1962, Churchill College: GSNR 1/5.
[127] Steiner, 21 September 1962, Churchill College: GSNR 1/5.

Stendhal.[128] But with Steiner ensconced in Churchill, but not yet welcomed into Cambridge, no such praise would again be forthcoming.[129]
He had cast aside the dream of mocking the "small tradition" at the
gates of Downing, and now confessed instead that he desired Leavis's
respect.[130] Snow and Steiner remained friends – Steiner read from
Dostoevsky at his memorial service in 1980 – but their correspondence
never regained the warmth of those exhilarating months prior to
Steiner's arrival in Cambridge. Steiner and Churchill English moved
on, and, although pained by his failure to secure a critical base in
Cambridge, so, too, did Snow.

Downing English

The traffic between Churchill English and Downing English was surprisingly brisk during this period. One of Churchill's first nominees for a
fellowship in English was Frank Lee, educated at Downing in the 1920s
and an honorary fellow since 1960; one of its first research fellows was
Ian Robinson, a student of Leavis's and Downing graduate of 1958.[131]
The year after Leavis delivered the annual Richmond Lecture in
Downing, Snow, accompanied by Barzun and Steiner, ambled across
town to do the same (his measured address on education disappointed
any students who might have hoped to witness a good row).[132] Leavis
delivered "Luddites? *or* There is Only One Culture," the second lecture
in his campaign against university expansion and establishment orthodoxies, at the invitation of students from Churchill College.[133] And
around the same time Q. D. Leavis was supervising English students
from Churchill.[134]

But the most arresting exchange between the two colleges was Brian
Vickers, a brilliant Renaissance scholar from Trinity. Vickers's research
on "Francis Bacon as a Literary Artist" made him an ideal candidate for
a position in English at Cambridge's new science college.[135] But Vickers
was not entirely happy at Churchill, and when another opening emerged

---

[128] Steiner, "The Master Builder," pp. 41–43.
[129] Steiner, 21 September 1962, Churchill College: GSNR 1/5.
[130] Steiner, 27 March 1962, Churchill College: GSNR 1/5.
[131] Fellowship Electors, 2 March 1960, Churchill College: CCGB 130/1.42; Ian
MacKillop, *F. R. Leavis: A Life in Criticism* (London: Allen Lane, 1995), p. 304.
[132] C. P. Snow, "Education and Sacrifice," *New Statesman*, 17 May 1963, pp. 746–750.
[133] F. R. Leavis, *Nor Shall My Sword: Discourses on Pluralism, Compassion and Social Hope*
(London: Chatto and Windus, 1972), pp. 28–29.
[134] MacKillop, *F. R. Leavis*, p. 352.
[135] "Churchill College Junior Research Fellowship Election 1964: Brian Vickers,"
Churchill College: CCGB 133/2/5.

in Cambridge he expressed interest; that position was at Downing, and it had been created by Leavis's retirement. When the Governing Body appointed Vickers, rather than his own candidate, Leavis abruptly terminated his association with the college to which he had devoted his career. When the dust finally settled, Vickers – the "two cultures" scholar from the college that Snow had helped found – was Downing's new Director of Studies in English.

Established in 1800 as a site of "law, physic, and the other useful arts and learning," Downing's modern, pragmatic bent was codified in its restriction that only two fellows represent holy orders.[136] During its first century of existence, study at Downing primarily focused upon law and medicine. Science was also a priority: Downing was one of the first Cambridge colleges to house its own laboratory, during the 1870s one of its fellows led the campaign to build university laboratories, and in 1896 another fellow established Cambridge's Department of Pharmacology.[137] Leavis brought international attention to the arts side of the college: the college history proudly recalls the era of Leavis's English School, when "young men . . . clamoured to come to Downing to hear their scrawny, earnest-faced open-shirted Pope expound the pure doctrine with the intolerance and fervour of an Old Testament prophet."[138] But with Leavis's resignation in 1964, as English faded in prominence in the college, law and medicine resumed their historical preeminence.[139] In another respect, though, Leavis was perfectly in tune with college tradition: the official history remarks that Downing will continue to thrive so long as "the buildings are not destroyed by a nuclear holocaust, or the idea smothered by egalitarian ignorance."[140] Science, technology, and equality: if Leavis's English School had any single purpose, it was to stand in defiance of the worship of these three idols of the twentieth century.

Leavis first arrived at Downing when his probationary university lectureship expired in 1931; the following year he was appointed the college's Director of Studies in English.[141] He gained another university lectureship in 1936, thus enabling Downing to elect him a fellow. Downing was not a wealthy college, but it provided a base for Leavis's teaching and writing. It was in this period that it became possible to speak of "Downing English," or, in Leavis's idiom, the "English School." By the late 1930s, Downing English was distinguishing itself

---

[136] Stanley French, *The History of Downing College Cambridge* (Downing College Association, 1978), p. 82.
[137] *Ibid.*, pp. 132, 135–136.   [138] *Ibid.*, p. 138.   [139] *Ibid.*, p. 140.   [140] *Ibid.*
[141] MacKillop, *F. R. Leavis*, p. 153.

within Cambridge, and gaining attention beyond Cambridge as well: in 1938 Downing students won four out of eight firsts in Part I of the English Tripos, a feat the *Observer* called "a triumph for what may be called the Downing School of Literature," and the next year Downing men earned four out of seven firsts in Part II.[142] Despite these successes, Leavis's English School was emphatically not geared towards producing "first-class men" – instead, Leavis imagined it as the antithesis of the corrupted system that replicated itself through exam-savvy students.

Leavis offered his vision for the English School in a series of articles in *Scrutiny* beginning in 1940, published as *Education and the University* in 1943.[143] The book proposed an agenda for literary studies, and for the university, after the war. The first chapter, "The Idea of a University," identified a historical crisis in the emergence of the "technical complexity of civilization" simultaneous with "social and cultural disintegration."[144] The proliferating specializations of modern society resulted in the loss of the general intelligence that could provide that society with direction. The result was uncoordinated change, with no purpose other than its own acceleration, and the resource that could provide the necessary guidance was the cultural tradition. The ideal university would function as the site where that tradition thrived, and where it could be transmitted, but even the university was not immune to the specialization and fracturing that characterized modern civilization. Rather than functioning as a cultural center, and relating diverse specializations together in a unified consciousness, the university was on the verge of becoming another appendage to the machinery of modern civilization.

The second chapter, "Sketch for an English School," positioned literary studies at the core of a redeemed university. English assumed this privileged position not out of disciplinary purity, but because the study of literature necessarily led into other domains. Working with the model of the two-part Cambridge Tripos, Leavis proposed that students approach Part II of the English Tripos from other fields and disciplines. He then sketched a model of learning centered around discussions rather than lectures, and evaluated through papers composed over time rather than examinations against the clock. The aim was not to foster recall of literary history or to encourage glib cultural facility, but rather to

---

[142] *Ibid.*, p. 160.

[143] F. R. Leavis, *Education and the University: A Sketch for an "English School"* (London: Chatto and Windus, 1943). See also Richard Storer, "*Education and the University*: Structure and Sources," in *F. R. Leavis: Essays and Documents*, ed. Ian MacKillop and Richard Storer (Sheffield Academic Press, 1995), Chapter 7.

[144] Leavis, *Education and the University*, pp. 22–23.

stimulate intelligence and develop sensibility – a dual mandate for which literary studies, conceived as the rigorous pursuit of true judgment, was ideally suited. Alongside these progressive characteristics, Leavis's program fiercely resisted democratic tendencies: the English School was explicitly charged with the task of educating an elite. "It is an intelligence so trained," Leavis explained, "that is best fitted to develop into the central kind of mind, the co-ordinating consciousness, capable of performing the function assigned to the class of the educated."[145]

The final chapter, "Literary Studies," illustrated Leavis's idea of literary education. Such an education rejected literary history and rote memorization, and was not even concerned primarily with interpretation; instead, the training would focus on attentive reading and correct judgment. This insistence upon the possibility of normative judgments of literary work – that is, upon the possibility of determining a work's creative success or failure – is where Leavisian criticism is most unlike academic criticism today. Leavis himself occasionally slipped on this point, sometimes stating that the student should bear in mind "the one right total meaning" (a matter of interpretation, which can be right or wrong), and other times explaining that the student should aim for "true judgment" (a matter of evaluation, for which no standard exists).[146] The ease with which Leavis moved between these competing senses demonstrates that, in his mind, they were not competing at all. Interpretation and evaluation for Leavis were the same act, the product of an attentive reading that created an experience in the mind of the reader – not the understanding of an experience, but *an actual experience*. Leavis believed that people once experienced language this way in the idiom of their daily lives, but that from the seventeenth century this relationship to language became confined within a marginalized tradition. *Education and the University* positioned the university as the place where that tradition must be sustained, and argued that literary studies should transmit the capacity to recognize and respond to it. Tradition, crisis, minority, center, standards, *life* – to Leavis's critics these were the overworked talismans of an obscure critical orthodoxy, but to his allies they pointed to the urgency of the mission before Downing English.

Leavis wrote *Education and the University* during the war, a time he believed to be at once threatening (because of the accelerating efficiency of civilization at war) and auspicious (because of the opportunities provided by postwar reconstruction). In Leavis's mind, education was every bit as important as the war effort, and he was infuriated by the government's refusal to postpone a small number of enlistments in order

[145] *Ibid.*, p. 55.   [146] *Ibid.*, pp. 72, 71.

to train teachers for after the war. But he anticipated that education reform would follow the war, and he wrote his book with the goal of influencing that debate. His proposals were enthusiastically received: the *Times Literary Supplement* declared that "*Education and the University* deserves a wide public. Its subject, indeed, is nothing less than the mental health of the nation."[147] The *Times Educational Supplement* agreed: "The present reviewer finds [Leavis's proposal] exciting to contemplate, and can see no reason why an experiment along these lines should be regarded as impracticable."[148] Leavis had secured valuable allies for his effort to reshape education in postwar Britain.

This public support boosted the English School within Downing. After the war, Leavis believed that the time had come to establish Downing as the center he had envisioned. He seized every opportunity to proselytize to his colleagues on the Governing Body, and he expressed satisfaction with the reception his ideas met in the college.[149] Leavis sought to translate his ideas and ideals into institutional form, for instance by stocking the college library with books appropriate to an English School – an effort that demanded all of his wiles in the face of the college librarian who refused to stock any novels (when that librarian retired, however, he left behind a catalogue testifying to Leavis's success: "Accessions to the Library during the years 1934–1956, bearing on English History of the Seventeenth Century").[150] In terms of under-graduate admissions, Leavis maintained unusual control for a Director of Studies by running a distinct scholarship exam for Downing, apart from the group examinations used by other colleges. Through these examinations Leavis exerted influence in schools and sixth forms throughout the country, as headmasters and students considering Downing needed to incorporate the curriculum set out in *Scrutiny*, *Culture and Environment*, and *Education and the University*.[151] Once they arrived at Downing, undergraduates could count on attention from their

---

[147] "Readers and Citizens," *Times Literary Supplement*, 15 January 1944, p. 31.

[148] "The Idea of a University," *Times Educational Supplement*, 1 January 1944.

[149] Leavis to Geoffrey Walton, 4 February 1947, Downing College: DCPP/LEA/7 Leavis, F. R.

[150] Robin Williams, "Some Memories of F. R. Leavis and Other Downing Dons in the Early 1950s," Downing College: DCHR/1/2/FRL Leavis, F. R.; Governing Body Minutes, Downing College, Vol. 220, 6 June 1957, p. 418, Minute 7.

[151] When Downing's separate examination was challenged in the 1950s, Leavis unsuc-cessfully opposed efforts to collapse its examination in with those of other colleges. "English as a Group Scholarship Subject," 20 January 1953, Downing College: D/M/P/1. For more on the scholarship system, see MacKillop, *F. R. Leavis*, pp. 154–155. The essential teaching text before *Education and the University* was *Culture and Environment: The Training of Critical Awareness* (London: Chatto and Windus, 1933), written with Denys Thompson.

supervisors, camaraderie among their peers, and the satisfaction of being engaged in a renegade enterprise – all of which resulted from Leavis's infectious conviction that literary studies was *the* essential discipline.

Yet those same convictions meant that there were two things that Downing English students could not necessarily count on: brushes with fame, and examination success. This is not to suggest that no eminent critics passed through the gates of Downing – after all, Leavis himself was one of the most influential literary critics in the English-speaking world. But by contrast with Snow's approach at Churchill, Leavis paid little mind to international reputation or academic records when seeking help in the college. Whereas to Snow any association of an eminent scholar promised to benefit Churchill, to Leavis eminence itself was suspect in this fallen world. He therefore rarely looked beyond his own circle for assistance – a habit that, as we shall see, put him out of step with the priorities of his college. Leavis also believed that examinations were a poor indicator of quality. Downing men garnered their share of firsts, especially in the 1930s when Leavis was initially making his mark as a teacher. But success on examinations testified to a kind of literary facility that Leavis saw as the opposite of education.[152] As an examiner himself, then, he looked for something different: when scrawled in the margins of a paper he was marking, "unsophisticated" could be a compliment, signifying a welcome unawareness of critical trends, whereas "accomplishment and facility" might doom a student to membership in King's, where they went in for that sort of thing.[153] His students internalized (or at least performed) a similar indifference: "Among my circle of friends there was an affectation of despising Tripos results," one student recalled. "We were particularly hostile to what we called 'working for a First', something that we supposed successful examinees did cynically and mechanically."[154]

In truth Leavis cared about the performance of his students – as he himself lamented, "All my firsts get two-twos."[155] Another former student offered several explanations: Leavis discouraged his students from attending the lectures of his nemeses on the English faculty, he insisted that his students read more widely than required for the Tripos,

---

[152] Leavis, *Education and the University*, pp. 45, 50–51.
[153] As MacKillop explained in his biography, Leavis used old student examinations as scratch paper, and these comments on student essays are taken from the reverse sides of the manuscript for "Scrutiny: A Retrospect," held at Harvard University: Houghton Library, MS Eng 1218.2.
[154] Neil Roberts, "'Leavisite' Cambridge in the 1960s," in *F. R. Leavis: Essays and Documents*, ed. MacKillop and Storer, p. 278.
[155] Williams, "Some Memories of F. R. Leavis"; Leavis to David Matthews, 19 June 1951, Emmanuel College, Cambridge (Emmanuel): ECA COL 9.59a.113.

and he encouraged them to read subjects other than English for Part II.[156] On one occasion Leavis expressed dismay at the examiners who were judging his best students poorly, and he anticipated the likely defense that those examiners frequently published – a "justification" that condemned them, and the system in which they thrived.[157] Downing English stood as the antithesis to that system.

Expansion and science

The increases in undergraduate numbers after the war, emphasizing the natural sciences in particular, threatened Leavis's idea of a university. His ideal centered around the English School, which would be responsible for sustaining intellectual standards. Standards, of course, meant selection, but in the end an elite benefited the whole of society by synthesizing, coordinating, and sustaining human creation: they imposed intelligence and sensibility upon the relentless advance of modern civilization. Whereas Leavis advocated small numbers of students centered around literary studies, postwar policy instead increased numbers and prioritized science. Nevertheless, to interpret Leavis's stance as opposition to "science" is a mistaken "two cultures" reductionism. On the contrary, Leavis insisted that he respected scientists because they shared his commitment to rigorous standards, and he maintained that he would prefer to discuss the university with a scientist than with "an academic humanist."[158] For Leavis, the drive towards expansion communicated disregard for the principle that the university must be restricted to a minority, and the prioritizing of the sciences smacked of the instrumentalism the university was supposed to counter.

Like many Cambridge colleges, Downing experienced significant growth between 1945 and 1960. Immediately after the war, the college allowed for increased numbers of undergraduates in order to accommodate returning servicemen.[159] In 1938 Downing had had 228 students in residence, but by 1960 that number had risen to 360. To manage these increases, a building program added sixty new rooms, renovated existing buildings to accommodate twenty-three additional students, and expanded facilities such as the sick bay, chapel, and

---

[156] Williams, "Some Memories of F. R. Leavis." Williams also includes Leavis's own preferred explanation, the English faculty's animus against him and his students.
[157] Leavis to Matthews, 19 June 1951, Emmanuel: ECA COL 9.59a.113.
[158] "I would rather discuss the function of the university with a mathematician or a physicist than with an academic humanist." *English Literature in Our Time and the University* (London: Chatto and Windus, 1969), p. 40.
[159] "Admissions," 19 January 1961, Downing College: D/M/P/8.

library – a project that cost this unwealthy college more than £200,000. In the same period, spending on scholarships more than doubled, and the number of fellows increased from eleven to twenty-one. The changes affected the college's character as well as its structure: in 1955 the Governing Body adjusted its admissions policies to allow students to arrive straight out of school, and in 1957 they agreed to increase the percentage of students in the sciences to 50 percent.[160] The 1950s at Downing, in short, were characterized by expansion, crowding, and construction.

Toward the end of the decade the college began to resist further expansion. As argued in a report prepared for a university committee in 1960, "[T]o turn Peterhouse (or Downing) into a Trinity-sized college overnight would produce not another Trinity but a featureless chaos."[161] In January 1958 the Tutorial Committee began planning for a reduction in the size of the college, estimating that a plan initiated the following year could reduce the undergraduate population to any number the Governing Body desired as soon as 1963.[162] Six days later, the Governing Body agreed to begin reducing numbers immediately, aiming to achieve a number of 350 total students (this figure was later allowed to rise to 365).[163] The following year, looking ahead to changes facing the university within the next five years, the Governing Body agreed that any effort to force Downing to increase student numbers must be resisted.[164] And with regard to the sciences, when the Senior Tutor reported in 1959 that other colleges were increasing their numbers of scientists, he explained that Downing had already been doing so for years – and that, if anything, they should consider reducing the numbers of scientists within their college.[165] Long before Lionel Robbins's committee had been appointed, then, Downing had experienced expansion and shifts toward the sciences – so much, in fact, that by the

---

[160] "Memorandum from Downing College," 6 November 1960, Downing College: D/M/P/8; Governing Body Minutes, Downing College, Vol. 220, 3 May 1957, p. 410, Minute 22 (e).
[161] "Memorandum from Downing College," 6 November 1960, Downing College: D/M/P/8.
[162] Tutorial Committee Minutes, 11 January 1958, held with the supplements to the Governing Body Minutes, 1957–1958, Downing College: D/M/P/6.
[163] Governing Body Minutes, Downing College, Vol. 220, 17 January 1958, pp. 475–476, Minute 22 (a); Governing Body Minutes, Downing College, Vol. 220, 16 January 1959, pp. 568–569, Minute 7 (b).
[164] Governing Body Minutes, Downing College, Vol. 220, 12 February 1960, p. 680, Minute 8.
[165] Tutorial Committee Minutes, 5 December 1959, held with the supplements to the Governing Body Minutes, Downing College: D/M/P/7.

end of the 1950s the college felt that it had already done its part, and might even have gone too far.

Having lived and worked through these developments, Leavis shared the conviction that expansion had gone far enough. This was no quixotic dream: we now know that Robbins was just beyond the horizon, but Leavis and the Governing Body did not. From their perspective, expansion had *already* happened, and – with some difficulty – the bulge in numbers had been managed. As the literary scholar Richard Storer observes, "[N]umbers had stabilised by the mid-1950s, and the government had changed, which perhaps explains Leavis's misplaced confidence that it shared his assumptions."[166] These assumptions were predicated on the principle that a limited number of students were capable of benefiting from university education, a principle that assumed that the university existed as a center of excellence. Excellence, not access: to Leavis – as to the founders of Churchill College – this was the "problem" confronting the university, but it was not the problem motivating Macmillan, Robbins, and other reformers.

Leavis composed his Richmond Lecture in the context of these discussions about the future of the university. Delivered early in February 1962, the lecture fell squarely between the establishment of Robbins's committee in 1961 and its report in 1963 – the period of "waiting for Robbins." Towards the end of his lecture, after he had challenged Snow's authority and argument, Leavis turned to his vision for the university. He insisted that the university must amount to more than a collection of specialist departments. Charged with the task of providing a "consciousness (and conscience) for our civilisation," his ideal university would be centered around the English School.[167] The English School, he explained, was not merely an annex of great books, but a creative force that maintained "the full life in the present – and life is growth – of our transmitted culture."[168] As long as the universities remained dominated by figures such as Snow and (later) Robbins, the English School must serve as the repository not only of the transmitted culture, but indeed of the very idea of the university. That is, the English School needed to be to the university what Leavis insisted *Scrutiny* had once been to Cambridge: "We were, and knew we were, Cambridge – the essential Cambridge in spite of Cambridge."[169] Not for the first time, and not for the last, Leavis was fighting to reclaim and redeem the university from keepers who appeared bent on its destruction.

---

[166] Richard Storer, "F. R. Leavis and the Idea of a University," *Cambridge Review*, November 1995, p. 98.
[167] Leavis, *Two Cultures?*, p. 30.   [168] *Ibid.*, pp. 28–29.   [169] *Ibid.*, p. 29.

Leavis Agonistes

It was at Downing that Leavis would make his stand. He exercised more influence in his college than in the English faculty, with which he had long feuded.[170] In October 1961, as his retirement approached, he expressed his hope that his work would continue at Downing, and that Downing would continue to serve as a place where the ideal university was realized.[171] In order to achieve that goal, he turned his attention to securing his successor in English. This task had been on his mind since the demise of *Scrutiny* in 1953, when he had expressed worry that his work in Cambridge might vanish upon his retirement.[172] As the decade advanced, Leavis's concerns for English increasingly dominated discussions by Downing's Governing Body.[173] In 1961 the college commissioned a portrait of Leavis by Peter Greenham, but Leavis was not impressed: he said that he instead wished that the Governing Body would commit to continuing his life's work.[174] A few months later, when his final academic year had begun, Leavis settled on a plan: he would arrange things so that, when the time came, he could impose his preferred candidate as Director of Studies in English.[175]

As Leavis fought these battles within Downing, his behavior was shaped by his peculiar conception of how politics worked. In response to the familiar refrain that "politics is the art of the possible," Leavis insisted, "*We* create possibility."[176] As discussed in Chapter 2, Leavis thought of politics differently than did Snow: rather than a matter of maneuvering and persuasion in assembling coalitions, Leavis thought of politics as something like the working of a machine. Not being part of the machine himself, his best chance to influence it was to bang on it

---

[170] Appointments were not strictly the preserve of the Faculty Board, but of an Appointments Committee consisting of members of the faculty. From Leavis's perspective, it amounted to much the same thing, and he was correct that no student or associate of his had made it through the process as of 1961. Leavis to David Holbrook, 7 September 1961, Downing College: DCPP/LEA/4 Leavis, F. R. (4).

[171] Leavis to Stanley French, 5 October 1961, Downing: DCHR/1/2/FRL Leavis, F.R.

[172] MacKillop, *F. R. Leavis*, p. 282.

[173] *Ibid.*, p. 311. The minutes of 21 October 1960 record that Leavis addressed the Governing Body on the subject of English after his retirement – an extraordinary instance, in these reticent minutes, of naming a particular fellow and subject. Governing Body Minutes, Downing College, Vol. 221, 21 October 1960, p. 19, Minute 8.

[174] Leavis to Walton, 10 June 1961, Downing College: DCPP/LEA/7 Leavis, F. R.

[175] Leavis to Walton, 7 November 1961, Downing College: DCPP/LEA/7 Leavis, F. R. For an account of Leavis's concerns during this period, see Dan Jacobson, *Time and Time Again* (New York: Atlantic Monthly Press, 1985), pp. 126–136.

[176] F. R. Leavis, " 'Believing In' the University," *The Critic as Anti-Philosopher* (Athens: University of Georgia Press, 1983), p. 172.

periodically. To Leavis, then, politics consisted of confrontations and provocations, in hopes of forcing a moment of recognition for someone on the inside. Such an attitude could make for a difficult colleague, but the source of the difficulty was not that Leavis was irrational – on the contrary, in his own way, he was as calculating as Snow.

Upon retirement, Leavis agreed to remain active at Downing as an advisor, examiner, and honorary fellow.[177] The question of his successor as Director of Studies in English remained open. Leavis's own candidate was Morris Shapira, who had graduated from Downing in 1953. Shapira's record was solid, if not stellar: he entered Downing with a minor scholarship, earned a second in Part I (English) and a first in Part II (Modern and Medieval Languages), and had studied for a year at Harvard.[178] In 1957 Downing elected Shapira to a three-year Research Fellowship, and he proved a committed teacher of undergraduates and a loyal supporter of Leavis.[179] In July 1962, at the moment of his official retirement, Leavis appeared to achieve the victory he sought: despite commitments to offer fellowships to two other English scholars should they receive university appointments, the Governing Body named Shapira the college's Director of Studies in English.[180] When the next academic year commenced, the succession seemed secure: Leavis accepted his honorary fellowship on the same day that Shapira was named examiner in the English scholarship examination.[181]

Yet the matter was not settled completely. Downing could not afford to award a college fellowship to someone who did not have a stipendiary university post. Perhaps because of his commitment to teaching – as he put it, "thirty to forty hours a week trying to eradicate conventionalities and clichés of thought" – Shapira had not even finished his PhD, and no university lectureship beckoned.[182] In the spring of 1964, at the end of

---

[177] Governing Body Minutes, Downing College, Vol. 221, 5 October 1962, p. 159, Minute 4.

[178] Supplements to Governing Body Minutes, 3 February 1956, Downing College: D/M/P/4.

[179] Governing Body Minutes, Downing College, Vol. 220, 26 July 1957, p. 430, Minute 6. Shapira's fellowship officially dated from 1 October 1957, and his first attendance at a meeting of the Governing Body followed on 4 October 1957. MacKillop, however, dated Shapira's fellowship from 1955: F. R. Leavis, p. 294.

[180] Governing Body Minutes, Downing College, Vol. 221, 23 July 1962, p. 155, Minute 16. The standing commitments were to G. D. Klingopulos and H. A. Mason. The focus here is on the events leading to the end of Leavis's affiliation with Downing; for the retirement saga, including the origins and fate of the F. R. Leavis Lectureship Trust, see MacKillop, F. R. Leavis, Chapter 10.

[181] Governing Body Minutes, Downing College, Vol. 221, 5 October 1962, pp. 159, 162, Minutes 4, 14.

[182] MacKillop, F. R. Leavis, p. 347; this narrative follows pp. 340–350.

the second year of this situation, the college began to take steps to secure a fellow in English. They offered a fellowship to John Newton, the first student of Leavis's to have secured a university lectureship, but Newton – not wanting to displace Shapira – turned it down.[183] The Governing Body then agreed to inquire into two other recently appointed lecturers, one of whom was Brian Vickers.[184] After Vickers dined in the college, the Governing Body unanimously elected him to a fellowship in July 1964.[185] Upon hearing of the appointment, Leavis immediately resigned his fellowship.[186] Frustrated with the drama inflicted upon them by their irascible colleague, the Governing Body responded by resolving not to reappoint Shapira, to reduce the number of students accepted to read English, and to move immediately towards securing a new fellow.[187] Leavis requested that his name be removed from the college books, thus terminating his association with Downing.[188] After further back and forth, in the summer of 1965 Vickers moved from Churchill to Downing as Fellow and Director of Studies in English. In February of that year, the Governing Body had voted 16–0 not to admit any students in English for 1966, and with that, after a tumultuous sequence, the Governing Body had finally reached a consensus on English in the college.[189]

The termination of Leavis's association with the college that housed his English School is puzzling. He had invested over three decades into building Downing English, and had worked for the previous decade to secure his legacy – only to repudiate the college in an instant. An important clue to understanding Leavis's behavior lies in his reaction to the end of *Scrutiny* in 1953. Leavis was distraught by the demise of the journal that he and his wife had run as an alternative to mainstream intellectual culture. When Snow (of all people) wrote to offer condolences, Leavis made no secret of the fact that he read the fate of *Scrutiny* as a failure: he was saddened, he admitted to Snow, not least because the end of *Scrutiny* represented a failure to sustain a rallying ground for *life*.[190] To another correspondent, Leavis despondently concluded that it had proved impossible to sustain a living center in Cambridge.[191] Over

---

[183] Governing Body Minutes, Downing College, Vol. 221, 8 May 1964, p. 280, Minute 7.
[184] *Ibid.*, Minute 8.   [185] *Ibid.*, 22 July 1964, p. 302, Minute 5.
[186] *Ibid.*, 2 October 1964, p. 309, Minute 4 (b). This is the official notification, but MacKillop suggested that Leavis resigned immediately upon learning of Vickers's appointment from the Master (p. 342).
[187] *Ibid.*, 23 October 1964, p. 319, Minute 9 (b), (c), (g).
[188] *Ibid.*, 27 November 1964, p. 334, Minute 23.
[189] *Ibid.*, 19 February 1965, p. 354, Minute 7.
[190] Leavis to Snow, 6 January 1954, HRC: Snow 132.10.
[191] Leavis to Holbrook, 3 December 1953, Downing College: DCPP/LEA/4 Leavis, F. R. (1).

time, however, the demise of *Scrutiny* was transformed into its ultimate vindication. After all, as long as it was running the journal remained in danger of corruption, as the need for copy and contributors threatened to force the Leavises to compromise their standards. Ceasing publication prevented such compromise, and its twenty volumes would forever testify to the possibility of maintaining standards in criticism. Moreover, *Scrutiny*'s end itself demonstrated the power of the enemies it had opposed, forcing (from Leavis's perspective) the world to acknowledge their reality once and for all. By the time Cambridge University Press agreed to reprint the whole series for sale to libraries, Leavis viewed the end of *Scrutiny* very differently than he had in 1954. Now, he insisted, *Scrutiny* represented not defeat but victory, affirming the possibility of maintaining a center of criticism in the face of overwhelming opposition.[192]

Similarly, for Leavis the end of the English School confirmed its place in history. After his resignation it ceased to exist, and so it would never be compromised by the professional ethos that increasingly pervaded the college, the English Faculty, and the university. Under Leavis, Downing had stood for something other than that ethos, an achievement made all the more impressive when its ultimate failure demonstrated the power of the forces it had opposed. By terminating the English School, Leavis sacrificed the physical institution to preserve the idea of the college. He was aware of the finality of this last desperate measure, writing after the fact that he had used his "H-Bomb."[193] He knew his resignation to be as permanent as it was devastating: in a final, terrible act of strength, F. R. Leavis had pulled the walls of Downing English down around him.

Conclusion

This chapter has explored an extended moment in university reform in postwar Britain. After the Second World War, universities were refashioned according to the demands of a technocratic state and culture. The assumptions governing the university remained hierarchical, but in the interests of national survival that hierarchy was opened to a broader proportion of society. In this context, rather than a definitive policy break, the Robbins Report is significant as evidence of a moment when the mission of the university was opened to reconsideration.

---

[192] F. R. Leavis, "A Retrospect," in Vol. 20 of *Scrutiny: A Quarterly Review* (Cambridge University Press, 1963), pp. 1–24.
[193] Leavis to David Matthews, 26 September 1964, Emmanuel: ECA COL 9.59.a.116.

Into that moment were thrust various ideas and ideals, and the Rede and Richmond lectures offered two such visions. Snow envisioned the university as a site of professional training, equipping future generations with the tools and dispositions that would enable Britain to prosper in an international economy. Leavis envisioned the university as a center of social criticism, a check upon – and counterbalance to – advancing specialization and instrumentalism in modern civilization. These two programs – of a university integrated with the economy and society, and of a university secured against the corruptions of economy and society – contended at once in the realm of ideas (as lectures offered in public) and politics (as policies advanced in colleges). As Snow and Leavis each worked to translate these ideals into institutional forms, they proceeded according to contrary conceptions of how politics worked. For Snow, politics consisted of tactical maneuvering and coalition building; whereas for Leavis, politics demanded deliberate intransigence and targeted outrage. Snow's efforts met with institutional success when he inserted an ally into a Cambridge college, but ended in ideological failure when that ally refused to endorse Snow's work; Leavis's efforts met with institutional failure when he precipitated the destruction of his English School, but they ended in ideological success to the extent that that failure was recast as testimony of his victory.

This competition between Snow and Leavis – and, by extension, the competition between their respective ideals – extended beyond the institutional confines of their colleges and the geographical confines of Cambridge. Snow and Leavis were offering contrary interpretations of what they understood to be modern civilization, and, as the next chapter shows, these interpretations turned on their readings of history.

4   The making of English social history

Human science or a human face?

The "two cultures" debate raged in the letters pages of the *Spectator* throughout March 1962, and it spiked again upon the hardback publication of Leavis's lecture in October. By the end of the year their feud might have seemed to have run its course, but Snow – still seething – was waiting for the opportunity to respond. Then, in the spring of 1963, he received a letter from the Cambridge historian Peter Laslett.[1] Laslett had already established himself as a historian of early modern political thought, but in the early 1960s his interests were shifting from individual thinkers to broader social structures.[2] His research lacked support in Cambridge, however, so he contacted Snow in hopes of securing a benefactor. Recognizing Laslett as a potential ally in his argument against Leavis, Snow agreed to assist Laslett's nascent Cambridge Group for the History of Population and Social Structure. The following year, when Laslett sent a draft of the first five chapters of *The World We Have Lost*, Snow was delighted: here was a new social history, employing the tools of the social sciences to demolish the romantic delusions of his critics.[3] But despite his overall approval, Snow objected to the penultimate sentence of Laslett's first chapter: "Time was when the whole of life went forward in the family, in a circle of loved, familiar faces, known and fondled objects, all to human size." In this – what was to become one of the most famous lines of historical prose of its era – Snow detected the very nostalgia that the new social history was supposed to eradicate.[4]

---

[1] Peter Laslett to C. P. Snow, 18 May 1963, Harry Ransom Humanities Research Center (HRC): Snow 132.3.
[2] John Locke, *Two Treatises of Government*, ed. Peter Laslett (Cambridge University Press, 1960).
[3] "I think it is a remarkable achievement, and will transform the whole of this kind of study." Snow to Laslett, 5 March 1964, HRC: Snow 132.3.
[4] "I was struck by the closing paragraph of your Chapter I when you talk about a life surrounded by the 'loved familiar faces'. This phrase seems to me to pre-judge the emotional experience." Snow to Laslett, 4 March 1964, HRC: Snow 132.3.

This collaboration between Snow and Laslett stands at the intersection of two stories from the 1960s: the development of a scientific style of history, and the "two cultures" controversy.[5] History assumed center stage in the Snow–Leavis controversy in two ways. First, their Rede and Richmond lectures advanced competing interpretations of the Industrial Revolution: Snow thought industrialization to have been a good thing, believing it to have provided material prosperity and social opportunity to the majority of the population; whereas Leavis was critical of industrialization, believing it to have nearly destroyed the last vestiges of the organic community and the language it sustained. These contrary interpretations of the Industrial Revolution emerged as central to the "two cultures" debate because they supported contrary assessments of the present.[6] Second, these arguments about historical interpretation coincided with an ongoing reorientation of the discipline more generally. Social history already had a long pedigree as the study of daily life rather than high politics, but in the early 1960s the field was being recast as a modern, quantitative social science.[7] This effort to refashion social history inspired controversies of its own, most notably the "standard of living debate" between E. J. Hobsbawm, E. P. Thompson, T. S. Ashton, R. M. Hartwell, and others.

These independent developments – the attempted "scientization" of history, and the "two cultures" controversy – improbably intersected when Snow endorsed a scientific social history, whereas Leavis defended a more literary orientation for the field. These positions might seem to

---

[5] On developments in social history (chronologically): Adrian Wilson, ed., "A Critical Portrait of Social History," *Rethinking Social History: English Society 1570–1920* (Manchester University Press, 1993), pp. 9–58; Miles Taylor, "The Beginnings of Modern British Social History?" *History Workshop Journal* 43 (Spring 1997), pp. 155–176; Jim Obelkevich, "New Developments in History in the 1950s and 1960s," *Contemporary British History* 14 (Winter 2000), pp. 125–142, published together with the transcript of a witness seminar held at the Institute of Historical Research, 29 April 1998; William H. Sewell, Jr., "Whatever Happened to the 'Social' in Social History?" in *Schools of Thought: Twenty-Five Years of Interpretive Social Science*, ed. Joan W. Scott and Debra Keates (Princeton University Press, 2001), pp. 209–226; David Cannadine, "Historians in 'The Liberal Hour': Lawrence Stone and J. H. Plumb Re-Visited," *Historical Research* 75 (August 2002), pp. 316–354; E. J. Hobsbawm, *Interesting Times: A Twentieth-Century Life* (London: Allen Lane, 2002), Chapter 17; John Brewer, "New Ways in History, or Talking About My Generation," *Historein* 3 (2001), pp. 27–46. Cannadine discusses social history and the "two cultures" in "The Age of Todd, Plumb, and Snow: Christ's, the 'Two Cultures,' and the 'Corridors of Power'," in *Christ's: A Cambridge College over Five Centuries*, ed. David Reynolds (London: Macmillan, 2005).

[6] See Stefan Collini, "The Literary Critic and the Village Labourer: 'Culture' in Twentieth-Century Britain," *Transactions of the Royal Historical Society* 14 (2004), pp. 93–116, especially pp. 112–116.

[7] Wilson, "A Critical Portrait of Social History"; Taylor, "The Beginnings of Modern British Social History?"

map onto a reading of their argument as a dispute between advocates of the arts and the sciences, and correspond with a reading of the "standard of living controversy" as a conflict between optimistic, quantitative historians and their pessimistic, literary colleagues. Upon closer examination, however, these divisions break down, and they do so in a way that suggests that the alliances in the effort to forge a new social history were structured by ideological commitments rather than disciplinary inclinations. In their particular corner of this broader conflict – a corner that included key British historians, as well as major figures among the New Left – Snow and Leavis each secured powerful allies in their efforts to translate ideological visions into disciplinary forms.

Social history in the 1960s

History was a thriving discipline when Snow delivered the Rede Lecture in 1959. As the welfare state supplied increasing numbers of students, economic prosperity provided matching resources. The number of students in higher education was in the process of doubling between 1954 and 1966, and in 1963 the Robbins Report promised continuing – indeed, accelerating – growth.[8] As David Cannadine writes, "Undeniably, the period from the late 1940s to the early 1970s was indeed a Golden Age for professional British historians, a time when academe in general was an affluent society, and when Clio in particular had never had it so good."[9] At the same time, historians throughout the West were rethinking the methods and perspectives of the field. In France, the historians associated with Fernand Braudel and the *Annales* school were demoting the significance of personalities and political events in favor of the analysis of long-term population trends, climate, and geography. In the United States, the "cliometricians" were employing a combination of neo-classical economics, statistical analysis, and data-processing technologies to revisit major questions in American history. And in Britain, the historians of the Communist Party Historians' Group, established in 1946 and including Rodney Hilton, Christopher Hill, E. P. Thompson, and E. J. Hobsbawm, spread out across the centuries to reconfigure the entire landscape of British history.[10]

---

[8] Hobsbawm, "Growth of an Audience," *Times Literary Supplement*, 7 April 1966, p. 283; *Higher Education: Report of the Committee Appointed by the Prime Minister under the Chairmanship of Lord Robbins, 1961–1963* (London: HMSO, 1963; cmnd. 2154).

[9] Cannadine, "The State of British History," *Times Literary Supplement*, 10 October 1986, p. 1139.

[10] On the history of historiography: Georg G. Iggers, *New Directions in European Historiography* (Middletown, Conn.: Wesleyan University Press, 1975); Iggers, *Historiography*

The members of the group went their separate ways following the convulsions in international communism in 1956, but their concern to widen the scope of historical inquiry and reorient its perspective informed the developing field of social history. Nowhere could that development be better seen than in the journal they had established: *Past and Present* introduced the *Annales* demographers to a British readership, and it provided a forum for debates over the transition from feudalism to capitalism. During the 1950s economic history, the history of the poor, and the history of everyday life combined to create a more confident role for the increasing number of social historians.[11] By 1960 social history looked to be the most promising area for young historians to enter, and in 1966 Keith Thomas demonstrated the field's confidence when he declared in the *Times Literary Supplement*, "The social history of the future will . . . not be a residual subject but a central one, around which all other branches of history are likely to be organized."[12] John Brewer recalls the appeal of these trends to university students at the time – trends that seemed to promise emancipation from Victorian constraints, and that were in sync with the politics of popular culture and Labour revisionism.[13] Social history was situated at the vanguard of these trends, its advocates and practitioners investing methodological innovations with the powerful appeal of scientific modernization.

Social history had not always been associated with technical innovation. In 1903 G. M. Trevelyan, who later penned the landmark *English Social History* (1942), challenged the contention of J. B. Bury, Regius Professor at Cambridge, that history was a science. Trevelyan insisted

---

in the Twentieth Century: From Scientific Objectivity to the Postmodern Challenge (Hanover, NH: Wesleyan University Press, 1997); in the United States, Michael Kammen, ed., *The Past Before Us: Contemporary Historical Writing in the United States* (Ithaca: Cornell University Press, 1980); in Britain, Dennis Dworkin, *Cultural Marxism in Postwar Britain: History, the New Left, and the Origins of Cultural Studies* (Durham: Duke University Press, 1997), Chapter 1. Taylor points to a non-Marxist lineage of social history in "The Beginnings of Modern British Social History?"; Hobsbawm recounts the history of the Historians' Group in "The Historians' Group of the Communist Party," in *Rebels and Their Causes*, ed. Maurice Cornforth (London: Lawrence and Wishart, 1978), pp. 21–47.

[11] Wilson, "A Critical Portrait of Social History"; Hobsbawm, "From Social History to the History of Society," *Daedalus* 100 (Winter 1971), pp. 20–45, especially pp. 21–22.

[12] Keith Thomas, "The Tools and the Job," *Times Literary Supplement*, 7 April 1966, p. 276. The claim about the field's commanding position by 1960 is from Lawrence Stone, *The Past and the Present Revisited* (London: Routledge, 1987), p. 12. Thomas has since revisited both his essay, and that issue of the *TLS*, in "History Revisited," *Times Literary Supplement*, 11 October 2006, reprinted as "The Changing Shape of Historical Interpretation," in *Penultimate Adventures with Britannia: Personalities, Politics, and Culture in Britain*, ed. Wm. Roger Louis (London: I. B. Tauris, 2008), pp. 43–51.

[13] Brewer, "New Ways in History, or Talking About My Generation."

that history remained a literary endeavor, and during the next century he and Bury defined the opposite poles in an identity crisis that bedeviled the profession.[14] With Trevelyan as its advocate, social history fell on the literary side of the divide – so much so that the great Elizabethan historian John Neale later recalled his frustration with the term "social history," due to its connotations of "the old pretty-pretty, descriptive stuff, void of intellectual guts."[15] After the Second World War social historians began aligning their field with the more rigorous social sciences, but in some ways science had long served as a model for historians. Professionalizing historians had cast their field in the mould of the natural sciences since the 1870s, culminating in Bury's declaration in 1903 that "history is a science, no less and no more."[16] "Science" in this sense provided a professional model, and it referred to the production of specialized knowledge, based in the university, subject to peer review, and disseminated through journals. Then, from the 1930s, the actual content of historiography came to be influenced by the social sciences: first economics, then sociology.[17] *Annales* depicted history as a social science, a sentiment echoed in 1952 in the inaugural issue of *Past and Present*: "We believe that the methods of reason and science are at least as applicable to history as geology, paleontology, ecology or meteorology, though the process of change among humans is immensely more complex."[18]

During the next fifteen years these trends gained momentum, culminating in 1966 in a special issue of the *Times Literary Supplement* on "New Ways in History." Keith Thomas exhibited the confidence of the field in his bracing leading essay.[19] He depicted British historiography as finally emerging from fifty years of amateurism. By contrast with their counterparts in the United States and Europe, he argued, British historians had regrettably remained separated from sociology, and had pursued their work as a craft rather than a science. Recently, however, the social sciences had breathed new life into the field, and Thomas

---

[14] John Neale, "History in the Scientific Age," *Nature* 199 (24 August 1963), pp. 735–737. Trevelyan's essay is included in *Clio, a Muse: and Other Essays* (New York: Longman's, Green, and Company, 1931).

[15] Neale, "History in the Scientific Age," p. 736. On Trevelyan, see Cannadine, *G. M. Trevelyan: A Life in History* (London: Harper Collins, 1992).

[16] From Bury's inaugural lecture as Regius Professor, quoted in Iggers, *New Directions in European Historiography*, p. 4. On the model of the natural sciences in the professionalization of British history, see T. W. Heyck, *The Transformation of Intellectual Life in Victorian England* (New York: St. Martin's Press, 1982), Chapter 5.

[17] Stone, *The Past and the Present Revisited*, pp. 11, 15.

[18] "Introduction," *Past and Present* 1 (February 1952), p. iii.

[19] Thomas, "The Tools and the Job." Brewer recalls the impact of this essay in "New Ways in History, or Talking About My Generation."

predicted that the hidebound historians in Oxford, and at the *English Historical Review*, would soon be forced aside in favor of the new generation. For the first time, he continued, history was becoming safe for professionals, and computerized analysis was no longer exclusive to economic history: "*All historical propositions* relating to the behaviour of large groups, for example, about illiteracy or religious activity, are susceptible of treatment in this way, *and indeed permit of no other.*"[20] Thomas's essay was methodology as manifesto, serving notice that the future of history had arrived – and that future was a scientific social history.

This is not to deny the diversity of social history in this period. Trevelyan's *English Social History* could hardly have been more different from the work of the Historians' Group of the Communist Party, both of which contrasted again with Thomas's liberal, modernizing sensibility. And although the appeal of quantitative social science was prominent, it was by no means unanimous – as attested to by E. P. Thompson's warning in the same number of the *Times Literary Supplement*: "A quantitative methodology," he wrote, "must not be allowed to remain uncriticized which obliterates (as 'literary' or as 'atypical') whole categories of evidence."[21] These trends generated outright opposition as well: Hugh Trevor-Roper warned of "the creeping paralysis of professionalism" in the journals, conferences, and jargon attending the growth of the discipline, and Geoffrey Elton warned that the new approaches amounted to "false gods."[22] Rather than the emergence of a monolithic "social history," the early 1960s should be viewed as a period of diverse possibilities for a field whose disparate origins and methodological catholicity rendered it attractive to a range of practitioners. These practitioners had the opportunity to influence the methodology, perspective, content – indeed, the very definition – of a field that seemed poised to establish the parameters of inquiry for the coming generation. And when the Robbins Report stressed the need to double undergraduate places in five years, promised to increase postgraduate numbers in the social sciences and humanities, and endorsed the founding of six new universities, it became clear that the opportunities were institutional as well as intellectual.[23] To adapt Trevelyan's famous phrase,

[20] Thomas, "The Tools and the Job," p. 276 (emphasis mine).
[21] E. P. Thompson, "History From Below," *Times Literary Supplement*, 6 April 1966, pp. 279–280.
[22] Trevor-Roper quoted in Thomas, "The Tools and the Job," p. 276; Elton quoted in *Recent Historians of Great Britain: Essays on the Post-1945 Generation*, ed. Walter Arnstein (Ames: Iowa State University Press, 1990), p. 7.
[23] Robbins, *et al.*, *Higher Education*, pp. 259, 279, 284.

social history was history with the politics very much *in* – and it was in this context that Snow and Leavis advanced their alternative visions for the field.

Literary optimists

Snow's collaboration with Laslett testifies to his interest in establishing history as a social science, and it might seem in accord with a reading of the "two cultures" debate as a disciplinary battle between advocates of the arts and the sciences. But Snow's interest in social history actually predated his association of it with social science. His primary motivation was not to ground history in scientific methodology, but rather to advance his interpretation of the material progress afforded by industrialization. As the "two cultures" debate unfolded in the early 1960s, Snow armed this optimistic reading of history with the language of science and modernization – advocating a new social history, but never losing sight of his primary aim.

Snow had been interested in social history since his first statement on the "two cultures," three years before his Rede Lecture in Cambridge.[24] Writing in the *New Statesman*, he claimed that, while little of the "traditional" culture interested scientists, they avidly read social history. By "social history" Snow meant not quantitative analysis, but "the sheer mechanics of living, how men ate, built, traveled, worked," and he pointed in particular to the work of G. M. Trevelyan, the supervisor of his friend J. H. Plumb.[25] Plumb had arrived in Cambridge in 1933, and, after working on code-breaking during the war, he was elected a Fellow of Christ's College in 1946. He soon figured at the forefront of social history, and edited *Studies in Social History* as a tribute to Trevelyan in 1955. This collection attested to the literary orientation of the field at this time, as Plumb's dedication praised Trevelyan as one "who for more than fifty years has maintained the tradition that history is literature." To Plumb that tradition flowed into the new social history, the field that he thought promised the greatest insights of the coming generation.[26]

Although they frequently followed the parlance of the day in referring to their politics as "socialist," by the early 1960s – after more radical

[24] Snow, "The Two Cultures," *New Statesman and Nation*, 6 October 1956, pp. 413–414.
[25] *Ibid.*, p. 413.
[26] J. H. Plumb, ed., *Studies in Social History: A Tribute to G. M. Trevelyan* (New York: Longman's, Green, and Company, 1955); Plumb on the promise of social history is on page xiv. On Plumb, see Cannadine, "Sir John Plumb," *History Today* (February 2002), pp. 26–28; Cannadine, "John Harold Plumb," *Proceedings of the British Academy* 124 (2004), pp. 269–309; "Historians in 'The Liberal Hour'."

beginnings – Plumb and Snow shared liberal commitments. Like Snow, Plumb considered himself left of center, progressive but not Marxist, and he supported Hugh Gaitskell and Harold Wilson in Britain and John F. Kennedy in the United States. Apropos of his own journey from Leicester to Cambridge, the cornerstone of Plumb's creed was the industrious individual, and he, too, believed that the ideal society would enable individuals to realize their potential. Plumb's embrace of Thatcherism in the 1980s would surprise his friends and colleagues, in part because his politics in the 1960s were in line with the modernizing, technocratic wing of the Labour Party – of which his friend Snow was a prominent representative. This political vision was inextricable from their reading (and writing) of history.

The year of the debut of Snow's "two cultures" thesis also saw publication of Plumb's *Sir Robert Walpole: The Making of a Statesman*.[27] Plumb had written his PhD dissertation in the shadow of Lewis Namier, but in the years afterward he came to view his work as a challenge to Namier.[28] His taste for narrative conflicted with Namier's structural histories, and he confided to Snow that "there is a deep resistance in the Namier school to what I am trying to do." That resistance, he knew, was well-founded: "I stand for something quite different to the Namier school."[29] Snow shared this hostility to Namierite history, because he believed that Namier's static analysis failed to acknowledge progress over time.[30] Snow wanted to see Namier's influence challenged, because he believed that his stature and methods prevented recognition of the fact of material betterment over time.[31] This reading of history as progress, but as the unfolding of material betterment rather than political liberty, might be labeled a "new Whiggery" – and just as the Whigs had overcome a series of Papist, Jacobite, and French threats to English liberty, in the new Whiggery the agents of prosperity were continually beset by reactionary rivals. In the Rede Lecture, Snow identified these opponents of material betterment – somewhat surprisingly – as the literary intellectuals of the previous two centuries.

---

[27] J. H. Plumb, *Sir Robert Walpole: The Making of a Statesman* (London: Cresset, 1956).

[28] In "The Age of Todd, Plumb, and Snow," Cannadine discusses Namier's influence on Plumb's early work, especially his doctoral thesis: "Elections to the House of Commons in the Reign of William III," unpublished PhD thesis, University of Cambridge (1936).

[29] Plumb to Snow, 19 April 1956, 28 April 1956, HRC: Snow 166.6. For another challenge to Namier at this time, see Herbert Butterfield, *George III and the Historians* (London: Collins, 1957).

[30] Snow to Plumb, 9 January 1956, Cambridge University Library (CUL): Plumb papers, Box "C.P. Snow + Pam: 1946 to 1968," File "Snow 1946 to 1968."

[31] Snow to Plumb, 25 June 1958, CUL: Plumb papers, Box "C.P. Snow + Pam: 1946 to 1968," File "Snow 1946 to 1968."

This optimistic interpretation of the Industrial Revolution was central to Snow's argument in *The Two Cultures*. In a ringing phrase – one that would become fiercely contested – Snow insisted that laboring people had eagerly welcomed industrialization: "For, with singular unanimity, in any country where they have had the chance, the poor have walked off the land into the factories as fast as the factories could take them."[32] He argued that they had benefited accordingly: "Health, food, education; nothing but the industrial revolution could have spread them right down to the very poor."[33] And he insisted that the lesson for the present was plain: "For, of course, one truth is straightforward. Industrialization is the only hope of the poor."[34] Rejection of this assessment, Snow believed, revealed suspect political sympathies: "The industrial revolution looked very different according to whether one saw it from above or below"; and creative writers proved particularly incapable of understanding the benefits of industrialization: "Plenty of them shuddered away . . . some, like Ruskin and William Morris and Thoreau and Emerson and Lawrence, tried various kinds of fancies which were not in effect more than screams of horror."[35] These screams, Snow suggested, betrayed reactionary incomprehension: "Intellectuals, in particular literary intellectuals, are natural Luddites," and the successors to these Luddites, the Modernist writers of the early twentieth century, were implicated in the worst crimes to follow: "Didn't the influence of all they represent bring Auschwitz that much nearer?"[36] In *The Two Cultures*, Snow sought to establish the interpretation of the Industrial Revolution as the litmus test of contemporary morality.

"The New Left boys"

Publicly Snow named his opponents as "literary intellectuals" or the "traditional culture," but privately he directed his animus and efforts against the emerging New Left. He wrote to ask Raymond Williams about his connections to *Universities and Left Review* and the *New Reasoner*, which were soon to amalgamate into the *New Left Review*. In these radicals, Snow thought that he spotted a familiar type: romantic intellectuals who were blind to the misery of the past, and who consequently opted out of meaningful, reformist politics in the present. He differentiated what he took to be their critique of modern society – mere "existential discontent" – from his own preference for pragmatic

---

[32] Snow, *The Two Cultures and the Scientific Revolution* (Cambridge University Press, 1959), p. 25.
[33] *Ibid.*, p. 26. [34] *Ibid.*, p. 24. [35] *Ibid.*, pp. 26, 24. [36] *Ibid.*, pp. 21, 7.

politics.[37] Snow was repeating advice that he had already offered to Williams, having implored Williams (and Richard Hoggart) to read J. D. Bernal's *World Without War*. "*Of course*, there is a great deal wrong with industrial society as we now know it," he had written. "The thing to do is to find ways to put that right, not dream ourselves into a myth of an eighteenth century which never existed."[38] This plea of 1958 anticipated the argument – and even the language – of his Rede Lecture six months later: "Industrialization is now, as it always has been, the one hope of the poor."[39] In order to foster meaningful change in the present, Snow believed it imperative to embrace the progress afforded by recent history – and, in his view, the New Left erred on both counts.

In 1960, Norman Podhoretz – a rising star among New York intellectuals, who had recently been named editor of *Commentary* – pressed his friend Snow for an article about the British New Left. Snow agreed, but he told Podhoretz that he wanted to widen his scope to consider progressive politics more generally. This would include the *New Left Review* circle, but not be limited to them: "As you will easily guess," he wrote, "I have not much use for a lot of them; politics is not simply, or even mainly, a matter of existential discontent."[40] When Podhoretz pressed him again about the article, his verdict sharpened: "I shall have to read a certain amount of the more or less half-baked outpourings of the New Left here," Snow wrote. "The more I think of them the more hopelessly inept I think they are, and they have about as much relation to real politics as they have to major league baseball."[41] Snow was particularly skeptical of their reading of history, and – although he respected Williams and Hoggart – he viewed them as the inheritors of a socialism derived from those archetypal Luddites, Ruskin and Morris – a tradition, he noted more than two years before the Richmond Lecture, they arrived at through F. R. Leavis.[42]

---

[37] Raymond Williams to Snow, 3 December 1959, HRC: Snow 210.1. For more accurate accounts of the New Left, see Dworkin, *Cultural Marxism in Postwar Britain*; Michael Kenny, *The First New Left: British Intellectuals after Stalin* (London: Lawrence and Wishart, 1995).

[38] Snow, "Act in Hope," *New Statesman*, 15 November 1958, p. 699 (emphasis in original).

[39] *Ibid.*   [40] Snow to Podhoretz, 2 February 1960, HRC: Snow 165.10.

[41] Snow to Podhoretz, 9 March 1960, HRC: Snow 165.10.

[42] "Williams and Hoggart are perfectly serious characters, but as you have perceived, most of their kind of socialism derives from Morris and Ruskin seen through the eyes of F. R. Le[a]vis. This means the practical relevance is pretty small. (Williams is a more complex case. He contrived to be a Leavisite and a Marxist at the same time. This gave him a nervous breakdown.)" Snow to Podhoretz, 2 February 1960, HRC: Snow 165:10. In the end, Snow decided not to write the article after all: Snow to Podhoretz, 24 January 1961, HRC: Snow 165.11.

Snow was correct to be wary of Leavis. In the Richmond Lecture of February 1962, Leavis confronted Snow squarely on the ground of history: "[Snow] knows nothing of history," he declared. "He has no notion of the changes in civilisation that have produced his 'literary culture'."[43] Leavis particularly targeted Snow's reading of industrialization: "[O]f the human history of the Industrial Revolution, of the human significances entailed in that revolution ... it is hardly an exaggeration to say that Snow exposes complacently a complete ignorance."[44] He rejected Snow's assertion that the poor had eagerly left the land for the factories: "This, of course, is mere brute assertion, callous in its irresponsibility ... If one points out that the actual history has been, with significance for one's apprehension of the full human problem, incomparably and poignantly more complex than that, Snow dismisses one as a 'natural Luddite.'"[45] He ridiculed the crass materialism that could tolerate such a charge: "The upshot is that if you insist on the need for any other kind of concern, entailing forethought, action and provision, about the human future – any other kind of misgiving – than that which talks in terms of productivity, material standards of living, hygienic and technological progress, then you are Luddite."[46] Yet Leavis insisted, "I am not a Luddite," and his Richmond Lecture amounted to a denunciation of Snow, his credentials, and his thesis – a moral judgment, to be sure, but one that he leveled on the terrain of history.[47]

Despite their impulse to dismiss Leavis's lecture as the outburst of a paranoid outcast, Snow and Plumb knew that their opponents on these questions extended well beyond Leavis. Plumb connected Leavis to Williams and Hoggart, and cast them all in the tradition of "the dangerous descendants of the craft-socialists – the Chestertons, Coles, ultimately ... Morrises, who worked to turn their back on industrialization and, as most people do, tried to find an historical justification for their attitude and found it – uncritically – in Barbara and J. L. Hammond."[48] Their counterattack, then, needed to aim at their rivals' intellectual bulwark. In the *Spectator* debate, Plumb – who had recently celebrated Trevelyan's insistence that history was literature – now invoked the social sciences, particularly anthropology, psychology, and economics, against Leavis's romantic misreading of history.[49] Snow, meanwhile, assured Podhoretz, "The English social historians are getting very tired of what they and I regard as a mis-reading of the

[43] Leavis, *Two Cultures? The Significance of C. P. Snow* (London: Chatto and Windus, 1962), p. 16.
[44] *Ibid.*, p. 10.   [45] *Ibid.*, p. 24.   [46] *Ibid.*, p. 19.   [47] *Ibid.*, p. 26.
[48] Plumb to Snow, 1 July 1962, HRC: Snow 166.9.
[49] Plumb, "Letters," *Spectator*, 30 March 1962, p. 396.

eighteenth and nineteenth century social condition here, as performed by the New Left Boys."[50] When he finally revisited the "two cultures," the new social history took center stage.[51]

Social history, a second look

"The Two Cultures: A Second Look" appeared in the *Times Literary Supplement* in October 1963. The essay registered a shift in Snow's tactics, from historical interpretation to historical methodology. Snow reported that he discerned a third culture coming into existence, ranged across various disciplines that were all committed to the empirical investigation of human existence: sociology, demography, political science, government, economics, medicine, psychology, architecture – and social history. Snow had already been aware of the social sciences at the time of his Rede Lecture, in which he acknowledged that his friends in social history and sociology would resent being classed with literary intellectuals.[52] In 1959 Snow had judged that his argument benefited from the clarity offered by the "two cultures" dichotomy, but in 1963 his goal was to mobilize allies. "A Second Look" devoted considerable attention to the "third culture," especially social history. Snow brazenly challenged his critics to produce evidence of a past golden age, so that the social historians could settle the matter once and for all.[53] Their investigations into the effects of industrialization – which Snow identified as "the fighting point of this whole affair" – required that these historians remain in contact with their scientific colleagues.[54] These historians worked in a mode rather different from Trevelyan, whom Snow had identified with social history seven years before. Their approach was scientific (if not a science), and Snow lauded them as lovers of truth, professionals who analyzed fact rather than sentiment, and who communicated their findings in the "dry but appallingly eloquent language of statistics."[55] Ranged against them were purveyors of myth, peddlers of lies, and advocates of "false social history," who stubbornly clung to "the stereotypes of fifty years ago."[56] But Snow

---

[50] Snow to Podhoretz, 25 May 1962, HRC: Snow 165.12.
[51] Snow, "The Two Cultures: A Second Look," *Times Literary Supplement*, 25 October 1963, pp. 839–844; the following citations refer to its publication, together with *The Two Cultures*, as *The Two Cultures: and A Second Look* (Cambridge University Press, 1964).
[52] Snow, *The Two Cultures*, pp. 8–9.
[53] Snow, *The Two Cultures: and A Second Look*, p. 84.   [54] *Ibid.*, p. 70.
[55] *Ibid.*, p. 83.   [56] *Ibid.*, p. 84.

declared that the tide was with the emerging third culture, citing in particular the demographers in France and Laslett in Britain.

Laslett was the driving force behind the most ambitious project in quantitative historical analysis in Britain. He and E. A. Wrigley would soon establish the Cambridge Group for the History of Population and Social Structure, which scoured parish registers to assemble data on fertility, mortality, and marriage patterns for the whole of society from the Tudors to Victoria. Laslett's language when soliciting funding stressed the group's scientific pedigree: their method would be "systematic," their technique "statistical." The Cambridge Group was Britain's answer to the *Annales*, employing modern concepts, techniques, and methods to answer questions about society before and during industrialization; Laslett ultimately hoped their findings would transform curricula in Cambridge and beyond.[57] Snow became captivated by this research as he was preparing his response to Leavis. "Do you know Peter Laslett?" he asked George Steiner. "I was deeply impressed by his piece in *The Listener* this week."[58] Snow's enthusiasm for Laslett's methodological innovations was of a piece with his ideological stance: "I have been meaning to write to you for some time," he later told Laslett. "I think [your demographic researches] are an essential foundation for any society that you and I and people like us now want."[59] A society, that is, that would acknowledge the fact of material progress, attribute that progress to industrialization, and export them both throughout the world. In order to advance this program, they first needed to win the historical argument.

In 1963, however, the prospects for Snow's new allies were bleak. When he urged Laslett to drive his research students forward, Laslett had to reply that he only had a library assistant and three volunteers. They were applying for a grant, though, and Laslett hoped they might use Snow as a reference.[60] The next year, their application faced a critical juncture: Laslett believed they were on the verge of receiving £5,000, but they actually needed three times that amount. Might Snow intervene? "[F]or if we fail with the Gulbenkian now," Laslett wrote despondently, "it will be at least six months before we can screw up another Foundation to the point Thornton has now reached and by then I may have lost the support of my volunteer assistants, and the university may well have decided that the lack of Foundation support demonstrates

[57] Calouste Gulbenkian Foundation (London), Annual Report for 1964, Entry 43.
[58] Snow to George Steiner, 7 February 1963, HRC: Snow 191.4.
[59] Snow to Laslett, 20 May 1963, HRC: Snow 132.3.
[60] *Ibid.*; Laslett to Snow, 27 May 1963, HRC: Snow 132.3.

that the project is no good."[61] Anticipating a Labour victory in the
upcoming election, Snow had already offered to introduce Laslett to
their spokesperson on education and science, Richard Crossman.[62] Now
he responded to Laslett's latest request by insisting that it was in the
public interest that the Cambridge Group receive financial support. He
immediately wrote to the Gulbenkian Foundation, and also began to think
about raising funds in the United States.[63] The recourse to American
money proved unnecessary: Laslett informed Snow that the Gulbenkian
Foundation had awarded the Cambridge Group £8,000 – not as much as
they hoped for, but enough to establish them in Cambridge.[64]

The first product of this research was Laslett's landmark account of
pre-industrial society, *The World We Have Lost* (1965).[65] His findings
showed that early modern families tended to be nuclear rather than
extended, that marriages occurred later than historians had thought, and
that populations evidenced unexpected mobility. He also confronted
rivals on two fronts: Marxist scholars, and "impressionist" historians.
He had already announced the death of "class" as a category in 1958,
explaining that "class is on the way out for historians: it is going fast, and
faster among the English economic historians than anywhere else."[66] By
1965 his impatience with Marxism was total: *The World We Have Lost*
denied the utility of "class" in discussions of pre-industrial society,
dismissed "alienation" as twentieth-century cant, insisted that the
English Revolution was no social revolution, and proposed that the
major historical division was between pre-industrial and industrial
(rather than feudal and capitalist) society. Empirical investigation,
Laslett explained, was finally disposing of the Marxist framework:
"It would, if it were possible, be far better to lay 'The Rise of the Gentry'
carefully alongside 'The Rise of the Middle Classes', and to place them
reverently together in the great and growing collection of outmoded
historians' idiom."[67] Impressionist historians – those who relied on
literary evidence – fared little better at Laslett's hands. Instead of relying
upon misleading snippets of literary evidence, demographic analysis
promised to ground historical knowledge on the basis of fact. On the

[61] Laslett to Snow, 28 February 1964, HRC: Snow 132.3.
[62] Snow to Laslett, 20 May 1963, HRC: Snow 132.3.
[63] Snow to Laslett, 5 March 1964, HRC: Snow 132.3.
[64] Laslett to Snow, 4 June 1964, HRC: Snow 132.3.
[65] Peter Laslett, *The World We Have Lost* (London: Methuen, 1965). Laslett stated in the
   introduction that the book was not a publication of the Cambridge Group, but the
   identification of the book with the Cambridge Group was inevitable. See, for instance,
   the review in the *Times Literary Supplement* of 9 December 1965 (discussed below).
[66] Peter Laslett, "Engels as Historian," *Encounter*, May 1958, pp. 85–86.
[67] Laslett, *The World We Have Lost*, p. 168.

question of the average age of brides, for instance, "[The evidence] decidedly does not confirm the impression made by Shakespeare and the other literary sources. Their evidence must be called systematically deceptive in this matter. It is best to look at the facts in a table."[68]

Tables, facts, demography: *The World We Have Lost* announced a new era of historical science. Dispensing with Marxist categories and literary evidence, history could finally take its place alongside statistics, economics, sociology, and anthropology.[69] And although his title suggested regret for a lost golden age, Laslett leveled a severe verdict on life before the Industrial Revolution: "[T]he coming of industry cannot be shown to have brought economic oppression and exploitation along with it. It was there already."[70] In the world we had lost, he emphasized, infant mortality was higher, life expectancy shorter, living harsher – and only industry made possible the improvements enjoyed in the twentieth century.[71] Snow was thrilled when he read his draft of the first five chapters of *The World We Have Lost*, writing to Laslett twice in two days. Here was the emerging "third culture" that he had fostered privately and endorsed publicly, employing the tools of the social sciences against Marxism and romanticism. Yet his question about Laslett's conclusion to that first chapter is a reminder of his priorities: despite the scientific rhetoric, methodological innovations, and modernizing appeal, Snow's interest in the new social history in 1964 derived from the same impulse as his favorable reference to the old social history in 1956. A scientific social history was not an end, but a means to an end: it was a Trojan horse carrying a liberal reading of industrial progress into classrooms and lecture halls throughout Britain.

Leavis's alternative "social" history

The *Times Literary Supplement* of December 9, 1965 featured a knockabout critique of *The World We Have Lost*.[72] Entitled "The Book of Numbers," the review began by declaring, "The engagement has been long announced, but some will be surprised to learn that the marriage between History and Sociology has already been solemnized . . . *The World We Have Lost* is a manifesto of the new science."[73] It mocked Laslett's scientific pretensions, challenged his use of social science, and defended the use of literary sources. Laslett's failing, according to the

---

[68] *Ibid.*, p. 82.   [69] *Ibid.*, p. 239.   [70] *Ibid.*, p. 3.   [71] *Ibid.*, pp. 126, 94, 45.
[72] "The Book of Numbers," *Times Literary Supplement*, 9 December 1965, pp. 1117–1118.
[73] *Ibid.*, p. 1117.

reviewer, was not that he employed the demographic techniques that had been developed by French historians, but rather that he did so in a slipshod manner: "The new science gives rise to statements about social structure which are, too often, bathetic or wholly imprecise."[74] Laslett was accused of "guessing a little," he was excoriated for his "unsatisfactory manner of treating scanty data," and he was chastized for his failure to employ "expertise" and "objectivity" when handling evidence.[75] The tables were confusing, the documentation thin, the text in need of proofreading. The critique thus targeted the methodological competence upon which Laslett based his intellectual authority. It was not an attack upon social history, but a call for a different kind of social history – one that neither exaggerated claims for quantitative evidence, nor dismissed the value of literary evidence. The anonymous reviewer was E. P. Thompson.[76]

Thompson remarked that *The World We Have Lost* was written for an audience that included Lord Snow, and this was not the first time that Thompson brushed up against Snow. As commentators in *Encounter* gravely attended to the "two cultures" problem, Thompson recognized the political stakes buried within Snow's formulation: "Herod (the liberal) is never more boring than when he appears in the guise of the ameliorative man of science," he wrote in 1960. "[H]ence that schizophrenic feature of Natopolitan ideology, the 'two cultures': the one a vast Cain armed with the Bomb, the other an acquiescent, pietistic Abel, baring his genteel hair-shirt for the blow."[77] Three years later, in *The Making of the English Working Class*, Thompson entered the "two cultures" debate: "When Sir Charles Snow tells us that 'with singular unanimity . . . the poor have walked off the land into the factories as fast as the factories could take them', we must reply, with Dr. Leavis, that the 'actual history' of the 'full human problem [was] incomparably and poignantly more complex than that'."[78] Leavis and Thompson undoubtedly shared literary affinities: Thompson's English teacher at school had been influenced by Leavis, and after the war Thompson had read English in Cambridge.[79] But in an argument in which the primary

---

[74] *Ibid.*   [75] *Ibid.*, p. 1118.
[76] *The Times Literary Supplement Centenary Archive*, available at www.tls.psmedia.com/. Not surprisingly, given Thompson's distinctive prose, E. A. Wrigley later recalled that the identity of the author was soon common knowledge.
[77] E. P. Thompson, "Outside the Whale," in *Out of Apathy* (London: New Left Books, 1960), p. 157.
[78] E. P. Thompson, *The Making of the English Working Class* (London: Gollancz, 1963), p. 445.
[79] E. P. Thompson, *Making History: Writings on Politics and Culture* (New York: New Press, 1994), p. 254.

axis of disagreement was *political*, Thompson (with his commitment to socialist humanism) and Leavis (with his visceral hostility to socialism) made for strange bedfellows indeed. How did they find themselves aligned against Snow and a scientific social history?

From his base in the English School, Leavis advanced an alternative social history. He insisted that the sources for understanding social conditions and historical change were not parish registers but great writers, and that the historian must pay careful attention to this incomparable body of evidence. In 1966, speaking at Cornell and Harvard, Leavis insisted that Dickens, as a great novelist, was in fact a great social historian; the following year, delivering the Clark Lectures in Cambridge, he extended the line of novelist–historians to include the great writers from Dickens to Lawrence.[80] In Leavis's anti-materialist worldview, literature provided the best available gauge of the health of any civilization, and by studying literature the historian would be led to considerations beyond the words on the page:

What, as a civilization to live in and be of, did England offer at such and such a time? As we pass from now to then, what light is thrown on human possibilities – on the potentialities and desirabilities of civilized life? In what respects might it have been better to live then than now? What tentative conception of an ideal civilization are we prompted towards by the hints we gather from history?[81]

To attend to these questions, the historian required training and expertise quite different from that of demographers or statisticians: the ability to read attentively and sensitively. Leavis, no less than Snow, was offering both an interpretation of history and a methodology to effect it.

Leavis subsequently became discouraged by the very trends that so excited Snow. He had previously been critical of Trevelyan's tendency to use literature as an ornament, rather than a source in its own right, but he nevertheless read Trevelyan's work with respect and appreciation.[82] Trevelyan, Leavis thought, had demonstrated the potential for social history to become the study of the whole civilization (even if his use of literary evidence testified to the need to reconfigure the relationship between literature and history). But the next generation of historians seemed to have taken a wrong turn. Leavis blasted Plumb for siding with Snow on the consequences of industrialization, and Plumb later found a

---

[80] F. R. Leavis, *Nor Shall My Sword: Discourses on Pluralism, Compassion and Social Hope* (London: Chatto and Windus, 1972), p. 81; Leavis, *English Literature in Our Time and the University* (London: Chatto and Windus, 1969), pp. 170, 174.

[81] Leavis, "Sociology and Literature," *Scrutiny* 13 (Spring 1945), p. 80.

[82] *Ibid.*, pp. 74–81.

place in the litany of the enlightened who endured Leavis's ridicule.[83] Harold Perkin ran afoul as well: although Leavis employed evidence from *The Origins of Modern English Society* (1969) to refute Snow and Plumb on the migration of the poor into the factories, he also chastized England's first Professor of Social History for his "uncritically enthusiastic" assessment of the Industrial Revolution.[84] Q. D. Leavis thought that Perkin exhibited the failings of a historian who privileged journalistic "facts" over the testimony of creative writers.[85] As her husband insisted, historians neglected literary evidence at their peril: "A study of human nature is a study of social human nature, and the psychologist, sociologist, and social historian aren't in it compared with the great novelists."[86] As Snow wanted, but as Leavis resented, the social historian had joined the company of the psychologist and sociologist.

Leavis's critique of social history was thus part of his argument against the social sciences. This position was not animated by a rejection of social science as such: after all, Q. D. Leavis's *Fiction and the Reading Public* (1932) advocated a variety of sociological analysis, and Leavis and his associates referred to their own approach as "anthropologico-literary."[87] *Scrutiny* related literary production to the society that sustained (or inhibited) it, even as it resisted what it represented as the Marxist tendency to read literature as an expression of social relations. In the early 1940s, speaking to students at the London School of Economics, Leavis explained that his conception of society fell somewhere between the Romantics (who isolated the individual from society) and the Marxists (who collapsed the individual within society). He sought to position himself between these extremes, allowing that the individual was always part of society, but insisting that their relationship was intellectual and spiritual rather than material and economic.[88] After the

---

[83] "Pluralism, Compassion and Social Hope" and "Elites, Oligarchies and an Educated Public," delivered in 1970 and 1971, respectively, at the University of York, published in *Nor Shall My Sword*.

[84] Harold Perkin, *The Origins of Modern English Society, 1780–1880* (London: Routledge, 1969); Leavis, *Nor Shall My Sword*, pp. 193–195.

[85] Q. D. Leavis to D. F. Pocock, 10 August 1971, Emmanuel College, Cambridge: ECA COL 9.59a.121.24.

[86] F. R. Leavis, "Anna Karenina: Thought and Significance in a Great Creative Work," originally in the first number of the *Cambridge Quarterly* in 1965, and later reprinted in Leavis, *Anna Karenina and Other Essays* (London: Chatto and Windus, 1967).

[87] Q. D. Leavis, *Fiction and the Reading Public* (London: Chatto and Windus, 1932). Ian MacKillop, *We Were That Cambridge: F. R. Leavis and the 'Anthropologico-Literary' Group* (Austin: University of Texas, 1993).

[88] F. R. Leavis, "Literature and Society," *Scrutiny* 12 (Winter 1943), pp. 2–11, reprinted in *The Common Pursuit* (London: Chatto and Windus, 1952), pp. 182–194.

war Leavis became increasingly hostile towards trends in sociology, psychology, and linguistics. By wrapping themselves in the language and pretensions of science, he believed, these disciplines were cutting themselves off from the insights of poets and novelists. But especially alarming, from Leavis's point of view, was the Robbins Report's contention that the humanizing complement to natural science could in the future be provided by these social sciences.[89] Leavis continued to sharpen his case, and eventually welcomed Stanislav Andreski's *Social Sciences as Sorcery* (1972).[90] Critics such as Andreski were all too rare, though, and the respect the university paid to the social sciences only confirmed the dire predicament facing *life* itself.

Yet the "two cultures" dichotomy explains Leavis's position no better than Snow's: Leavis directed this critique not against *science*, but against the *social*. In *The Two Cultures*, Snow contrasted the individual condition (ultimately tragic, because destined to die a solitary death) with the social condition (for which there remained the hope of collective improvement). To Leavis, this dichotomy between the *individual* and the *social* drained the latter of life and rendered it an abstraction, an aggregate to be manipulated by technocrats such as Snow and Robbins. "To use the word 'social'," he explained, "as Lord Snow does, is to evacuate 'society' and leave it empty of life."[91] Leavis believed that this conception of society had a history of its own, one that dated from the seventeenth century. He conceived of "society," by contrast, as the meeting of minds in what he called the "third realm," or the "human world." This meeting was possible through language, which was itself the textured inheritance of generations of collaboration; this collaboration then made further creation possible, building on the living language and transmitting it through time. "Human life lives only in individuals," Leavis told those students at the LSE. "I might have said, the truth that *it is only in individuals that society lives*."[92] There was no

---

[89] The Robbins Report is a recurring topic in *English Literature in Our Time and the University, Nor Shall My Sword*, and *The Living Principle* (London: Chatto and Windus, 1975).

[90] Stanislav Andreski, *Social Sciences as Sorcery* (London: Deutsch, 1972), discussed in Leavis, *The Living Principle*, Chapter 1. Andreski had come to Leavis's attention when he had difficulty finding a publisher for *The African Predicament: A Study in the Pathology of Modernisation* (London: Michael Joseph, 1968), which criticized plans to end hunger in Africa through the establishment of bureaucracies along Western lines: Leavis, *Nor Shall My Sword*, pp. 190–191. See Chapter 6 for further discussion of the intellectual connections between Leavis and Andreski.

[91] Leavis, *Nor Shall My Sword*, p. 172.

[92] Leavis, *The Common Pursuit*, p. 185 (emphasis mine). On the "third realm" or "human world," see Dan Jacobson, *Time and Time Again* (New York: Atlantic Monthly Press, 1985), pp. 126–136, especially pp. 126–127.

society apart from the individual, Leavis was saying, and the distinction between them was but another regrettable consequence of the seventeenth century.

Leavis's hostility to social science thus followed from his critique of modern civilization. This is why, despite their ideological differences, Leavis and Thompson found themselves allied against Snow and *The Two Cultures*. Leavis's position was predicated upon an idealized past, and in the 1960s he defiantly advocated an elite university against the democratic tide; whereas Thompson was a democratic socialist, and he placed his faith in ordinary people. But both Leavis and Thompson recognized that Snow's case rested upon his optimistic faith in the progress brought about by industrial civilization, and so their critiques closed in around him at once from the right and the left.

Conclusion

By 1970, Snow's hopes for social history had been dashed. In his final major comment on the "two cultures," he expressed regret that the empirical questions he had raised in "A Second Look" still remained unanswered. Instead of proving the benefits of industrialization, historians seemed to have rejected the notion of progress itself.[93] Elsewhere he explained that he had learned that history differed from science because it was not "automatically progressive": whereas science could not help but show the direction of time's arrow, professional historians had abandoned their commitment to narrative in favor of detailed studies of marginal significance.[94] But Snow had identified a new field in which to invest his hopes: the history of science. A decade before he had suggested that the history of science might function as a bridge between the two cultures, but his interest had now shifted along familiar lines: the history of science appealed not as a bridge between cultures, but because it seemed certain to provide a refuge for progressive narratives in history.[95] In the early 1960s, then, Snow endorsed a scientific social history in the hope that it would confirm his progressive reading of history, and in 1970 he shifted his attention to the history of science for precisely the same reason. In both cases Snow hoped to realize his

---

[93] Snow, "The Case of Leavis and the Serious Case," *Times Literary Supplement*, 9 July 1970, pp. 737–740.

[94] Snow, "The Role of Personality in Science," University of Texas at Austin, 1970 (n.d.), British Library, National Sound Archive: Cassette 1CA0012643.

[95] Snow, "Recent Thoughts on the Two Cultures," Foundation Oration, Birkbeck College, London, 12 December 1961, British Library: WP 8944/39.

optimistic vision in disciplinary form, and in each case the discipline and its methodology were secondary to this ideological goal.[96]

This chapter has examined one aspect of the development of social history in the 1960s. That story consists of two parts: the development of social scientific approaches (a question of method), and the "standard of living" debate (a question of content). These two developments dovetailed to the extent that proponents of quantitative methodologies overlapped with optimistic historians on the question of industrialization, while their pessimistic critics defended qualitative approaches. Previous accounts have tended to collapse these two stories, depicting a single contest between scientific optimists and literary pessimists over social history, but that interpretation is problematized by the intersection of these developments with the "two cultures" controversy. Snow, Leavis, and their respective allies certainly clashed over the interpretation of the Industrial Revolution, but they did so in ways that did not necessarily align with the dichotomies of optimist/pessimist and quantitative/qualitative. Hence Snow's alliance with fellow optimist J. H. Plumb, and the sympathy of both with the literary G. M. Trevelyan; and hence Leavis's alliance with fellow pessimist E. P. Thompson, who invoked (rather than disputed) the need for "precision," "objectivity," and "social science" in criticizing Peter Laslett. This chapter has sought to disentangle disciplinary inclinations from ideological commitments, so as to reveal the ways in which the former could prove malleable in service of the latter.

---

[96] See Chapter 7 for discussion of the ways in which subsequent developments in the history of science would have again frustrated Snow's hopes.

5   The rise of national "decline"

Declinism

The historian of postwar Britain confronts an embarrassment of riches. "Riches" both in the sense of the wealth of available narratives that might be told about recent British history, and of the place of wealth in those narratives. After all, since 1945 Britain has in many ways become a more prosperous, tolerant, and democratic society, and in deciding what stories to tell about that period the historian may elect to emphasize the establishment of the welfare state and subsequent improvement in living standards, the transition in international relations from the British Empire to the European Union, or the increased opportunities available to women, minorities, and the working class. A more critical eye, of course, may be drawn towards any number of competing narratives, such as the partial dismantling of the welfare state in the name of national efficiency, the maintenance of a warfare state in the name of national prestige, or the rise of racism and xenophobia in the name of national identity.

But the historian can tell only so many stories, and the historiography of postwar Britain has tended to emphasize national decline. Perry Anderson's *tour de force* in the *New Left Review* in 1964, "Origins of the Present Crisis," took the anemic state of Britain's economic and political position to be a fact so obvious that it demanded a reinterpretation of the entire course of British history.[1] Declinist historiography flourished in the following decades, most notably in the work of Martin Wiener and Correlli Barnett.[2] Anderson has recently returned to the theme, suggesting that "the British way of coming down in the world might itself be termed a mediocre affair," and comparing Britain's lackluster descent with the more "spectacular failure" enjoyed by France. The story of

---

[1] Perry Anderson, "Origins of the Present Crisis," *New Left Review* 23 (January–February 1964), pp. 26–53.
[2] Martin Wiener, *English Culture and the Decline of the Industrial Spirit, 1850–1980* (Cambridge University Press, 1981); Correlli Barnett, *The Audit of War: The Illusion and Reality of Britain as a Great Nation* (London: Macmillan, 1986). For further discussion of this literature, see the Introduction.

postwar Britain is one of such ineptitude, it seems, that even its decline has been second rate.[3]

There are two general ways of explaining the prominence of "decline" in these accounts of postwar British history. An economic explanation would presume that discussions of decline reflected material developments, such as the trade imbalances and currency crises resulting from Britain's decreasing share of world trade. As the Introduction discussed, however, historians have challenged this interpretation on a number of fronts, to the point that the economic historian Jim Tomlinson now advises that decline "be treated with the same scepticism with which, for example, historians of the sixteenth and seventeenth centuries would now deal with the idea of the 'decline of the gentry.' "[4] A cultural explanation for the prominence of decline, by contrast, resists granting priority to material factors, and instead treats "decline" as a political discourse that itself shaped interpretations of economic change.[5] By contrast with disagreements about the reality or significance of relative economic decline, there is no denying that the discourse of decline – or, to adopt the historian's term, *declinism* – figured prominently in postwar British culture. But if declinism did not simply reflect economic developments, how did it come to occupy so prominent a position in postwar British culture?

Discussions of decline were indeed pervasive in the 1960s, surfacing even in a "two cultures" debate that was ostensibly about the relationship between scientific and literary intellectuals. This chapter, then, follows C. P. Snow and F. R. Leavis as their arguments and ideologies

---

[3] Perry Anderson, "Dégringolade," *London Review of Books*, 2 September 2004, p. 3.

[4] Jim Tomlinson, "Economic 'Decline' in Post-War Britain," in *A Companion to Contemporary Britain, 1939–2000*, ed. Paul Addison and Harriet Jones (Oxford: Blackwell, 2005), p. 164. For overviews of these debates, see Richard English and Michael Kenny, eds., *Rethinking British Decline* (London: Macmillan, 2000); Peter Clarke and Clive Trebilcock, eds., *Understanding Decline: Perceptions and Realities of British Economic Performance* (Cambridge University Press, 1997). The revisionist historiography includes (chronologically): D. N. McCloskey, *If You're So Smart: The Narrative of Economic Expertise* (University of Chicago Press, 1990), pp. 40–55; David Edgerton, *England and the Aeroplane: An Essay on a Militant and Technological Nation* (Basingstoke: Macmillan 1991); Edgerton, *Science, Technology, and the British Industrial "Decline", 1870–1970* (Cambridge University Press, 1996); Jim Tomlinson, "Inventing 'Decline': The Falling Behind of the British Economy in the Postwar Years," *Economic History Review* 49 (1996), pp. 731–757; Tomlinson, *The Politics of Decline: Understanding Post-war Britain* (Harlow: Longman, 2001).

[5] The terminology of "economic" and "cultural" here refers to the general approaches of economic and cultural history, rather than the self-identifications of prominent exemplars in these debates: so Wiener is a cultural historian (who takes the reality of an economic fact as his starting point), whereas Tomlinson is an economic historian (who treats interpretations of economic developments as the outcomes of political arguments).

intersected with national debates about Britain's economic and international position. To varying degrees, Snow and Leavis both attached their arguments to concerns about national decline, in ways that reveal how declinism offered a malleable set of assumptions and anxieties that could be harnessed to competing – indeed, contradictory – ends. Declinism, that is, flourished in part because it offered a rhetorical weapon to advocates of various positions in the cultural politics of postwar Britain.[6]

What's wrong with Britain?

It will come as no surprise that Britain struggled to find its feet after the Second World War. The outlines of this story are familiar: with the end of war the United States abruptly terminated lend-lease and begrudgingly granted Britain an emergency loan, and shortly thereafter the Americans assumed the dual burdens of communist containment and European development through the Truman Doctrine and the Marshall Plan. Clement Attlee's Labour government, meanwhile, took the decision to develop an atomic bomb while withdrawing from India, abandoning Palestine, and extending the welfare state. The trajectory of this story of domestic and international challenges is familiar, continuing into the 1950s in Winston Churchill's disappointed efforts to play the honest broker *vis-à-vis* the United States and the Soviet Union, Anthony Eden's disastrous intervention at Suez, and Harold Macmillan's acceptance of the transformation of empire into commonwealth.

Yet despite these developments, evidence at both the popular and elite levels complicates a narrative of steady decline. In 1951 the planners of the Festival of Britain promoted a modern, optimistic, and scientific vision of the nation's future, and in 1953 the coronation of Queen Elizabeth II provided occasion for the celebration of continuing – indeed, renewed – national greatness.[7] Even after Suez many Britons remained proud of their country's international stature, particularly its

---

[6] My thinking about "decline" in the 1960s is related to Daniel Ritschel's treatment of "planning" in the 1930s: *The Politics of Planning: The Debate on Economic Planning in Britain in the 1930s* (Oxford: Clarendon, 1997). Ritschel points to related debates over "collectivism" in the 1890s, "national efficiency" before the First World War, "rationalization" in the 1920s, and "reconstruction" during both world wars (p. 12). See also my " 'Decline' as a Weapon in Cultural Politics," in *Penultimate Adventures with Britannia: Personalities, Politics, and Culture in Britain*, ed. Wm. Roger Louis (London: I. B. Tauris, 2008), pp. 201–214.

[7] Becky Conekin, *'The Autobiography of a Nation': The 1951 Festival of Britain* (Manchester University Press, 2003). Ross McKibbin links the festival and the coronation in *Classes and Cultures: England 1918–1951* (New York: Oxford University Press, 1998), p. 535.

position as the first among equals in Europe. Kenneth Morgan suggests that Moscow continued to behave as though Britain remained a military and industrial power, and even the humiliation of Suez did not keep the Conservative government from cruising to re-election less than three years later. Tory Britain was affluent Britain, as memorialized in Macmillan's famous remark on the stump, "You've never had it so good."[8] The key point is that, while developments overseas helped create a context in which discussions of decline could flourish, they did not automatically generate those discussions in and of themselves.

If not the direct result of an obvious experience, how had the concept of decline become so prominent in British culture by the early 1960s? It is necessary to distinguish here between three concepts, "declinism," "economic decline," and "national decline." *Declinism* refers to the articulation and manipulation of anxieties related to Britain's shifting economic and international status – it is a historian's term for a cultural phenomenon, and another way of referring to the same idea would be to put decline in quotation marks ("decline"). *National decline* predated the postwar decades and surfaced in any number of discussions, making it at once a more amorphous and tenacious concept, and it achieved particular resonance with the retreat of the empire, especially after Suez. But this sense of national decline is something different from the more specific claim of *economic decline*, which did not figure prominently in political discussion until the end of the 1950s. Tomlinson has shown that this concept was only made thinkable as a result of developments in the assessment of economic and government performance.[9] Indices such as consumer inflation and wage increases provided new ways of comparing national economic performances, while *growth* supplanted *employment* as the key indicator of government performance. Analysts' acceptance of these measures – an acceptance that itself testifies to a robust economy – made economic decline thinkable in ways it had not been a decade before. Paradoxically, then, the notion of economic decline emerged during one of the first decades of the century to have ended in better economic shape than it had begun.[10]

But in addition to being measurable, economic decline also had to seem plausible. The plausibility of "decline" resulted in part from the grafting of these new worries about economic decline onto older concerns about national prestige. Relative economic decline was thus

---

[8] This paragraph draws from Kenneth Morgan, *The People's Peace: British History, 1945–1989* (New York: Oxford University Press, 1990).

[9] Tomlinson, *The Politics of Decline*, especially Chapter 2.

[10] Tomlinson dates it from 1959–1960 in "Conservative Modernisation, 1960–64: Too Little, Too Late?" *Contemporary British History* 11 (Autumn 1997), p. 18.

presented as evidence of more profound problems, and the two concepts became conflated into a single phenomenon: national decline. Between Suez in 1956 and Labour's victory in 1964, laments of this malaise flourished in Penguin's "What's Wrong with Britain?" series, Andrew Shonfield's *British Economic Policy since the War* (1958), Michael Shanks's *The Stagnant Society* (1961), Bryan Magee's *The New Radicalism* (1962), Anthony Sampson's *Anatomy of Britain* (1962), and Anderson's "Origins of the Present Crisis" (1964).[11] These writers had no doubt that Britain faced a grave crisis, but they ranged so widely in their diagnoses and prescriptions that they can hardly be said to have been discussing the same thing at all. As with the calls for a more "scientific" history (discussed in the previous chapter), "decline" proved so compelling that it was yoked to a range of positions – from Shonfield's critique of international overstretch, to Shanks's critique of Shonfield. The common ground in each case was the assumption that *something* was wrong with Britain, a lament so familiar that *Private Eye* offered an "All-Purpose 'What's-Wrong-With-Britain' Graph," consisting of five lines steadily descending since 1900 – the implication being that, whatever might want measuring, it surely must have been getting worse.[12] The declinist craze peaked by the mid 1960s, but not before it had made an indelible mark on public discourse.[13]

One of the most influential statements of declinism appeared as a special issue of *Encounter* magazine. In July 1963 the entire number of *Encounter* was devoted to a single topic, the "Suicide of a Nation?". Arthur Koestler – Hungarian-émigré-turned-British-man-of-letters – proposed the theme to the editors, who responded by inviting Koestler to edit the number himself. He enlisted seventeen writers, including Malcolm Muggeridge, Cyril Connolly, and John Vaizey, as well as Shanks and Shonfield, to discuss the crisis confronting Britain. Defining the terms of analysis in his opening essay, Koestler insisted that Britain's decline was economic, not imperial, and that its causes were cultural,

---

[11] Andrew Shonfield, *British Economic Policy since the War* (Baltimore: Penguin, 1958); Michael Shanks, *The Stagnant Society: A Warning* (Baltimore: Penguin, 1961); Bryan Magee, *The New Radicalism* (New York: St. Martin's Press, 1962); Anthony Sampson, *Anatomy of Britain* (London: Hodder and Stoughton, 1962); Anderson, "Origins of the Present Crisis." For historical discussions of this literature, see Tomlinson, *The Politics of Decline*, pp. 21–26; David Edgerton, *Warfare State: Britain, 1920–1970* (Cambridge University Press, 2006), Chapter 5.

[12] Christopher Booker, Richard Ingrams, William Rushton, *et al.*, *Private Eye's Romantic England: The Last Days of Macmilian* (London: Weidenfeld & Nicolson, 1963), p. 31. The vogue of decline is evident in the book's subtitle, which deliberately evokes comparison with the Roman Empire.

[13] Tomlinson, *The Politics of Decline*, p. 21.

not structural. "Suicide" was an appropriate term, since the consensus emerged that – far from the inevitable adjustments of a former imperial power – Britain was dying by its own hand. "What ails Britain is not the loss of Empire," Koestler declared, "but the loss of incentive."[14]

As the issue proceeded, its indictment of a hidebound establishment gathered momentum. Instead of a meritocracy, Britain was a "mediocracy," and instead of management by experts it was governed by amateurs.[15] The essays demanded the modernization of education, industry, and government, purging them of these dilettantes and replacing them with experts instead. When Henry Fairlie and Malcolm Muggeridge dissented from this consensus, Koestler dismissed their contributions as "antributions," and suggested that their essays illustrated the sort of thinking that was actually the problem.[16] He concluded by restating the problem as the development of a culture in which "blueprint," "technocrat," and "efficiency" (not to mention "washing machine" and "detergents") were bandied about as "hate-slogans." Instead, Koestler urged his readers to accept the unavoidable reality: "The new structure which is taking shape is the society of managers, technocrats, official planning, chromium, motels, and motorways."[17] The path to the future was clear, and the only question was whether Britain would take it.

"Suicide of a Nation?" articulated a deep and widespread commitment to techno-nationalist modernization. 'Techno-nationalist modernization' refers to the belief that national achievement depended upon technological advance, which alone could foster the social and economic modernization that were essential to domestic prosperity and international competitiveness. The establishment of Churchill College as a training ground for a scientific and technological elite was one product of these assumptions, as was its enthusiastic reception by a national media convinced of the links between national survival and scientific technology. The Robbins Report of 1963 relied upon similar assumptions, justifying the expansion of the university system and its continued

---

[14] Arthur Koestler, "Introduction: The Lion and the Ostrich," *Encounter*, July 1963, p. 8. For further discussion of this number's context, one that relates it to the many works that echoed these themes at this time, see Peter Mandler, *The English National Character: The History of an Idea from Edmund Burke to Tony Blair* (New Haven: Yale University Press, 2006), pp. 215–228.

[15] In addition to Koestler, see Goronwy Rees, "Amateurs and Gentleman, or The Cult of Incompetence," pp. 20–25; Michael Shanks, "The Comforts of Stagnation," pp. 30–38; Austen Albu, "Taboo on Expertise," pp. 45–50, all in *Encounter*, July 1963.

[16] Henry Fairlie, "On the Comforts of Anger," pp. 9–13; Malcolm Muggeridge, "England, Whose England?" pp. 14–17, both in *Encounter*, July 1963.

[17] Koestler, "Postscript: The Manager and the Muses," *Encounter*, July 1963, pp. 115, 113.

reorientation toward science and technology by their promised contribution to national competitiveness.[18] Two years later the physicist
R. V. Jones echoed these sentiments on the BBC: "With colonies gone,
our easy markets and our easy supplies have disappeared. Science and
technology provide our main hope of recovery."[19] Born of concerns
about Britain's supposedly faltering economic performance in the
1950s, declinism fueled a widespread commitment to modernization –
and nobody tapped into this zeitgeist better than the Labour Party of
Hugh Gaitskell and, especially, Harold Wilson.[20]

White heat

The political potential for a campaign of scientific modernization was
proved by the case of Tony Benn. Upon the death of Lord Stansgate in
November 1960, the young, handsome, centrist MP from Bristol South
East assumed his father's title – and was immediately ordered out of
the House of Commons. First elected to the House of Commons in
1950, Benn had already attempted to renounce his right to the title, but
the Lords refused his petition. In 1961, then, he and his constituents
launched the "Bristol Campaign," circulating a petition protesting the
rule that disqualified hereditary peers from serving in the Commons.[21]
It soon became clear that the Bristol Campaign had ramifications beyond
parliamentary procedure: the petition depicted the rule that disqualified
Benn as "a symbol of a deeper malaise in Britain today: namely, our
failure to adapt ourselves to modern life, our fear of the future and our
preference for living in the comfortable after-glow of past glories." His
campaign was really about the "case for modernisation," and it was
"set . . . against a world background of scientific, economic and political
change." In a few steps, Benn's challenge to an old rule had become a
struggle on behalf of "the practical application of the fabulous scientific
opportunities now available to mankind." The Bristol Campaign widened
the terms of the conflict, elevating a personal matter into a national crisis –
and this was a deliberate strategy, as Benn confided to Snow: "We plan

[18] Desmond King and Victoria Nash, "Continuity of Ideas and the Politics of Higher
Education Expansion in Britain from Robbins to Dearing," *Twentieth Century British
History* 12 (2001), pp. 185–207.
[19] R. V. Jones, "In Search of Scientists – I," *Listener*, 23 September 1965, p. 447.
[20] On the scientific, technological, and modernizing zeitgeist, see Dominic Sandbrook,
White Heat: A History of Britain in the Swinging Sixties (London: Little, Brown, 2006),
pp. 41–60.
[21] Papers from the Bristol Campaign are held with Snow's papers at the Harry Ransom
Humanities Research Center (HRC): Snow 205.10. The following quotations come
from a memorandum prepared by Benn, dated March 1961 and included in that file.

to broaden the campaign out into an attack on everything that is old-fashioned in Britain today."[22] The battle lasted more than two years, ultimately meeting with success in the spring of 1963 when Benn – having relinquished his title – triumphantly returned to the Commons. The Bristol Campaign demonstrated the political punch packed by laments about decline, demands for modernization, and calls for scientific opportunity – a lesson not lost on the leaders of a Labour Party then reeling from three consecutive defeats. But in the campaign to come there would be one essential difference: whereas Benn found support across the political spectrum, brandishing the signature of Winston Churchill and the acquiescence of the Conservatives and Liberals, in Labour's hands modernization would be presented as the preserve of a single party.

Labour seemed to be improving its electoral prospects under new leader Hugh Gaitskell. The centrist Campaign for Democratic Socialism had infiltrated the constituency parties, and Gaitskell had warded off the advocates of nuclear disarmament at the party conference of 1961. During the next year he succeeded in acting the part of a prime-minister-in-waiting, until unexpectedly dying in January 1963. He was succeeded by a former Oxford economist, Harold Wilson. Wilson inherited a party prone to disputes over nationalization, taxation, unilateralism, and so on. While Gaitskell had resolved these conflicts by siding with the party's right, Wilson preferred to transcend them by fusing the fortunes of socialism and science. He boasted of his membership in the Society of Statisticians – a fortuitous contrast with his Conservative counterpart, the fourteenth Earl of Home, who famously confessed to doing his sums with matchsticks. Home himself had recently taken over a government rocked by scandal: a tawdry affair of sex and spies, in which Macmillan's acceptance of John Profumo's denials smacked of an obsolete set of gentlemanly values.[23] If Wilson had his way, the choice between the Conservatives and Labour would be a choice between aristocrats and technocrats, between tradition and modernization, and between the past and the future.[24]

Wilson solidified this impression in one of the most famous speeches in the history of British politics, his address to the Labour Party Conference at Scarborough on October 1, 1963 (the very year, not coincidentally, of Benn's victory, the Robbins Report, and "Suicide of

---

[22] Benn to Snow, 27 March 1961, HRC: Snow 205.10.
[23] Dominic Sandbrook, *Never Had It So Good: A History of Britain from Suez to the Beatles* (London: Little, Brown, 2005), Chapter 17.
[24] Morgan, *The People's Peace*, Chapter 6.

a Nation?"). He opened by repeating his call of four years before, that science and socialism be fused together to ready Britain for the future. Deftly reading the language of class onto a linear model of history, he cast conservatives as antiquated aristocrats, and socialists as progressive meritocrats: the Tories conceived of the international system as an "old-boy network," when in truth no nation would henceforth have a position greater than it earned; the Tories thought they were leading a nation of "Gentlemen," when in truth they confronted international "Players."[25] The world had entered a period of scientific and technological advance, Wilson said, in which the very technologies that promised gains in productivity also threatened to reduce employment. Private enterprise had proved not up to the task of managing these developments, but socialist planning was. Wilson then laid out a four-point plan for science, including educating more scientists, keeping them in the country, deploying them within industry, and maximizing their potential. His plan would require changes in education, from opening access to increasing places, which only a Ministry of Science could accomplish. Wilson then spoke of the need to restate socialism in terms of this scientific revolution, a revolution that mandated fundamental changes: "The Britain that is going to be forged in the white heat of this revolution will be no place for restrictive practices or for outdated methods."[26] The white heat of the scientific revolution, Wilson declared, would prove inhospitable to privilege, pedigree, and the past.

Labour's manifesto the next year, *The New Britain*, read like a combination of Koestler in *Encounter* and Wilson at Scarborough.[27] It insisted on the need to reverse "the decline of the thirteen wasted years," lashed out against the "old-boy network," and pledged to bring Britain up to speed in the "scientific age" through a combination of modernization, technology, and – especially – planning.[28] The manifesto concluded with a pledge, in capital letters, to make the British "THE GO-AHEAD PEOPLE WITH A SENSE OF NATIONAL PURPOSE, THRIVING IN AN EXPANDING COMMUNITY WHERE SOCIAL JUSTICE IS SEEN TO PREVAIL."[29] Recognizing a good thing when they saw it, the Conservatives attempted to harness the appeal of science and modernization to their own cause.[30] In the end, though, their belated

---

[25] Harold Wilson, "Labour's Plan for Science," *Purpose in Politics* (London: Weidenfeld & Nicolson, 1964), pp. 14, 28.
[26] *Ibid.*, p. 27.
[27] *Let's Go with Labour for the New Britain: The Labour Party's Manifesto for the 1964 General Election* (London: Victoria House Printing Co., 1964).
[28] *Ibid.*, pp. 3, 10, 5, and *passim.*   [29] *Ibid.*, pp. 4, 24.
[30] Tomlinson, "Conservative Modernisation, 1960–64: Too Little, Too Late?".

efforts fell short, and in October 1964 Labour secured its first parliamentary majority since 1951.

"Decline" thus flourished in the late 1950s and early 1960s as a rhetorical weapon employed on behalf of a center-left critique of contemporary Britain. The declinist critique maintained that Britain was being run into the ground by a cabal of old boys, who were incapable of responding to the scientific revolution that was transforming industry throughout the world. In place of amateur gentlemen doing sums by matchsticks, Britain needed professional experts in science and technology. This is not to suggest that science and technology had never been celebrated in Britain before, but rather that an inherited commitment to science and technology was now being yoked to an ambitious program of modernization by experts.[31] To adapt a phrase, from the Festival of Britain in 1951 to the victory of Harold Wilson's Labour Party in 1964, British culture was being forged in the white heat of a technocratic revolution. Snow's Rede Lecture of 1959 advanced precisely these themes.

The corridors of power

Snow ceaselessly warned of the impending decline that threatened Britain, unless its economic, educational, and governing institutions underwent dramatic transformation. This diagnosis put him in the company of other critics of British society and institutions, such as Arthur Koestler, Anthony Sampson, and Perry Anderson (among many others). In Snow's hands, decline seemed capable of explaining nearly anything: for instance, in attempting to account for a generation of radical intellectuals who were trending conservative, he concluded that this "irregular right" was the product of a social democracy "getting internally tidier at a time when its external power is, relative to the outside world, going down."[32] On another occasion, while sympathetically portraying a team of nuclear scientists, Snow depicted decline not as an experience endured, but an obstacle avoided, thanks to the work of Britain's scientists and administrators.[33] And in between, decline surfaced in connection with the "two cultures" when Snow explained that Britain was "in danger of deluding ourselves into a grandiose Spanish

---

[31] Edgerton, *England and the Aeroplane*; Frank Miller Turner, "Public Science in Britain, 1880–1919," *Isis* 71 (December 1980), pp. 589–608.
[32] C. P. Snow, "The Irregular Right: Britain without Rebels," *Nation*, 24 March 1956, p. 239.
[33] C. P. Snow, "The Men of Fission," *Holiday*, April 1958, pp. 95, 108–115.

twilight," citing that past empire to inspire present reforms.[34] Generally, though, Snow invoked decline as a warning of the fate that would befall Britain if certain reforms were not realized – and, despite periodic references to Spain or Sweden, the Republic of Venice tended to serve as his favorite example.[35]

In putting decline to work on behalf of a program of technocratic modernization, Snow subscribed to the same reading of British history and culture as the "Suicide of a Nation?" team. Together they believed that Britain's economic, social, and political structures required complete overhaul, replacing gentlemanly ethics with professional expertise. Writing affectionately of the technocrat, Snow said, "It is that kind of man, formidably intelligent, imaginative, prepotent, that any technical society needs to do some of its most difficult jobs."[36] With such men in charge, benefits would follow: "[T]he managerial society is in the long run men's best source of social hope."[37] To Snow, the managerial society was no mere fantasy: he believed that large scientific establishments, such as the nuclear facility at Harwell, represented the realization of an ideal society, one that was run by competent, disinterested, technical experts.[38] This was, of course, a political program – the "technocratic liberalism" discussed in Chapter 1 – but an essential component of the program was its denial of politics: the technocrat boasted expertise, not ideology. For this reason, Snow saw little difference between Soviet bureaucrats and American managers, as they were all engaged in the identical work of solving large problems through the complex structures of modern society.

In his writing Snow explored the world of this "bureaucratic man." The primary attribute of bureaucratic man was that he got things done, and getting things done required assembling coalitions, navigating power structures, and – especially – understanding the game. It was in this sense, which he referred to as "closed politics," that Snow considered himself (and was considered by others) a master of politics. Closed politics were rational and pragmatic, but they could also prove unpredictable and volatile; the assembling of coalitions was painstaking,

---

[34] C. P. Snow, "Britain's Two Cultures: A Study of Education in a Scientific Age," *Sunday Times*, 10 March 1957, p. 12.

[35] In addition to Snow, *The Two Cultures and the Scientific Revolution*, see Snow, "Phase of Expansion," *Spectator*, 1 October 1954, p. 406; Snow, "New Minds for the New World," *New Statesman*, 8 September 1956, pp. 279–282; Snow, "Miasma, Darkness, and Torpidity," *New Statesman*, 11 August 1961, pp. 186–187; Snow, *Variety of Men* (London: Macmillan, 1967), p. 152.

[36] C. P. Snow, "Industrial Dynamo," *New Statesman*, 16 June 1956, p. 703.

[37] C. P. Snow, "The Corridors of Power," *Listener*, 18 April 1957, p. 620.

[38] Snow, "The Men of Fission."

and the work could be undone by a single incomprehensible act. By definition, closed politics precluded recourse to a wide public; instead, this was the politics of experts, in positions of power, bearing ultimate responsibility. These were the themes of Snow's Godkin Lectures at Harvard in 1960, a cautionary tale featuring Lord Cherwell, Churchill's scientific advisor during the Second World War. Snow argued that Cherwell had successfully secured a monopoly of power, yet displayed appalling judgment in matters of life and death. Snow's sympathies lay with Cherwell's rival, Henry Tizard, but his overall point concerned the dangers inherent in the rise of any single "scientific overlord" – a problem that emerged from the growing gap between the experts who understood problems and the politicians who made decisions.[39]

Snow examined these problems in his most anticipated novel, *Corridors of Power* (1964).[40] The story features Roger Quaife, a rising star among Conservative MPs in the late 1950s. Quaife's colleagues expect him to bide his time, with the goal of attaining office – perhaps the highest office – sometime in the future. But Quaife is a man of action, and, after conferring with scientific experts, and then securing an ally in the Civil Service, he commences upon an intricate plan ultimately aimed at abandoning Britain's nuclear deterrent. Snow was writing subsequent to the launch of the Campaign for Nuclear Disarmament (CND), and his timing was deliberate: while not necessarily opposed to CND's goals, Snow wanted to show that constructive political action resulted not from unruly social movements, but from restrained and responsible maneuvering inside the corridors of power.[41] To Snow, although the potential for action by any individual was slight, it was only through a series of individual nudges that movement could be achieved. "I sometimes wonder how much freedom any of us have to make decisions?" Quaife asks at one point. "Politicians, I mean. I wonder if the limits of freedom aren't tighter than one's inclined to think."[42] In a world of technical experts, scientific knowledge, and administrative bureaucracy, popular democracy was becoming meaningless: as Quaife tells the House of Commons at the book's climax, "The problems we're trying to handle

---

[39] C. P. Snow, *Science and Government* (Cambridge, Mass.: Harvard University Press, 1960).

[40] C. P. Snow, *Corridors of Power* (London: Macmillan, 1964); these quotations come from the omnibus edition: Snow, *Strangers and Brothers* (New York: Scribner's, 1972), vol. III. Snow told Norman Podhoretz that the connections between this novel and his Godkin Lectures were deliberate: Snow to Podhoretz, 9 March 1960, HRC: Snow 165.10.

[41] Snow repeatedly declined requests of support from representatives of CND. HRC: Snow 68.8–68.9.

[42] Snow, *Strangers and Brothers*, pp. 162–163.

are very difficult. So difficult that most people in this country – people who are, by and large, at least as intelligent as we are – can't begin to understand them."[43] Given the population's ignorance, the MP's role was clear: "We are trying to speak for them. We have taken a great deal upon ourselves. We ought never to forget it."[44] Quaife's plea to his colleagues was Snow's creed of the expert: the problems are complex, the solutions are available, the responsibility is great. In the end, however, even Quaife's formidable skills prove no match against parliamentary inertia: in one of Snow's most gripping scenes, Quaife – having lost the crucial vote – exits the chamber with his head down, ignoring the shouts of "Resign! Resign!" that rain down upon him.[45] Snow's message was clear: only an individual working inside the corridors of power can hope to accomplish anything, but even such an individual cannot expect to accomplish much.

In a perceptive review of *Corridors of Power*, the sociologist Edward Shils identified a tension in Snow's oeuvre. As a democrat, Shils wrote, Snow was presumably suspicious of closed politics, yet he was also clearly fascinated by it.[46] In the late 1950s and early 1960s, the analyst of politics increasingly became a participant as well. Events pushed the tension Shils had identified to the fore, but as they did it became clear that his observation derived from a misconception: although he was fascinated by closed politics, Snow was not quite a democrat.

The Gaitskell Group

Historians have long attempted to identify the origins of the "white heat," Harold Wilson's positioning of Labour as the party of science and modernization. Kenneth Morgan notes precursors in the social scientific analysis of the Fabians before 1914, and also in the scientific utopianism of the young H. G. Wells.[47] Gary Werskey calls attention to scientific socialists from the 1930s such as Joseph Needham, J. B. S. Haldane, Lancelot Hogben, and Hyman Levy; the key work being J. D. Bernal's *The Social Function of Science* (1939).[48] Other candidates include Solly Zuckerman's dining club, the "Tots and Quots," in the 1930s, and the Association of Scientific Workers after the war. But more immediate precursors can be identified in a series of private meetings between eminent scientists and senior Labour politicians between 1956 and 1964.

---

[43] *Ibid.*, p. 263.   [44] *Ibid.*   [45] *Ibid.*, p. 265.
[46] Edward Shils, "The Charismatic Centre," *Spectator*, 6 November 1964, pp. 608–609.
[47] Morgan, *The People's Peace*, p. 232.
[48] J. D. Bernal, *The Social Function of Science* (London: Routledge, 1939); Gary Werskey, *The Visible College* (London: Allen Lane, 1978).

These meetings were the brainchild of Marcus Brumwell, and they included scientists such as Bernal, Jacob Bronowski, Solly Zuckerman, and Patrick Blackett, as well as politicians such as Harold Wilson, Jim Callaghan, and Richard Crossman. Labour leader Gaitskell attended from the outset, and the meetings became known as the "Gaitskell Group."[49]

The Gaitskell Group's first meeting took place at the Reform Club in London on July 17, 1956. Present were an impressive array of scientific figures, including Blackett, Bronowski, and Zuckerman; Callaghan attended as Labour's shadow coordinator for science.[50] Brumwell prepared a document to set the meeting's agenda: "The Labour Party and Science" explained that a failure to fund and direct science and technology was crippling British industry.[51] British science, it continued, was underfunded, understaffed, misdirected, and uncoordinated. Five objectives would remedy this problem: supporting basic research, integrating science with the economy, training a greater numbers of scientists, educating more people in general science, and contributing to international science. The group met once more between this initial meeting and the summer of 1958, when they began to focus on helping Labour win office. It was with an eye towards formulating their policy program into an electoral pitch that, in June 1958, Brumwell approached Snow.[52]

Science was only compatible with socialism, Snow responded, and from June 1958 he became an active member of the Gaitskell Group.[53] The next September he also began meeting with a more select group, the Senior Scientists Group, focusing on questions of manpower (as a veteran scientific recruiter for the Civil Service) and communication (as a successful novelist and commentator).[54] The scientists set about drafting papers to guide future Labour ministers in decisions on science, which addressed "Scientific and Technical Manpower," "Fundamental Science," "Science and Industry," "Civil Research and Development," and "Government Machinery." Snow penned the paper dealing with manpower, which began: "All previous estimates of the need for scientists,

---

[49] Copies of the records of the Gaitskell Group are held with the papers of P. M. S. Blackett at the Royal Society (London): Blackett E.24–E.34. The term "Gaitskell Group" is Blackett's. See also Mary Jo Nye, *Blackett: Physics, War, and Politics in the Twentieth Century* (Cambridge, Mass.: Harvard University Press, 2004), pp. 158–159.

[50] Gaitskell Group, 17 July 1956, Royal Society: Blackett E.24.

[51] "The Labour Party and Science (Notes to start a discussion, 17 July 1956)," Royal Society: Blackett E.25.

[52] Brumwell to Snow, 20 June 1958, HRC: Snow 65.10; Brumwell to Blackett, 4 September 1959, Royal Society: Blackett E.29.

[53] Gaitskell Group, 27 June 1958, Royal Society: Blackett E.26.

[54] Senior Scientists Group, 26 September 1958, Royal Society: Blackett E.27.

engineers, technologists, and technicians have proved in the event to have been seriously understated."[55] Scientific and technical advance required fundamental shifts in priorities and resources, Snow continued, as well as an end to the specialization in British schools. The world was undergoing a scientific revolution, from atomic energy to automation, and meeting the needs, challenges, and opportunities demanded increased numbers of trained staff. Britain needed more programs in science and technology, as well as the establishment of new universities and technical colleges. Meeting these targets meant that the pool of applicants must be extended to include all classes and both sexes, tapping into unused talent. "Political leadership can to some extent alter the climate," concluded the author of *Corridors of Power*. "But a small number of personal appointments could go a long way to determine the success or failure of the entire operation."[56] Snow's contribution read like a civil servant's version of the recommendations of his Rede Lecture – which is precisely what it was.

In the summer of 1959, with an election expected later that year, the papers were bound together into a red volume, "A Labour Government and Science." The documents proved influential, with Gaitskell declaring that he would embrace the proposals the moment Labour won office. Wilson agreed, but his keen eye was particularly drawn towards the rhetorical potential promised by aligning Labour with science, planning, and a pioneering spirit. He wanted to make clear that the party was not offering a "soulless technocracy," but that it proposed to make full use of science – which, he thought, would give Labour the "right image" in the election. Snow agreed, and offered to write something within a fortnight.[57] The leaflet he produced became the basis for a pamphlet released just before the election, but it was not enough: the election of October 8, 1959 proved a heartbreaking defeat, as Labour won nineteen fewer seats than four years before.[58]

Despite the defeat, Brumwell determined that the Gaitskell Group must continue its work. They convened in June 1960 to assess their accomplishments and plan for the future, and their confidence that science could prove critical to Labour's eventual success had only increased. Bronowski noted that science was the "magic word" these days, and that it could well prove to be useful propaganda. Wilson, the

[55] "Scientific and Technical Manpower," in "A Labour Government and Science: Papers for Mr. Gaitskell," p. 3, Royal Society: Blackett E.28.

[56] *Ibid.*, pp. 8–9.   [57] Gaitskell Group, 27 August 1959, Royal Society: Blackett E.28.

[58] From the finding aid to Blackett's papers, Royal Society, p. 218. Confirmed in a document titled "Progress Report on 'Labour and Science'," Royal Society: Blackett E.30.

senior politician in attendance, agreed, and he even floated the idea of a television debate on the subject.[59] Despite defeat at the polls, spirits remained high, but within two years the scientists were growing restless. Brumwell opened the meeting of June 5, 1962 by sharing his concern that Labour was not sufficiently enthusiastic about science.[60] The scientists were frustrated with the low priority given to the Shadow Minister for Science, the failure to challenge the government on its scientific policies, and the lack of integration of scientists onto non-scientific committees. Their formal complaint read: "It would appear that science is accorded a very low priority in *practice* whatever may be *said* about its importance."[61] Bronowski was especially frustrated – "I see no point in going on with these delightful but frustrating dinner parties" – and he circulated a list of complaints.[62] In a letter later referred to as the "ultimatum," on November 1, 1962 the group sent their complaints directly to Gaitskell.[63] Gaitskell received the note warmly, but without any urgency; a week later he replied with the bland assurance that he would take their concerns under consideration.[64] After six years of meetings, morale had reached its low point, as the prospects for an alliance between Labour and science seemed dim.

Within three months, however, the Gaitskell Group enjoyed a complete reversal of fortune. Upon Gaitskell's death in January 1963, Wilson secured the party leadership, and he immediately proved an enthusiastic ally of the senior scientists. "In the new situation," Brumwell wrote Blackett, referring to the changed leadership, "it appears that the whole activity of pepping up the Labour Party's attitude towards science has taken a violent and admirable step forward."[65] Wilson had always been the political liaison to the group who was most enthusiastic about science.[66] He now appointed Richard Crossman as Shadow Minister of Science, satisfactorily addressing one of the scientists' complaints.[67] Wilson and Crossman both attended the next meeting of the senior members, when Wilson laid out an ambitious program of economic planning, the establishment of new ministries, and challenges to the

[59] Gaitskell Group, 27 June 1960, Royal Society: Blackett E.30.
[60] Gaitskell Group, 5 June 1962, Royal Society: Blackett E.32.
[61] "Science and the Labour Party," Royal Society: Blackett E.33.
[62] Bronowski to Brumwell, 13 July 1962, Royal Society: Blackett E.32.
[63] Gaitskell Group to Hugh Gaitskell, 1 November 1962, Royal Society: Blackett E.33.
[64] Letter from Gaitskell, 8 November 1962, Royal Society: Blackett E.33.
[65] Brumwell to Blackett, 27 February 1963, Royal Society: Blackett E.33.
[66] A minute from the meeting of June 23, 1961 is typical: "Harold Wilson emphasized that the Labour Party is now science minded." Gaitskell Group, 23 June 1961, Royal Society: Blackett E.31.
[67] Brumwell to Blackett, 27 February 1963, Royal Society: Blackett E.33.

Treasury – in short, he promised a "violent revolution" that would "explode the system of government into a proper realization of how to deal with life in a scientific world."[68] The meeting established seven steps for action, including a "Labour Party and Science" conference, a fresh set of cabinet papers, a new association of Labour scientists, and an election manifesto focusing upon science – a task that immediately secured the assistance of Bronowski and Snow.[69]

The journey that had begun with the first meeting of the Gaitskell Group in 1956 was now on the course that would lead to Scarborough and, eventually, to Downing Street. As for Snow, even without his volunteer work for the Labour Party, these were extraordinarily busy years. The Rede Lecture of 1959 had transformed him from a successful novelist into an international figure; in 1960 he delivered the Godkin Lectures at Harvard, and then spent a term at Berkeley; and in 1962 he served as Rector of St. Andrews. Also that year, in addition to undergoing two serious surgeries for a detached retina, he twice endured a maelstrom of publicity attending the Richmond Lecture: first upon its delivery, and again upon its publication. And this was also the time when he was busy with the founding of Churchill College. There was thus no shortage of claims upon Snow's time and energy during the most active years of the Labour scientists, a fact reflected in his frequent absences from their semi-annual meetings.

Within the Gaitskell Group itself, Snow remained a prized asset. As early as 1958 the issue had been raised of granting him a peerage, so that his talents could be utilized in Parliament.[70] Had Labour won the election in 1959, Snow expected to be offered a government position.[71] Three years later, when Wilson wanted a meeting with two senior scientists, Snow received an invitation, along with J. D. Bernal – somewhat to Snow's embarrassment, as he reminded Brumwell that he was not a practicing scientist.[72] Wilson's subsequent rise brought Snow increasingly close to the political office he insisted he did not want. And in some ways, Snow did not need to enter Parliament to have his voice heard: in a speech in the Commons in 1961, Wilson borrowed Snow's own favorite image regarding national decline: "We meet the challenge of the modern world," he said, "with *an effete Venetian oligarchy*, a government

---

[68] Gaitskell Group, 24 June 1963, Royal Society: Blackett E.34.   [69] *Ibid.*

[70] Cecil Gordon to the Gaitskell Group, 18 September 1958, Royal Society: Blackett Papers.

[71] Snow to J. II. Plumb, 15 September 1959, Cambridge University Library (CUL): Plumb papers, File: "Snow 1946 to 1968," Box "C. P. Snow + Pam, 1946 to 1968."

[72] Brumwell to Snow, 10 July 1962, HRC: Snow 65.10; Snow to Brumwell, 12 July 1962, HRC: Snow 65.10.

who themselves reflect that nation's besetting weakness of family connection and aristocratic recruitment."[73] According to Crossman, Snow
was the person Wilson most trusted on science; and, before the 1964
election, Snow was functioning as an informal clearing house for civil
servants needing to send a message to the Leader of the Opposition.[74]

Having campaigned by promising the "white heat" of the scientific
revolution, upon victory Wilson placed Snow in the House of Lords to
show that he meant it.[75] Snow became Parliamentary Secretary to the
Ministry of Technology, a new ministry headed by the trade union
veteran, Frank Cousins. For Snow, son of a clerk in a Leicester factory,
membership in the most elite club in Britain was quite a thrill. Baron
Snow included in his coat of arms a crossed pen and telescope, sym-
bolizing the two cultures, and his maiden speech on November 18, 1964
received widespread praise. Despite his initial reservations, it seemed
that Snow might come to enjoy his new role.[76] But before long, Lord
Snow of Leicester ran into the difficulties examined by C. P. Snow the
novelist: the room for maneuver was narrow, while the margin for error
proved wide.

MinTech

Plans for the Ministry of Technology were developed in part by Patrick
Blackett, an active member of the Gaitskell Group. In September 1964
Blackett submitted "The Case for a Ministry of Technology" to Wilson,
which argued that the failure of British industry stemmed from a failure
of management.[77] He claimed that, during the previous thirteen years,
private industry had shown that it could not sufficiently modernize on
its own. While Blackett was writing, the various possibilities to address
this problem included expanding the Board of Trade or creating a
Ministry of Industry, but Labour's need for quick results rendered both
options unacceptable. Instead, Blackett proposed a small Ministry of
Technology. The ministry would direct civil research and development,
identifying areas of strength and weakness, and setting targets accordingly. The assumptions behind the formation of the ministry, then, were

---

[73] This extract from Wilson's speech is dated April 18, 1961, and is held at the Royal
Society: Blackett E.40 (emphasis mine).
[74] Plumb to Snow, May 1963, HRC: Snow 166.10; Snow to Barzun, 21 July 1964,
quoted in Caroline Nobile Gryta, "Selected Letters of C. P. Snow: A Critical Edition,"
unpublished PhD dissertation, Pennsylvania State University (1988), pp. 310–311.
[75] *Times Literary Supplement*, "Technology and Humanism," 29 July 1965, pp. 641–642.
[76] Philip A. Snow, *A Time of Renewal: Clusters of Characters, C.P. Snow, and Coups* (London: Radcliffe, 1998), pp. 86–88.
[77] Blackett, "The Case for a Ministry of Technology," Royal Society: Blackett E.49.

(1) managerial failure, (2) technological backwardness, (3) economic decline, and (4) the efficiency of planning. From the moment the new ministry was announced on October 28, 1964, its structure and responsibilities differed substantially from what Blackett had proposed; but Blackett remained influential as Deputy Chairman of the Advisory Council on Technology, as well as Scientific Advisor to the Ministry.[78]

Snow represented the new ministry as Parliamentary Secretary from the House of Lords. Snow's red boxes at MinTech were filled with papers relating to four industries: computers, machine tools, electronics, and aircraft, with the occasional inclusion of telecommunications and atomic energy; the minister also oversaw the Atomic Energy Authority and National Research Development Corporation. The ministry carried out technical and economic studies of industrial needs, prepared programs of research and development, guided technological education at all levels, and funded ten research laboratories. In short, MinTech was charged with the task of monitoring and directing technological research and development; or, as Snow explained (echoing the Labour manifesto), "The Ministry of Technology has the general responsibility of guiding and stimulating a major national effort to bring advanced technology and new processes into British industry."[79] Not exactly scintillating, but this was the life of bureaucratic man – the mundane, but crucial, world of competents and competence.

Snow quickly grew frustrated with the difficulty of accomplishing his goals. He composed forests of memoranda on efficiencies of scale, measurement standards, and the civil service, some of which displayed the novelist's flair ("I think the trouble about this country is as follows: We can't afford to have a revolution: and we can't afford not to have one"), but most of which did not ("I suspect that this type of personnel management is going to become increasingly important").[80] He began to devote more energy to projects that promised more immediate gratification: a plea for Wilson to deliver a witty speech on the metric system, the establishment of a "Unit for Minor Bright Ideas" to solicit ideas from creative artists, and hopes of founding a mathematical Olympiad for schoolchildren. Snow also weighed in about political initiatives, such as the suggestion that Wilson make "a bit of a song and dance" about women's issues, since he had observed how excited women became by a

---

[78] Finding aid to the Blackett papers, Royal Society, p. 228. For a discussion of the differences between Blackett's proposals and the actual ministry, see Edgerton, *Warfare State*, Chapter 6.

[79] Snow to Harry Mitchell, 26 May 1965, HRC: Snow 106.11.

[80] Snow to Frank Cousins, 16 August 1965, HRC: Snow 106.12; Snow to Cousins, 12 January 1965, HRC: Snow 106.11.

mildly feminist speech.[81] This is not to suggest that Snow was negligent in government: he was a diligent administrator, but he clearly preferred to write about, rather than endure, the limits to individual action.

To make matters worse, Snow was dogged by a series of missteps throughout his sixteen months in office. He got off on the wrong foot by asking Wilson for an official car (generally a benefit reserved for the Minister); in April 1965 he received criticism for continuing to accept fees for his appearances and reviews while in office; and in 1966 a reporter's phone call to his home embarrassingly confirmed his intention to resign.[82] He clashed with Cousins over policy, and embarrassed the more democratically minded Crossman by referring to him as "Minister."[83] Snow was not particularly fond of Crossman, and the feeling was mutual: although he reviewed Snow's *Science in Government* favorably in 1961, Crossman thought Snow's appointment "a bit crazy," and he anticipated that the novelist would not be effective in government.[84] But Snow had certainly managed to catch Wilson's eye, and Crossman acknowledged that Snow's word on science, technology, and education carried real weight.[85] These were relatively minor issues, perhaps inevitable in a political culture that thrives on gossip and personality conflicts, but the defining event of Snow's tenure, the "Eton Affair," cannot be so easily dismissed.

On February 10, 1965, during a debate in the House of Lords over the government's plans for comprehensive education, Viscount Eccles stunned Lord Snow by asking why he was sending his own son to Eton. Snow, caught off-guard, disastrously replied that it would be a mistake to educate one's children in a manner differently from their peers. So impolitic an explanation surely resulted from the fact that Snow had

[81] Snow to Wilson, 1 June 1965, HRC: Snow 106.11.   [82] HRC: Snow 106.14.
[83] Snow to Cousins, 28 May 1965, HRC: Snow 106.11; the anecdote about Crossman is from an obituary of Snow by Alan Watkins: "Laureate of Meritocracy," *Observer*, 6 July 1980.
[84] Richard Crossman, "Secret Decisions," *Encounter*, June 1961, pp. 86–90; Crossman, *The Diaries of a Cabinet Minister: Volume One, Minister of Housing, 1964–1966* (London: Hamish Hamilton and Jonathan Cape, 1975), p. 42. Crossman later confessed to "grave doubts" about Snow (p. 117). Crossman and Wilson were dismissive of Snow's performance in politics: David Cannadine, "C. P. Snow, 'The Two Cultures,' and the 'Corridors of Power' Revisited," in *Yet More Adventures with Britannia*, ed. Wm. Roger Louis (London: I. B. Tauris, 2005), p. 110. Compare with Snow's recollection in John Halperin, *C. P. Snow: An Oral Biography, Together with a Conversation with Lady Snow (Pamela Hansford Johnson)* (New York: St. Martin's Press, 1983), p. 188. Roy Jenkins, Home Secretary at the time, referred to Snow as the "improbable Sancho Panza" to the Minister, the trade unionist Frank Cousins: *A Life at the Center: Memoirs of a Radical Reformer* (New York: Random House, 1991), p. 171.
[85] Plumb to Snow, May 1963, HRC: Snow 166.10. Crossman recalled the meeting at which Snow dazzled Wilson in *The Diaries of a Cabinet Minister*, p. 42.

never given much thought to the matter, as most Labour ministers sent their children to public schools. But regardless, a merciless lashing commenced in the press, and the file in Snow's papers on the "Eton Affair" is easily the thickest from his period in government.[86] A critic in the *Spectator* suggested, "Rarely, I think, has a public man exploded his own reputation so effectively." He noted that Snow's claim was especially rich, given that he had spent the previous two decades hectoring the British about their outmoded social system, and he then concluded archly, "Now at last I know what Lord Snow means by the two cultures."[87] Christopher Hollis, also in the *Spectator*, expressed his disdain in verse:

> It will surely come to pass,
>   Says Lord Snow,
> That the Lower Middle Class
>   (Vide Snow),
> Will go by general rule
> To a Comprehensive School,
> Where the cultures can be mixed
> And the answers can't be fixed,
>   C. P. Snow.
>
> But where, O tell me, where,
>   C. P. Snow,
> Are the Snows of yesteryear
>   Baron Snow?
> Since he'll spend his Finest Hour
> In the Corridors of Power,
> He says his boy must go
> Where the chaps are nice to know,
>   Poor young Snow.[88]

Either Snow never understood what caused the uproar, or he refused to back down on a matter of principle. In either case, he responded to the many letters pouring into his office with two defenses, astonishing in their political tone-deafness. First, he said, it was simply a fact that society was divided, so his son should indeed be educated in the fashion of his peers. Second, he explained, his son was regarded by his teachers as having particular promise, and he even stood a chance for a scholarship. Snow offered this response to an angry comprehensive teacher, along with the added touch of inquiring, "Incidentally, what is the nearest good comprehensive school to Cromwell Road?"[89] Snow's

---

[86] HRC: Snow 225.1.
[87] "Spectator's Notebook," *Spectator*, 19 February 1965, p. 225.
[88] Christopher Hollis, "Snows of Tomorrow Year," *Spectator*, 26 February 1965, p. 254.
[89] Snow to Brian Bastin, 26 February 1965, HRC: Snow 225.1.

defenses changed over time, but not necessarily for the better: his wife claimed that Eton was the only school attempting to rectify the "two cultures" problem.[90] Snow survived the controversy, but the frustrations steadily mounted, until one day when he declared in public: "Chucking bricks at Frank Cousins and myself has become a kind of national sport."[91] On February 10, 1966 – a year to the day after the Eton Affair began – Snow tendered his resignation. Hoping to avoid further distractions, Wilson requested that he remain through the election, before allowing Snow to return to his writing on April 5, 1966.[92]

The Eton Affair sums up Snow's tenure at MinTech: a ministry founded for public relations that foundered upon public relations; hopes for dramatic modernization that proved excruciatingly dull; an effort to heal class divisions that ended up reinforcing them; and the master of the political novel who proved a political liability. Most importantly, the episode exposed the fault Shils had identified: although a member of a party committed to social equality, Snow was no egalitarian. In its unreflective honesty, Snow's wooden response in the House of Lords made this fact plain. Despite periodic gestures towards democracy, equality, and feminism, Snow remained a committed liberal – that is, his commitment was to a fluid social hierarchy, not social equality, and during the remainder of the decade this stance would harden.

Science and planning

Wilson and Labour confronted vigorous opposition, but that opposition did not take the form of hostility to science and modernization. Wilson succeeded to the extent that he managed to depict modernization as a party issue, with Labour in favor and the Conservatives against. In truth, though, from 1960 the Conservatives had embraced their own program of economic modernization. Macmillan, for instance, could have been composing an essay for "Suicide of a Nation?" when he wrote, "We have now reached a stage in our post-war history where some more radical attack must be made upon the weakness of our economy."[93] As the Labour Party was discussing ways to reform and reinvigorate the economy,

[90] Pamela Hansford Johnson to Harry Levin, 17 August 1965, Harvard University: Houghton Library, Levin papers, MS Am 2461 (918), Storage 342, Box 18, "Snow, C. P."
[91] Quoted in John Stevenson, "When a Man is Sick of Power," *Daily Sketch*, 24 February 1966, p. 6.
[92] Philip A. Snow, *A Time of Renewal*, p. 105.
[93] Macmillan, "Modernization of Britain," 3 December 1962, Public Records Office (Kew): CAB 129/111, quoted in Tomlinson, "Conservative Modernisation, 1960–64," p. 18.

the Conservatives sought to implement modernizing reforms of their own. But while members of both parties were convinced of the need for modernizing reforms, the ministries responsible for translating directives into policy remained skeptical. The result, as Tomlinson shows, was bureaucratic resistance to Conservative modernizing policies, until Labour's victory in 1964 altered the possibilities for reform.[94] Nevertheless, in the early 1960s, whatever the issue and whichever the party, modernization was the order of the day – as suggested by the *Private Eye* spoof of a Conservative campaign poster, "Tory weather is modern weather."[95]

One consequence of this program of Conservative modernization was the establishment in 1959 of a new cabinet position, the Minister for Science. The first Minister for Science was Lord Hailsham, Quintin Hogg. Hailsham had no ministry, but he nevertheless succeeded in streamlining the funding of Britain's scientific establishment. He proved a vigorous minister in the House of Lords, regularly denouncing the rigidity and inefficiency of outmoded customs and technologies.[96] He pledged to reform the apprentice system, bringing industrial training onto scientific footing, and he scolded the engineering industry for failing to adopt new technologies.[97] Yet rather than welcoming this minister for science and his modernizing initiatives, the Gaitskell Group consistently criticized Hailsham. Their criticism suggests that they were motivated by something more than a commitment to science and modernization.

A primary issue dividing left from right in this period was not science or modernization (about which, as we have seen, members of both parties broadly agreed), but rather planning. The scientists, bureaucrats, and politicians of the Gaitskell Group advocated the rational, disinterested, and coordinated planning of science and technology, whereas their rivals – including, as we shall see, the Minister for Science – strenuously opposed centralized planning. The Gaitskell Group, and the Labour Party more generally, believed that private companies fundamentally lacked impartiality, vision, and resources, and that as a result the state needed to direct economic development. This thinking led to the establishment of the Ministry of Technology, born of frustration with the failures of industry, and a testament to confidence in the ability of the state to do better. The word for such a program of rational,

[94] Tomlinson, "Conservative Modernisation, 1960–64," pp. 18–19, 33–34.
[95] Booker, *et al.*, *Private Eye's Romantic England*, p. 56.
[96] Quintin Hogg (Baron Hailsham of St. Marylebone), *A Sparrow's Flight* (London: Collins, 1990), pp. 330–331.
[97] "Science and the Nature of Politics," *Nature*, 27 October 1962, p. 301.

dispassionate management is *technocracy* – precisely the term that made Koestler giddy, Wilson skittish, and Fairlie furious.

Fairlie's contribution to "Suicide of a Nation?" rejected calls for an infusion of managerial expertise. He valued individualism and liberty rather than experts and management, and he believed individualism and liberty to be threatened by programs boasting such labels as "dynamism," "efficiency," and "greatness."[98] In the guise of attacks upon amateurs, Fairlie detected the politics of managers, and he knew another word for these managers: "The voice of the manager then, now the voice of the *technocrat*, proclaiming, as does every opponent of free institutions, that freed from the necessity to consult ordinary people, he could run their lives for them far more efficiently and beneficently than they can themselves."[99] Fairlie then issued an improbable rallying cry: "It is time that, against their evil doctrine, we re-asserted our right to be inefficient."[100] The "right to inefficiency" struck a discordant note at the height of the technocratic moment, and Koestler breezily dismissed Fairlie's contribution as an "antribution," his argument not refuted so much as refused.

The same year, Britain's Minister for Science offered his own argument against the planning of science. In *Science and Politics*, Hailsham invoked the politics of liberal individualism in explaining the function of his office.[101] Science, he argued, needed to be funded, but it must never be planned, because research and discovery depended upon the initiative and instincts of the individual scientist. The scientist's freedom needed to be protected: "Thus the duty of organizing science in a free society, like all other important duties, begins with the individual," he wrote. "Government . . . is not, and cannot be, directory and executive."[102] Hailsham's next chapter followed this argument against scientific planning with a critique of *The Two Cultures*. Hailsham suggested that Snow's thesis, a misreading of the inevitable and harmless fact of specialization, reflected attitudes in the Senior Common Room rather than the real world: "Neither in exegetical nor in fundamental terms does it stand up to examination."[103] He did not make the point explicitly, but Hailsham recognized the technocratic impulse behind Snow's argument. After all, there is no reason why an argument against the administrative direction of science (*Science and Politics*) should have been followed by an argument about the dichotomy between the arts and the sciences

---

[98] Henry Fairlie, "On the Comforts of Anger," *Encounter*, July 1963, p. 10.
[99] *Ibid.*, p. 11.   [100] *Ibid.*
[101] Quintin Hogg, *Science and Politics* (London: Faber and Faber, 1963).
[102] *Ibid.*, p. 19.   [103] *Ibid.*, p. 33.

(*The Two Cultures*), but it is not at all surprising that an argument against the planning of science should have led into criticism of Snow's plea for the technocratic modernization of science and the state.

Labour worked to defuse arguments about the threat planning posed to freedom in its 1964 election manifesto. "Here is the case for planning," it declared, and then attempted to counter the anticipated attack: "And here, in this manifesto, is the answer to the Tory gibe that Planning could involve a loss of individual liberty."[104] The manifesto promised to establish a Parliamentary Commissioner to investigate abuses of government power against individuals. It is not clear that the establishment of a government official would assuage worries about the growth of the state, but the manifesto pressed forward: "Labour firmly puts the freedom of the individual FIRST."[105] On the issue of individual freedom, Labour had a plan – and, in 1964 at least, that was good enough.

Ordeal by planning

The 1960s were good times for advocates of planning, but Hailsham and Fairlie did find allies in their efforts to defend individual freedom. During and after the Second World War, a pair of liberal economists, John Jewkes and Friedrich von Hayek, attacked the extension of wartime controls in the form of a welfare state. The titles of their polemics made their arguments clear: *Ordeal by Planning* had an unpleasant ring, especially if it led down *The Road to Serfdom*.[106] They argued that economic systems were too complicated, unpredictable, and uncontrollable to be managed or directed. Innovation derived not from the disinterested and omniscient intervention of the state – which would prove ineffective, if not counterproductive – but rather from the actions of enterprising individuals. The ideas of these liberal economists found parallels in the philosophy of science of Michael Polanyi. Polanyi maintained that scientific progress resulted from adjustments, modifications, and additions to a collective body of knowledge. The key figure in this process was the individual scientist, who identified problems, made observations, and offered explanations, all of which cumulatively revised existing knowledge. Any external directives or guidance, he believed, would complicate, and possibly undermine, the scientific process. Polanyi devoted much energy after the war to the Society for

---

[104] Labour Party, *Let's Go with Labour for the New Britain*, p. 3.   [105] *Ibid.*, p. 4.
[106] John Jewkes, *Ordeal by Planning* (New York: Macmillan, 1948); Friedrich von Hayek, *The Road to Serfdom* (University of Chicago Press, 1944).

Freedom in Science, an anti-Marxist organization that was committed to countering the interference of planners in scientific research.[107]

Hailsham, Jewkes, Hayek, and Polanyi shared a conviction about the folly of interfering with complicated systems, as well as a corresponding commitment to defending the individual from the reach of the state. The major figure in these discussions at the time was Karl Popper, who published *The Open Society and Its Enemies* in 1945.[108] Yet Snow and Leavis rarely engaged with Popper and his ideas: on one occasion a critic of Snow cited *The Open Society* against him, and Leavis occasionally suspended his disdain for philosophy long enough to express gratification at having been classed alongside Popper.[109] These fleeting indications of their respective stances towards Popper fit with the picture that is emerging here, but in order to apprehend their ideas on the relationship between individuals and systems it is necessary to move beyond their relationships to that familiar public figure.

The ideas of Hailsham, Jewkes, Hayek, and Polanyi about matters of epistemology correlated with their mutual hostility towards planning and socialism. They would likely have said that their understanding of the futility of attempting to manage complicated systems led them to oppose collectivist politics, but it is at least equally plausible that their opposition to collectivist politics predisposed them to adopt a skeptical stance towards efforts to direct the production of knowledge. In either case there were clear connections between their ideas and their politics, which help to explain Snow's opposition to both. Whereas Polanyi insisted that scientists created knowledge in unpredictable, and thus undirectable, ways, Snow believed that scientists began with a sense of the conclusions they wanted to confirm.[110] Professional success, in that vision, resulted from finding ways to confirm ideas already in mind – a process, Snow explained, that was actually identical to the work of politicians. For this reason Snow endorsed both scientific administration and technocratic politics: both science and politics proceeded by the realization of targets, so he believed that they both could be directed by rational management – or, in the parlance of the day, planned.

---

[107] On Polanyi's political work, see Jessica Reinisch, "The Society for Freedom in Science, 1940–1963," unpublished MSc thesis, University of London (2000), p. 19. See also Mary Jo Nye, "Michael Polanyi (1891–1976)," *HYLE* 8 (2002), pp. 123–127.
[108] Karl Popper, *The Open Society and Its Enemies* (London: Routledge, 1945).
[109] Israel Shahak, "Letters," *Spectator*, 2 May 1969, p. 596.
[110] C. P. Snow, "Less Fun Than Machiavelli," *New Statesman*, 9 January 1970, p. 50. Snow was reviewing a book that purported to explain how the complex system of politics worked, which is why he paused to explain that he personally favored planning.

Three conclusions follow from this brief consideration of the relationship between knowledge and politics. First, within the minds of these figures (e.g. Polanyi or Hayek), their political commitments were connected to their sense of knowledge production. Second, among figures compatible with one another (e.g. Polanyi and Hayek), that compatibility derived from a combination of intellectual (anti-systematic) and political (anti-socialist) sympathies. And third, across the divide between figures who differed from one another (e.g. Polanyi and Snow), their incompatibility similarly derived from a combination of intellectual and political antagonisms. The point here is not to identify the precise factors leading to particular sympathies and other antipathies, but merely to suggest that these overlapping networks of sympathies and antipathies were more than a coincidence. They were differences of thought and of politics, and they had little (if anything) to do with disciplinary inclinations. That is, attitudes towards planning, rather than science, animated and ordered a significant vector of politics in postwar Britain.

Leavis among the liberals

While browsing through a bookshop one day in Cambridge, Leavis came across a collection of essays by Michael Polanyi. It seems likely that the third essay, "The Two Cultures," would have first caught his eye.[111] Like Snow, Polanyi had been trained as a physical chemist, but their common training did not prevent Polanyi from launching an attack on *The Two Cultures*. He challenged Snow's premise that science was marginalized in modern culture, noting instead that the claims and authority of science were dangerously comprehensive. Through the twin idols of Freud and Marx, he argued, scientific claims of interpretive authority threatened to displace individual creativity and human humility. Science had been responsible for great progress, to be sure, but in order for that path to be recovered, human pretensions to control over vast and complicated systems needed to be demolished. "A humanist revisionism can be secured," Polanyi concluded, "only by revising the claims of science itself."[112] The necessary first step would be to discard the ideal of impersonal objectivity, which Polanyi dated as having emerged during the seventeenth century.

---

[111] Michael Polanyi, "The Two Cultures," *Knowing and Being: Essays*, ed. Marjorie Grene (London: Routledge, 1969), pp. 40–46. The essay originally appeared in *Encounter*, September 1959, pp. 61–64.

[112] *Ibid.*, p. 46.

Leavis was intrigued. Here was a scientist against Snow, critical of the ideal of impersonal objectivity, hostile to Marxism, and locating the fateful transition in the seventeenth century. Leavis began referring students and readers to Polanyi and his chief expositor, the philosopher of biology Marjorie Grene, both of whom began to figure prominently in his writing.[113] Polanyi was especially useful to Leavis in two ways. His standing as a scientist fortified Leavis's defense against charges that his position derived from hostility to science: "It is the extra-literary nature of [Polanyi's] approach, that of a distinguished scientist whose impelling interest was the nature of scientific discovery, that makes him so valuable an ally."[114] But more importantly, Polanyi's emphasis upon the inseparability between *knowing* and *being* corresponded with Leavis's ideas about language. Recall that Leavis contrasted his sense of the creative use of language, the collaborative extension of a shared human consciousness, against notions of it as merely descriptive, a matter of finding words to describe things. He believed that since humans think through language, there could be no conception of things apart from language, and he further insisted that there were no abstract criteria against which the critic assessed the use of language. As he became fond of saying (no doubt mischievously) towards the end of his life, his friend Ludwig Wittgenstein had been "comparatively naive . . . about language."[115] A poem did not need to measure itself against some independent standard, as implied by the philosopher's search for evaluative criteria: it succeeded or failed to the extent that it created an experience in the mind of the reader. Leavis employed these concepts throughout his career, most clearly in his exchange with René Wellek in 1937, but this later engagement with Polanyi provided the occasion to further develop his ideas.[116]

The value of Grene and Polanyi for Leavis became most clear in his final two books, *The Living Principle* (1975) and *Thought, Words, and Creativity* (1976).[117] There he identified the culprit that his reading of history had lacked, the "Cartesian dualism."[118] Leavis's critique of

---

[113] F. R. Leavis, *Nor Shall My Sword: Discourses on Pluralism, Compassion and Social Hope* (London: Chatto and Windus, 1972); Leavis, *The Living Principle: "English" as a Discipline of Thought* (London: Chatto and Windus, 1975).

[114] Leavis, *The Living Principle*, p. 39.   [115] *Ibid.*, p. 13.

[116] F. R. Leavis, "Literary Criticism and Philosophy: A Reply," *Scrutiny* 6 (June 1937), pp. 59–70, reprinted in *The Common Pursuit* (London: Chatto and Windus, 1952).

[117] F. R. Leavis, *Thought, Words and Creativity: Art and Thought in Lawrence* (New York: Oxford University Press, 1976).

[118] Leavis used the term in *Nor Shall My Sword*, and relied on it extensively in *The Living Principle*.

modern civilization had long lacked precision, inviting commentators to read him as hostile to capitalism, or democracy, or industry, or science. Leavis certainly regretted the turn taken towards each of these things during the seventeenth century, but it was no mere oversight that he consistently resisted equating that turn with any one of them in particular. To avoid anachronism I have substituted "modern civilization" as the object of his critique, but in the 1970s, with the help of Grene and Polanyi, Leavis identified his target more precisely. The disaster of modern civilization was its erection of a division between words and things, between language and reality, and this development had its origin in the introduction of the dualism associated with Newton and, especially, Descartes. "The point to be stressed is that, whatever was gained by the triumph of 'clarity', logic and Descartes, the gain was paid for by an immeasurable loss," Leavis explained. "[Y]ou can't . . . subscribe to the assumptions implicit in 'clear' and 'logical' as criteria without cutting yourself off from most important capacities and potentialities of thought which of its nature is essentially heuristic and creative."[119] While not expressed in these terms until the engagement with Polanyi, this perspective had long informed Leavis's criticism – including, not least, his critique of *The Two Cultures*.

The compatibility between Polanyi and Leavis, along with their mutual antagonism towards Snow, points towards something more significant than mere intellectual agreement. The connections between ideas and politics could be intricate: Polanyi's essay against *The Two Cultures* had been published in *Encounter*, which was funded by the Congress for Cultural Freedom, and both *Encounter* and the CCF were established and funded by the CIA to provide a cultural and political forum for liberal ideas amid the Cold War.[120] As with Leavis's antipathy towards Keynes, and Hailsham's resemblances to Jewkes, the point here is not to identify ironclad linkages, so much as to build the case that these overlapping relationships were too regular to be mere coincidence. Leavis's sense of language, creation, and knowledge fit into the same family of ideas as Hailsham on industrial innovation, Hayek and Jewkes on economic enterprise, and Polanyi on scientific discovery. Whatever the differences between these various figures, when attempting to locate and explain Leavis's ideological position we repeatedly find ourselves led towards an individualist liberalism.

---

[119] Leavis, *The Living Principle*, p. 97.
[120] Frances Stonor Saunders, *Who Paid the Piper? The CIA and the Cultural Cold War* (London: Granta Books, 1999).

Decline redux

Despite living at the heart of a century characterized by vast ideological struggles for hearts, minds, and territory, Leavis wrote little about politics as conventionally defined. He simply did not see the point, believing that both political parties were committed to identical assumptions regarding economic growth and university expansion. Although certainly no Tory, he did tend to direct a greater share of his opprobrium against the left than the right – as, for instance, on the occasion when he squeezed into the margin of a letter the reminder that he hated Marx, Bentham, the *Guardian*, and the *New Statesman*.[121]

More than anything, perhaps, Leavis felt isolated from politics. His assumptions about the individual and society were broadly in sync with ideas circulating among "One Nation" conservatives and the Tory grassroots, but Leavis was too hostile to established mores and powers to imagine himself as a conservative.[122] Invoking Snow's phrase, he explained that he was cut off from the "corridors of power" in Cambridge (to say nothing of Westminster).[123] He had occasional brushes with politicians, such as on one occasion when friends arranged a meeting with Labour's Shadow Minister of Education, Richard Crossman. Leavis startled Crossman by declaiming Greek verse, but the meeting was not a success, and Leavis was particularly frustrated by what he thought of as Crossman's meaningless promise to "smash the oligarchy."[124] Leavis did collect a handful of political endorsements: Hailsham praised his war against "enlightened" educational reformers such as Robbins, and three ex-ministers of education (including R. A. Butler) offered support for his campaign on behalf of the elite university.[125] During the 1964 general election campaign, Leavis took the unusual step of publicly declaring his intention to vote Liberal, only to regret it when the local Liberal candidate declared his commitment to comprehensive education.[126] Leavis concluded that he wanted nothing to do with party politics. "Politicians must aim at winning elections," he realized. "And

[121] Leavis to A. I. Doyle, 9 September 1965, Downing College: DCPP/LEA/2 Leavis, F. R.
[122] E. H. H. Green, *Thatcher* (London: Hodder Arnold, 2006), pp. 41–46, 191–193.
[123] Leavis to D. F. Pocock, 25 July 1961, Emmanuel College (Emmanuel): ECA COL 9.59a.121.20.
[124] Ian MacKillop, *F. R. Leavis: A Life in Criticism* (London: Allen Lane, 1995), p. 374. The meeting took place in the home of Richard and Jean Gooder, and I am grateful to the Gooders for sharing their recollections with me.
[125] G. Singh, *F. R. Leavis: A Literary Biography* (London: Duckworth, 1995), p. 193.
[126] F. R. Leavis, *English Literature in Our Time and the University* (London: Chatto and Windus, 1969), p. 30.

I have been forced to abandon the illusion that I could show my sense of political responsibility by believing, or trying to believe, in any party."[127]

Yet Leavis was determined to be heard inside the corridors of power. Rather than supporting candidates or endorsing policies, his relationship to national politics came to consist of an effort to attach tin cans to the trousers of the great and the good. He decided that, if no public figures would admit the need for elites, and if they continued instead to recycle platitudes about democracy, he would publicly call attention to their insincere posturing.[128] The Richmond Lecture figured as the first in a series of forays against Britain's "enlightened" orthodoxy, and it inaugurated a decade of protests against what Leavis viewed as their pernicious clichés.[129] But the reception of the Richmond Lecture revealed a problem: Leavis had sought to expose the historical crisis that had created Snow's inflated reputation, but the ensuing discussion was devoted to defending Snow from Leavis's attack. How, then, could Leavis draw attention to the issues he wanted to raise, without having his argument so misunderstood?

Leavis established the relevance of his critique in part by relating it to anxieties about national decline.[130] "That [society] has a malady it is very much aware," he told an audience in 1969. "[E]veryone has heard of that lack of 'a sense of purpose'."[131] The national crisis, according to Leavis, consisted of two parts: a lack of purpose at home, and the prospect of being overshadowed abroad. His prescription differed fundamentally from Snow's: whereas Snow cited Venice in order to secure support for reforms that might maintain Britain's economic position, Leavis detected an opportunity when inherited assumptions about what constituted "success" might be open to challenge. "[I]mperial 'greatness' cannot be 'great' in the old way," he noted, and likewise dismissed the significance of "bigness, wealth, and brute power."[132] From Leavis's perspective, by rejecting these ideals, "purpose" could at last be understood as something other than the manufacture and satisfaction of material wants. Leavis was advocating the rethinking of the materialist – and materialistic – foundations of modern civilization. "If this country could generate in a decisive way the kind of creative effort I have described," he assured his audience, "that would be its true greatness in

---

[127] Leavis, *English Literature in Our Time and the University*, p. 30.

[128] Leavis to David Holbrook, 12 December 1968, Downing College: DCPP/LEA/4 Leavis, F. R. (5).

[129] Leavis, *Nor Shall My Sword*.

[130] Leavis, *English Literature in Our Time and the University*, Chapter 6; *Nor Shall My Sword*, Chapters 4, 5, 7.

[131] Leavis, *English Literature in Our Time and the University*, p. 183.   [132] *Ibid.*, p. 35.

192 The Two Cultures Controversy

history reaffirmed."[133] Leavis was connecting long-standing commitments to contemporary worries. He continued to advance his critique of modern civilization, but in order to make that case he seized upon anxieties about national decline, molded them to his purposes, and wielded them against his rival.

Conclusion

This chapter has explored some of the issues animating national politics in Britain from the end of the Second World War through the early 1970s. Its focus has fallen between the Suez crisis of 1956 and Labour's victory of 1964, when economic decline first emerged as a political problem. Given the coincidence of its emergence with unprecedented prosperity, it was by no means inevitable that economic decline should have come to figure as a primary way of understanding this period. Declinist anxiety was initially pressed forward by center-left advocates of technocratic modernization, who blamed Britain's economic decline on the failed leadership of an amateurish establishment. Facilitated by the emergence of new ways of thinking about economic performance, and situated in the context of long-term adjustments to Britain's international position, declinism quickly moved to the center of narratives of postwar British history.

By following Snow and Leavis through their engagements with national politics in this period, two major arguments have emerged. First, whereas political actors of all persuasions were convinced of the importance of science and technology, their attitudes towards planning revealed stark lines of ideological difference. Indeed, commitments to science that might have seemed to suggest unity – such as the Conservative government's appointment of a Minister for Science, at the same time that the Labour Party was soliciting advice from the Gaitskell Group – belied contradictory attitudes towards centralized planning of scientific research. And these differences about planning extended beyond debates about the role of the state, organizing more general considerations of the relationship between the individual and the complex systems of modern society. Second, after its initial emergence among modernizing critics of a hidebound establishment, declinism flourished in part because it provided a powerful resource for advocates of various positions. The fact that declinist anxiety was invoked from various quarters attests to the fact that it was indeed central to culture and politics during this period, but the fact that it could be yoked to

---

[133] Leavis, " 'English', Unrest, and Continuity," in *Nor Shall My Sword*, p. 133.

competing agendas suggests that it is best understood less as a common experience than as a common *resource*.

Yet any discussion of Britain's "decline" after 1945 must also consider the global dimensions. After all, as one colony after another secured independence, commentators turned their attention to Britain's changing relationship to the wider world – and, as if on cue, the "two cultures" controversy provided an opportunity to discuss precisely that question.

6   Post-colonial developments

Imagined terrain

The "two cultures" controversy might have become just another argument about the arts and the sciences, but instead it intersected with simultaneous debates about the mission of the university, the interpretation of history, and the state of the nation. The reason for this expansive brief lay in the fact that, in the early 1960s, an injection of "science" as advocated in *The Two Cultures* was frequently being presented as a necessary component of institutional modernization. This nexus of associations between science, modernization, and existing institutions points to something larger at work in these discussions than merely the embrace of "science" as such. The advocates of scientific modernization were advocates of their society more generally: they believed that, whatever its faults, society as it existed in Britain and the West offered material and social benefits to the majority of the population, and they advocated modernizing reforms because they wanted to see that society rejuvenated at home and extended abroad. Their opponents, likewise, were critical not merely of "science" but of their society, and therefore they challenged these proposals for its rejuvenation and extension. These competing views of the present rested upon contrary readings of history, and the "two cultures" debate ignited in part because it was charged by disagreements over these broader issues.

The retreating British Empire emerged as the ultimate terrain where these arguments about the past, present, and future were joined. In their Rede and Richmond lectures, C. P. Snow and F. R. Leavis advanced rival assessments of the civilization they believed had first emerged in Britain, as well as contrary answers to the question of whether that civilization should now be extended throughout Asia and Africa. Snow urged this process forward: in *The Two Cultures* he argued that the Industrial Revolution had spread prosperity throughout British society, that China and the Soviet Union had recently engineered industrializations of their own, and that Britain and the West had a moral obligation to propel the rest of the world along the same path. "It is technically possible," he declared, "to carry out the scientific revolution in India, Africa, South-east Asia, Latin America, the Middle East, within fifty years."[1] It was precisely this program that filled Leavis with dread. Leavis had long denounced the civilization that he believed had emerged in England during the seventeenth century, and his Richmond Lecture rejected Snow's proposals to extend it still further. "Who will assert," he inquired skeptically, "that the average member of a modern society is more fully human, or more alive, than a Bushman, an Indian peasant, or a member of one those poignantly surviving primitive peoples, with their marvellous art and skills and vital intelligence?"[2] Snow's defenders, such as the historian J. H. Plumb, derided this claim as insincere and mistaken, while Leavis's defenders, such as the historian E. P. Thompson, maintained hope that battles lost in English history might yet be won elsewhere.[3] In these arguments, "Asia" and "Africa" figured in part as imagined locations, the sites where competing visions of Britain's past, the West's present, and the world's future all met in one place.[4]

These readings of history as a linear process echoed the "modernization theory" of American social science, but despite these similarities the argument in Britain should not be entirely conflated with discussions taking place in very different contexts.[5] That is, just as the exchange between Snow and Leavis should not be slotted into a longer history because of a superficial similarity of subject matter, neither should it be collapsed into far-flung discussions because of a coincidence of chronology. This point becomes clear through comparison of the differing ways that the Cold War figured in the debate, particularly in the most prominent American discussion of the controversy: Lionel Trilling's essay in *Commentary* magazine in June 1962 (itself not to be conflated

---

[1] C. P. Snow, *The Two Cultures and the Scientific Revolution* (Cambridge University Press, 1959), p. 43.

[2] F. R. Leavis, *Two Cultures? The Significance of C. P. Snow* (London: Chatto and Windus, 1962), p. 26.

[3] J. H. Plumb, "Letters," *Spectator*, 30 March 1962, p. 396; E. P. Thompson, *The Making of the English Working Class* (London: Gollancz, 1963), p. 13. Thompson endorsed Leavis on p. 445; on their mutual sympathies, and the place of history in the debate, see Chapter 4. Thompson made a related argument two years later, when he suggested that "something of the same moral economy" that had persisted into the late eighteenth century in England and France "endures in parts of Asia and of Africa today." Thompson, "The Peculiarities of the English," *Socialist Register, 1965*, ed. Ralph Miliband and John Saville (New York: Monthly Review Press, 1965), p. 354.

[4] This chapter examines these competing ideological positions among British intellectuals, rather than the attempted implementation of these policies in the colonial and post-colonial worlds – a subject that falls outside the scope of this book, and that is best examined by specialists in these fields.

[5] On modernization theory, see Nils Gilman, *Mandarins of the Future: Modernization Theory in Cold War America* (Baltimore: Johns Hopkins University Press, 2003).

with the work of modernization theorists).[6] Trilling's analysis soon emerged as a touchstone in discussions of the Snow–Leavis controversy, but Snow himself confessed, in "The Two Cultures: A Second Look," that he could not quite understand it.[7] Snow was confused because, although he and Trilling were ostensibly addressing the same topic, they were actually discussing different things. To Snow, living in London and lecturing in Cambridge, it seemed obvious that *The Two Cultures* addressed the future of Britain's former colonies; whereas to Trilling, living in New York and teaching at Columbia, it seemed equally clear that *The Two Cultures* related to the stand-off between the United States and the Soviet Union. These arguments did share one important similarity, however: the wider world figured in both as an imagined site of conflict for arguments close to home.

The view from New York

Snow believed that the divisions of the Cold War could be bridged by cultural exchanges and mutual understanding. In his view, the communist East and capitalist West represented not rival systems, but simply different iterations of modern society. He occasionally proved willing to harness Cold War anxieties, as when he warned in *The Two Cultures* that, if the West did not assist the developing world, the Communists would get there first. But for the most part he avoided Cold War rhetoric, and *The Two Cultures* generally treated the United States and Soviet Union as Britain's natural comparators. This tri-partite analysis, however, did not always translate into the American context, where Snow's divisions between Britain, the United States, and the Soviet Union tended to become collapsed into the more familiar binary of East against West.

Some commentators rushed to a Cold War reading of the debate more quickly than others. William F. Buckley, America's leading conservative intellectual, lacerated Snow in *National Review* for having suggested in an interview that he would feel equally at home in Russia or America.[8] Buckley introduced his readers to Snow, whose lecture *The Two Cultures*, he explained, had become "the talk-talk of the highbrow set." Snow's

---

[6] Lionel Trilling, "Science, Literature, and Culture: A Comment on the Leavis–Snow Controversy," *Commentary*, June 1962, pp. 461–477.

[7] C. P. Snow, "The Two Cultures: A Second Look," *Times Literary Supplement*, 25 October 1963, pp. 839–844, published as *The Two Cultures: and A Second Look* (Cambridge University Press, 1964).

[8] William F. Buckley, Jr., "The Voice of Sir Charles," *National Review*, 22 May 1962, p. 358. All quotations in this paragraph are from this essay.

reputation had spiraled steadily upwards, Buckley wrote, until it was finally challenged by "a crusty Oxford [*sic*] don, F. H. [*sic*] Leavis." Leavis had attacked Snow's literary pretensions, but Buckley thought something more thorough was required. Snow, he suggested, espoused an abhorrent relativism that treated the United States and the Soviet Union as moral equivalents. Buckley blamed this sort of relativism for blinding cosmopolitan intellectuals to Communist brutality, and thereby "draining the moral content out of our struggle against Communism." Summit meetings, cultural exchanges, and a White House invitation to Linus Pauling all became for Buckley "steps on the road to C. P. Snow," that is towards a society that would inform "a subject people whose martyrs are slaughtered every day on their stomachs, stopped by machine gun bullets" that "the West is no different from what they are fleeing from, dying of." For Buckley, as for so many others, *The Two Cultures* presented an ideal opportunity to air prior grievances.

Buckley's conflation of the recognition of Linus Pauling with the murder of political refugees was typical of the relentless binaries of Cold War polemics, but it nevertheless serves as a reminder of the political context in which he wrote. Even a brief timeline of events between Snow's initial remarks on the "two cultures" in 1956 and Leavis's rejoinder in 1962 conveys a sense of the stakes of geo-politics in this period as seen from New York: in 1956 the Soviet Union invaded Hungary; in 1957 the Soviet Union launched Sputnik; in 1958 Khrushchev called for the withdrawal of troops from Berlin; in 1959 Fidel Castro led the revolution in Cuba; in 1960 an American spy plane was shot down over Soviet territory; and in 1961 construction began on the Berlin Wall – indeed, construction began the day after Snow's interview aired.[9] From Buckley's perspective these events transpired in a world divided between East and West, but in truth there were significant variations within those supposedly hegemonic blocs. Britain had Cold Warriors of its own, and (as we shall see) they too criticized Snow, but it was also a place where the establishment's newspaper of record could respond to Yuri Gagarin's spaceflight by acknowledging the achievements of centralized planning.[10] That there was less room for maneuver in the American context is illustrated not by the eager polemics of Buckley, but by the more thoughtful reservations – but reservations still – of Lionel Trilling.

[9] Malcolm Muggeridge, "Appointment with Sir Charles Snow," interview broadcast 18 August 1961, typescript held in the Harry Ransom Humanities Research Center (HRC): Snow 8.1.
[10] "The Plough and the Stars," *Times*, 26 April 1961, p. 15.

Trilling's essay, "Science, Literature, and Culture: A Comment on the Leavis-Snow Controversy," appeared in *Commentary* in June 1962. *Commentary* was an influential periodical of politics and culture, broadly liberal in outlook (although it would later emerge as a leading neo-conservative journal). Its editor was the precocious Norman Podhoretz, and we have met these figures before. Trilling was Professor of English at Columbia University, and in the 1950s Podhoretz had been one of his most brilliant students. Podhoretz then read English with Leavis in Cambridge, before returning to New York and, from 1960, editing *Commentary*. In 1955 Trilling warmly reviewed Snow's novel *The New Men*, suggesting that, while Snow might never write a great novel, he was steadily producing good ones; in 1958 Podhoretz published a favorable review of *The Conscience of the Rich*, praising Snow's novels for their intelligence and insight.[11] It was during this period that the Snows became friendly with the Podhoretzes and the Trillings (as well as with Trilling's colleague at Columbia, Jacques Barzun), and on trips across the Atlantic the couples arranged their schedules to make room for dinners.[12] But Podhoretz had also remained friendly with Leavis, so the attack by his former teacher on his new friend placed him in an awkward position. Caught between mentors and friends, Podhoretz did his best: he secured Trilling's assessment of the controversy for *Commentary*, and offered both Leavis and Snow opportunities to respond.[13] Neither accepted his offer, and all of these relationships were strained by the affair.[14]

Trilling's essay unfolded in his characteristic style. It opened with a series of telling observations, proceeded to peel back layer after layer of meaning, and eventually arrived at a penetrating conclusion. He began by relating the argument between Snow and Leavis to the previous

[11] Lionel Trilling, "The Novel Alive or Dead," *Griffin*, February 1955, pp. 4–13; Norman Podhoretz, "England, My England," *New Yorker*, 10 May 1958, pp. 143–146.

[12] The development of these relationships becomes apparent through their correspondence: Snow/Trilling in HRC: Snow 197.21, Snow/Podhoretz in HRC: Snow 165.10–165.13, Snow/Barzun in HRC: Snow 56.1–56.7. Podhoretz's memoirs provide accounts of literary culture in New York during this period, the emergence and trajectory of neo-conservatism, and his relationship with Lionel and Diana Trilling: Podhoretz, *Making It* (New York: Random House, 1967); Podhoretz, *Breaking Ranks* (New York: Harper and Row, 1979); Podhoretz, *Ex-Friends* (New York: Free Press, 1999).

[13] Podhoretz to Snow, 22 May 1962, HRC: Snow 165.12.

[14] *Ibid.*; Snow to Podhoretz, 13 March 1980, HRC: Snow 165.13. On the trajectory of Snow's relationship with Podhoretz, including the renewal of their correspondence towards the end of Snow's life, see Chapter 7. Trilling's relationship with Leavis was similarly strained, much to his dismay and despite his best efforts: Richard Hoggart, *A Measured Life: The Times and Places of an Orphaned Intellectual* (New Brunswick: Transaction, 1994), p. 291.

century's exchange between Thomas Huxley and Matthew Arnold, allowing that "the new power of science perhaps justifies a contemporary revival of the Victorian question."[15] He then approached Snow's Rede Lecture by moving backward in time, beginning with the hubbub in the *Spectator*, and pausing over Leavis's lecture long enough to register discomfort with its "impermissible tone."[16] These introductory observations were followed by sustained attention to *The Two Cultures* itself. Snow's initially even-handed lament, Trilling noted, actually advanced a moral indictment of literature that could not be sustained; Snow's claim that the traditional culture managed the Western world was mistaken; and Snow's faith in international cooperation among scientists betrayed a naive denial of the realities of politics. Leavis, Trilling thought, should have been up to the task of justifying the moral function of literature against Snow's claims, but despite its ferocity his critique failed to confront Snow's actual premises.

Trilling took this uncharacteristic failure of criticism as an invitation to consider how much Snow and Leavis actually shared in common. He pointed to their mutual commitments to the creation of a new social class, one that would be based on taste rather than privilege. Yet in the modern age – "an age dominated by advertising" – this commitment to taste revealed the limits of "culture" as a basis of judgment: "In our more depressed moments," Trilling wrote, "we might be led to ask whether there is a real difference between being The Person Who defines himself by his commitment to one or another idea of morality, politics, literature, or city-planning, and being The Person Who defines himself by wearing trousers without pleats."[17] From this perspective, he continued, Snow's preference for the lifestyles of scientists, Leavis's preference for D. H. Lawrence, and the *Spectator* reader's preference for Snow or Leavis all became evidence of the extent, but also the limitations, of "the cultural mode of thought."[18] Trilling concluded by suggesting that these limitations reminded him of the need for an alternative basis of assessment, "the idea of Mind" – a foundation of judgment less bound by the constraints of time and place.[19]

[15] Trilling, "Science, Literature and Culture," p. 462.
[16] *Ibid.*, pp. 463–464.   [17] *Ibid.*, p. 476.   [18] *Ibid.*, p. 477.
[19] *Ibid.*, pp. 476–477. For a contemporary critique of Trilling's argument, one that Snow cultivated in private and cited in public, see Martin Green, "Lionel Trilling and the Two Cultures," *Essays in Criticism* 13 (1963), pp. 375–385. Green contacted Snow in 1960 after *The Two Cultures* inspired him to study science as an adult; Snow initially kept his distance, but, during the controversy with Leavis, Green earned his trust by proving a staunch ally. HRC: Snow 109.1–109.3.

Trilling recognized the centrality of politics to the controversy. "[I]f we consent to involve ourselves in the new dialectic of the old controversy," he wrote, "we must be aware that we are not addressing ourselves to a question of educational theory, or to an abstract contention as to what kind of knowledge has the truest affinity with the human soul. We approach these matters only to pass through them. What we address ourselves to is politics."[20] Snow and Trilling might have agreed on that point, but it soon became clear that they had different conceptions of the "politics" at hand. In Trilling's presentation, Snow's argument turned on two pivots: first at its mention of the human condition, when the even-handed analysis turned into an indictment of literary intellectuals, and then at its shift to a global perspective, when the focus on the failings of literature gave way to discussion of the more hopeful future offered by science. Trilling suggested that, in Snow's presentation, the common culture among scientists transcended even the most intractable of divisions: "For the real message of *The Two Cultures*," he wrote, "is that an understanding between the West and the Soviet Union could be achieved by the culture of scientists, which reaches over factitious national and ideological differences."[21] Trilling thus read Snow's "real message" as a plea to transcend the Cold War – a denial of politics that he could not endorse: "[W]e can be perfectly certain that the world will not be saved by denying the actualities of the world. Among these actualities politics is one."[22] He summarized his analysis this way: "In short, Sir Charles, seeking to advance the cause of understanding between the West and the Soviet Union, would seem to be saying that this understanding will come if we conceive . . . that politics cannot be judged (because it does not really exist)."[23] It was a position that Trilling thought fundamentally mistaken.

This criticism caught Snow by surprise, but the seeds of Trilling's objection had actually been apparent for years. In 1955 Trilling had called *The Masters* "a paradigm of the political life," and that favorable review sparked both Snow's career and their friendship.[24] The same review, however, noted Snow's reluctance to blame even those characters who seemed most to deserve it. Snow wrote sympathetically of progressive scientists who had sided with Communism in the 1930s, leading Trilling to protest: "I can't help thinking of the failure of intelligence that was involved with the good will, of the laziness of scientific minds that interpreted so badly the inadequately-gathered evidence, of the arrogance of scientific minds that were sure that politics and human good are

---

[20] Trilling, "Science, Literature and Culture," p. 462.   [21] *Ibid.*, p. 469.
[22] *Ibid.*, p. 470.   [23] *Ibid.*, p. 471.   [24] Trilling, "The Novel Alive or Dead," p. 9.

so easily comprehended."[25] In 1955 Trilling hurried to acknowledge his own "disagreeable" impulse to blame, and praised Snow by comparison for his capacity for forgiveness. By 1962, however, Trilling's reservations towards Snow's reluctance to judge had developed into more substantial concerns about Snow's apparent refusal to acknowledge politics at all.

Snow responded to Trilling's criticism the following year in "The Two Cultures: A Second Look." He protested that he had arguably written as much about politics as any living person – how could Trilling possibly have read him as denying the existence of politics? He sought to resolve this conundrum by unpacking Trilling's argument. Critics such as Trilling, he explained, "mean by 'politics' something more limited than most of us can accept . . . They mean . . . the waging of the cold war."[26] Rather than disputing this observation, Snow embraced it: "[Trilling's] criticism amounts to saying that I did not relate the lecture to the cold war, as it was being waged in 1959: or, more sinister still, that I did not accept the cold war as the prime absolute of our age, and of all ages to come. Of course I didn't."[27] In short, Trilling had been correct to observe that Snow refused to read international politics through the lens of the Cold War, and the reasons for that refusal explain why Snow rejected a Cold War interpretation of the debate in favor of an alternative perspective from post-imperial Britain.

Beyond the Cold War

Snow's impatience with Cold War divisions, and his efforts to direct attention to Asia, Africa, and elsewhere instead, were closely related to his argument in *The Two Cultures*. The Rede Lecture proposed that Britain and the West send capital and personnel throughout the world to facilitate economic development. "Scientists," Snow assured his audience, "would do us good all over Asia and Africa."[28] The ambition was to propel underdeveloped nations along a historical continuum that culminated in industrial development and economic prosperity. This program depended upon a linear reading of history, one that Snow made even more explicit in *A Second Look*.[29] He explained that the globe

---

[25] *Ibid.*, p. 10. [26] Snow, *The Two Cultures: and A Second Look*, p. 97.
[27] *Ibid.* [28] Snow, *The Two Cultures*, p. 46.
[29] On the colonial, and military, origins of this ostensibly post-imperial, liberal program, see Priya Satia, "Developing Iraq: Britain, India, and the Redemption of Empire and Technology in the First World War," *Past and Present* 197 (November 2007), pp. 211–255. Moreover, given Snow's commitment to a linear reading of history – a commitment shared by advocates of modernization theory – it is interesting to note that this program had its origins in a very different set of assumptions: "Developing Mesopotamia," Satia writes,

resembled "a vast sociological laboratory in which one can observe all kinds of society from the neolithic to the advanced industrial," and that parish registers from early modern France told a story currently taking place in Asia and Latin America.[30] From this perspective, the Cold War posed problems of two sorts: it obscured the reality that industrialized nations were more alike than different, and it diverted attention from the actual – and tragic – disparities among nations at different stages of development. When Snow turned his attention to international affairs, therefore, he hoped to resolve divisions of two sorts: the presumption of political differences between East and West, and the reality of economic differences between North and South.

The first of these goals inspired Snow to attempt to soothe Cold War tensions. He befriended the Soviet literary critic Valentina Ivasheva, and in 1961 he confided his hope that his recent novel, *The Affair*, might resonate with Soviet readers: "It is what I am trying to say by every means open to me," he explained. "If this is pointed out by someone writing the introduction[,] then perhaps the book will be seen to contain a message of hope."[31] He was referring to a passage depicting Lewis Eliot's defense of a fellow-traveler who has been accused of scientific fraud. Eliot urges the college's judiciary council not to confuse the man with the politics: "Wasn't it the chronic danger of our time, not only practical but intellectual, to let the world get divided into two halves?"[32] Eliot worries that the "fog of prejudice" had become "so thick that people on the two sides were ceasing to think of each other as belonging to the same species," and he pleads with the council to see common humanity despite contrary ideologies.[33] Snow hoped *The Affair* would be read in the Soviet Union as a show of good faith from a friendly Western writer, and as evidence that a future was being imagined beyond the politics of confrontation.

Snow's literary success in the United States and the Soviet Union encouraged him to think of himself as a bridge between the two nations. It was for this reason that he declined Harold Macmillan's invitation to serve on Lionel Robbins's committee on higher education: "The Americans have taken my books up in a fairly big way," Snow informed the Prime Minister, "and, very oddly, I am also somewhat in demand in Moscow."[34] He wanted to use this opportunity to attempt to speak to both sides, and in order to help him find his audience he continued

"was an act of restoration, not transformation, a refitting of it, through modern technology, to resume its traditional role in a modern world" (p. 231).
[30] Snow, *The Two Cultures: and A Second Look*, pp. 81, 83.
[31] Snow to Valentina Ivasheva, 15 May 1961, HRC: Snow 123.7.
[32] C. P. Snow, *The Affair* (London: Macmillan, 1960), p. 327.   [33] *Ibid.*
[34] Snow to Harold Macmillan, 26 January 1961, HRC: Snow 142.9.

cultivating relationships with Soviet intellectuals. The figures he was most interested in knowing were writers rather than scientists, and establishment figures rather than dissidents. In addition to Ivasheva, then, he also befriended the writer (and future Nobel laureate) Mikhail Sholokhov. The Soviet Writers' Union, the institutional locus of Socialist Realism, invited him to visit their offices in Moscow, and Snow returned from that visit eager to promote Soviet writers in Britain.[35] He began a correspondence with the editor of *Soviet Literature*, Vasili Azhayev. Snow promised that he would publicize *Soviet Literature* in Britain, and Azhayev in turn kept him posted on the reception of his novels in the Soviet Union.[36] It is difficult to assess the impact of such efforts on something so vast as the Cold War, but they paid dividends of another kind: in 1963 Snow was awarded an honorary doctorate from Rostov State University, and in 1965 his sixtieth birthday was marked by a conference in Moscow on his novels.[37]

Snow also sought to persuade his publisher to become the main British house for Soviet literature. "I am very anxious for Macmillans really to establish themselves as the main contact for the most interesting developments in Soviet literature," he told Alan Maclean towards the end of 1967.[38] He urged Maclean to send an editor to the offices of *Soviet Literature*, but Maclean – courteously keeping his distance – replied that the firm could not afford to lose a staff member for a month.[39] Snow then ran the suggestion past Harold Macmillan, and Macmillan assured him that he wanted to assist where he could.[40] Early the next year, when the Soviet translator of Ernest Hemingway planned a visit to London, Snow tried to arrange a meeting with the firm.[41] For various reasons these efforts came to nothing, but the relationships that were forged proved more lasting. In March 1968 Ivasheva sent Snow a dismissive rejection letter that she had received from a British publisher, along with the melodramatic inscription: "Do you remember saying once, the rest of our lives would be dedicated to the building of bridges between our two great countries?"[42] Motivated by just such a combination of idealism and self-interest, Snow's efforts to build those bridges occupied much of his energy during the two decades after his Rede Lecture.

---

[35] HRC: Snow 199.11.
[36] Snow to Vasili Azhayev, 11 August 1961, HRC: Snow 55.7; Azhayev to Snow, 4 May 1962, HRC: Snow 55.7.
[37] "Tribute to Lord Snow," *Soviet News* (London), 15 October 1965.
[38] Snow to Alan Maclean, 29 November 1967, HRC: Snow 143.9.
[39] Maclean to Snow, 5 December 1967, HRC: Snow 143.9.
[40] Macmillan to Snow, 15 December 1967, HRC: Snow 142.10.
[41] Snow to Maclean, 4 January 1968, HRC: Snow 143.9.
[42] Ivasheva to Snow, 25 March 1968, HRC: Snow 123.11.

Snow's indulgence towards the Soviet Union attracted criticism as well. In 1960 the writer and critic John Wain returned from a trip to the Soviet Union and contradicted Snow's positive assessment of conditions there. In "An Open Letter to My Russian Hosts," published in the *Observer*, Wain delivered a blunt assessment of publishing, tourism, and education in the Soviet Union – all of which he characterized as propaganda, manipulated by the state to impress credulous Westerners.[43] The following year, reviewing an edition of Russian short stories that included an introduction by the Snows, the *Spectator* rejected their insistence upon the need to distinguish between art and politics when reading Soviet literature, arguing that the very interest of contemporary Russian fiction lay in its negotiations of the constraints imposed by Socialist Realism.[44] In 1962, as Leavis's Richmond Lecture caused Snow to become increasingly sensitive to public criticism, Snow brought (and won) a libel suit against Bernard Levin for having suggested that he was a fellow-traveler.[45] He brought that suit because he thought of himself as pro-Russian rather than pro-Communist, a distinction that lay at the heart of his impatience with the Cold War.

In 1968, in a survey of the Russian scene since 1956 – the pivotal year of Khrushchev's secret speech, the Soviet invasion of Hungary, and the splintering of the British Communist Party – Snow approved of the emergence of "liberal Communism" in eastern Europe. Liberal Communism, he explained, was a non-ideological position that rejected Stalinism, yet accepted the need for public ownership, state planning, and Communist Party leadership.[46] He said that liberal Communists recognized that they were situated within a complex society, and – rather than lashing out – they wanted to work through that society to extend justice and welfare throughout the population. "If the year of my birth (1905) had remained unchanged, but I had been born a Russian," he concluded, "I suppose I should be a liberal Communist."[47] Snow's characterization of Soviet society exactly mirrored his understanding of

---

[43] John Wain, "An Open Letter to My Russian Hosts," *Observer*, 7 August 1960, p. 13; Snow responded in the next issue.

[44] Ronald Bryden, "With a Difference," *Spectator*, 15 December 1961, p. 908.

[45] Bernard Levin, "My Concern Is Not the Play But What Is Behind It," *Daily Mail*, 7 September 1962, p. 3; *Times*, 1 August 1963, p. 8. This affair is recounted in Paul Boytinck, *C. P. Snow: A Reference Guide* (Boston: Hall, 1980), B581.

[46] C. P. Snow, "Liberal Communism: The Basic Dogma, the Scope for Freedom, the Danger in Optimism," *Nation*, 9 December 1968, pp. 617–623, reprinted in Snow's introduction to Georgi Dzhagarov, *The Public Prosecutor: A Play*, trans. Marguerite Alexieva, adapted for the stage by C. P. Snow and Pamela Hansford Johnson (London: Owen, 1969). On the cultural thaw in the Soviet Union, and on revisionism in eastern Europe, see Tony Judt, *Postwar* (New York: Penguin, 2005), pp. 422–449.

[47] Snow, "Liberal Communism," p. 619.

British society – indeed, of societies throughout the industrialized world. Where others saw differences of ideology, Snow saw similarities of function: he believed that modern societies, whether nominally communist, socialist, or capitalist, represented various iterations of an advanced socio-economic system. This system generated and distributed economic prosperity, and in *The Two Cultures* (and elsewhere) Snow implored his audience to see beyond the Cold War so as to extend that prosperity throughout the wider world.

The expert's burden

If one part of Snow's international agenda was to identify common ground despite the Cold War, his other ambition was to mobilize intellectual and political support for economic development. Snow's position on the Cold War is significant in this regard not because it represents widely held views, but because it complicates conventional terms of analysis. That is, his denial of the existence of meaningful differences between East and West does not fit into the dichotomies of Cold War polemics, and as such it points to the need to attend to variations within positions that presented themselves as hegemonic.[48] Snow's position on the post-colonial world, however, is significant for the opposite reason: not because it is atypical, but because it is representative. His ideas about Asia and Africa at the moment of decolonization provide a point of entry into broader conversations about Britain's shifting international position in a world after empire.[49]

International politics looked different when viewed through the lens of imperial retreat rather than the Cold War. The years after 1956 were no less eventful for the British than the Americans: this was the period of Mau Mau, the "wind of change," and rapid decolonization.[50] Dean

---

[48] The historiography on the Cold War is vast, but for a helpful survey of the issues and literature as they pertain to Britain, see Harriet Jones, "The Impact of the Cold War," in *A Companion to Contemporary Britain, 1939–2000*, ed. Paul Addison and Harriet Jones (Oxford: Blackwell, 2005), pp. 23–41.

[49] This perspective – of a colonial, North–South axis, rather than a Cold War, East–West one – was also evident in France during this period: Joseph Morgan Hodge, *Triumph of the Expert: Agrarian Doctrines of Development and the Legacies of British Colonialism* (Athens: Ohio University Press, 2007), p. 209. Tony Judt notes, and warns against, a tendency among American scholars to read European affairs at this time through the concerns of Washington: *Postwar*, pp. 281–282.

[50] As in the case of the Cold War, the historiography on decolonization is enormous; Bill Schwarz offers an interpretive introduction, and a bibliographical essay, in "The End of Empire," in *A Companion to Contemporary Britain, 1939–2000*, ed. Paul Addison and Harriet Jones, pp. 482–498. See also Wm. Roger Louis, *The Ends of British Imperialism: The Scramble for Empire, Suez, and Decolonization* (London: I. B. Tauris, 2006).

Acheson's remark that Britain had lost an empire but not yet found a role does not exactly capture the state of that relationship: Britain may have been losing an empire, but familiar assumptions as to its role nevertheless persisted. The form of that role may have been shifting from master to champion, from administration to education, and from exploitation to assistance, but within changed parameters old habits persisted. Britain was frequently depicted as having reached an advanced stage of economic, social, and political development, and its future position in the world was expected to derive from that fact. While in the past that position had been secured through political administration, in the future it would derive from education and development. But in both cases – and in the characteristic move of any ideology – the interests of the (former) colonizer were thought to be aligned with the needs of the (formerly) colonized. Snow's assessment of Britain's international position in a world after empire adhered closely to this position.

The debate about *The Two Cultures* emerged as one site of discussion of these issues. The lecture's concluding section was entitled "The Rich and the Poor," and this theme was so central to his argument that Snow considered employing that title for the lecture as a whole.[51] He identified the gap between the rich and poor nations of the world as the most pressing issue of contemporary morality and politics. As we have seen, Snow believed that this gap existed because some economies had industrialized whereas others had not – a state of affairs, he assured his audience, that would not, and should not, last much longer. The question facing Britain, and indeed the whole West, was whether they would rise to the challenge of assisting India, Africa, Southeast Asia, Latin America, and the Middle East in their inevitable pursuit of industrial development and economic prosperity. This commitment to industrial, rather than agricultural, development placed Snow at odds with much of the late-colonial intellectual and political establishment – a reminder of the variations and tensions that existed even among advocates of "development" broadly understood.[52] Snow, for his part, fervently believed in the directed industrialization of the "scientific revolution," and therein lay the connection between the global crisis and the "two cultures" problem: he argued that the education system of Britain in particular, and of the West more generally, was failing to

---

[51] Snow, *The Two Cultures*, pp. 38–48.
[52] Hodge, *Triumph of the Expert*, p. 267. On prior conceptions of colonial "development," see Satia, "Developing Iraq," especially pp. 213–215, 254–255.

produce the personnel required for this task. The reform of education was but one step, then, towards a greater end: in *The Two Cultures* Snow called for Britain and the West to send capital and personnel throughout the world to foster industrialization.

Snow frequently returned to this argument in the years after his Rede Lecture. In 1960, addressing the American Association for the Advancement of Science, he urged his audience to combat the global crises of nuclear war, hunger, and overpopulation.[53] Three years later, in "The Two Cultures: A Second Look," he insisted that science and technology held the potential to alleviate poverty and suffering the world over: "We cannot avoid the realisation that applied science has made it possible to remove unnecessary suffering from a billion individual human lives."[54] Snow explained that he was speaking of healing the sick, feeding the hungry, providing shelter, and preventing overpopulation, and he argued that the knowledge to resolve each of these crises was readily available – only the failure, or the refusal, to acknowledge the relationship between *development* and *progress* stood in the way. Snow was advocating something much more ambitious than mere financial assistance: he hoped that, in the wake of economic development, the institutional structures of industrial economies and modern societies would follow. He was talking about "[t]rade unions, collective dealing, the entire apparatus of modern industry," and he believed this apparatus a good thing in and of itself: "I don't think anyone knows how inextricably these liberties depend on our existing political, social, and economic institutions."[55] In short, with regard to economies, societies, and polities, Snow believed that the world had problems and the West had solutions, and the problem with Western civilization was only that it lacked the will to replicate itself around the globe.

Snow had no shortage of company in advocating Western assistance with international development. According to Joseph Morgan Hodge, "The self-assurance and the faith in science, technology, and the ability of state and international organizations to manage development and human progress were perhaps never greater."[56] An intellectual godfather to this program was Snow's own hero, H. G. Wells, whose *Open Conspiracy* (1928) had sounded the call to lead the world's "backward races" towards material betterment through the planning and development of science,

---

[53] C. P. Snow, "The Moral Un-neutrality of Science" (1960), reprinted in *Public Affairs* (New York: Scribner's, 1971).
[54] Snow, *The Two Cultures: and A Second Look*, p. 78.
[55] *Ibid.*, p. 89; Snow, "The Cold War and the West," *Partisan Review*, Winter 1962, p. 82.
[56] Hodge, *Triumph of the Expert*, p. 267.

technology, and industry.[57] On the British left this position was endorsed by such figures as J. D. Bernal in *World Without War* (1958), and Peter Worsley in *Out of Apathy* (1960).[58] One of its most respected proponents was Snow's friend Patrick Blackett, who enjoyed the unusual distinction of being simultaneously esteemed on the political left, within the Labour Party, and among his scientific peers.[59] In 1957 Blackett anticipated Snow's arguments in an article, "Technology and World Advancement," which was reprinted in *Nature* and the *Listener*, and generated discussions in the *Observer* and the *Economist*.[60] A decade after Snow's Rede Lecture, Blackett – then President of the Royal Society – repeatedly sounded the call for economic development to alleviate poverty around the world in a series of lectures, including the Nehru Lecture (1968), the Gandhi Memorial Lecture (1969), and the Rede Lecture (1969).[61]

Snow generally avoided the term "modernization," and British imperial projects should not be conflated with American Cold War ambitions, but these ideas about development did share common assumptions with modernization theory. Modernization theory flourished in American social science after the Second World War, and it found political influence in the White House during the 1960s. The theory posited specific criteria constituting "modernity," such as economic growth, social mobility, political participation, and secularization.

---

[57] H. G. Wells, *The Open Conspiracy: Blue Prints for a World Revolution* (London: Gollancz, 1928), especially pp. 113–114. In the 1930s Snow challenged the English Tripos in Cambridge for neglecting Wells, and in the 1960s Snow appreciatively revisited Wells. See Stefan Collini's "Introduction," in *The Two Cultures* (Cambridge University Press, 1993), pp. xxiii–xxv, as well as Snow, *Variety of Men* (London: Macmillan, 1967), pp. 63–85.

[58] J. D. Bernal, *World Without War* (London: Routledge and Paul, 1958); Peter Worsley, "Imperial Retreat," in *Out of Apathy*, ed. E. P. Thompson (London: New Left Books, 1960), pp. 139–140.

[59] Mary Jo Nye, *Blackett: Physics, War and Politics in the Twentieth Century* (Cambridge, Mass.: Harvard University Press, 2004)

[60] P. M. S. Blackett, "Technology and World Advancement," *Advancement of Science*, September 1957, pp. 3–11, reprinted in the *Listener* (5 September 1957), *Discovery* (September 1957), *Nature* (7 September 1957), *Science and Culture* (October 1957), and *Bulletin of the Atomic Scientists* (November 1957); the article was also discussed, among other places, in the *Economist* (7 September 1957) and the *Observer* (8 September 1957).

[61] The Jawaharlal Nehru Memorial Lecture was delivered in 1968 and published as "Science and Technology in an Unequal World," *Jawaharlal Memorial Lectures, 1967–1972* (Bombay: Bharatiya Vidya Bhavan, 1973); the Gandhi Memorial Lecture was delivered in 1969 and published as *Reflections on Science and Technology in Developing Countries* (Nairobi: East African Publishing House, 1969); the Rede Lecture was delivered in Cambridge in 1969 and published as *The Gap Widens* (Cambridge University Press, 1970).

By registering the achievement (or absence) of these and other attributes, nations could be placed along a continuum that culminated in the universal goal of modernity. A key tract in this literature derived from a set of Cambridge lectures delivered the year before Snow's Rede Lecture, W. W. Rostow's *The Stages of Economic Growth*.[62] Rostow, Professor of Economic History at MIT, took the Industrial Revolution in Britain as a model in order to identify the steps towards modernity. He went on to serve in the Kennedy and Johnson administrations, and his book sold 260,000 copies in English between 1960 and 1972. The subtitle of his book – *A Non-Communist Manifesto* – reflects the Cold War imperative of the context in which these ideas flourished: modernization theory provided an intellectual rationale for policies aimed at moving "Third World" nations along the path of development, pushing them towards modernity along Western, rather than Soviet, lines.[63]

Forms of development were also embraced by political leaders and scientific intellectuals within the former empire. Indeed, for many nationalist leaders, the colonial state's emphasis upon agricultural reform obstructed the more pressing – and promising – pursuit of industrial development, and one goal of independence was to seize control of the state so as to direct its energies towards the latter.[64] A powerful advocate of industrialization was the theoretical physicist (and 1979 Nobel laureate) Abdus Salam, who had been born in 1926 in western Punjab. After the Second World War he took a doctorate at Cambridge, and then briefly taught mathematics in Pakistan at Government College and the University of Lahore. In 1954 Salam returned to Cambridge as a lecturer, and from 1957 he was Professor of Theoretical Physics at Imperial College London – a position that he retained while founding and directing the International Centre for Theoretical Physics in Trieste (ICTP).[65] Salam firmly believed in the links between scientific,

---

[62] W. W. Rostow, *The Stages of Economic Growth: A Non-Communist Manifesto* (Cambridge University Press, 1960).

[63] Gilman emphasizes that Rostow's engagement with Marxism was more complicated than simple opposition: *Mandarins of the Future*, pp. 199–202. On modernization theory in the United States, see also Howard Brick, *Age of Contradiction: American Thought and Culture in the 1960s* (Ithaca: Cornell University Press, 1998), pp. 44–65. Hodge detaches the British and American projects, and instead recovers the imperial history into which the postwar British case fits, in *Triumph of the Expert*. For a historical account of the rise and fall of the "development" paradigm, including citations to the extensive historiography on the subject, see Barbara Weinstein, "Developing Inequality," *American Historical Review* 113 (February 2008), pp. 3–9.

[64] Hodge, *Triumph of the Expert*, p. 266.

[65] In 1997 the ICTP was renamed the Abdus Salam International Centre for Theoretical Physics. On Salam, including his relationship with Snow, see Alexis de Greiff, "The International Centre for Theoretical Physics, 1960–1979: Ideology and Practice in a

technological, and economic development, and in 1961 he delivered a rousing speech along these lines to the All Pakistan Science Conference in Dhaka. This speech echoed Snow's *The Two Cultures*, it cited Rostow's *The Stages of Economic Growth*, and its peroration called for scientific development harnessed to the goal of economic prosperity. Anticipating Harold Wilson's rhetoric at the Labour Party conference two years later, Salam declared: "Let us be absolutely clear about the nature of the revolution we are trying to usher in. It is a technological and scientific revolution, and thus it is imperative that top-most priorities are given to the massive development of the nation's scientific and technological skills."[66] Salam connected the development of those skills to the fight against poverty, and he concluded by calling for growth in Pakistan as rapid as that which had already been achieved in Russia and China.

With his message being echoed by figures from the political left, the Anglo–American establishment, and the British Commonwealth, Snow would hardly have recognized similarities between his proposals for industrialization and older justifications for imperialism. Indeed, he was mindful of the tradition of European meddling in other peoples' affairs: "Plenty of Europeans, from St. Francis Xavier to Schweitzer, have devoted their lives to Asians and Africans, nobly but paternally," he said in *The Two Cultures*, but he insisted that he was advocating something different: "These are not the Europeans whom Asians and Africans are going to welcome now. They want men who will muck in as colleagues, who will pass on what they know, do an honest technical job, and get out."[67] Scientists were ideally suited for this work, Snow argued, not only because they possessed the requisite technical knowledge, but because their international collaborations rendered them comparatively free of racial prejudice. Snow himself had no patience for racism: later that decade, speaking in the House of Lords, he denounced the expression of opinions that would comfort white settlers in Rhodesia or white southerners in America.[68] In place of the old pattern of paternalism, racism, and imperialism, *The Two Cultures* offered what Snow believed to be a new program of technocracy, democracy, and development.

United Nations Institution for Scientific Cooperation and Third World Development," unpublished PhD thesis, University of London (2001); T. W. B. Kibble, "Salam, Muhammad Abdus (1926–1996)," *Oxford Dictionary of National Biography* (Oxford University Press, 2004).

[66] Salam, "Technology and Pakistan's Attack on Poverty," address to the All Pakistan Science Conference (Dhaka, 1961), HRC: Snow 177.8.

[67] Snow, *The Two Cultures*, p. 45.

[68] Snow, Speech to the House of Lords, 18 June 1968, *Parliamentary Debates*, Lords, 5th ser., vol. 293 (11 June 1968–28 June 1968), cols. 539–548.

Yet the assumptions behind this prescription betrayed habits of mind that had been forged during a previous era. In this view Britain had a duty to assist its former colonies, to provide them with technical – even linguistic – training, and to guide them towards a metropolitan stage of economic, social, and political development. Agency and knowledge both remained close to home, and programs of modernization and development promised a familiar role for Britain in delivering them to the very lands and peoples they had until recently administered. In *The Two Cultures*, as in related discussions at the height of decolonization, long-standing ideas about Britain's relationship to its former colonies were not being overhauled so much as updated.[69]

Dissent on development

Leavis did not share Snow's access to British prime ministers and Soviet intellectuals, but in the Richmond Lecture and subsequent statements he, too, connected his argument to the issues of decolonization and development. Indeed, this position informed one of the most puzzling comments in his Richmond Lecture: "[I]f you are enlightened," he had said, eyebrow fully cocked, "you see that the sum of wisdom lies in expediting the processes which will ensure the Congolese, the Indonesians, the Bushmen *(no, not the Bushmen – there aren't enough of them)*, the Chinese, the Indians, their increasing supplies of jam."[70] What Leavis meant by this ironic exception for the "bushmen" becomes clear through consideration of his ideas about social and economic development more generally. While Snow advocated intervention to improve material conditions throughout Asia and Africa, Leavis detected a rare opportunity when Britain and the West might be prevented from making things worse. This position found few allies in the "two cultures" controversy of 1962, but by the end of that decade a critical stance towards development was becoming less marginal in intellectual discourse. This fact does not necessarily testify to the extent of Leavis's influence, so much as to a broad ideological shift that created more receptive conditions for positions that he had long advanced.

Despite their differences, Leavis and Snow actually shared common assumptions with regard to international affairs. Leavis, no less than Snow, viewed the Cold War less as a clash between rival systems than as

---

[69] On the continuities – of both personnel and ideas – between the late-colonial and post-colonial development programs, see Hodge, *Triumph of the Expert*, pp. 254–276. James Vernon makes a related point in *Hunger: A Modern History* (Cambridge, Mass.: Harvard University Press, 2007), pp. 272–273.

[70] Leavis, *Two Cultures?*, p. 25 (emphasis mine).

a division within a civilization; and they both presumed a linear reading of historical development, in which Asia and Africa figured as the next battleground between forces that had previously clashed in England's past. Their similarities even extended to the level of tactics, as they both sought to harness British anxieties about the ascendance of the United States: Snow warned in his Rede Lecture that "this country will be the *enclave* of an *enclave*," while Leavis seized opportunities to harness unease about Britain's likely position in a world dominated by America (both of which echoed Jimmy Porter in *Look Back in Anger*: "It's pretty dreary living in the American age – unless you're an American of course").[71] In short, when Snow and Leavis turned their attention to the world beyond Britain, they focused on the former empire rather than the Cold War, and in order to persuade their audiences to do the same they dangled the prospect that Britain still retained a role on that part of the world stage.

Within this broadly shared framework, however, Snow and Leavis differed profoundly in their assessments of the end towards which history was hurtling. While Snow interpreted the contemporary crisis as a failure to export industrialization, Leavis feared that the job was being accomplished with frightening efficiency. The difference was partly over the question of whether material improvement constituted an adequate social and political goal, but more fundamentally they differed as to whether elements that had developed in one society could – and should – be transplanted onto alien soil. In *The Two Cultures*, for example, Snow proposed sending English teachers, along with scientists and technologists, throughout Asia and Africa, but in 1970 – as their argument flared one final time – Leavis pronounced himself "not in the least tempted to think of English as the evangelizing presence among lesser breeds who must be taught the way to salvation."[72] Later, in *A Second Look*, Snow suggested that the whole apparatus of industrial society would benefit developing nations, but Leavis later said that he thought it "ludicrous" to believe that Africa or India could sustain the imposition of Western democracy or bureaucratic government.[73] In both of these cases – regarding

---

[71] Snow, *The Two Cultures*, p. 47 (emphasis in original); F. R. Leavis, *Nor Shall My Sword: Discourses on Pluralism, Compassion and Social Hope* (London: Chatto and Windus, 1972); John Osborne, *Look Back in Anger, A Play in Three Acts* (London: Faber and Faber, 1957), quoted in David Edgar, "Stalking Out," *London Review of Books*, 20 July 2006, p. 10.

[72] In the Rede Lecture Snow called for "scientific teachers from this country and the US, and what is also necessary . . . teachers of English." *The Two Cultures*, p. 46. Leavis responded in "Pluralism, Compassion and Social Hope," *Nor Shall My Sword*, quotation p. 186. See Chapter 7 for further discussion of their 1970 argument.

[73] Snow, *The Two Cultures: and A Second Look*, p. 89; Leavis, *Nor Shall My Sword*, pp. 190–191.

cultural transfer (in the form of language), and social development (in the form of institutions) – Snow hoped to propel external transformation, whereas Leavis wanted to defend internal integrity. As a result of this difference, they repeatedly found themselves on opposite sides of the modernizing divide.

When the "two cultures" debate raised these issues in the early 1960s, the balance of opinion fell on Snow's side of the argument. Responding to *The Two Cultures*, the distinguished biologist C. H. Waddington recalled his prior experience in Nigeria. The technologies of industrial civilization had hardly been evident, he said, so even the ordinary utensils of everyday life were the products of extraordinary craftsmanship. "Almost every single article the ordinary people used was beautiful," Waddington wrote affectionately – but he nevertheless suspected that those craftsmen would have preferred access to Western medicine: "If those people were given the choice, and they are given it, of living twice as long and not suffering from trachoma, filiarisis, sleeping sickness, yellow fever, and the rest of it, can anyone seriously argue that they are wrong in the choice they have made, to take the life and try to let the pots follow?"[74] When Leavis disputed this position in the Richmond Lecture, suggesting that the skills and intelligence invested in those pots represented something that must not be abandoned, Snow's allies responded in a way that made clear their convictions that their modernizing sympathies advanced the interests of the poor. Plumb, for instance, inquired, "Has Dr Leavis ever seen an Indian peasant, a Bushman, or a primitive people exercising their vital intelligence?"[75] He surmised that Leavis had not, otherwise he could not possibly have suggested that their lives were in any way better than those of ordinary people in a modern society. Snow, Waddington, Plumb, and others recognized no distinction between being on the side of indigenous peoples, and being in favor of the extension of their own industrial civilization.

Leavis rejected the notion that he was "against" those peoples while Snow and his supporters were "for" them, but in order for that point to register he needed to disrupt the associations between *development* and *improvement*. To Leavis, development meant the imposition of a destructive civilization, one that valued material ends at the expense of cultural continuity – a process, he thought, that should hardly be depicted as "progress" for the people who were forced to endure it. In

---

[74] C. H. Waddington, "Humanists and Scientists: A Last Comment on C. P. Snow," *Encounter*, January 1960, p. 72. David Riesman approved of the developmental dimension of Snow's argument in "The Whole Man," *Encounter*, August 1959, pp. 70–71.
[75] Plumb, "Letters," p. 396.

the early 1960s Snow's position was more likely to garner public support, but towards the end of the decade Leavis began to sense a turning of the tide. In 1970, departing for a moment from his beleaguered pose, he observed that "[s]ince . . . the Rede Lecture won that near-unanimity of applause . . . the climate has changed."[76] He pointed in particular to the convulsions in American society and culture in the late 1960s, and to their echoes in Britain in the forms of trade union militancy, sexual promiscuity, student unrest, and feminist agitation.[77] None of these developments garnered Leavis's approval, and the zeal with which he challenged "progressivist" values led him to denounce immigration into Britain, and to question the nation's readiness to become a "multiracial" society, no less than development in Africa.[78] But however distasteful he found its expression, he nevertheless believed that the emergence of widespread discontent despite material prosperity confirmed his prediction that rising living standards would never satisfy human aspirations.

Meanwhile, optimistic assessments of industrial development were coming under assault from other quarters as well. In April 1968, thirty intellectuals gathered in Rome to discuss new global crises, and the Club of Rome subsequently worked to place limits to growth on the international agenda. "[W]e must prepare for self-restraint and self-discipline," declared Aurelio Peccei, the club's chair and founder, "and direct our knowledge and technology towards protecting nature, or what is left of it, and other forms of life, instead of overexploiting them."[79] In 1972 the United Nations convened a "Conference on the Human Environment" in Stockholm, which sought to reconcile the apparently contradictory agendas of developmentalism and environmentalism.[80] And during the 1970s, in the humanities and social sciences, modernization theory was increasingly challenged by the critical perspectives of dependency theory.[81] Leavis, for his part, was certainly aware of a conflict between ecological balance and industrial society: a student recalled him as having said in 1964, "You don't see so many butterflies nowadays. They're killing them off with insecticide." He continued in this vein, and added a dig at Snow: "All they care about is the Industrial Society – not

---

[76] Leavis, *Nor Shall My Sword*, p. 179.   [77] *Ibid.*, pp. 179–181.
[78] *Ibid.*, pp. 169, 190–191.
[79] Aurelio Peccei, quoted in Willem L. Oltmans, ed., *On Growth: The Crisis of Exploding Population and Resource Depletion* (New York: G. P. Putnam's Sons, 1974), p. 474.
[80] Hodge, *Triumph of the Expert*, p. 270. See also Holger Nehring, "The Growth of Social Movements," in *A Companion to Contemporary Britain, 1939–2000*, ed. Paul Addison and Harriet Jones, pp. 395–397.
[81] Weinstein, "Developing Inequality," pp. 3–4.

that I've got anything against industry, but they're just callous brutes, like old what's his name, Lord Corridor of Power."[82] Snow, too, recognized tensions between the programs of developmentalism and environmentalism, and he made no secret as to which he himself favored: in 1969, when he received an invitation to a debate in the House of Lords about the environment, Snow pointedly replied that he was preoccupied at the moment with much larger problems.[83] And the suspicion was mutual: in *Small is Beautiful* (1973), an environmental protest against unsustainable growth, E. F. Schumacher explicitly challenged Snow and *The Two Cultures*.[84]

Shared discontent was one thing, but Leavis had to look harder to find actual allies – until, in the early 1970s, they began to emerge. In 1976, in the conclusion of his final book, Leavis praised the controversial economist at the London School of Economics, P. T. Bauer. Bauer, like Leavis, was a self-styled scourge of conventional wisdom, and in a series of publications he had challenged the assumption that foreign aid stimulated economic growth.[85] Leavis thought Bauer a flawed prophet ("Bauer, of course, is an economist; but he is an intelligent one"), but he appreciated his eye for the "fallacies, falsities, dishonesties, contradictions, and nonsensicalities" of received views.[86] Bauer became known as a prominent critic of state-centered development, and also a key

[82] Neil Roberts, "'Leavisite' Cambridge in the 1960s," in *F. R. Leavis: Essays and Documents*, ed. Ian MacKillop and Richard Storer (Sheffield Academic Press, 1995), p. 268.

[83] Lord Byers to Snow, 12 February 1969; Snow to Byers, 14 February 1969, HRC: Snow 224.7.

[84] E. F. Schumacher, *Small is Beautiful: Economics as if People Mattered* (New York: Harper and Row, 1973), pp. 80–82. On Schumacher, and on one strand of the intellectual origins of environmentalism in Britain, see Meredith Veldman, *Fantasy, the Bomb, and the Greening of Britain: Romantic Protest, 1945–1980* (Cambridge University Press, 1994). On the emergence of critiques of "modernity" and development theory in the American context, see Brick, *Age of Contradiction*, pp. 58–65; Weinstein, "Developing Inequality," pp. 3–9. Gilman dates the transition in the fortunes of modernization theory, and of the assumptions that sustained it, between 1965 and 1975: "by the early 1970s," he writes, "it seemed as if attacks were coming from virtually every direction." Gilman, *Mandarins of the Future*, p. 205; on the turn versus growth in particular, see p. 251. The focus here is on transformations in metropolitan ideas about science, technology, and development, but events on the ground provided challenges of their own to the premises and promises of development theorists: see, for instance, J. S. Hogendorn and K. M. Scott, "The East African Groundnut Scheme: Lessons of a Large-Scale Agricultural Failure," *African Economic History* (1981), pp. 81–115. The groundnut scheme is also discussed in Hodge, *Triumph of the Expert*, pp. 209–214.

[85] Keith Tribe, "Bauer, Peter Thomas, Baron Bauer (1915–2002)," *Oxford Dictionary of National Biography* (Oxford University Press, 2006). P. T. Bauer, *Dissent on Development: Studies and Debates in Development Economics* (London: Weidenfeld & Nicolson, 1971).

[86] F. R. Leavis, *Thought, Words and Creativity: Art and Thought in Lawrence* (New York: Oxford University Press, 1976), p. 147.

participant in the neoliberal turn in economic thought. Another unorthodox academic who met with Leavis's approval was the Polish-born sociologist, Stanislav Andreski. Andreski was the author of *The African Predicament: A Study in the Pathology of Modernisation*, which controversially sought to shift responsibility for the "African predicament" from external causes (such as European imperialism) to the internal dynamics of African societies.[87] His iconoclastic argument, and his preference for internal analysis, suggested that Leavis had found a like-minded ally, a suspicion that was confirmed by Andreski's next book. *Social Sciences as Sorcery* challenged the scientific pretensions, objective posturing, and quantitative analysis of contemporary social science, and Leavis so appreciated its critique of intellectual abstraction that he began to assign it in his seminars at York.[88]

Leavis was not especially interested in policies towards Africa, but it nevertheless makes sense that he was drawn to these books by Bauer and Andreski: among metropolitan intellectuals in this period, "Africa" could function as an imagined location where arguments about their own society were joined. Leavis, as we have seen, believed that modern civilization had first emerged in England, that it was characterized by a rupture between language and thought, and that it was on the verge of being extended throughout the world. His embrace of Andreski's critique of abstraction, and of Bauer and Andreski's skepticism towards development, help to explain that puzzling aside in his Richmond Lecture. "[I]f you are enlightened," Leavis had said, "you see that the sum of wisdom lies in expediting the processes which will ensure the Congolese, the Indonesians, the Bushmen *(no, not the Bushmen – there aren't enough of them)*, the Chinese, the Indians, their increasing supplies of jam."[89] These peoples counted, Leavis was saying, only if they could be counted. By pointing out that the "bushmen" were too few in number to register in the developers' calculations, Leavis was mocking the moral pretensions of those (such as Snow) who claimed to have ordinary people in mind as they sought to extend their own civilization. Leavis had long opposed modern civilization, its tendency towards abstraction, and its celebration by a complacent establishment – and, at this historical moment, "Africa" figured as the location where each of these arguments met in one place.

---

[87] Stanislav Andreski, *The African Predicament: A Study in the Pathology of Modernisation* (London: Michael Joseph, 1968), praised in Leavis, *Nor Shall My Sword*, p. 191.
[88] Andreski, *Social Sciences as Sorcery* (London: Deutsch, 1972); Leavis, *The Living Principle: "English" as a Discipline of Thought* (London: Chatto and Windus, 1975), pp. 25–26.
[89] Leavis, *Two Cultures?*, p. 25 (emphasis mine).

Conclusion

In the fifteen years following the debacle at Suez – a period when assumptions about the empire did not necessarily recede as rapidly as the thing itself – the question arose whether, in Asia, Africa, and elsewhere, the new nations of the former British Empire should pursue policies of industrial development. In their Rede and Richmond lectures, and in the public debates that followed, Snow, Leavis, and their respective allies clashed over precisely this question, projecting their competing interpretations of British history onto the non-Western world's future.

In the course of these disputes, however, the ideological terrain began to shift beneath their feet. Snow had equated concern for the world's poor with support for industrial development, but by the late 1960s the sustainability of this program was being challenged. In 1968 he delivered a speech in Fulton, Missouri – the site of Winston Churchill's "Iron Curtain" address a generation before – about the paralysis among liberals that seemed to prevent them from confronting the world's crises; he also warned of the emergence of a dangerous new counterculture, one that seemed more interested in criticizing society than improving it.[90] Two years later, when collecting his addresses from the previous decade for publication in a single volume, beginning with "The Two Cultures" and concluding with "The State of Siege," Snow planned to add a final section about the remaining possibilities for a liberal attitude: *Public Affairs* was published in 1971, but that optimistic conclusion never got written.[91]

Leavis had his own reasons for challenging the pursuit of development, reasons that did not include countercultural sympathies. Nevertheless, his long-standing critique of modern civilization increasingly threatened to earn him unlikely new allies. In 1972 a writer in the *Guardian* noted that "intellectual fashion" had "caught up" with Leavis, in the form of ecological anxieties, criticisms of growth, and skepticism towards technocracy; although Leavis had retired from Cambridge a

---

[90] Snow, "The State of Siege," in *Public Affairs*, pp. 199–221.
[91] The proposed section was to be called "A Place to Stand." Snow to Maclean, 28 October 1970, HRC: Snow 143.14. Snow did include a brief epilogue, which testified to his despair. Looking to the future, he said that he anticipated "a prolonged period of hardship, sporadic famine rather than widespread, commotion rather than major war. To avoid worse will require more foresight and will than men have shown themselves capable of up to now" (p. 224). He concluded by placing his hope in the next generation, who – in a depiction nearly identical to his portrayal of scientists in *The Two Cultures* – he explained had moved beyond the prejudices of race and nation, but who faced nearly insurmountable economic and political obstacles.

decade before, the writer anticipated a renewed surge in his reputation.[92] Four years later, responding to Leavis's final book, Richard Hoggart reported on the emergence of "quite a strong backlash in developing countries ... to the cruder, two-dimensional operational thrust of development programmes." Hoggart noted that Western architecture, for instance, was being rejected in favor of local traditions, and that Western notions of progress, development, and growth were being questioned where they had until recently been embraced.[93]

Neither Snow nor Leavis had altered their positions, but in the changed contexts of changing times existing positions were being thrown into different relief. In 1959 Snow had confidently equated science, industrialization, and progressive politics, but a decade later these connections were being challenged by a more radical left. This reshuffling of ideological positions is one facet of the complicated developments associated with "The Sixties," and the next chapter seeks to explain this process by tracking the arguments of Snow and Leavis during and after the "two cultures" controversy.

[92] W. L. Webb, "New Year's New Reading II," *Guardian*, 13 January 1972.
[93] Richard Hoggart, "Persuaded into Words," *Guardian*, 26 August 1976.

7   The eclipse of the meritocratic moment

When equality threatened

In the spring of 1970, Snow's opportunity for a public rejoinder finally presented itself. Leavis was embarked upon his "higher pamphleteering," a series of lectures denouncing the democratic – and hence pernicious – principles that plagued discussions of education. He frequently related the commitment to mass education to the notion that a computer could write a poem: both propositions, he argued, derived from a utilitarian mindset that was itself the problem, a mindset that he branded "technologico-Benthamism."[1] When the *Times Literary Supplement* printed a lecture along these lines, one that included a few swipes at Snow, its editor Arthur Crook privately urged Snow to respond.[2] Snow had long chafed at the restraint he had shown in not replying directly to Leavis, and now he spotted an irresistible opening: Leavis had said that other critics claimed for Dickens little more than "entertainment value," when that was in fact the assessment – indeed, nearly the words – from *The Great Tradition*.[3] In his last major statement on the "two cultures," then, Snow set out to nail his nemesis on a matter of historical fact, literary interpretation, and professional ethics.

---

[1] F. R. Leavis, " 'Literarism' versus 'Scientism': The Misconception and the Menace," *Times Literary Supplement*, 23 April 1970, pp. 441–444, reprinted in *Nor Shall My Sword: Discourses on Pluralism, Compassion and Social Hope* (London: Chatto and Windus, 1972), pp. 137–160.

[2] Crook – himself an occasional target of Leavis's derision – was not disinterested, and provided Snow with a special "science" number of the *TLS* to use against Leavis. Snow to George Steiner, 26 March 1970, HRC: Snow 191.8; Crook to Snow, 6 May 1970, HRC: 196.14. See also Derwent May, *Critical Times: The History of the Times Literary Supplement* (London: Harper Collins, 2001), pp. 364–365.

[3] Snow frequently wondered whether it had been wise to refrain from responding to Leavis, for instance in a letter to Harry Levin of 11 October 1966 (HRC: Snow 133.16). He was correct in catching Leavis on this point: Leavis had written, "That Dickens was a great genius and is permanently among the classics is certain. But the genius was that of a great entertainer, and he had for the most part no profounder responsibility as a creative artist than this description suggests." *The Great Tradition* (London: Chatto and Windus, 1948), p. 19.

219

Yet the essay that he wrote, "The Case of Leavis and the Serious Case," revealed very different priorities from those of 1959.[4] Absent were the issues that had animated *The Two Cultures*: the incomprehension between scientific and literary intellectuals, their contrary assessments of the Industrial Revolution, and the need to foster global industrialization. Now Snow reduced the distinctions between the "two cultures" to the progressive nature of science versus the static disposition of the humanities, but for the most part he did not address the "two cultures" at all. The essay's opening section concluded by endorsing truth over moral relativism, and the majority of the text defended the need to cultivate an elite. A decade earlier, in *The Two Cultures* (1959) and in *A Second Look* (1963), Snow had situated scientists to the left of their literary counterparts: scientists, he said, were averse to racial prejudice and sympathetic to the poor. Leavis responded to Snow's thesis with his anti-modern critique, and he rejected calls for democratized education by insisting upon the need to cultivate a critical minority. In 1970 neither Snow nor Leavis had abandoned these posi-ions, but changed circumstances were throwing their arguments into different relief: Snow's concern for the poor now led him to defend the elites who provided for them, while Leavis's attacks upon the materialism of "modern civilization" threatened to earn him unwelcome new allies on the cultural and political left.

These changing allegiances offer the opportunity to explore one fault along the vast tectonic shift of "The Sixties" (a label of convenience referring to a number of developments that reached into the 1970s). The 1960s and 1970s were a *moment*, but "The Sixties" were a *movement*, and the historical effort to apprehend its meaning is underway.[5] A distinctive feature of the twentieth century was the fact that, for those who happened to live in the prosperous West, the achievement of economic and social equality could figure as a pragmatic program. This state of affairs was made possible by a combination of *motives* (from the left's point of view, a mature body of socialist thought; from the right's point of view, the need to mollify social upheaval) and *means* (the existence of

---

[4] C. P. Snow, "The Case of Leavis and the Serious Case," *Times Literary Supplement*, 9 July 1970, pp. 737–740, reprinted in *Public Affairs* (New York: Scribner's, 1971), pp. 81–97.

[5] Arthur Marwick, *The Sixties: Cultural Revolution in Britain, France, Italy, and the United States, c.1958–c.1974* (Oxford University Press, 1998); Dominic Sandbrook, *Never Had It So Good: A History of Britain from Suez to the Beatles* (London: Little, Brown, 2005); Sandbrook, *White Heat: A History of Britain in the Swinging Sixties* (London: Little, Brown, 2006). For the American story, in addition to the relevant sections of Marwick, see Howard Brick, *Age of Contradiction: American Thought and Culture in the 1960s* (Ithaca: Cornell University Press, 1998).

a state capable of redistributing wealth on a national scale).[6] The con-
fluence between these motives and means climaxed in "The Sixties,"
when a number of movements challenged the presumption that inequality
was ineradicable. These challenges, in turn, generated responses that
shaped political culture during the remainder of the century: on the right,
the emergence of a revised rationale for social inequality in the form of
marketplace ideals; on the left, a shift in attention from materialist analysis
to cultural critique. If "The Sixties" can be understood as the moment
when equality threatened (or, at least, when it could be seen to have
threatened), the left subsequently attempted to explain what had gone
wrong, while the right sought to ensure that it would not happen again.

This abstract explanation of the reshufflings associated with "The
Sixties" can be illustrated through consideration of the responses of particular individuals to particular issues at particular times. As we have seen,
despite their many differences, Snow and Leavis shared a mutual commitment to a fluid social hierarchy. They wanted to see inherited hierarchies supplanted – not by societies of equals, but by hierarchies of talent.
Since they believed that inequality was inherent and inevitable, they
thought that education should develop (rather than deny) differences of
talent. During the 1960s and 1970s, however, this meritocratic commitment seemed under threat from the egalitarian ideals driving comprehensive education and university expansion. Snow and Leavis responded
to this challenge with their meritocratic polemics, insisting upon the
inevitability of social hierarchies and defending the institutions that sustained them, but their arguments led them down different paths. When
the dust finally settled, with the political landscape dominated by marketplace ideals rather than meritocratic commitments, Snow and Leavis
each found themselves in the company of some surprising new allies.[7]

---

[6] This two-part model of historical causation derives from Daniel Headrick, *Tools of Empire: Technology and European Imperialism in the Nineteenth Century* (New York: Oxford University Press, 1981).

[7] By mapping this social, political, and intellectual shift, I am pursuing the suggestive insights of John Guillory and David A. Hollinger. According to Guillory, "While the predominantly conservative political orientation of criticism continued into the 1960s, that orientation was completely reversed in the space of a decade, largely as a result of *external* factors (everything that is evoked by 'the sixties'). The political orientation of the humanist professoriate shifted massively from the Right to the Left at the same time that the scientific professoriate was to some extent depoliticized (or in some sectors, pro-pelled to the Right). After a long hiatus . . . the reemergence of cultural criticism in the seventies and eighties made it possible to renew the conflict of the faculties once again as a war between Left and Right, but with the political affiliations of the two cultures reversed." Guillory, "The Sokal Affair and the History of Criticism," *Critical Inquiry* 28 (Winter 2002), p. 503. Hollinger writes: "Snow had hit a nerve, and he did so just when some literary critics were brooding among themselves over their own misgivings about canonical modernism . . . Some of this literary cohort withdrew, one might say, and

The sleep of reason

Snow offered a highly moralistic vision of scientific practice. His experience at Cambridge in the 1930s, and then in recruiting scientists during the war, exposed him to a great many scientists (by his own estimate, "as many as anyone in the world").[8] During that time he compiled a number of informal observations, ranging from the aversion of scientists to notions of class, nation, and race, to their better-than-average records as husbands and fathers (the instinctive omission of "wives and mothers" offers more insight into the masculine conception of the scientist than the actual sociology of science at mid century).[9] Snow believed that scientists were truthful by training and progressive by instinct: "There is a built-in moral component right in the core of the scientific activity itself," he claimed. "The desire to find the truth is itself a moral impulse . . . To scientists, who are brought up in this climate, this seems as natural as breathing."[10] The certainty of truth compelled honesty, the search for truth facilitated cooperation, and the combination of both resulted in a moral inclination that no other profession could match – a characterization that caused Snow to link science and the left, most prominently in *The Two Cultures*.

Snow's presumption of a link between science and the left derived from his personal experience between 1930 and 1960. Any such connections were not the result of a necessary relationship between scientific practice and progressive politics, as he suggested, but rather of the political context of this particular period. It is well known that the scientific left was prominent in Cambridge during the 1930s.[11] Like so many others, the scientific establishment and scientific workers earned

---

regrouped, and came out some years later under the cover of Michel Foucault and postmodernism to attack science as itself cryptofascist and to claim for literature the badge of democracy and equality and human decency." Hollinger, "Science as a Weapon in *Kulturkämpfe* in the United States During and After World War II," *Isis* 86 (September 1995), p. 449.

[8] C. P. Snow, "The Moral Un-neutrality of Science," *Public Affairs* (New York: Scribner's, 1971), p. 187. Originally delivered to the American Association for the Advancement of Science in 1960.

[9] On race and class, see C. P. Snow "New Minds for the New World," *New Statesman*, 8 September 1956, pp. 279–282; Snow, "The Age of Rutherford," *Atlantic Monthly*, November 1958, pp. 76–81. The claim about family life is from "The Moral Un-neutrality of Science," pp. 187–188. On women in British science before, during, and after the Second World War, see David Edgerton, *Warfare State: Britain, 1920–1970* (Cambridge University Press, 2006), pp. 172–180.

[10] Snow, "The Moral Un-neutrality of Science," p. 192.

[11] Gary Werskey, *The Visible College: The Collective Biography of British Scientific Socialists of the 1930s* (London: Allen Lane, 1978); J. G. Crowther, *The Social Relations of Science* (New York: Macmillan, 1941). See also Werskey, "The Marxist Critique of Capitalist

their anti-fascist stripes during the war, after which some of Britain's most prominent intellectuals, such as J. D. Bernal and P. M. S. Blackett, were equally at home in the lab and on the left. Blackett was not a Marxist, whereas Bernal was, and their relatively peaceful co-existence points towards a general consensus on the left in this period about the value of science, technology, and industry – a creed most spectacularly affirmed when the Labour Party aligned itself with science from 1963. Snow may have been romanticizing things when he posited the existence of necessary affinities between scientists and the left, especially in light of the intimate connections between science, the military, and the state, but he was correct to suggest that the left at mid century was broadly in favor of the economic and historical development promised by the combination of science, technology, and industry.[12]

Snow himself straddled a number of fissures in the politics of the left after the war. He knew well the economic, social, and professional opportunities that a career in science could offer a talented child not born of privilege, and for that he was quick to credit science itself (rather than expanding opportunities in the professions more generally).[13] He believed in opening access, spreading a wide net, and tapping into talent – positions that caused him to employ the language of democracy, but always in service of a position best understood as meritocracy.[14] For example, he consistently advocated the education of women: not because of a commitment to women's liberation necessarily, but because of his desire to see Britain maximize its available talent.[15] He identified himself as a liberal, but always voted Labour; he occasionally called himself

Science: A History in Three Movements?", www.human-nature.com/science-as-culture/werskey.html.

[12] On the connections between science, the state, and the political right, see David Edgerton, *England and the Aeroplane: An Essay on a Militant and Technological Nation* (Basingstoke: Macmillan, 1991); Edgerton, *Warfare State*; S. Waqar H. Zaidi, "Barnes Wallis and the 'Strength of England'," *Technology and Culture* 49 (2008), pp. 62–88.

[13] Harold Perkin, *The Rise of Professional Society: England since 1880* (London: Routledge, 1989), Chapter 9. In this regard, it is interesting that Snow's protagonist, Lewis Eliot, ascended the social and professional ranks not through science but law; the fact that Eliot was Snow's alter-ego suggests that Snow may indeed have credited his own upward mobility to having entered the professions in general, rather than science in particular.

[14] A clear statement of Snow's position on education was his Richmond Lecture at Downing College, delivered the year after Leavis's lecture in the same venue: "Education and Sacrifice," *New Statesman*, 17 May 1963, pp. 746–750.

[15] Snow's desire to cultivate the talent of women was sincere, surfacing even in his anonymous contribution to the policy papers assembled for Hugh Gaitskell: "A Labour Government and Science: Papers for Mr. Gaitskell," 31 July 1959, Royal Society: Blackett E.28.

a socialist, but never endorsed socialism.[16] In short, despite the occasional invocation of radical rhetoric or gesture towards left-wing positions, Snow believed in the fluid social hierarchy and the institutions it staffed, and he thought science an admirable domain because it seemed to operate in accord with these principles.

During the 1960s, however, the latent fissures on the left increasingly became exacerbated. From 1945 a socialist government enacting the policies of liberal grandees had garnered the support of a broad coalition, and during the first half of the 1950s the Communist Party contained many of the nation's most brilliant and irascible minds. That changed when the Soviet Union invaded Hungary in 1956, as radical intellectuals abandoned the party but not their convictions. And just as the resulting New Left was developing its critique of British institutions, demographic change was applying pressure upon those institutions. The Education Act of 1944 yielded more students qualified for higher education than ever before, and plans for comprehensive schools reignited the always controversial subject of secondary education. Expanded access to education led more children of manual workers into the professions, where class distinctions did not necessarily align with, or melt away before, professional hierarchies. And during the 1960s, two of the developments that were most to change British society gathered momentum: Commonwealth immigration, and women's equality. All of this was unfolding in the context of a polarized (and nuclearized) Cold War world, and against the backdrop of the war in Vietnam – a war it could never be certain that Britain would not join. While it is important not to exaggerate the "consensus" that existed prior to the 1960s, it seems fair to suggest that these developments and experiences applied pressure upon heretofore unspoken assumptions and uneasy alliances.

At the time of the Rede Lecture, between addressing national issues in public and advising the Labour Party in private, Snow was as politically involved as he had ever been. Already there arose occasional glimpses of the frustrations that would test his commitments. The Campaign for Nuclear Disarmament (CND) was established in 1958, but whenever its representatives contacted Snow to request a speech or a signature (as they did frequently), he politely declined.[17] Meanwhile the New Left was reinvigorating a movement battered by international disillusionments

---

[16] When S. Gorley Putt stood for Parliament as a Liberal, Snow complained that he should have run as a Labour candidate; Putt thought this odd, since Snow himself was a liberal, but in Snow's mind there was no contradiction between being a liberal and voting Labour – indeed, this was the course he followed throughout his life. Snow to Putt, 5 August 1945, HRC: Snow 134.8.

[17] HRC: Snow 68.8–68.9.

and domestic defeats. Snow was wary of this New Left from the outset, and he conveyed his doubts about their politics to Raymond Williams.[18] To Snow, CND and the New Left represented movement politics and social criticism, two enterprises for which he had no patience. His response was to write *Corridors of Power* (1964), an effort to illustrate what he believed to be a more realistic and responsible approach to political change, and at the same time he was writing and speaking tirelessly about the benefits afforded by modern society.[19] In short, Snow did not want to question modern society, he wanted to extend it, and this commitment set him squarely against more radical efforts on the horizon.

Snow's hostility to movement politics was joined by a visceral distaste for challenges to manners and mores. Snow was of a generation that did not cultivate regional accents, they lost them – such was the fate of his own Midlands accent, and of Lewis Eliot's as well: "Except for the odd scientist like Walter Luke," Eliot said, "people of our origins, making their way into the professional life, tried to take on the sound of the authoritative class. It was a half-unconscious process, independent of politics."[20] In Cambridge during the 1930s the affable Snow honed a flair for social mixing, which served him well as he climbed the social and professional ladders. But in the 1950s he became infuriated as the roughneck manner of Kingsley Amis came to be interpreted as a political statement. In private, Snow contrasted the "lower-class manners" and "upper-class politics" of Amis with his own preference for upper-class manners and progressive politics; and in his novels, he skewered Amis in the character of Lester Ince, who enacted his brand of non-politics through a tendency to swear while wearing casual clothing.[21] On one occasion, Eliot reminded his son of the distinction between transgressive manners and progressive politics: "I brought out the old aphorism that when young men rebel against social manners, they end up by not rebelling against anything else." His son brushed off the comment, leaving Eliot unsettled: "[A]re these really our successors? Will they ever be able to take over?"[22]

---

[18] Williams to Snow, 3 December 1959, HRC: Snow 210.1. See also Chapter 4.

[19] C. P. Snow, *Corridors of Power* (London: Macmillan, 1964).

[20] C. P. Snow, *Last Things* (London: Macmillan, 1970), reprinted in *Strangers and Brothers* (New York: Scribner's, 1972), vol. III, p. 807. Snow's experience (like Eliot's) was typical: Perkin, *The Rise of Professional Society*, pp. 267–268. Audio of Snow is available at the Harry Ransom Humanities Research Center in Austin, Texas, and at the National Sound Archive in London.

[21] Snow to Harry Hoff, 1 November 1960, HRC: Snow 118.3.

[22] Snow, *Last Things*, p. 693.

The naiveté of young radicals and the dangers of the permissive society emerged as prominent themes in Snow's novels between 1968 and 1972. The title of the penultimate installment in the Lewis Eliot sequence, *The Sleep of Reason* (1968), conveyed his verdict on the times.[23] Between 1963 and 1965, in a notorious episode, three children were found murdered on the moors near Manchester, and in 1966 Snow and Pamela Johnson attended the trial of the accused.[24] Johnson quickly produced *On Iniquity: Some Personal Reflections Arising out of the Moors Murder Trial* (1967), which was replete with anxieties about an "increasingly permissive society, some compost-heap of rottenness out of which such ugly weeds could flourish and grow lush."[25] Johnson linked pornography to fascism, and in the profusion of sex and violence she thought she detected trends that had previously led to Auschwitz.[26] She insisted that perverted sexuality, glorified illiteracy, and disregard for religion had created these monsters. *Time* magazine may have recently celebrated "Swinging London," but Johnson feared the atmosphere in Britain's cities "may result in a grave infection to our social health."[27] Postwar Britain, she thought, was beginning to resemble Weimar Germany, a state of affairs so distressing that no argument could be too blunt: "All right," she wrote, "what happened after that? Hitler."[28] Johnson's book – filled with ideas about the genetic basis of criminality, connections between avant-garde aesthetics and depraved immorality, and frustrations with the egalitarian pieties of the left – articulated worries that were coming to preoccupy her husband as well.[29]

Snow's response to the trial, *The Sleep of Reason*, explored the episode's meaning through the tale of two lesbians on trial for the murder of a young boy. The murderers' actions may have been irrational, Snow thought, but they were not inexplicable. He portrayed his characters as acting out of an extreme libertarian creed, which maintained that personal behavior must not be constrained by social norms, and he associated this notion with the permissive society. His depiction of the villains as lesbians, while certainly gratuitous, was consistent with his earlier portrayals of science and scientists as heterosexual and masculine (see Chapter 1). To Snow, heterosexuality and masculinity constituted the bounds of the norm, and to step outside these bounds was to

---

[23] C. P. Snow, *The Sleep of Reason* (London: Macmillan, 1968).

[24] David Shusterman, "C. P. Snow," *Dictionary of Literary Biography, Vol. 15: British Novelists, 1930–1959; Part 2: M–Z*, ed. Bernard Oldsey (Detroit: Gale, 1983), pp. 484–485.

[25] Pamela Hansford Johnson, *On Iniquity: Some Personal Reflections Arising out of the Moors Murder Trial* (New York: Scribner's, 1967), p. 11.

[26] *Ibid.*, p. 26.   [27] *Ibid.*, pp. 34, 37, 129, 45.   [28] *Ibid.*, pp. 50–51.

[29] *Ibid.*, pp. 29, 87–88, 118–119. Johnson was a Christian, Snow was not religious.

depart from reason itself. He had previously argued that literary intellectuals had rejected reason when they fostered the anti-social ethos that
led to Auschwitz, and now he suggested that his villains did the same
when their libertarian creed led them to abandon social constraints.
Snow wanted to stigmatize the flight from reason that he believed
characteristic of the period, and to make that point he depicted his
characters existing outside the bounds of "normal" behavior – and thus
as lesbians. The novel's secondary plot portrays the embattled Vice-
Chancellor of a new university struggling to uphold academic standards
against faculty and students alike. One of the defendants is a student at
the university, and the epigraph by Francisco Goya connected the dots
to distill Snow's argument: "The sleep of reason brings forth monsters."

Mindful of his restless youth in Leicester, and with a talented teenage
son of his own at home, Snow was by no means hostile to youth *tout
court* – indeed, his next two novels presented sympathetic accounts of
idealistic young people.[30] But he desperately wanted the next generation
to reject what he viewed as nihilistic radicalism, and to embrace the
pragmatic style of politics that he strongly favored. On balance, though,
while applauding the energy and idealism that animated the young,
Snow – like many others of a certain age in uncertain times – could not
entirely suppress his unease with the cultural transformations they had
wrought.

The excellence of elites

However uncomfortable Snow may have been with these trends, none of
them presented him with a crisis of conscience. He dismissed CND as
ineffective, the New Left as marginal, the Angry Young Men as reactionary, nihilism as irrational, and young radicals as immature. These
developments struck him as irritating sideshows, and he thought of them
much as Lewis Eliot did the works of J. R. R. Tolkien: the whimsies and
fantasies of dreamers, inexplicably capable of stirring up passion, but
with little ultimate significance.[31] Understanding how the world oper-
ated, and working to make it better, was Snow's credo as a novelist, an
administrator, and a public figure – as he explained, "You've got to
understand how the world ticks, if you're going to have any chance of
making it tick better."[32] Implicit in that creed was the principle Snow
held most dear: *some people* were capable of understanding how the

---

[30] Snow, *Last Things*; Snow, *The Malcontents* (London: Macmillan, 1972).
[31] Snow, *Last Things*, p. 792.
[32] Snow, "Science, Politics, and the Novelist," *Kenyon Review* 23 (Winter 1961), p. 15.

world ticked, and *those* people had a responsibility to make it tick better. This position was predicated upon the assumption of inherent human difference, and Snow consistently advocated reforms to existing institutions so as to better develop and deploy the abilities of the talented. This program could withstand the irritating noises made by intellectuals and novelists, but there was one principle that it could neither accommodate nor ignore: equality.

For the final fifteen years of his life, from the day that he was ambushed in the House of Lords in 1965 to the day that he died in London in 1980, few subjects animated Snow more readily than the need to defend hierarchies against advocates of equality. This is not to suggest that Snow opposed practical measures designed to make life more fair or less miserable for the majority of the population – to the contrary, he evidenced a consistent commitment to creating social opportunity and alleviating material poverty, in Britain and throughout the world. It was not the *fact* of economic or social equality that troubled Snow, because he did not believe it existed; rather, it was the *principle* of equality that he resisted. He believed that the drive for equality was based upon a wilful denial of innate human differences. He recognized that the embrace of the egalitarian principle – however admirable the motives behind it, and however implausible the goals it advanced – threatened support for the idea of inherent excellence. Snow opposed the principle of equality, then, because it threatened the presumption of inequality upon which his meritocratic worldview depended.

This opposition generally took the form of justifying the existence of, and need for, various kinds of elites. The concern was not a new one: liberals had long confronted the need to justify the continuation of elites and inequality, and as early as 1938 Snow described his novel sequence as an exploration of innate versus environmental factors in human development.[33] And he was by no means alone in his embrace of social inequality: as discussed in the Introduction, society and culture during the postwar decades were characterized by widespread acceptance of, and faith in, hierarchies of expertise. For example, the need for an elite was taken for granted in the proposals to establish Churchill College, which was established not to train scientists (the contribution of a single college would be too small to make a difference nationally), but scientific *leaders*.[34] Similar assumptions repeatedly recurred in postwar culture,

---

[33] David Wootton, "Liberalism," *The Oxford Companion to Twentieth-Century British Politics*, ed. John Ramsden (Oxford University Press, 2002), pp. 380–381. Snow's commitment to exploring these issues through his novels is quoted in William Cooper, "C. P. Snow," in *British Writers*, ed. Ian Scott-Kilvert (New York: Scribner's, 1984), vol. VII, p. 333.
[34] See Chapter 3.

from theater programs to spy novels to political campaigns – after all, more than anything else, it was the identification, training, and valorization of experts that promised to prevent the "suicide" of a nation.[35] In short, there was nothing sinister or secretive about Snow's belief that a prosperous society required elites – on the contrary, that was a fundamental assumption of education, politics, and culture in Britain after 1945.[36]

As developments applied pressure upon these assumptions, Snow adjusted his arguments accordingly. *The Two Cultures* suggested that British education was excessively geared to the training of a tiny elite, and as late as 1963 Snow was prioritizing the need for educational expansion.[37] To be sure, at this time Snow already believed in the need for an elite, but he argued for educational expansion because he did not think that principle under any threat. Subsequent developments did not change his mind on the need for mass education, but they did force him to rearrange his priorities and arguments. He became consumed by anxiety that egalitarian ideals were threatening the commitment to the training of elites. The 1965 controversy in the House of Lords over sending his son to Eton functioned as a moment of personal recognition, when his social democratic sympathies were exposed as an awkward fit with the egalitarian wing of the Labour Party.[38] When crafting his arguments in defense of these assumptions, Snow identified a dual threat in the claim that differences in achievement resulted from differences of environment. In the discussions to follow, then, he pursued parallel tracks: insisting upon the need for elites, and challenging the notion that inequality resulted from environmental factors.

The battleground for these questions emerged as education, where Snow's insistence upon the need to identify and train talented students challenged the commitment to comprehensive education. To Snow, the premise that students began with equal aptitude was patently false, and the point of education was to develop, rather than deny, variable talents. "When handing out the genes," he argued, "God or fate deals one a hand of cards: the best that education can do is to teach one to play it

---

[35] Arthur Koestler, ed., *Suicide of a Nation? An Enquiry into the State of Britain Today* (London: Hutchinson, 1963).

[36] Becky Conekin, Frank Mort, and Chris Waters, eds., *Moments of Modernity: Reconstructing Britain, 1945–1964* (London: Rivers Oram, 1999), pp. 14–15 and *passim*.

[37] "We teach, of course, a far smaller proportion of our children up to the age of eighteen: and we take a far smaller proportion even of those we do teach up to the level of a university degree. The old pattern of training a small *élite* has never been broken, though it has slightly bent." Snow, *The Two Cultures*, p. 32. See also his Richmond Lecture, "Education and Sacrifice," p. 747.

[38] See Chapter 5.

properly."[39] In December 1966 he addressed the House of Lords, connecting Britain's "brain drain" to a reluctance to valorize excellence, and proposing the establishment of "centers of excellence" to redress this crisis. When Noel Annan questioned this proposal, Snow reassured his friend of his support for equality, but could not resist adding one qualification: "I do feel increasingly," he wrote, "that [egalitarianism] must not be allowed to destroy our sense of the really good [sic] or the institutions which, by historical chance, have a world reputation."[40] At times there seemed little that Snow thought a renewed respect for elites could not accomplish: he advised a government commission that the best way to recruit a more comprehensive civil service would be, counterintuitively, to establish a more elite civil service. He explained that anybody with a second-class degree would in truth make an adequate administrator, but for various reasons such people did not aspire to the civil service. The best way to recruit them, therefore, would be to establish an elite executive class, thereby making the profession as a whole more attractive.[41]

Snow pressed his campaign on behalf of excellence at every opportunity. In assessing new literature for the *Times Literary Supplement*, he advised aspiring novelists that what class had been to the Victorians, elites were to contemporary society. That is, far from anything sinister or treacherous, they were an unavoidable social fact, and thus worthy of the novelist's attention.[42] As a founding member of the program in British Studies at the University of Texas, Snow delivered lectures on three topics: *The Two Cultures*, *The Masters*, and "Elite Education in England."[43] And just two years before his death, Snow addressed the Socratic Society at Churchill College on the subject of elitism.[44] Indeed, throughout the 1970s, the defense of elites figured as a leitmotif in Snow's reviews for the *Financial Times*: any author who pejoratively employed terms such as "mandarin" or "elitism" received a swift rebuke.[45] To offer but one final example: when, as discussed at the outset of this chapter, Snow worked

---

[39] C. P. Snow, review of J. B. S. Haldane, *The Man with Two Memories* (London: Merlin Press, 1976), typescript in HRC: Snow 34.2.

[40] Snow, "The Brain Drain," House of Lords, 20 December 1966; Annan to Snow, 21 December 1966; Snow to Annan, 29 December 1966, HRC: Snow 224.3.

[41] Snow to T. J. Pitt (Research Secretary of the Labour Party), 4 October 1966, HRC: Snow 131.4.

[42] C. P. Snow, "In the Communities of the Elite," *Times Literary Supplement*, 15 October 1971, pp. 1249–1250.

[43] Wm. Roger Louis, ed., *Yet More Adventures with Britannia: Personalities, Politics, and Culture in Britain* (London: I. B. Tauris, 2005).

[44] HRC: Snow 74.10.

[45] HRC: Snow, Boxes 33–34, *passim*. For instance, he defended Chinese mandarins in reviewing Peter Kellner and Lord Crowther-Hunt, *The Civil Servants* (London:

the case for elites into his statement on the "two cultures" in 1970, his essay prompted a reply from Lionel Robbins. Robbins agreed with Snow about the need to emphasize excellence at the level of graduate education, but he confessed to doubts about the desirability of separating schoolchildren by ability. Snow reiterated his commitment to special education for talented children, before revealing his deeper motivations: "My real reason is more complicated," he confided to Robbins. "I suspect we are going to have a hard fight to get people to continue to recognise that academic excellence is a good thing in itself."[46] *Excellence in itself*: it was the defense of the very principle of inequality that was motivating Snow. These were fundamental differences indeed: after all, neither Annan nor Robbins was a wild-eyed leftist, but there was proving to be plenty of room for even a liberal to sit to Snow's left.

Essential inequality

The second facet of Snow's position required that he challenge the notion that inequality resulted from environmental factors rather than innate qualities. This commitment led in some surprising directions. In *The Two Cultures*, and in related statements, Snow explained that one of the most striking features of scientists was their impatience with notions of nation and race. Engaged as they were in an international enterprise, scientists' horizons transcended those of others engaged in more parochial pursuits. As a result, he asserted, scientists had no doubt of two facts: their peers in Asia and Africa were as capable as they were, and the nations of Asia and Africa were certain to develop their economies. Since scientists recognized the equality of aptitude across nations and races, he continued, they cheerfully accepted this state of affairs – and not only did they accept it, but their progressive orientation and fraternal fellow-feeling ensured that they were eager to drive international development forward.

Snow never abandoned his stance on the equality of races, but – through that ongoing process of shifting priorities – he came to admire science less because it embraced equality than because it had the potential to confirm *inequality*. The key field in these discussions was genetics. Snow had been trained as a physical chemist, and he had long been fascinated by physics, but genetics was not a field in which he

Macmillan, 1980) and Brian Sedgemore, *The Secret Constitution* (London: Hodder and Stoughton, 1980), HRC: Snow 33.3.
[46] Snow to Robbins, 4 August 1970, in response to Robbins's letter of 9 July 1970, HRC: Snow 172.8.

claimed any expertise. During the 1970s, however, his reviews and speeches referred to genetics as frequently as chemistry or physics.[47] In an admirable contrast to other thinkers on these issues, Snow never made claims about the inferiorities of particular racial groups, and instead he preferred to make his case by pointing to the intellectual accomplishments of Jewish people.[48] However, unpleasant consequences were implicit in this logic: if success could be explained with reference to innate and heritable qualities, then failure should be as well. But Snow did not pursue such claims, and, given the statements he made on race throughout his career, he certainly would have rejected them. His aim was not to elevate or denigrate any particular group, but rather to affirm the existence of something that contributed to achievement *yet remained impervious to the environment*. Yet Snow soon learned that the combination of genetics and the meritocracy could prove controversial in any form.

In 1969, in his remarks upon receiving an honorary doctorate from Hebrew Union College, Snow speculated about the existence of racial gene pools. He surmised that these pools might explain Jewish intellectual achievements, and he suggested that genetic inheritance was more influential than environment or luck in determining achievement.[49] Snow had ventured related thoughts eight years before, but at that time he stressed *environmental* factors in determining achievement, while cautioning that racial thinking *in any form* degraded humanity.[50] By 1969, though, his priorities had shifted, and at Hebrew Union College he emphasized genetic inheritance over environmental factors in determining achievement. Back in Britain the Labour government's Minister for Education and Environment immediately denounced the Labour peer's remarks, branding Snow's ideas inimical to the principles guiding government policy on education, and this response prompted a pair of columns and a flurry of letters in the *Spectator*.[51] Snow intervened in the debate to suggest that biogenetics was on the verge of becoming as controversial as Darwin had been a century before, and he cast his critics in the forthcoming battles in the unhappy role of Bishop Wilberforce. The charges were spiraling, and – as is often the case in such public

---

[47] Snow, "Two Addresses by Lord C. P. Snow," Pace University, 26–27 April 1977, HRC: Snow 35.6; "The Two Cultures and Medicine," November 1978, HRC: Snow 35.7.

[48] For example, in a review of *The French Right*, ed. J. S. McClellan (London: Cape, 1970), typescript in HRC: Snow 33.5.

[49] Reconstructed from George Gale, "Saying the Unsayable," *Spectator*, 25 July 1970, pp. 65–66.

[50] Snow, introducing Arnold Rogrow, *The Jew in a Gentile World* (New York: Macmillan, 1961), pp. xv–xvii.

[51] Denis Brogan, "Inequality and Mr. Short," *Spectator*, 18 April 1969, p. 505; letters followed from 2 May 1969 to 14 June 1969.

debates – the race was on for the ultimate rhetorical weapon; the next letter, from Israel Shahak in Jerusalem, duly connected Snow with the Nazis (Snow, perhaps sensing that he had lost the arms race on this occasion, did not reply). A final comment by another writer complained of the bias at work in these debates: "It is acceptable to liberals for scientists to seek to prove that environment counts for more than heredity in determining measurable intelligence, but not vice versa."[52] Snow would have agreed with the point, but he had not put it that way – yet.

Breaking ranks

Developments were challenging Snow's worldview at its foundations, forcing breaches – in different ways, for different reasons – in his sympathies with the Labour Party, the intellectual left, the working class, gay rights advocates, and the culture at large.[53] Like his friend J. H. Plumb, Snow was frequently frustrated by radical idealists and irritable intellectuals who denounced the "structures" of modern society, while failing to recognize that it was the best society to have yet come along.[54] Towards the end of the 1960s, Snow began to complain about what he called the "liberal package deal," by which he meant a number of measures that liberally minded people seemed expected to support without reservation. He initially invoked the term to refer to support for comprehensive education, but over time the "liberal package deal" came to include quotas in education, the repeal of censorship laws, the apparent prohibition on speaking about genetics, and the belief that social ills resulted from environmental factors.[55]

[52] Gale, "Saying the Unsayable," p. 66. Philip A. Snow recounts the affair in *Stranger and Brother: A Portrait of C. P. Snow* (London: Macmillan, 1982), pp. 174–175.

[53] Snow's problems with the Labour Party stemmed from their plans for comprehensive state education, discussed in this chapter; his differences with the left were apparent in his campaign against the New Left, examined in Chapter 4; his frustration with the working class became apparent in his review of John Julius Norwich, *Venice: The Rise to Empire* (London: Allen Lane, 1977), vol. I, in which Snow unfavorably contrasted industrial relations in contemporary Britain to the Venetian arsenal workers' loyalty to state and nation (HRC: Snow 34.7). Snow was not hostile to homosexuals, but he expressed irritation with writers who, he thought, regarded their work as what he called "the public relations department of gay lib," and, invoking the catch-all complaint against contemporary culture, he suggested that the "permissive society" was to blame. Review of Brian Finney, *Christopher Isherwood* (New York: Oxford University Press, 1979), typescript in HRC: Snow 33.3.

[54] Plumb to Snow, 25 August 1970, HRC: Snow 166.13. The naiveté of complaining about social "structures" is also subject of conversation in *Last Things*.

[55] Snow to Amis, 5 July 1967, HRC: Snow 51.14; Snow, "Two Addresses by Lord C. P. Snow"; Review of Norman Podhoretz, *Breaking Ranks*, *Financial Times*, 16 February 1980 (discussed below).

Snow remained a member of the Labour Party, but in 1976 even that lifelong loyalty was tested. That year the government passed the 1976 Education Act, compelling Local Education Authorities to submit plans reorganizing secondary schools along comprehensive lines.[56] In October – less than two weeks before Prime Minister James Callaghan delivered a landmark speech at Ruskin College, initiating a national debate over the government's role in education – Snow penned a passionate letter to Shirley Williams, Minister of Education and Science.[57] Snow explained that he was writing for himself, but also "for others *who try hard to be social democrats* and who are at the same time occupied with some sort of intellectual or creative life . . . All these people have never voted anything but Labour in their lives, but they are appalled by the Government's educational policy." He said that he was speaking for figures such as Iris Murdoch, J. B. Priestley, and himself, all of whom believed in the existence of, and the need for, a talented elite. "Such an elite is to be trained or given social esteem," Snow insisted. "All present policy suggests that political opinion is hardening the other way." Having thus implicitly threatened to defect at the ballot box, Snow then turned up the heat still further: he reminded Williams that Britain had signed the Declaration of Human Rights, which, in an effort to protect religious education, had guaranteed the right to education outside the state system. "[I]ndependent education is here to stay," he noted, adding, "It will also increase." He insisted that professional people who wanted quality education for their children were not selfish – in fact, he explained, they were already establishing scholarships so that other children could attend the elite private schools to which they sent their children. "This is the kind of call to which professional people respond," Snow declared, with a flourish of class pride. He concluded by acknowledging that the development of these scholarships would be gradual, but he suggested that this was the sort of education reform he could endorse: expanding access, but maintaining excellence.

Snow was following the path taken by many liberals during this period, a rightward shift known in the American context as "neoconservatism."[58] "Neoconservatives" were liberal intellectuals who rejected radicalism in the 1960s, shifted their political orientations in the 1970s, and embraced

---

[56] Roy Lowe, "Education," in *A Companion to Contemporary Britain, 1939–2000*, ed. Paul Addison and Harriet Jones (Oxford: Blackwell, 2005), p. 288.

[57] Snow to Shirley Williams, 7 October 1976, HRC: Snow 210.1; Williams replied in a letter of October 25, 1976, HRC: Snow 210.1. The following quotations are from Snow's letter of 7 October.

[58] John de la Mothe discusses Snow's increasingly despondent politics in *C. P. Snow and the Struggle of Modernity* (Austin: University of Texas, 1992).

Ronald Reagan in the 1980s.[59] By 1966 the editor of *Commentary* magazine, Norman Podhoretz, had become concerned by what he saw as the anti-Americanism of the New Left, and in 1970 he declared that *Commentary* would henceforth oppose radical movements. As the historian Howard Brick explains, Podhoretz's declaration represented "one of the first signs that a camp of liberals and former radicals were drifting, first in cultural matters and a few years later in political and economic affairs, toward a 'neoconservatism' destined to flourish in the 1970s."[60] In the face of challenges to American institutions domestically and American policies internationally, neoconservatives recognized that their sympathies and loyalties lay on the side of those institutions and policies. They therefore advocated policies that would preserve American institutions at home, in addition to policies that would extend American ideals abroad. In international affairs they emerged as idealists and hawks: suspicious of global institutions, unwavering in support of Israel, and relentless in their criticism of the Soviet Union. It is somewhat misleading that they came to be known as "conservatives," since their idealistic, transformative global vision might best be understood as a muscular liberalism (although shorn of the tolerance and caution that restrained their former colleagues).

Neoconservatism generally refers to an American phenomenon, but the affinities with Snow's experience are revealing. While far from a Cold War hawk, Snow believed in the virtues and promises of his society, and when he encountered radicals who adopted more critical perspectives he found himself moving – incrementally, but steadily – towards the right. But the connections between Snow and the neoconservatives are more than a matter of mere intellectual affinity: Snow and Podhoretz had been friends since 1958, and he had also corresponded with Irving Kristol. When Podhoretz became editor of *Commentary* in 1960, he and Snow continued to discuss politics and culture, and Podhoretz requested the

---

[59] Irving Kristol suggests that the term was coined by his critics in the 1980s, but he thought it apt and subsequently adopted it: Kristol, *Neoconservatism: The Autobiography of an Idea* (New York: Free Press, 1995). The historiography of the movement remains thin, most accounts having been written by participants or journalists; one insightful account is the documentary by Joseph Dorman, *Arguing the World* (New York: First Run/Icarus Films, 1997). See also Peter Steinfels, *The Neoconservatives: The Men Who Are Changing American Politics* (New York: Simon and Schuster, 1979); John Ehrman, *The Rise of Neoconservatism: Intellectuals and Foreign Affairs, 1945–1994* (New Haven: Yale University Press, 1995); Godfrey Hodgson, *The World Turned Right Side Up: A History of the Conservative Ascendancy in America* (Boston: Houghton Mifflin, 1996). The major work on American conservatism, which ends too soon to fully consider the new right, is George Nash, *The Conservative Intellectual Movement in America, since 1945* (New York: Basic Books, 1976).

[60] Brick, *Age of Contradiction*, p. 176.

article about the New Left that Snow so dreaded writing.[61] The "two cultures" controversy, however, placed a strain on their friendship. Podhoretz informed Snow that he had turned down Leavis's offer to publish his Richmond Lecture in *Commentary*, but he also solicited what turned out to be an influential, critical assessment from Lionel Trilling.[62] Worse still, when Podhoretz offered Snow space to respond, he felt obliged to mention that he had remained friendly with his former teacher from Cambridge, Leavis.[63] That act of betrayal, combined with Podhoretz's failure to intervene publicly on Snow's behalf, proved too much for their friendship to bear, and for the next dozen years Snow and Podhoretz went separate ways.

Then, towards the end of his life, Snow reached out to Podhoretz. Reviewing Melvin Lasky's *Utopia and Revolution* (1976) for the *Financial Times*, Snow cited Podhoretz and *Commentary* as the potential intellectual base that the right had long lacked.[64] Shortly thereafter, he wrote Podhoretz directly: "I have been following with close attention your efforts to produce a kind of respectable neo-conservatism," Snow wrote. "With the greater part of it . . . I am in entire sympathy, and have in fact been saying similar things over here."[65] He cited his opposition to affirmative action (which did not exist in Britain) as one area of agreement, while registering reservations about Podhoretz's aggressive military stance. Then, in February 1980, Snow favorably reviewed Podhoretz's explosive memoir, *Breaking Ranks*. He declared Podhoretz "brilliant," and sympathetically differentiated the neoconservative stance from right-wing attacks upon the welfare state. Although *Breaking Ranks* had been written in an American context, Snow identified lessons for a British audience: "Most English readers will find warnings in *Breaking Ranks*, especially in the campaigns that *Commentary* is fighting against the sillier items in the liberal package deal."[66]

Snow died on July 1, 1980, less than five months after his warm review of Podhoretz. His obituary in the *Observer* ran under the fitting headline, "Laureate of Meritocracy."[67] And so he was: as a novelist, commentator, and public figure, Snow spent his career advocating a society that would identify, cultivate, and esteem talent. Not only

---

[61] See Chapter 4.

[62] Lionel Trilling, "Science, Literature, and Culture: A Comment on the Leavis–Snow Controversy," *Commentary*, June 1962, pp. 461–467 (discussed in Chapter 6).

[63] Podhoretz to Snow, 22 May 1962, HRC: Snow 165.12.

[64] Snow, review of Melvin Lasky, *Utopia and Revolution* (London: Macmillan, 1977), typescript in HRC: Snow 34.7.

[65] Snow to Podhoretz, 13 November 1978, HRC: Snow 165.13.

[66] Snow, review of Podhoretz, *Financial Times*, 16 February 1980.

[67] Alan Watkins, "Laureate of Meritocracy," *Observer*, 6 July 1980.

would such a society enable individuals to realize their abilities, he believed, but it also promised to ensure a decent life for all, and in Snow's estimation industrial society represented the best prospect for realizing this meritocratic vision. In the final fifteen years of his life, however, this vision had been subjected to relentless assault, a process that left Snow increasingly exasperated. It is impossible to know for certain, and he might well have become a founding member of the Social Democratic Party, but, had he lived, it is not impossible to imagine Snow having joined his old friend from Leicester on one final journey, J. H. Plumb's rightward trek towards Thatcherism during the 1980s.

Exit right

If one story in the cultural and political history of postwar Britain is the rise of a new right, another is the emergence of the New Left. The first part of that history has been well told: it begins with the exodus of socialist intellectuals from the Communist Party in 1956, follows the union between northern activists and a younger, Oxford-based generation in the *New Left Review* in 1960, and climaxes in the purge of that journal's editorial board by the theoretically inclined wing of the movement led by Perry Anderson.[68] That story is satisfying in part because it is discrete and coherent: it is one episode in the history of Marxism, with a clear beginning and end. Yet it is also part of the history of the intellectual and political left since 1945 more generally, and that history is neither so discrete nor so coherent. It is an account not of a "rise and fall" but of a mutation, a shift in emphasis from materialist analysis to cultural critique. That shift brought surprising implications for the fate of Leavis's stance.[69]

From the time of his retirement in 1962, Leavis enjoyed a remarkable series of triumphs. In 1963 Cambridge University Press reprinted the entire run of *Scrutiny* (which had published its final issue a decade before); in 1965 his work was translated into Japanese, Italian, and Swedish; in 1966 he and Q. D. Leavis visited Harvard and Cornell;

---

[68] Dennis Dworkin, *Cultural Marxism in Postwar Britain: History, the New Left, and the Origins of Cultural Studies* (Durham: Duke University Press, 1997); Michael Kenny, *The First New Left: British Intellectuals after Stalin* (London: Lawrence and Wishart, 1995).

[69] On this shift, see Dworkin, *Cultural Marxism in Postwar Britain*. On the conservative dimensions of Leavis's criticism, thought, and practice, see Anne Samson, *F. R. Leavis* (University of Toronto Press, 1992); Francis Mulhern, *The Moment of "Scrutiny"* (London: New Left Books, 1979).

238 The Two Cultures Controversy

and in 1967 he delivered the Clark Lectures in Cambridge.[70] This
phase of Leavis's career (much like those previous) featured a series of
dramatic confrontations. The narrative of these confrontations was
frequently ironic, their plots following one of two scripts: Leavis might
be embraced, to which he would respond by denouncing his admirer; or
he might issue a fierce denunciation, which would be met with an
enthusiastic embrace. An example was his relationship with the University of York: Leavis identified university expansion as a step towards
the elimination of the standards that sustained the capacity for *life*, and
York offered him a professorship. There were exceptions to this pattern,
as when an enemy responded with malice (as did Snow), but the relationships often developed along these lines. While scholars and participants (frequently, participant-scholars) have offered psychological
explanations for these developments, they might instead be understood
as part of the process of shifting alliances and antipathies that characterized the 1960s.

Leavis's relationship to student activism offers another example of this
process. Throughout his career Leavis imagined himself as the anti-
establishment figure *par excellence*: it was part of his legend that the
Home Office had investigated him in the 1920s for attempting to import
a copy of *Ulysses*, an episode that inspired an undergraduate magazine to
establish the "Leavis Prize for Pornography."[71] The Leavises envisioned
Scrutiny as a renegade enterprise, and Leavis tended to depict his literary
judgments as affronts to received wisdom. In that more formal time,
Leavis was known for his open-necked shirt, and when classroom
authority was social authority, Leavis could treat students as collaborators and equals.[72] Indeed, in his battles with the English Faculty in the
early 1960s, Leavis knew that he could count on undergraduate support,
and he believed that support provided him with a certain moral
authority.[73] Later that decade, however, when undergraduates began to
protest against the university, Leavis wanted nothing to do with them.

[70] The lectures at Cornell and Harvard, along with those of Q. D. Leavis, were published
as *Lectures in America* (London: Chatto and Windus, 1969); the Clark Lectures as
English Literature in Our Time and the University (London: Chatto and Windus, 1969).
[71] Ian MacKillop, *F. R. Leavis: A Life in Criticism* (London: Allen Lane, 1995), pp. 88–91.
For the legal details, see A. D. Harvey, "Leavis, *Ulysses*, and the Home Office,"
Cambridge Review, October 1993, pp. 123–128.
[72] "[H]e had a truer secret weapon possessed by none of his great contemporaries – an
instinct for academic democracy. He treated adolescents like Trevor Nunn, Simon
Gray, and John Cleese as equals or potential equals." John Ezard, "The Max Miller of
the Lecture Circuit," *Guardian*, 18 April 1978.
[73] Leavis to Harding, 27 November 1963, Emmanuel College, Cambridge (Emmanuel):
ECA COL 9.59a.129.

However critical he may have been of the examination system, he opposed their efforts to reform it; however much he resented the academic establishment, he sided with Vice-Chancellors against student leaders; and however disgusted he may have been with contemporary society, he found the counterculture even more repulsive.[74] Norman Podhoretz and Raymond Williams both noted affinities between Leavis and the student radicals, but Leavis himself viewed those students as enemies of standards and of the university, and he denounced them as such.[75]

Leavis had never been at a loss for things to denounce, but in retirement he was especially flush with targets. A partial list of his targets would include egalitarianism, democracy, unions, immigration, feminism, Marxism, and sexual emancipation; among politicians he was equally hostile to Harold Wilson and Edward Heath; his tirades against the establishment came to include Noel Annan, Lionel Robbins, Alex Todd, and J. H. Plumb (in addition to Snow). The transistor radio, bingo halls, and package holidays to Spain came in for his derision, and he interpreted "pluralism, compassion and social hope" as the watchwords of a dispiriting malaise.[76] Each of these targets, Leavis thought, testified to misplaced priorities: egalitarianism valued equality over elites, democracy valued participation over direction, unions valued wages over meaningful labor, and so forth. Leavis believed that politicians were constrained to the point that they could not talk about matters of importance, so instead they paid lip service to egalitarian principles they could not possibly hold. Meanwhile, establishment figures (such as Annan and Snow) uttered clichés about "pluralism" and "social hope," while remaining blissfully unaware of how hollow such promises ultimately were. In short, when Leavis surveyed the social, cultural, and political scene in the 1960s, he saw something far more terrifying than a society on the wrong track: he saw a society that had been on the wrong track for so long that it no longer recognized its predicament. Through his lecturing, teaching, and writing, Leavis endeavored to induce recognition of the threat that conventional wisdom posed to intelligence, discrimination, and creation.

---

[74] On Leavis's support for York's Vice-Chancellor against a "student revolt," see Leavis to Holbrook, 12 December 1968, Downing College: DCPP/LEA/4 Leavis, F. R. (5).

[75] Raymond Williams, "A Refusal to be Resigned," *Guardian*, 18 December 1969; Norman Podhoretz, "F. R. Leavis: A Revaluation," *The Bloody Crossroads: Where Literature and Politics Meet* (New York: Simon and Schuster, 1986); Leavis, *Nor Shall My Sword, passim.*

[76] This list only begins to identify Leavis's targets, but *Nor Shall My Sword* contains them all.

Leavis descried this threat everywhere, not least in Cambridge English. Raymond Williams occupied a towering position on the intellectual left in this period, and from 1961 he was also Leavis's colleague on the Cambridge English Faculty. Williams acknowledged his intellectual debts to Leavis, as well as their very different political stances, and by all indications the two enjoyed a courteous, if distant, working relationship.[77] Privately, however, Leavis was quick to place distance between Williams and himself, and he was correct to identify antagonisms between Williams's work and his own: Williams admitted, for instance, that his undergraduate lectures on the novel mounted a sustained argument against *The Great Tradition*.[78] Leavis occasionally identified the alternative that Williams represented explicitly, remarking that he was seen to exercise a "Marxising" influence in the faculty.[79]

The hostility was mutual. In the *New Left Review* in 1968, Perry Anderson published a dazzling survey of academic disciplines in Britain, "Components of the National Culture."[80] Anderson confronted a problem that, in his view, plagued British intellectual life more generally: the absence of a critical perspective such that flourished in Europe. "The culture of British society is organized about an absent centre," he wrote, "an overall account of itself, that could have been either a classical sociology or a national Marxism."[81] The absence of such a center had created a vacuum, into which Leavis had thrust the unlikely candidate of literary studies: "This claim was certainly unique to England: no other country has produced a critical discipline with these pretensions."[82] In the 1930s, Anderson continued, Leavis and *Scrutiny* had routed vulgar Marxism, and the subsequent Leavisian alternative stimulated the few works of cultural criticism and socialist theory to have emerged in Britain – most notably, Williams's *Culture and Society* (1958) and *The Long Revolution* (1961).[83] Anderson was acknowledging Leavis's achievement, but also identifying that achievement as a problem to move beyond.[84]

As old quarrels resumed, new antagonisms emerged as well. Leavis dismissed nineteenth-century feminism as "contrary to nature," but by

---

[77] Fred Inglis, *Raymond Williams* (London: Routledge, 1995), pp. 182–183.

[78] Williams, quoted in Inglis, *Raymond Williams*, p. 183.

[79] Leavis, "The State of English" (letter), *Times Literary Supplement*, 3 March 1972.

[80] Perry Anderson, "Components of the National Culture," *New Left Review* 50 (July–August 1968), pp. 3–57, reprinted in *English Questions* (London: Verso, 1992), pp. 48–104.

[81] Anderson, *English Questions*, p. 103.   [82] *Ibid.*, p. 96.

[83] Raymond Williams, *Culture and Society, 1780–1950* (London: Chatto and Windus, 1958); *The Long Revolution* (London: Chatto and Windus, 1961).

[84] On this point, see also Mulhern, *The Moment of "Scrutiny."*

1976 the feminist movement was attracting his ire.[85] In his Richmond Lecture he had derided the ideal of "equality," quoting D. H. Lawrence to suggest that difference, not equality, was the essential fact of human nature: he quoted Birkin from *Women in Love*, "We are all abstractly and mathematically equal, if you like . . . But spiritually, there is pure difference and neither equality nor inequality counts."[86] In 1976 – in an argument that was identical to, and simultaneous with, Snow's campaign against comprehensive education – Leavis again criticized feminism, which he thought denied the fact of natural difference in favor of a commitment to equality.[87] Leavis included the book's epigraph, another quotation from Lawrence, as a riposte to such claims: "Man or woman, each is a flow, a flowing life. And without one another, we can't flow, just as a river cannot flow without banks. A woman is one bank of the river of my life, and the world is the other." He derided "the passion for equality" as a product of the "religion of egalitarianism," and he remarked that any functioning society required social differentials of various sorts (for instance, of power, authority, and opportunity).[88] Feminism, Leavis thought, sought to deny this reality: it "proclaimed . . . 'equality' of women and men," he argued, "whereas *difference* is the essential fact."[89] Leavis insisted that the issue was "not a matter of inequality or 'underprivilege'," but rather the natural, inevitable, and necessary fact of "difference."[90] Snow couched his anti-egalitarian arguments in terms of the need to cultivate individual talent and prevent national decline, but Leavis – constitutionally unable to be so politic – directed his arguments against the ideal of equality itself.

Even in retirement, then, the confrontations never ceased. Leavis confronted a number of irritants during his final two decades, from student activism to Marxist criticism to resurgent feminism. He fought these battles the way he always had, through his literary and social criticism, but even as he wrote the discipline that he had shaped was moving away from him. Not that Leavis lost sleep over the direction of the field: his books found readers, the *Times* printed his letters, and his teaching and lecturing remained in demand. But while his career in criticism had been devoted to identifying the tradition of writers who

---

[85] Neil Roberts, "'Leavisite' Cambridge in the 1960s," in *F. R. Leavis: Essays and Documents*, ed. Ian MacKillop and Richard Storer (Sheffield Academic Press, 1995), p. 268.

[86] F. R. Leavis, *Two Cultures? The Significance of C. P. Snow* (London: Chatto and Windus, 1962), p. 21.

[87] F. R. Leavis, *Thought, Words and Creativity: Art and Thought in Lawrence* (New York: Oxford University Press, 1976).

[88] *Ibid.*, pp. 141–142.   [89] *Ibid.*, p. 142 (emphasis mine.)   [90] *Ibid.*

exhibited minds in touch with *life*, by 1970 little in that project remained unproblematic.[91] To subsequent generations of students Leavis's vocabulary would appear as foreign as his concerns, and eventually he took his place alongside other displaced giants of the discipline's past.

The hidden network

Yet at the moment when Leavis was becoming a stranger in his own field, trends in the humanities were rendering elements of his stance more central than ever. In 1976 Malcolm Bradbury discussed a student's essay, "If You'll Be Frank, I'll Be Karl." The student recalled the impression Leavis had made upon him as an undergraduate at York, and he explained that Leavis remained an inspiration even as Marxism was pressing its way towards the center of the field. The shift from Leavis to Marx entailed tensions, but not necessarily contradictions: as Bradbury observed, "[W]here, in the present order and the present academy, can today's student, conscious that literature does embody a dissent from the established order and its preferences, go *except* to Marxism?"[92] For this reason, he explained, "a good deal of the cultural work done by the generation successor to *Scrutiny* has shifted this way."[93] To Bradbury, this recognition pointed to "the continuing force of Leavis himself," a sentiment that Terry Eagleton echoes in *Literary Theory*: "English students in England today are 'Leavisites' whether they know it or not."[94] The provocation in Eagleton's assertion lies in his anticipation of the reader's sense that literary criticism occupies a different ideological position today than it did at mid century.[95] Yet the field never changed beyond recognition, as literary scholars continued to work within a

---

[91] Michael Bell explains the timing of, and reasons for, this development: "[B]y the end of the sixties, the increasing dominance of Marxist analysis, the impact of feminist and minority ethnic writing, and the globalising of literary influence and creation, all made Leavis's methods and concerns seem outdated and parochial." Bell, "F. R. Leavis," in *The Cambridge History of Literary Criticism: Volume 7: Modernism and the New Criticism*, ed. A. Walton Litz, *et al.* (Cambridge University Press, 2000), p. 420.

[92] Malcolm Bradbury, "The Tip of Life," *New Statesman*, 1 October 1976, p. 453.

[93] *Ibid.*

[94] *Ibid.*; Terry Eagleton, *Literary Theory: An Introduction* (Minneapolis: University of Minnesota Press, 1983), p. 31. On Leavis's persistence, see Dworkin, *Cultural Marxism in Postwar Britain*, Chapter 3; Gary Day, *Re-reading Leavis: Culture and Literary Criticism* (New York: St. Martin's Press, 1996); Bill Reading, *The University in Ruins* (Cambridge, Mass.: Harvard University Press, 1996).

[95] On this historical shift, see Guillory, "The Sokal Affair and the History of Criticism"; Hollinger, "Science as a Weapon in *Kulturkämpfe* in the United States During and After World War II." For a longer perspective, primarily focused (as are Guillory and Hollinger) on the American story, see Gerald Graff, *Professing Literature: An Institutional History* (University of Chicago Press, 1987).

paradigm of social and cultural critique – a framework that had been forged by, and that was inherited from, a previous generations of critics. Tracking the fortunes of Leavis's ideas through this period reveals continuities through this process of disciplinary transformation. Leavis's ideas persisted in three major ways, the first of which was through institutions and personnel. He always resented the failure of his students to secure university positions in Cambridge, and by 1965 he accepted that his legacy would not be at his own Downing College, but he remained committed to continuing the battle elsewhere.[96] In 1962 the *Observer* published a feature on "The Hidden Network of Leavisites," which began: "Great men of ideas, innovators like Marx and Freud, never stand alone." Leavis's "disciples," it explained, had spread throughout the world, and they were especially prominent in schools and universities throughout Britain. The article specifically identified Denys Thompson, headmaster at Yeovil; G. D. Klingopulos, Senior Lecturer at Cardiff; G. H. Bantock, Reader at Leicester; Frank W. Bradbrook, Lecturer at Bangor; and R. G. Cox, Senior Lecturer at Manchester. But Leavis's impact, it continued, extended beyond the classroom: David Holbrook was a prominent poet, Andor Gomme and L. G. Salingar were extra-mural tutors, and Boris Ford was editor of the *Pelican Guide to English Literature*. Leavis was also credited with having influenced Richard Hoggart, Raymond Williams, and the British New Left. The article indulged in the melodramatic (at one point it suggested that, wherever three or four gathered in his name, Leavis was there among them), but it nevertheless testified to the reach of Leavis's influence.[97]

It was the existence of this "hidden network" that facilitated the break with Downing. Leavis precipitated (or acquiesced in) the end of his English School not because he was prepared to see his life's work eliminated in an instant, but because he already knew that the chances for its perpetuation lay elsewhere. University expansion, ironically, provided fertile ground. In 1965 Leavis shifted his attention to York, where Eric James – former High Master of Manchester Grammar School, and the new university's first Vice-Chancellor – recruited him to a visiting professorship. Having just opened its doors in 1963, York was

---

[96] Leavis to D. F. Pocock, 7 May 1965, Emmanuel: ECA COL 9.59a.121.22.

[97] "The Hidden Network of Leavisites," *Observer*, 11 March 1962. Graham Hough, one of Leavis's colleagues on the Cambridge English Faculty, begrudgingly agreed: "Universities are more numerous than ever; they have flourishing English departments; disciples of Dr. Leavis occupy prominent positions in most of them, not only in England, but all over the world, from Melbourne to New York. Yet the world is what it is." Hough, "The Ordered Carnival," *New Statesman*, 5 December 1969, pp. 817–818. For a brief, but fascinating, example of the way that students traveled along Leavisian networks, see Roberts, " 'Leavisite' Cambridge in the 1960s," p. 271.

an odd fit for the arch-critic of university expansion, but Leavis was happy there, taking the train up on Tuesdays and staying through Friday.[98] He enjoyed his status as a grand figure at York, with no obligations other than teaching, and he saw his responsibility as keeping the university aware of its purpose.[99] As part of the Department of English and Related Studies, English at York assumed something like the interdisciplinary form proposed in *Education and the University*, and the students had two weeks (rather than Cambridge's three hours) to complete their examinations.[100]

But long before students ever arrived at university, Leavis already exerted influence upon their educations. As Fred Inglis wrote in 1967, "The whole tenor of school English teaching has been altering out of all recognition these past few years."[101] Inglis was referring to the subterranean influence of Leavis and Denys Thompson, which manifested itself in A-level papers, O-level reforms, CSE work, English in schools, and the National Association for the Teaching of English. Leavis had long been aware of his influence in this regard, as the scholarship examinations that he administered at Downing provided him with connections into schools. Two decades later, as tensions between Leavis and Downing became the subject of newspaper stories, the *Sunday Times* reported that headmasters were already sending their best pupils to provincial universities where the English teachers had trained under Leavis.[102]

Leavis's influence, as Pendennis had suggested, extended beyond the realm of education. Three journals committed themselves to continuing the work of *Scrutiny*: *Cambridge Quarterly, Human World*, and *New Universities Quarterly*. Leavis's pupils secured positions in the state-subsidized theater, and included two future directors of the Royal Shakespeare Company, Peter Hall and Trevor Nunn (indeed, one observer claimed to identify Leavis's interpretation of *Othello* in a production starring Olivier).[103] According to Noel Annan, the *Guardian* provided a friendly home for Leavisian criticism, and Karl Miller read English with Leavis before serving as editor of the *Listener*, literary editor of the *Spectator* and *New Statesman*, and founding editor of the

[98] MacKillop captured the incongruity of Leavis in his new surroundings in *F. R. Leavis*, Chapter 11.
[99] Leavis to Denys Harding, 8 October 1967, Emmanuel: ECA COL 9.59a.83.
[100] Brian MacArthur, "The Outsider," *Guardian*, 13 June 1966.
[101] Inglis, in *New Society*, 16 November 1967, p. 700.
[102] "The Politics of Why Leavis Quit," *Sunday Times*, 1 November 1964.
[103] Noel Annan, *Our Age: English Intellectuals Between the World Wars – a Group Portrait* (New York: Random House, 1990), p. 322; Ezard, "The Max Miller of the Lecture Circuit."

London Review of Books.[104] And, as already noted, Boris Ford's *Pelican Guide to English Literature* read like a "Who's Who" of pupils and collaborators: according to Ford's calculations, about one in three contributors to the seven volumes had written for *Scrutiny.*[105] In short, Leavis's legacy is a far more concrete matter than the identification of tropes in a discourse, as his students and admirers carried his ideas and his style into schools, universities, and cultural institutions for decades to come.

The second dimension of Leavis's endurance was disciplinary. His importance to the history of literary studies in the English-speaking world is beyond question. Leavis was part of the first generation of undergraduates to read English in Cambridge, and he played a key role in establishing the credentials of a discipline that otherwise could have been (and elsewhere was) dismissed as "soft."[106] Not only did he demonstrate that literary studies demanded standards, rigor, and intelligence, but he insisted that it should be situated at the center of the university – not simply at the center of the arts, but at the core of humane education. Leavis pressed this case with particular determination, but he was by no means alone in this ambition: in the United States the New Critics asserted the critic's unique expertise, and in Britain the stature of T. S. Eliot lent powerful credence to the critic's claims to cultural authority. Today the English Department/Faculty occupies a prominent position in the British university, and "close reading" is accorded a methodological status on a par with the historian's recourse to the archives. These developments were not inevitable, and part of the explanation for why they occurred must lie with the agency and labor of this generation of teachers and critics.

Leavis's disciplinary legacies extended beyond the English department. Two of the key documents in the background to *Scrutiny* were *Fiction and the Reading Public* (1932) and *Culture and Environment* (1933).[107] Q. D. Leavis's *Fiction and the Reading Public* advanced a "sociological" approach to literature, relating literary texts to the society and culture in which they were produced, while *Culture and Environment* took the form of a teaching manual, guiding teachers and headmasters in

---

[104] Annan, *Our Age,* p. 322.

[105] Boris Ford, "Round and about the *Pelican Guide to English Literature,*" in *The Leavises: Recollections and Impressions,* ed. Denys Thompson (Cambridge University Press, 1984), p. 110.

[106] On Leavis's role in the development of Cambridge English, see Stefan Collini, "Cambridge and the Study of English," in *Cambridge Contributions,* ed. Sarah J. Omrod (Cambridge University Press, 1998), pp. 42–64.

[107] Q. D. Leavis, *Fiction and the Reading Public* (London: Chatto and Windus, 1932); F. R. Leavis and Denys Thompson, *Culture and Environment: The Training of Critical Awareness* (London: Chatto and Windus, 1933).

training their students to read advertising, for instance, as part of the civilization that produced it. While Leavis is sometimes conflated with the New Critics, this insistence upon the words *not* on the page differed from the New Critics' focus upon texts. By contrast, Leavis, Q. D. Leavis, Thompson, and their associates developed a method and rationale for "reading" culture critically, and with a different inflection that program later informed the emergent field of cultural studies.[108] The Centre for Contemporary Cultural Studies (CCCS) was established in Birmingham in 1964, and its first director was Richard Hoggart. The Leavises' influence upon Hoggart was clear – even to Leavis, who unkindly (and incorrectly) dismissed Hoggart's *The Uses of Literacy* (1957) as derivative of *Fiction and the Reading Public*.[109] In 1969 a new director, Stuart Hall, took the CCCS in a more radical direction, shifting its focus from the "left-Leavisism" of Hoggart and Williams, but decades later Eagleton detected the "residual Leavisite" in Hall after all.[110]

Another domain in which Leavis's approach found echoes was the history and sociology of science. In the interwar decades Leavis exhibited hostility towards the heritage of the Enlightenment, depicting the "progress" offered by science and technology as the unwelcome acceleration of a destructive civilization. As he developed this position in literary studies, philosophers and political theorists associated with the Frankfurt School on the continent were developing their critique of Enlightenment rationality.[111] An anti-Enlightenment stance found few early advocates in Britain, but then from the 1970s a critical orientation towards the assumptions of scientific practice found a home in the history and sociology of science. This is not to suggest that the history and sociology of science arose out of Leavis's ideas (their development owed much to the interwar work not of Leavis, but of Marxist historians of science), but their assumptions and approaches nevertheless corresponded with many of his ideas.[112] These developments were pressed

[108] Leavis's influence upon cultural studies was frequently noted in the retrospectives at the centenary of his birth in 1995: for instance, Malcolm Bradbury, "Whatever Happened to F. R. Leavis?" *Sunday Times*, 9 July 1995; Gary Day, "A Pariah in the Republic of Letters," *Times Higher Education Supplement*, 4 August 1995, p. 21.
[109] Richard Hoggart, *The Uses of Literacy: Aspects of Working-Class Life with Special Reference to Publications and Entertainments* (London: Chatto and Windus, 1957).
[110] Terry Eagleton, "The Hippest," *London Review of Books*, 7 March 1996, p. 3. On the origins, founding, and direction of the CCCS, see Dworkin, *Cultural Marxism in Postwar Britain*, Chapter 3.
[111] Theodor Adorno and Max Horkheimer, *Dialektik der Aufklärung: Philosophische Fragmente* (Amsterdam: Querido, 1947); Martin Jay, *The Dialectical Imagination: A History of the Frankfurt School and the Institute of Social Research, 1923–1950* (Boston: Little, Brown, 1973).
[112] See Werskey, "The Marxist Critique of Capitalist Science."

forward by Bob Young, for instance in the volume he edited on *Changing Perspectives in the History of Science* (1973), and at the University of Edinburgh, in the program in the Sociology of Scientific Knowledge (SSK).[113] Scientists were shown to have been pursuing alchemy, eugenics, and power in addition to truth and knowledge, findings that complicated their public images as pioneers of progress.[114] Indeed, in the competition to attract the interest of historians, the triumphs of science came to be joined – and often displaced – by the assumptions of scientists.[115] These assumptions had histories of their own, and their interrogation led outside the history of science and into the history of society.[116] As a result, while *The Two Cultures* ensures that Snow remains the more cited figure in the history of science, in many ways Leavis's ideas remain more familiar.

But it was Leavis's emphasis upon language that retained the most subsequent currency even through apparently hostile intellectual developments.

[113] Examples of these developments include Thomas Kuhn, *The Structure of Scientific Revolutions* (University of Chicago Press, 1962); Robert Young and Mikulas Teich, eds., *Changing Perspectives in the History of Science: Essays in Honor of Joseph Needham* (London: Heinemann Educational, 1973). For a critical history of Kuhn's thesis, see Steve Fuller, *Thomas Kuhn: A Philosophical History for Our Times* (University of Chicago Press, 2000). Major figures of the Edinburgh school include David Bloor and Barry Barnes; key early works include Barnes, *T. S. Kuhn and Social Science* (London: Macmillan, 1982); Bloor, *Wittgenstein: A Social Theory of Knowledge* (New York: Columbia University Press, 1983). On Young, and on science studies in Britain during the twentieth century, see Werskey, "The Marxist Critique of Capitalist Science."

[114] For example (chronologically): Paul Forman, "Weimar Culture, Causality, and Quantum Theory, 1918–1927," *Historical Studies in the Physical Sciences* 3 (1971), pp. 1–116; Betty Jo Teeter Dobbs, *The Foundations of Newton's Alchemy: or, "The Hunting of the Greene Lyon"* (New York: Cambridge University Press, 1975); Spencer Weart, *Scientists in Power* (Cambridge, Mass.: Harvard University Press, 1979); Stephen Jay Gould, *The Mismeasure of Man* (New York: Norton, 1981); Donald MacKenzie, *Statistics in Britain, 1865–1930: The Social Construction of Scientific Knowledge* (Edinburgh University Press, 1981); Stephen Kern, *The Culture of Time and Space, 1880–1914* (Cambridge, Mass.: Harvard University Press, 1983).

[115] Simon Schaffer, "Godly Men and Mechanical Philosophers: Souls and Spirits in Restoration Natural Philosophy," *Science in Context* 1 (1987), pp. 55–85; Steven Shapin, "The House of Experiment in Seventeenth-Century England," *Isis* 79 (September 1988), pp. 373–404; Shapin, " 'The Mind Is Its Own Place': Science and Solitude in Seventeenth-Century England," *Science in Context* 4 (1990), pp. 191–218; Shapin, *A Social History of Truth: Civility and Science in Seventeenth-Century England* (University of Chicago Press, 1994); Theodore Porter, *Trust in Numbers: The Pursuit of Objectivity in Science and Public Life* (Princeton University Press, 1995); Andrew Warwick, *Masters of Theory: Cambridge and the Rise of Mathematical Physics* (University of Chicago Press, 2003).

[116] Steven Shapin and Simon Schaffer, *Leviathan and the Air-Pump: Hobbes, Boyle, and the Experimental Life* (Princeton University Press, 1985); Stephen Toulmin, *Cosmopolis: The Hidden Agenda of Modernity* (New York: Free Press, 1990); Bruno Latour, *Pandora's Hope: Essays on the Reality of Science Studies* (Cambridge, Mass.: Harvard University Press, 1999).

Chapter 2 discussed the centrality of language to Leavis's ideas about history, literature, and culture since the seventeenth century: he believed that a rich linguistic inheritance had been fractured at that time, leading to the erection of a false dichotomy between *language* and *reality* – a dichotomy that Leavis believed to be characteristic of modern Western thought. He criticized this false opposition in the Richmond Lecture, pointing instead to a "human world" that preceded any intellectual edifice created by scientists – after all, ideas about nature were only made possible by the language they inherited.[117] Leavis continued to develop these ideas after his Richmond Lecture, and by the early 1970s he was identifying the target of his critique as the "Cartesian dualism."[118] The contrast with Snow's ideas is revealing: in 1960 Snow wrote that facts were "hypnotic . . . neutral . . . innocent," but in his penultimate book Leavis insisted that facts were never apprehended apart from values, experience, and – especially – language.[119] However foreign subsequent developments might have rendered many of Leavis's assumptions, his lifelong insistence upon the primacy of language to experience – that is, his insistence that language always precedes, and therefore shapes, human experience – was to find unlikely echoes in such subsequent developments as post-structuralist theory.[120]

A third dimension of Leavis's persistence was ideological. Leavis shared common antagonisms with subsequent cultural critics, antagonisms that included Western civilization and Marxist materialism. Leavis, as we have seen, believed that modern civilization had its origins in the seventeenth century, and that one of its most salient characteristics was its relentless materialism. Leavis's opposition to that civilization, and thus to its materialism, led him to adopt a critical stance towards intellectual positions that prioritized economic relationships (such as Marxism), and towards political projects that prioritized standards of living (such as the welfare state at home, and development theory abroad). He believed that the acceptance of these priorities testified to the extent to which modern civilization had already advanced, and through his literary and social criticism he wanted to expose and oppose the intellectual

---

[117] "[T]here is a prior human achievement of collaborative creation, a more basic work of the mind of man (and more than the mind), one without which the triumphant erection of the scientific edifice would not have been possible: that is, the creation of the human world, including language." Leavis, *Two Cultures?*, p. 27.

[118] Leavis, *Nor Shall My Sword*; Leavis, *The Living Principle: 'English' as a Discipline of Thought* (London: Chatto and Windus, 1975); Leavis, *Thought, Words, and Creativity* (1976).

[119] C. P. Snow, *The Affair* (London: Macmillan, 1960), p. 315; Leavis, *The Living Principle*, p. 34 and *passim*.

[120] Day, *Re-reading Leavis*.

suppositions and political ambitions that would extend it still further. This position led him into a series of polemical confrontations, including his arguments against Marxism during the 1930s and his challenges to development theory during the 1960s. Then, from the 1970s, as another generation of literary and cultural critics developed critiques of Western civilization and Marxist analysis, critiques that eventually developed into post-colonial and post-modern theory, they found that Leavis had already been there. Or, more precisely, they found a congenial home in the discipline of literary studies that Leavis had done so much to establish as a home for social and cultural criticism.

In summary, while the discipline of literary criticism underwent enormous changes during the second half of the twentieth century, it also exhibited important continuities. Leavis's position persisted in several ways, even when the moment of his intervention had passed. Because there is no denying that that moment has passed, as Leavis's critical approach or literary judgments do not occupy anything like the standing they enjoyed at mid century. But Leavis's influence nevertheless persisted, through institutions and personnel (schools, universities, the public culture), disciplinary lineages (literary studies, cultural studies, science studies), and ideological antagonisms (modern civilization, Marxist materialism). By no means would Leavis have embraced his new comrades, any more than they were particularly eager to acknowledge him, but the critical positions and ideological perspectives that animated his criticism continued to be pressed forward – in different forms, from different places – by unlikely successors.

From merit to the market

As their final fates suggest, Snow and Leavis shared much in common. They both married talented women, who made intellectual careers in a society that was less than accommodating, and their partnerships were professional as well as personal, as each couple collaborated to publish together. In literature, Snow and Leavis reviled the Bloomsbury Group, the ultimate insiders against whom their own programs were directed; they disdained Kingsley Amis, the "man-of-the-moment" whose success only attested to the superficiality of literary trends; and they endorsed Dickens, placing him beside Shakespeare in terms of historical importance.[121] In politics, they viewed the Soviet Union and United States as

---

[121] Snow initially praised *Lucky Jim*, and he remained friendly towards Amis as late as 1967, but privately his contempt was withering – hence his satirical portrait of Amis in the character of Lester Ince.

essentially similar; they saw little meaningful difference between the Labour and Conservative parties at home; and they both kept their distance from the British New Left.[122] Even their rhetoric could prove indistinguishable: "The cheerful passivity of millions under the influence of the mass media. The cheerful unstrenuousness of ninety-five percent of human beings. People preferring to watch games played well rather than playing them badly themselves. Spectator sports, the football pools, gambling. Alcohol. Sex. Spiritual emptiness." That might have been Leavis speaking in the hall of some new university, but in this case it was Snow writing in the *Financial Times*.[123]

Most importantly, Snow and Leavis shared a commitment to meritocratic ideals, along with a corresponding hostility towards egalitarian demands – both of which they expressed by defending elites. "Personally, I would take at least as much care of [the intellectually gifted] as we take of potential athletes," Snow noted in his retort to Leavis in 1970 – and, on that point at least, there was no difference between them.[124] The same year, Leavis insisted in a lecture that "there must always be 'elites'," a fact that he believed it hypocritical, if fashionable, for "progressivist" intellectuals to deny. "There are scientist elites, air-pilot elites, *corps d'élite*, and social elites (the best people)," he explained, "and the underprivileged masses know that professional footballers and BBC announcers are elites."[125] Elites, for Leavis, were undeniable and unavoidable, and he equated them here with the *experts* who occupied important positions in the social world of postwar Britain, and in the meritocratic ideal of the professional society. "Elitism," however, functioned for Leavis as a polemical charge, one that denied this social reality and challenged the meritocracy: "The word 'elitism'," he warned, "has its use (which is military) when it is a question of destroying the grammar schools or making the universities 'comprehensive'."[126] As their identical responses to comprehensive education suggest, Snow and Leavis both resisted egalitarian reforms. Born to the middle class within five years of the new century, they had internalized the meritocratic promise. They believed, that is, in a society in which individuals

[122] The assertion that Snow – a lifelong Labour voter, and eventually a Labour peer – saw little difference between Labour and the Tories might seem surprising, but he asserted just that (as well as the similarities between the United States and the Soviet Union) in an interview with Malcolm Muggeridge, "Appointment with Sir Charles Snow," 18 August 1961, HRC: Snow 8.1.

[123] Snow, review of Ralph Glasser, *Leisure: Penalty or Prize?* (London: Macmillan, 1970), typescript in HRC: Snow 34.1.

[124] Snow, "The Case of Leavis and the Serious Case," p. 739.

[125] Leavis, "Pluralism, Compassion and Social Hope," in *Nor Shall My Sword*, p. 169.

[126] *Ibid.*

could achieve positions commensurate with their talents: a stance at once radical in its assault upon privilege, and conservative in its hostility towards equality.

For approximately three decades after 1945, a period that Snow surmised would later be viewed as a golden age, the meritocratic ideal presumed unequal talents but promised equal opportunity.[127] This position navigated a long-standing tension between liberty and equality in liberal thought.[128] As the political theorist Sheldon Wolin explains, in discussing the problem that inequality had posed for nineteenth-century liberals, "*Elitism* provided the conduit by which liberalism transmitted aristocracy into the postrevolutionary world. That required a redefinition of aristocracy, not as a caste with inherited privileges, but as the embodiment of educated taste, ideals of public service and philanthropy, and earned superiorities."[129] By recasting social hierarchies as the product of earned superiorities rather than inherited privileges, elitism offered a justification for inequality in a democratic age. The acceptance of that explanation, as Walter Bagehot knew, required habits of deference, but elitism and deference could persist alongside meritocratic ideals so long as the differences they justified were understood to have been earned.[130] This sense of elitism – one that derived from *earned* superiorities, and that manifest itself in the expression of *educated* taste – structured the meritocratic commitments of Snow and Leavis alike.

As the 1960s proceeded, however, egalitarian demands increasingly challenged the meritocracy to deliver on its promises. After all, in an imperfect world, existing social inequalities might be the result not of innate differences of talent, but of imposed differences of environment. A true meritocracy, therefore, would constantly be required to address structural inequalities – an imperative that, if taken seriously, threatened to emphasize the pursuit of equal opportunity, even at the expense of the cultivation of unequal talents. Calls for such reforms as comprehensive education, university expansion, and gender equality applied pressure upon the meritocratic promise at precisely this point.[131] Snow and

---

[127] Snow to I. S. Cooper, 9 September 1975, quoted in Caroline Nobile Gryta, "Selected Letters of C. P. Snow: A Critical Edition," unpublished PhD dissertation, Pennsylvania State University (1988), p. 372.

[128] David Wootton, "Liberalism," *The Oxford Companion to Twentieth-Century British Politics*, ed. John Ramsden (Oxford University Press, 2002), pp. 380–381.

[129] Sheldon Wolin, *Tocqueville between Two Worlds: The Making of a Political and Theoretical Life* (Princeton University Press, 2001), p. 9 (emphasis mine). Thanks to Greg Downs.

[130] Walter Bagehot, *The English Constitution* (1867), ed. Paul Smith (Cambridge University Press, 2001); see especially Smith's discussion of deference, pp. xx–xxvii.

[131] For an introduction to three such movements, and to the scholarship on social movements in Britain during the twentieth century, see Holger Nehring, "The Growth

Leavis recognized in these demands a challenge to the principles upon which their worldviews depended, and so they responded by denouncing egalitarianism and defending elites. But the increasingly hostile receptions their arguments met, as evidenced by their steadily more embattled tones, pointed to the erosion of the assumptions that sustained liberal elitism, and thus to the need for a revised rationale to justify social inequality.

Such a rationale emerged during the final quarter of the twentieth century. Around the time that Margaret Thatcher replaced Edward Heath as leader of the Conservative Party, the *market* displaced *merit* as the liberal polity's preferred explanation for persistent inequalities. The "market" in this sense refers not to the act of buying and selling, but to the aggregate product of countless individual decisions.[132] This paradigm shift – from a meritocracy of experts, to a marketplace of consumers – offered a revised explanation for the fact of inequality. If the meritocracy's problem was that it could never be certain whether inequality stemmed from internal qualities or external conditions, shifting the cause of inequality from the capacities of the individual to the dictates of the market rendered its origins diffuse. Consider the example of education: in a society and culture organized around marketplace thinking, schools may be understood to produce differing rates of university students not because of differences in resources, but because of innumerable decisions made by parents, teachers, administrators, and councils. This explanation transfers responsibility from an institution to an abstraction – a shrewd move indeed, since an abstraction is difficult to identify, and even more difficult to remedy, especially by comparison with something so concrete as a school (a state institution, which needs more money). This is not to say that proponents of the market did

of Social Movements," in *A Companion to Contemporary Britain, 1939–2000*, ed. Paul Addison and Harriet Jones (Oxford: Blackwell, 2005), pp. 389–406. In the same volume, Janet Fink analyzes social inequality and efforts to address it in "Welfare, Poverty and Social Inequalities," pp. 263–280.

[132] E. J. Hobsbawm and S. M. Amadae identify related shifts. Hobsbawm discusses the rise of "market sovereignty," in which "the consumer takes the place of the citizen," and "private preferences" replace ideas about "common or group interests." Amadae, citing Hobsbawm, locates a transition from "the familiar language of citizenship," to an emphasis upon "consumers' choices" instead. Hobsbawm, Amadae, and I are all discussing a broad cultural shift during the late twentieth century, one characterized in part by a diffusion of responsibility. Hobsbawm, "Democracy Can Be Bad for You," *New Statesman*, 5 March 2001, p. 26; Amadae, *Rationalizing Capitalist Democracy: The Cold War Origins of Rational Choice Liberalism* (University of Chicago Press, 2003), p. 4. For further consideration of the causes of this shift, see Nils Gilman, *Mandarins of the Future: Modernization Theory in Cold War America* (Baltimore: Johns Hopkins University Press, 2003), pp. 244–249.

not exist before 1975, or that claims about merit disappeared after 1975 – indeed, Cambridge is certainly more "meritocratic" today than it was a half century ago. But *as a cultural ideal that organizes understandings of various social practices*, the *market* was to the age of Thatcher what *merit* was to the age of Snow.

As we have seen, Snow and Leavis committed themselves to denouncing egalitarianism and defending elites, but differences within their positions led them to adopt contrary stances with regard to the marketplace paradigm. By defending the need for elites, and by praising the genetic heritage of Jewish people, Snow made clear that his commitment was to inequality as such. He was no *laissez-faire* ideologue, but neither did he harbor hostility towards marketplace values – as suggested, for instance, by his suggestion that "money" provided aspiring writers with a rewarding subject.[133] In this context it is not surprising that his lifelong friend Jack Plumb proved receptive to neoliberal politics in the 1980s, or that Ronald Millar, the playwright who adapted his novels for the stage, emerged as a Thatcherite speechwriter.[134] Leavis, on the contrary, had long adopted an antagonistic stance towards marketplace values. Not only was the emergence of capitalism one of the deplorable developments of the awful seventeenth century, but the displacement of critical judgments by mass market taste threatened the capacity for recognition that was essential to continued creation. Leavis, therefore, could not possibly have followed the turn towards the market, and in fact his long-standing critique found new allies instead on the intellectual left.

Conclusion

In Agnieszka Holland's film *Europa, Europa* (1990), set in central Europe during the Second World War, a pair of ships carrying Jewish refugees pass each other while traveling in opposite directions. One ship appears to be fleeing the Soviets, the other the Nazis, and neither set of passengers can comprehend the suicidal journey being taken by the other.[135] At the dawn of the 1960s, in somewhat less dire circumstances,

---

[133] C. P. Snow, "The Pursuit of Money," *Sunday Times*, 23 January 1949.
[134] Philip A. Snow, *Stranger and Brother*, p. 121.
[135] Jan Gross explains that a related story circulated at the time: "An apocryphal story from this period has two trainloads of Jews passing each other in opposite directions at the Soviet–German border; passengers on each train gesticulate wildly to passengers in the other that they must be out of their minds to be going to where they are just coming from." *Revolution from Abroad: The Soviet Conquest of Poland's Western Ukraine and Western Belorussia* (Princeton University Press, 2002), p. 207. Thanks to Ben Frommer.

C. P. Snow and F. R. Leavis embarked upon journeys of their own. Snow had initiated the "two cultures" debate by attacking English departments from the left in the name of science, but a decade later he was invoking science to demonstrate the futility of egalitarian ideals. Leavis responded to Snow with a reactionary denunciation of the civilization that produced him, but a decade later the critique of that civilization was finding its allies on the intellectual left. Despite these contrary trajectories, their motivations were identical: Snow and Leavis were fleeing the specter of social equality, and it is amusing to imagine them, perhaps somewhat disoriented, as they passed each other en route.

This chapter has followed these intellectual shifts in order to shed light on the broader transformations of the 1960s. The point has not been to suggest that their ideas changed during this period, because for the most part they did not. Snow's interest in the relationship between ability and environment remained constant from the 1930s to the 1970s, as did Leavis's hostility towards the claims of Marxists and the platitudes of politicians. What did change, however, were the aspects of their positions that they emphasized, and the peers with whom they agreed. Nothing forced these changes more than the language and policies endorsing the goal of social equality, since egalitarian ideals threatened the delicate balance between equal opportunity and unequal capacity upon which meritocratic commitments depended. Snow reacted to this threat by insisting upon the inevitability of social hierarchy, while Leavis responded by attacking egalitarian ideals. Snow's arguments placed him in the company of other liberals who took a right turn when they confronted the radical implications of the 1960s, while Leavis's long-standing position proved amenable to a critique of a society organized around the market. In the end, of course, the social movements of the 1960s and 1970s did not eradicate inequality, but they did force the revision of the rationale that sustained it.

Conclusion

Last things

Today C. P. Snow and F. R. Leavis share a fate that neither would have wanted, bound together in history by the "two cultures" controversy. Snow hoped that his legacy would be as a novelist, but more than a quarter century after his death it is the Rede Lecture that sustains his reputation. *The Two Cultures* remains in print and in demand: the Canto edition has sold over thirty thousand copies since 1993, and during the same period it has been translated into seventeen languages.[1] It is ironic, then, that the lecture that secured Snow's place in intellectual history inspired the critique that imperiled his literary standing. 1962 truly was Snow's *annus miserabilis* – a year that included Leavis's lecture (which had to be twice endured, once upon delivery and again upon publication), a libel suit, and two difficult eye surgeries.[2] To be sure, Snow remained a public figure, and was even briefly a government minister; he continued to write novels, deliver lectures, and collect honorary degrees, and throughout the 1970s he wrote a weekly column for the *Financial Times*.[3] Yet his star never shined as brightly as it had before. Privately Snow blamed Leavis for having cost him the Nobel Prize, and, although they held up initially, from 1968 sales of his novels began to decline.[4] When Leavis died in 1978, Pamela Johnson conceded that his Richmond

---

[1] C. P. Snow, *The Two Cultures*, introduction by Stefan Collini (Cambridge University Press, 1993).

[2] Philip A. Snow, *Stranger and Brother: A Portrait of C. P. Snow* (London: Macmillan, 1982), p. 143; *A Time of Renewal: Clusters of Characters, C. P. Snow, and Coups* (London: Radcliffe Press, 1998), p. 75; Pamela Hansford Johnson, *Important to Me* (New York: Scribner's, 1974), pp. 217–221; C. P. Snow, *Last Things* (London: Macmillan, 1970).

[3] Snow hoped to collect a record number of honorary degrees; he wound up with thirty during his lifetime (plus one awarded posthumously): P. Snow, *Stranger and Brother*, pp. 193–194. David Cannadine suggests that Leavis's lecture did little damage in the short term: "C. P. Snow, 'The Two Cultures,' and the 'Corridors of Power' Revisited," *Yet More Adventures with Britannia*, ed. Wm. Roger Louis (London: I. B. Tauris, 2005), p. 108.

[4] P. Snow, *Stranger and Brother*, pp. 173, 169, 177.

Lecture had done damage to her husband's reputation; when Q. D. Leavis died three years later, Johnson clipped the obituary.[5] In historical perspective, then, 1962 figures as the year when Snow went from being the author of forthcoming novels to being the author of *The Two Cultures*.

1962 was a pivotal year for Leavis as well. He retired from official teaching in Cambridge that spring, and began to devote more attention to public lectures and social criticism – beginning by reaching his widest audience to date in the Richmond Lecture. He accepted a series of visiting and honorary appointments, and particularly enjoyed his teaching at the University of York. In 1966 he and Q. D. Leavis journeyed to the United States, delivering well-received lectures at Harvard and Cornell.[6] In fact, Leavis published as many books in retirement as in the previous three decades, but, as discussed in Chapter 7, developments in literary studies were rendering his criticism increasingly marginal to the field. He was awarded the Companion of Honour (CH) in 1978, the year of his death – as with so much else in his career, the award seemed belated recognition from an ungrateful establishment. Today Leavis continues to haunt the English Tripos in Cambridge, where students might be asked to analyze a passage from the point of view of a "Feminist, Leavisite, Marxist."[7] Some time after their deaths, the Leavises' former home on Bulstrode Gardens in Cambridge featured a plaque in the shape of a tombstone: "Home of F. R. and Q. D. Leavis from 1962–1981," the plaque read. "Their ashes lie nearby."[8]

This book began by asking how a topic as familiar as the relationship between the arts and the sciences could have generated such controversy in the 1960s; it has answered that question by showing that that inherited topic was invested with contemporary concerns. Snow and Leavis advanced contrary interpretations of what they understood to be modern civilization: Snow believed it to have produced an admirable society, which generated material prosperity and social opportunity for the majority of the population, whereas Leavis believed it to have produced an abhorrent society, one that required determined opposition

---

[5] P. Snow, *A Time of Renewal*, p. 198; the obituary of Q. D. Leavis is included in the collection of Johnson's papers at the Harry Ransom Humanities Research Center (HRC): Snow, Addition to His Papers, 7.4.

[6] F. R. and Q. D. Leavis, *Lectures in America* (London: Chatto and Windus, 1969).

[7] This particular example is from an English Tripos question of 30 May 1994: "Write a dialogue between two literary critics of differing views (e.g. Feminist, Leavisite, Marxist) discussing one or both passages in question 22." Richard Storer discussed Leavis as a ghostly figure in a fascinating paper: "The After-life of Leavis," Loughborough University, 20 April 2002.

[8] Unidentified newspaper clipping, Emmanuel College, Cambridge: ECA COL 9.59a.132.

from a critical minority. These positions collided in the "two cultures" controversy, which in turn intersected with simultaneous arguments about the mission of the university, the interpretation of history, the agenda of national politics, and the future of the former empire. In each of these cases, against the backdrop of calls for scientific modernization, Snow and his allies advocated a technocratic liberalism, while Leavis and others countered with radical critiques – a dynamic that animated not only the "two cultures" controversy, but issues of cultural politics throughout the 1960s. Yet despite their many differences, these arguments all unfolded within a shared meritocratic consensus, and the eventual challenge to that consensus was part of a broad ideological shift from the late 1960s – a shift that marginalized the positions of Snow and Leavis alike.

New bearings

Historians differ as to whose intervention proved decisive in the debate. Dominic Sandbrook suggests that "Snow's rather fatuous argument would probably have been forgotten had it not been for the furious response of F. R. Leavis," but David Edgerton is surely correct that "it is Snow [who] makes Leavis famous for most of the lay population."[9] In either case, the "two cultures" controversy ensures a place for both Snow and Leavis within two larger histories: the history of postwar Britain, and the tradition discussing the arts and the sciences. Although he bore scars from Leavis's attack for the remainder of his life, it was actually Snow who succeeded in establishing the terms through which not only their argument, but also these histories, were subsequently understood. Revising our interpretation of the "two cultures" controversy, therefore, revises our interpretations of these larger histories as well.

Snow argued that British society was dominated by an archaic establishment that favored the arts over the sciences, and that as a result it faced the prospect of imminent decline. This critique was part of Snow's ideological position, a technocratic liberalism: a faith in the ability of the state to turn talented individuals into trained experts, who would work through existing institutions to the benefit of society. In *The Two Cultures* Snow connected this position to anxieties about Britain's economic decline, anxieties that emerged in the 1950s and flourished

---

[9] Dominic Sandbrook, *White Heat: A History of Britain in the Swinging Sixties* (London: Little, Brown, 2006), p. 49; David Edgerton, *Warfare State: Britain, 1920–1970* (Cambridge University Press, 2006), p. 204.

in the 1960s. He did not invent the discourse of decline, but he was a prominent advocate of it, along with such figures as Anthony Sampson and Arthur Koestler. The social criticism they produced, including *Anatomy of Britain* (1962), *Suicide of a Nation?* (1963), *The Two Cultures* (1959), and *The Two Cultures: and A Second Look* (1964), subsequently informed the historiography of modern Britain – most notably in the work of Martin Wiener, who transformed this critique of British society into an influential history of British culture since 1850.[10] The assumptions structuring the historiography on Britain's economic decline, then, have their origins not in an objective assessment of economic data, but in a technocratic critique of postwar society.[11] Rather than adopting that critique, as in declinist historiography, this book has recovered the ideological position that it advanced.

But the "two cultures" formulation remains influential well beyond British historiography. Book reviews, letters to editors, radio talks, intellectual conferences, academic journals, and scholarly monographs continually invoke the "two cultures" to make a point, explain an argument, or initiate a discussion.[12] It is the presumed relevance of this dichotomy (rather than, say, Snow's endorsement of literary realism) that keeps *The Two Cultures* in print today – a fact that is evident even in the title of the current edition, shorn as it is of Snow's period reference to ". . . *the Scientific Revolution.*" This book has emphasized the significance of Snow's argument and the controversy it inspired, but by situating them both firmly in the context of postwar Britain it has also challenged ahistorical invocations of the "two cultures" as a category of

[10] Anthony Sampson, *Anatomy of Britain* (London: Hodder and Stoughton, 1962); Arthur Koestler, ed., *Suicide of a Nation? An Enquiry into the State of Britain Today* (London: Hutchinson, 1963); Martin Wiener, *English Culture and the Decline of the Industrial Spirit* (Cambridge University Press, 1981; 2nd edn., 2004).

[11] See also D. N. McCloskey, *If You're So Smart: The Narrative of Economic Expertise* (University of Chicago Press, 1990), pp. 40–55; David Edgerton, "The Prophet Militant and Industrial: The Peculiarities of Correlli Barnett," *Twentieth Century British History* 2 (1991), pp. 360–379; Jim Tomlinson, "Inventing 'Decline': The Falling Behind of the British Economy in the Postwar Years," *Economic History Review* 49 (1996), pp. 731–757.

[12] Michiko Kakutani, "Seduction and Reduction on a British Campus," *New York Times*, 5 June 2001; Mark S. Roulston, "Two Cultures" (letter), *Independent*, 3 May 2002; M. Lythgoe, "The New Two Cultures," Radio 4, 18 April 2007; W. Rüegg, ed., *Meeting the Challenges of the Future: A Discussion between 'The Two Cultures'* (Florence: Leo S. Olschki, 2003); Wai Chee Dimock and Priscilla Wald, "Literature and Science: Cultural Forms, Conceptual Exchanges," *American Literature* 74 (December 2002), pp. 704–715; Lennard J. Davis and David B. Morris, "Biocultures Manifesto," *New Literary History* 38 (2007), pp. 411–418; Ullica Segerstrale, ed., *Beyond the Science Wars: The Missing Discourse about Science and Society* (Albany: SUNY Press, 2000), pp. 15–28, 102–105, 185–187; Elizabeth Spiller, *Science, Reading, and Renaissance Literature: The Art of Making Knowledge, 1580–1670* (Cambridge University Press, 2004).

analysis. Indeed, the "two cultures" fails to describe even the argument between Snow and Leavis during the 1960s – not to mention those of the 1880s, or of the 1990s, or that are yet to come. With so many issues routinely packed into that familiar formulation, invocations of the "two cultures" should be taken not as a description of intellectual life or an explanation of its arguments, but rather as an *opportunity* to consider what else might be going on beneath the huffing and puffing of disciplinary squabbling.

Bibliography

Letters to editors, anonymous columns, and book reviews are not included. See footnotes for complete manuscript citations. The distinction between "primary" and "secondary" sources derives from their usage in the text. Where appropriate, individual contributions to collaborative volumes are included in addition to the entry for the volume as a whole.

MANUSCRIPT COLLECTIONS

British Library.

British Broadcasting Corporation Written Archives Centre, Reading (BBC WAC).

Calouste Gulbenkian Foundation, London.

Cambridge University Library (CUL).

Cambridge University Press (CUP).

Churchill College, Cambridge.

Downing College, Cambridge.

Emmanuel College, Cambridge.

Harry Ransom Humanities Research Center, Austin, Texas (HRC).

Houghton Library, Harvard, Cambridge, Massachusetts.

Reading University.

Royal Society, London.

PUBLISHED PRIMARY SOURCES

Adorno, Theodor and Horkheimer, Max, *Dialektic der Aufklärung: Philosophische Fragmente* (Amsterdam: Querido, 1947).

Albu, Austen, "Taboo on Expertise," *Encounter*, July 1963, pp. 45–50.

Allen, Walter, *et al.*, "A Discussion of C. P. Snow's Views," *Encounter*, August 1959, pp. 67–73.

Amis, Kingsley, *Lucky Jim* (London: Gollancz, 1954).

Anderson, Perry, "Components of the National Culture," *New Left Review* 50 (July–August 1968), pp. 3–57.

"Origins of the Present Crisis," *New Left Review* 23 (January–February 1964), pp. 26–53.

Andreski, Stanislav, *The African Predicament: A Study in the Pathology of Modernisation* (London: Michael Joseph, 1968).

Social Sciences as Sorcery (London: Deutsch, 1972).

Arnold, Matthew, "Literature and Science," in *The Complete Prose Works of Matthew Arnold*, ed. R. H. Super (Ann Arbor: University of Michigan Press, 1974), vol. X, pp. 53–73.

Bagehot, Walter, *The English Constitution* (1867), ed. Paul Smith (Cambridge University Press, 2001).

Bantock, G. H., "A Scream of Horror," *Listener*, 17 September 1959, pp. 427–428.

Bauer, P. T., *Dissent on Development: Studies and Debates in Development Economics* (London: Weidenfeld & Nicolson, 1971).

Beer, John, "Pools of Light in Darkness," *Cambridge Review*, 7 November 1959, pp. 106–109.

Bernal, J. D., *The Social Function of Science* (London: Routledge, 1939).

World Without War (London: Routledge and Paul, 1958).

Blackett, P. M. S., *The Gap Widens* (Cambridge University Press, 1970).

Reflections on Science and Technology in Developing Countries (Nairobi: East African Publishing House, 1969).

"Science and Technology in an Unequal World," *Jawaharlal Memorial Lectures, 1967–1972* (Bombay: Bharatiya Vidya Bhavan, 1973).

"Technology and World Advancement," *Advancement of Science*, September 1957, pp. 3–11.

Booker, Christopher, Ingrams, Richard, Rushton, William, *et al.*, *Private Eye's Romantic England* (London: Weidenfeld & Nicolson, 1963).

Bowden, F. P. and Snow, C. P., "Photochemistry of Vitamins A, B, C, D," *Nature*, 14 May 1932, pp. 720–721.

"Photochemistry of Vitamins A, B, C, D," *Nature*, 25 June 1932, p. 943.

Bradbury, Malcolm, "The Tip of Life," *New Statesman*, 1 October 1976, pp. 453–454.

Brogan, Denis, "Inequality and Mr. Short," *Spectator*, 18 April 1969, p. 505.

Bronowski, Jacob, "Architecture as a Science and Architecture as an Art," *Royal Institute of British Architects Journal* 62 (March 1955), pp. 183–189.

The Common Sense of Science (Cambridge, Mass.: Harvard University Press, 1951).

Science and Human Values (New York: Harper and Row, 1956).

Bronowski, Jacob and Mazlish, Bruce, *The Western Intellectual Tradition: From Leonardo to Hegel* (London: Harper and Row, 1960).

Bryden, Ronald, "With a Difference," *Spectator*, 15 December 1961, p. 908.

Buckley, Jr., William F., "The Voice of Sir Charles," *National Review*, 22 May 1962, p. 358.

Butterfield, Herbert, *George III and the Historians* (London: Collins, 1957).

Colville, John, "A Battle of Britain Still to Win," *Daily Telegraph*, 26 June 1958.

Conquest, Robert, "Letters," *Spectator*, 30 March 1962, pp. 395–396.

Cooper, William, "C. P. Snow," in *British Writers*, ed. Ian Scott-Kilvert (New York: Scribner's, 1984), vol. VII, pp. 321–341.

Memoirs of a New Man (London: Macmillan, 1966).

"Reflections on Some Aspects of the Experimental Novel," in *International Literary Annual*, ed. John Wain (London: John Calder, 1959).

Scenes from Provincial Life (London: Jonathan Cape, 1950).

Cornelius, David K. and St. Vincent, Edwin, eds., *Cultures in Conflict: Perspectives on the Snow–Leavis Controversy* (Chicago: Scott Foresman and Co., 1964).

Crosland, Anthony, *The Future of Socialism* (London: Jonathan Cape, 1956).

Crossman, Richard, *The Diaries of a Cabinet Minister: Volume One, Minister of Housing, 1964–1966* (London: Hamish Hamilton and Jonathan Cape, 1975).

"Secret Decisions," *Encounter*, June 1961, pp. 86–90.

Crowther, J. G., *The Social Relations of Science* (New York: Macmillan, 1941).

Dean, Robert, "The Tripos of 1961," *Cambridge Review*, 28 October 1961, p. 57.

Dzhagarov, Georgi, *The Public Prosecutor: A Play*, trans. Marguerite Alexieva, adapted for the stage by C. P. Snow and Pamela Hansford Johnson (London: Owen, 1969).

Eliot, T. S., *Selected Essays* (New York: Harcourt Brace, 1932).

Fairlie, Henry, "On the Comforts of Anger," *Encounter*, July 1963, pp. 9–13.

Ford, Boris, ed., *The Modern Age: Volume 7 of the Pelican Guide to English Literature* (Baltimore: Penguin Books, 1963).

Fuller, Roy, "The Critic and the Weekly," *New Statesman*, 14 July 1972, p. 56.

Galbraith, John Kenneth, *The Affluent Society* (Boston: Houghton Mifflin, 1958).

Gale, George, "Saying the Unsayable," *Spectator*, 25 July 1970, pp. 65–66.

Gardner, Helen, "The World of C. P. Snow," *New Statesman*, 29 March 1958, pp. 409–410.

Gerhardi, William, "Sir Charles Snow, Dr. F. R. Leavis, and the Two Cultures," *Spectator*, 16 March 1962, pp. 329–31.

Green, Martin, "Lionel Trilling and the Two Cultures," *Essays in Criticism* 13 (1963), pp. 375–385.

von Hayek, Friedrich, *The Road to Serfdom* (University of Chicago Press, 1944).

Heilbron, I. M. and Morton, R. A., "Photochemistry of Vitamins A, B, C, D," *Nature*, 11 June 1932, pp. 866–867.

Hogg, Quintin (Baron Hailsham of St. Marylebone), *Science and Politics* (London: Faber and Faber, 1963).

Hoggart, Richard, "Persuaded into Words," *Guardian*, 26 August 1976.

The Uses of Literacy: Aspects of Working-Class Life with Special Reference to Publications and Entertainments (London: Chatto and Windus, 1957).

Hollis, Christopher, "Snows of Tomorrow Year," *Spectator*, 26 February 1965, p. 254.

Hough, Graham, "The Ordered Carnival," *New Statesman*, 5 December 1969, pp. 817–818.

Huxley, Aldous, *Literature and Science* (London: Harper and Row, 1963).

Huxley, T. H., "Science and Culture," *Science and Education: Essays* (New York: D. Appleton, 1896), pp. 134–159.

Jewkes, John, *Ordeal by Planning* (New York: Macmillan, 1948).

Johnson, Pamela Hansford, *This Bed Thy Centre* (London: Chapman and Hall, 1935).

Important to Me (New York: Scribner's, 1974).

On Iniquity: Some Personal Reflections Arising out of the Moors Murder Trial (New York: Scribner's, 1967).

"The Sickroom Hush over the English Novel," *List*, 11 August 1949.

Jones, R. V., "In Search of Scientists – I," *Listener*, 23 September 1965, p. 447.

Kakutani, Michiko, "Seduction and Reduction on a British Campus," *New York Times*, 5 June 2001.

Koestler, Arthur, "Introduction: The Lion and the Ostrich," *Encounter*, July 1963, pp. 5–8.

"Postscript: The Manager and the Muses," *Encounter*, July 1963, pp. 113–117.

ed., "Suicide of a Nation?" *Encounter*, July 1963.

ed., *Suicide of a Nation? An Enquiry into the State of Britain Today* (London: Hutchinson, 1963).

Labour Party, *Let's Go with Labour for the New Britain: The Labour Party's Manifesto for the 1964 General Election* (London: Victoria House Printing Co., 1964).

Laslett, Peter, "Engels as Historian," *Encounter*, May 1958, pp. 85–86.

The World We Have Lost (London: Methuen, 1965).

Leavis, F. R., "Afterword," *The Pilgrim's Progress*, by John Bunyan (New York: New American Library, 1964).

"Anna Karenina" and Other Essays (London: Chatto and Windus, 1967).

"Anna Karenina: Thought and Significance in a Great Creative Work," *Cambridge Quarterly* 1 (Winter 1965–1966), pp. 5–27.

"'Believing In' the University," *The Critic as Anti-Philosopher* (Athens: University of Georgia Press, 1983), pp. 171–185.

The Common Pursuit (London: Chatto and Windus, 1952).

"Critic and Leviathan: Literary Criticism and Politics," *Politics and Letters* 1 (Winter–Spring 1948), pp. 58–61.

The Critic as Anti-Philosopher: Essays and Papers, ed. G. Singh (Athens: University of Georgia Press, 1983).

D. H. Lawrence: Novelist (London: Chatto and Windus, 1955).

Education and the University: A Sketch for an "English School" (London: Chatto and Windus, 1943).

"Elites, Oligarchies and an Educated Public," in *Nor Shall My Sword*, pp. 201–228.

English Literature in Our Time and the University (London: Chatto and Windus, 1969).

"English Poetry in the Eighteenth Century," *Scrutiny* 5 (June 1936), pp. 13–31.

"English Poetry in the Seventeenth Century," *Scrutiny* 4 (December 1935), pp. 236–256.

"'English', Unrest, and Continuity," in *Nor Shall My Sword*, pp. 103–133.

For Continuity (Cambridge: Minority Press, 1933).

The Great Tradition: George Eliot, Henry James, Joseph Conrad (London: Chatto and Windus, 1948).

"In Defence of Milton," *Scrutiny* 7 (June 1938), pp. 104–114.

"Introduction," in John Stuart Mill, *Mill on Bentham and Coleridge* (London: Chatto and Windus, 1950).

"'Lawrence Scholarship' and Lawrence," *Sewanee Review* 71 (January–March 1963), pp. 25–35.

"'Literarism' versus 'Scientism': The Misconception and the Menace," in *Nor Shall My Sword*, pp. 137–160.

"'Literarism' versus 'Scientism': The Misconception and the Menace," *Times Literary Supplement*, 23 April 1970, pp. 441–444.

"Literary Criticism and Philosophy: A Reply," *Scrutiny* 6 (June 1937), pp. 59–70.

"Literature and Society," *Scrutiny* 12 (Winter 1943), pp. 2–11.

The Living Principle: "English" as a Discipline of Thought (London: Chatto and Windus, 1975).

"Luddites? *or* There Is Only One Culture," in *Nor Shall My Sword*, pp. 77–99.

"The Marxian Analysis," *Scrutiny* 6 (September 1937), pp. 201–204.

Mass Civilisation and Minority Culture (Cambridge: Minority Press, 1930).

"Milton's Verse," *Scrutiny* 2 (September 1933), pp. 123–136.

"Mr. Eliot and Milton," *Sewanee Review* 57 (Winter 1949), pp. 1–30.

New Bearings in English Poetry: A Study of the Contemporary Situation (London: Chatto and Windus, 1932).

Nor Shall My Sword: Discourses on Pluralism, Compassion and Social Hope (London: Chatto and Windus, 1972).

"Pluralism, Compassion and Social Hope," in *Nor Shall My Sword*, pp. 163–198.

"Restatements for Critics," *Scrutiny* 1 (March 1933), pp. 315–323.

"A Retrospect," *Scrutiny: A Quarterly Review* (Cambridge University Press, 1963), vol. XX, pp. 1–24.

"Retrospect of a Decade," *Scrutiny* 9 (June 1940), pp. 70–72.

Revaluation: Tradition and Development in English Poetry (London: Chatto and Windus, 1936).

"Saints of Rationalism," *Listener*, 26 April 1951, p. 672.

"Sociology and Literature," *Scrutiny* 13 (Spring 1945), pp. 74–81.

Thought, Words and Creativity: Art and Thought in Lawrence (New York: Oxford University Press, 1976).

"The Two Cultures? The Significance of C. P. Snow," *Spectator*, 9 March 1962, pp. 297–303.

Two Cultures? The Significance of C. P. Snow, with an essay on "Sir Charles Snow's Rede Lecture" by Michael Yudkin (London: Chatto and Windus, 1962).

"Under Which King, Bezonian?" *Scrutiny* 1 (December 1932), pp. 205–215.

Valuation in Criticism and Other Essays, ed. G. Singh (Cambridge University Press, 1986).

Leavis, F. R. and Leavis, Q. D., *Dickens the Novelist* (London: Chatto and Windus, 1970).

Lectures in America (London: Chatto and Windus, 1969).

Leavis, F. R. and Thompson, Denys, *Culture and Environment: The Training of Critical Awareness* (London: Chatto and Windus, 1933).

Leavis, Q. D., *Fiction and the Reading Public* (London: Chatto and Windus, 1932).

Levin, Bernard, "My Concern Is Not the Play But What Is Behind It," *Daily Mail*, 7 September 1962, p. 3.

Locke, John, *Two Treatises of Government*, ed. Peter Laslett (Cambridge University Press, 1960).

Lovell, A. C. B., "A Unified Culture," *Encounter*, August 1959, p. 68.

MacArthur, Brian, "The Outsider," *Guardian*, 13 June 1966.

Magee, Bryan, *The New Radicalism* (New York: St. Martin's Press, 1962).
Mill, John Stuart, *Mill on Bentham and Coleridge*, with an introduction by F. R. Leavis (London: Chatto and Windus, 1950).
Three Essays (Oxford University Press, 1975).
Muggeridge, Malcolm, "England, Whose England?" *Encounter*, July 1963, pp. 14–17.
Neale, John, "History in the Scientific Age," *Nature* 199, 24 August 1963, pp. 735–737.
Newquist, Roy, *Counterpoint* (New York: Rand McNally, 1964).
Nott, Kathleen, "The Type to Which the Whole Creation Moves? Further Thoughts on the Snow Saga," *Encounter*, February 1962, pp. 87–88, 94–97.
Oltmans, Willem L., ed., *On Growth: The Crisis of Exploding Population and Resource Depletion* (New York: G. P. Putnam's Sons, 1974).
Osborne, John, *Look Back in Anger, A Play in Three Acts* (London: Faber and Faber, 1957).
Parsons, Ian, "Letters," *Spectator*, 23 March 1962, p. 365.
Plumb, J. H., "Letters," *Spectator*, 30 March 1962, p. 396.
Sir Robert Walpole: The Making of a Statesman (London: Cresset, 1956).
ed., *Studies in Social History: A Tribute to G. M. Trevelyan* (New York: Longman's, Green, and Company, 1955).
"Welfare or Release," *Encounter*, August 1959, pp. 68–70.
Podhoretz, Norman, *Breaking Ranks* (New York: Harper and Row, 1979).
"England, My England," *New Yorker*, 10 May 1958, pp. 143–146.
Polanyi, Michael, *Knowing and Being: Essays*, ed. Marjorie Grene (London: Routledge, 1969).
"The Two Cultures," *Encounter*, September 1959, pp. 61–64.
Popper, Karl, *The Open Society and Its Enemies* (London: Routledge, 1945).
Putt, S. Gorley, "Technique and Culture: Three Cambridge Portraits," *Essays and Studies* 14 (1961), pp. 17–34.
Read, Herbert, "Mood of the Month – X," *London Magazine*, August 1959, pp. 39–43.
Rees, Goronwy, "Amateurs and Gentleman, or The Cult of Incompetence," *Encounter*, July 1963, pp. 20–25.
Richards, I. A., *Practical Criticism: A Study of Literary Judgment* (London: Harcourt Brace, 1929).
Principles of Literary Criticism (London: Kegan Paul, 1924).
Science and Poetry (London: Kegan Paul, 1926).
Riesman, David, "The Whole Man," *Encounter*, August 1959, pp. 70–71.
Rogrow, Arnold, *The Jew in a Gentile World*, with an introduction by C. P. Snow (New York: Macmillan, 1961).
Rose, Kenneth, "Choosing Technology's Few," *Daily Telegraph*, 10 September 1958.
Rostow, W. W., *The Stages of Economic Growth: A Non-Communist Manifesto* (Cambridge University Press, 1960).
Russell, Bertrand, "Snobbery," *Encounter*, August 1959, p. 71.
Russell, Leonard, "Billiard-Room Talks," *Sunday Times*, 6 March 1960, p. 18.
Sampson, Anthony, *Anatomy of Britain* (London: Hodder and Stoughton, 1962).
Anatomy of Britain Today (London: Hodder and Stoughton, 1965).
Sayers, Dorothy, *Gaudy Night* (London: Victor Gollancz, 1935).

Schumacher, E. F., *Small is Beautiful: Economics as if People Mattered* (New York: Harper and Row, 1973).

Shahak, Israel, "Letters," *Spectator*, 2 May 1969, p. 596.

Shanks, Michael, "The Comforts of Stagnation," *Encounter*, July 1963, pp. 30–38.

The Stagnant Society: A Warning (Baltimore: Penguin, 1961).

Shils, Edward, "The Charismatic Centre," *Spectator*, 6 November 1964, pp. 608–609.

Shonfield, Andrew, *British Economic Policy since the War* (Baltimore: Penguin, 1958).

Sitwell, Edith, "Sir Charles Snow, Dr. F. R. Leavis, and the Two Cultures," *Spectator*, 16 March 1962, p. 331.

Snow, C. P., "Act in Hope," *New Statesman*, 15 November 1958, pp. 698–700.

The Affair (London: Macmillan, 1960).

"The Age of Rutherford," *Atlantic Monthly*, November 1958, pp. 76–81.

"Britain's Two Cultures: A Study of Education in a Scientific Age," *Sunday Times*, 10 March 1957, p. 12.

"The Case of Leavis and the Serious Case," in *Public Affairs*, pp. 81–97.

"The Case of Leavis and the Serious Case," *Times Literary Supplement*, 9 July 1970, pp. 737–740.

"Challenge to the Intellect," *Times Literary Supplement*, 15 August 1958, p. 2946.

"The Cold War and the West," *Partisan Review*, Winter 1962, p. 82.

The Conscience of the Rich (London: Macmillan, 1958).

"The Corridors of Power," *Listener*, 18 April 1957, pp. 619–620.

Corridors of Power (London: Macmillan, 1964).

"Cult of the Atrocious," *Sunday Times*, 16 October 1949.

Death under Sail (London: Heinemann, 1932).

"Education and Sacrifice," *New Statesman*, 17 May 1963, pp. 746–750.

George Passant (London: Faber and Faber, 1940). Originally titled *Strangers and Brothers*.

Homecomings (London: Macmillan, 1956).

"In the Communities of the Elite," *Times Literary Supplement*, 15 October 1971, pp. 1249–1250.

"Industrial Dynamo," *New Statesman*, 16 June 1956, p. 703.

"The Irregular Right: Britain Without Rebels," *Nation*, 24 March 1956, pp. 238–239.

Last Things (London: Macmillan, 1970).

"Less Fun Than Machiavelli," *New Statesman*, 9 January 1970, p. 50.

"Liberal Communism: The Basic Dogma, the Scope for Freedom, the Danger in Optimism," *Nation*, 9 December 1968, pp. 617–623.

The Light and the Dark (London: Faber and Faber, 1947).

The Malcontents (London: Macmillan, 1972).

"Man in Society," *Observer*, 13 July 1958, p. 12.

The Masters (London: Macmillan, 1951).

"The Men of Fission," *Holiday*, April 1958, pp. 95, 108–115.

"Miasma, Darkness, and Torpidity," *New Statesman*, 11 August 1961, pp. 186–187.

"The Moral Un-neutrality of Science," in *Public Affairs*, pp. 187–198.

New Lives for Old (London: Victor Gollancz, 1933) (anonymously).

The New Men (London: Macmillan, 1954).

"New Men for a New Era," *Sunday Times*, 24 August 1958, p. 12.

"New Minds for the New World," *New Statesman*, 8 September 1956, pp. 279–282.

"On Magnanimity," *Harper's*, July 1962, pp. 37–41.

"Phase of Expansion," *Spectator*, 1 October 1954, p. 406.

Public Affairs (New York: Scribner's, 1971).

"The Pursuit of Money," *Sunday Times*, 23 January 1949.

"A Revolution in Education," *Sunday Times*, 17 March 1957, p. 5.

"Science and Government," in *Public Affairs*, pp. 99–149.

Science and Government (Cambridge, Mass.: Harvard University Press, 1960).

"Science, Politics, and the Novelist, or, The Fish and the Net," *Kenyon Review* 23 (Winter 1961), pp. 1–17.

The Search (London: Victor Gollancz, 1934; New York: Scribner's, 1958).

The Sleep of Reason (London: Macmillan, 1968).

"The State of Siege," in *Public Affairs*, pp. 199–221.

Strangers and Brothers (London: Faber and Faber, 1940). Subsequently retitled *George Passant*.

Strangers and Brothers (London: Macmillan, 1972; New York: Scribner's, 1972), 3 vols.

"Technological Humanism," *Nature*, 8 February 1958, p. 370.

Time of Hope (London: Faber and Faber, 1949).

Trollope (London: Macmillan, 1975).

"The Two Cultures," *New Statesman and Nation*, 6 October 1956, pp. 413–414.

The Two Cultures, with an introduction by Stefan Collini (Cambridge University Press, 1993).

"The Two Cultures and the Scientific Revolution," *Encounter*, June 1959, pp. 17–24; July 1959, pp. 22–27.

The Two Cultures and the Scientific Revolution (Cambridge University Press, 1959).

"The Two Cultures: A Second Look," *Times Literary Supplement*, 25 October 1963, pp. 839–844.

The Two Cultures: and A Second Look (Cambridge University Press, 1964).

"The 'Two-Cultures' Controversy: Afterthoughts," *Encounter*, February 1960, pp. 64–68.

"Valedictory," *Sunday Times*, 28 December 1952, p. 7.

Variety of Men (London: Macmillan, 1967).

Steiner, George, "F. R. Leavis," *Encounter*, May 1962, pp. 37–45.

"The Master Builder," *Reporter*, 9 June 1960, pp. 41–43.

"The Retreat from the Word," *Kenyon Review* 23 (Spring 1961), pp. 187–216.

Tolstoy or Dostoevsky: An Essay in the Old Criticism (New York: Knopf, 1959).

Stevenson, John, "When a Man is Sick of Power," *Daily Sketch*, 24 February 1966, p. 6.

Storr, Anthony, "Sir Charles Snow, Dr. F. R. Leavis, and the Two Cultures," *Spectator*, 16 March 1962, pp. 332–333.

Thomas, Keith, "The Tools and the Job," *Times Literary Supplement*, 7 April 1966, p. 276.

Thompson, E P., "The Book of Numbers," *Times Literary Supplement*, 9 December 1965, pp. 1117–1118 (anonymously).

"History from Below," *Times Literary Supplement*, 6 April 1966, pp. 279–280.

Making History: Writings on Politics and Culture (New York: New Press, 1994).

The Making of the English Working Class (London: Gollancz, 1963).

ed., *Out of Apathy* (London: New Left Books, 1960).

"Outside the Whale," in *Out of Apathy*, pp. 141–194.

"The Peculiarities of the English," *Socialist Register, 1965*, ed. Ralph Miliband and John Saville (New York: Monthly Review Press, 1965), pp. 311–362.

Trevelyan, G. M., *Clio, a Muse: and Other Essays* (New York: Longman's, Green, and Company, 1931).

English Social History (London: Longmans, 1942).

Trilling, Lionel, *The Liberal Imagination* (New York: Viking, 1950).

Matthew Arnold (New York: Norton, 1939; London: George Allen and Unwin, 1955).

"The Novel Alive or Dead," *Griffin*, February 1955, pp. 4–13.

"Science, Literature, and Culture: A Comment on the Leavis–Snow Controversy," *Commentary*, June 1962, pp. 461–77.

Waddington, C. H., "Humanists and Scientists: A Last Comment on C. P. Snow," *Encounter*, January 1960, pp. 72–73.

Wain, John, "21 Years with Dr. Leavis," *Observer*, 27 October 1963.

"An Open Letter to My Russian Hosts," *Observer*, 7 August 1960, p. 13.

Wald, Richard C., "New Churchill College Slated to Open at Cambridge Oct. 1," *New York Herald Tribune*, 25 August 1960.

Watkins, Alan, "Laureate of Meritocracy," *Observer*, 6 July 1980.

Webb, W. L., "New Year's New Reading II," *Guardian*, 13 January 1972.

Wells, H. G., *The Open Conspiracy: Blue Prints for a World Revolution* (London: Gollancz, 1928).

Williams, Raymond, *Culture and Society, 1780–1950* (London: Chatto and Windus, 1958).

The Long Revolution (London: Chatto and Windus, 1961).

"A Refusal to be Resigned," *Guardian*, 18 December 1969.

Wilson, Angus, "Fourteen Points," *Encounter*, January 1962, pp. 10–12.

"If It's New and Modish, Is It Good?" *New York Times Book Review*, 2 July 1961, p. 1.

"A Plea Against Fashion in Writing," *Moderna Sprak* 55 (1961), pp. 345–350.

Wilson, Harold, *Purpose in Politics* (London: Weidenfeld & Nicolson, 1964).

Worsley, Peter, "Imperial Retreat," in *Out of Apathy*, ed. E. P. Thompson, pp. 101–140.

Wyndham-Goldie, Grace, *et al.*, *The Challenge of Our Time* (London: P. Marshall, 1948).

Young, Michael, *The Rise of the Meritocracy, 1870–2033: An Essay on Education and Equality* (London: Thames and Hudson, 1958).

Yudkin, Michael, "Sir Charles Snow's Rede Lecture," originally published in the *Cambridge Review*, and reprinted in F. R. Leavis, *Two Cultures? The Significance of C. P. Snow* (London: Chatto and Windus, 1962).

SECONDARY SOURCES

Addison, Paul, "The Impact of the Second World War," in *A Companion to Contemporary Britain, 1939–2000*, ed. Paul Addison and Harriet Jones, pp. 3–22.

Addison, Paul and Jones, Harriet, eds., *A Companion to Contemporary Britain, 1939–2000* (Oxford: Blackwell, 2005).

Amadae, S. M., *Rationalizing Capitalist Democracy: The Cold War Origins of Rational Choice Liberalism* (University of Chicago Press, 2003).

Anderson, Perry, "Dégringolade," *London Review of Books*, 2 September 2004, pp. 3, 5–9.

English Questions (London: Verso, 1992).

Annan, Noel, *Our Age: English Intellectuals between the World Wars – a Group Portrait* (New York: Random House, 1990).

Arnstein, Walter, ed., *Recent Historians of Great Britain: Essays on the Post-1945 Generation* (Ames: Iowa State University Press, 1990).

Baldick, Chris, *The Social Mission of English Criticism, 1848–1932* (New York: Oxford University Press, 1983).

Barnes, Barry, *T. S. Kuhn and Social Science* (London: Macmillan, 1982).

Barnett, Correlli, *The Audit of War: The Illusion and Reality of Britain as a Great Nation* (London: Macmillan, 1986).

"How Britain Squandered Her Post-war Chance," *Independent*, October 18, 2001.

The Lost Victory: British Dreams, British Realities, 1945–1950 (London: Macmillan, 1995).

Bateson, F. W., *Essays in Critical Dissent* (London: Longman, 1972).

Bell, Michael, "F. R. Leavis," in *The Cambridge History of Literary Criticism, Vol. 7: Modernism and the New Criticism*, ed. A. Walton Litz, Louis Menand and Lawrence Rainey (Cambridge University Press, 2000), pp. 389–422.

F. R. Leavis (London: Routledge, 1988).

Bernstein, George, *The Myth of Decline: The Rise of Britain since 1945* (London: Pimlico, 2004).

van Beusekom, Monica and Hodgson, Dorothy, "Lessons Learned? Development Experiences in the Late Colonial Period," *Journal of African History* 41 (2000), pp. 29–33.

Black, Lawrence, *The Political Culture of the Left in Affluent Britain, 1951–64: Old Labour, New Britain?* (Basingstoke: Palgrave Macmillan, 2003).

Black, Lawrence and Pemberton, Hugh, eds., *An Affluent Society? Britain's Post-war "Golden Age" Revisited* (Aldershot: Ashgate, 2004).

Bloor, David, *Wittgenstein: A Social Theory of Knowledge* (New York: Columbia University Press, 1983).

Booth, Alan, "The Manufacturing Failure Hypothesis and the Performance of British Industry during the Long Boom," *Economic History Review* 56 (2004), pp. 1–33.

Boytinck, Paul, *C. P. Snow: A Reference Guide* (Boston: Hall, 1980).

Bradbury, Malcolm, "Whatever Happened to F. R. Leavis?" *Sunday Times*, 9 July 1995.

Brand, J. C. D., "The Scientific Papers of C. P. Snow," *History of Science* 26 (June 1988), pp. 111–127.

Brewer, John, "New Ways in History, or Talking About My Generation," *Historein* 3 (2001), pp. 27–46.

Brick, Howard, *Age of Contradiction: American Thought and Culture in the 1960s* (Ithaca: Cornell University Press, 1998).

Briggs, Asa, *Victorian People: A Reassessment of Persons and Themes, 1851–1867*, rev. edn. (University of Chicago Press, 1972).

Broadberry, S. N. and Crafts, N. F. R., "British Economic Policy and Industrial Performance in the Early Post-war Period," *Business History* 38 (1996), pp. 65–91.

"The Post-war Settlement: Not Such a Good Bargain after All," *Business History* 40 (1998), pp. 73–79.

Budge, Ian, "Relative Decline as a Political Issue: Ideological Motivations of the Politico-Economic Debate in Post-war Britain," *Contemporary Record* 7 (Summer 1993), pp. 1–23.

Burnett, D. Graham, "A View from the Bridge: The Two Cultures Debate, Its Legacy, and the History of Science," *Daedalus* 128 (Spring 1999), pp. 193–218.

Cannadine, David, "C. P. Snow, 'The Two Cultures,' and the 'Corridors of Power' Revisited," in *Yet More Adventures with Britannia*, ed. Wm. Roger Louis (London: I. B. Tauris, 2005), pp. 101–118.

G. M. Trevelyan: A Life in History (London: Harper Collins, 1992).

"Historians in 'The Liberal Hour:' Lawrence Stone and J. H. Plumb Re-Visited," *Historical Research* 75 (August 2002), pp. 316–354.

"John Harold Plumb," *Proceedings of the British Academy* 124 (2004), pp. 269–309.

"Sir John Plumb," *History Today*, February 2002, pp. 26–28.

"The State of British History," *Times Literary Supplement*, 10 October 1986, p. 1139.

Catterall, Peter, "What (If Anything) is Distinctive about Contemporary History?" *Journal of Contemporary History* 32 (4) (October 1997), pp. 441–452.

Chainey, Graham, *A Literary History of Cambridge* (Cambridge: Pevensey, 1985).

Christiansen, Rupert, "Footsteps from the Floor Above," *Spectator*, 8 July 1995, p. 33.

Clarke, Peter, *Hope and Glory: Britain, 1900–1990* (London: Allen Lane, 1996).

Liberals and Social Democrats (Cambridge University Press, 1978).

Clarke, Peter and Trebilcock, Clive, eds., *Understanding Decline: Perceptions and Realities of British Economic Performance* (Cambridge University Press, 1997).

Coates, David, *The Question of UK Decline: State, Society, and Economy* (London: Harvester Wheatsheaf, 1994).

Collini, Stefan, *Absent Minds: Intellectuals in Britain* (Oxford University Press, 2006).

Arnold (Oxford University Press, 1988).

"Cambridge and the Study of English," in *Cambridge Contributions*, ed. Sarah J. Omrod (Cambridge University Press, 1998), pp. 42–64.

"HiEdBiz," *London Review of Books*, 6 November 2003, pp. 3, 5–9.

"Introduction," in C. P. Snow, *The Two Cultures* (Cambridge University Press, 1993).

"The Literary Critic and the Village Labourer: 'Culture' in Twentieth-Century Britain," *Transactions of the Royal Historical Society* 14 (2004), pp. 93–116.

"On Highest Authority: The Literary Critic and Other Aviators in Early Twentieth-Century Britain," in *Modernist Impulses in the Human Sciences, 1870–1930*, ed. Dorothy Ross (Baltimore: Johns Hopkins University Press, 1994), pp. 152–170.

Colville, John, *Footprints in Time* (London: Collins, 1976).

Conekin, Becky, *The Autobiography of a Nation: The 1951 Festival of Britain* (Manchester University Press, 2003).

"'Here is the Modern World Itself': The Festival of Britain's Representations of the Future," in *Moments of Modernity: Reconstructing Britain, 1945–1964*, ed. Becky Conekin, Frank Mort and Chris Waters, pp. 228–246.

Conekin, Becky, Mort, Frank and Waters, Chris, eds., *Moments of Modernity: Reconstructing Britain, 1945–1964* (London: Rivers Oram, 1999).

Conquest, Robert, *The Dragons of Expectations: Reality and Delusion in the Course of History* (New York: Norton, 2005).

Cooper, Frederick and Packard, Randall, eds., *International Development and the Social Sciences: Essays on the History and Politics of Knowledge* (Berkeley: University of California Press, 1997).

Cooper, William, "C. P. Snow," in *British Writers*, ed. Ian Scott-Kilvert (New York: Scribner's, 1984), vol. VII, pp. 321–341.

Corfield, Penelope J., *Power and the Professions in Britain, 1700–1850* (London: Routledge, 1995).

Cornforth, Maurice, ed., *Rebels and Their Causes* (London: Lawrence and Wishart, 1978).

Crafts, N. F. R., "The Golden Age of Economic Growth in Western Europe, 1950–1973," *Economic History Review* 48 (1995), pp. 429–447.

Cronin, James, *Labour and Society* (New York: Schocken, 1984).

Darnton, Robert, *The Great Cat Massacre, and Other Episodes in French Cultural History* (New York: Vintage, 1985).

Daunton, Martin, *Just Taxes: The Politics of Taxation in Britain, 1914–1979* (Cambridge University Press, 2002).

Daunton, Martin and Rieger, Bernhard, eds., *Meanings of Modernity: Britain from the Late-Victorian Era to World War II* (Oxford: Berg, 2001).

Davis, Lennard J. and Morris, David B., "Biocultures Manifesto," *New Literary History* 38 (2007), pp. 411–418.

Davis, Natalie Zemon, *The Return of Martin Guerre* (Cambridge, Mass.: Harvard University Press, 1983).

Day, Gary, "A Pariah in the Republic of Letters," *Times Higher Education Supplement*, 4 August 1995, p. 21.

Re-reading Leavis: Culture and Literary Criticism (New York: St. Martin's Press, 1996).

Dimock, Wai Chee and Wald, Priscilla, "Preface: Literature and Science: Cultural Forms, Conceptual Exchanges," *American Literature* 74 (December 2002), pp. 705–714.

Dobbs, Betty Jo Teeter, *The Foundations of Newton's Alchemy: or, "The Hunting of the Greene Lyon"* (New York: Cambridge University Press, 1975).

Dworkin, Dennis, *Cultural Marxism in Postwar Britain: History, the New Left, and the Origins of Cultural Studies* (Durham: Duke University Press, 1997).

Eagleton, Terry, "The Hippest," *London Review of Books*, 7 March 1996, pp. 3–5.

Literary Theory: An Introduction (Minneapolis: University of Minnesota Press, 1983).

Edgar, David, "Stalking Out," *London Review of Books*, 20 July 2006, pp. 8–10.

Edgerton, David, "C. P. Snow as Anti-Historian of British Science: Revisiting the Technocratic Moment, 1959–1964," *History of Science* 43 (June 2005), pp. 187–208.

England and the Aeroplane: An Essay on a Militant and Technological Nation (Basingstoke: Macmillan, 1991).

"The Prophet Militant and Industrial: The Peculiarities of Correlli Barnett," *Twentieth Century British History* 2 (1991), pp. 360–379.

"Science and the Nation: Towards New Histories of Twentieth-Century Britain," *Historical Research* 78 (February 2005), pp. 96–112.

Science, Technology, and the British Industrial 'Decline', 1870–1970 (Cambridge University Press, 1996).

Warfare State: Britain, 1920–1970 (Cambridge University Press, 2006).

Ehrman, John, *The Rise of Neoconservatism: Intellectuals and Foreign Affairs, 1945–1994* (New Haven: Yale University Press, 1995).

English, Richard and Kenny, Michael, eds., *Rethinking British Decline* (London: Macmillan, 2000).

Ezard, John, "The Max Miller of the Lecture Circuit," *Guardian*, 18 April 1978.

Feinstein, C., "Benefits of Backwardness and Costs of Continuity," in *Government and Economies in the Post-war World: Economic Policies and Comparative Performance*, ed. Andrew Graham and Anthony Seldon (London: Routledge, 1990), pp. 275–293.

"Structural Change in the Developed Countries during the Twentieth Century," *Oxford Review of Economic Policy* 15 (1999), pp. 35–55.

Ferns, John, *F. R. Leavis* (New York: Twayne, 2000).

Fink, Janet, "Welfare, Poverty and Social Inequalities," in *A Companion to Contemporary Britain, 1939–2000*, ed. Paul Addison and Harriet Jones, pp. 263–280.

Ford, Boris, "Round and about the *Pelican Guide to English Literature*," in *The Leavises: Recollections and Impressions*, ed. Denys Thompson, pp. 103–112.

Forman, Paul, "The Primacy of Science in Modernity, of Technology in Postmodernity, and of Ideology in the History of Technology," *History and Technology* 23 (March/June 2007), pp. 1–152.

"Weimar Culture, Causality, and Quantum Theory, 1918–1927," *Historical Studies in the Physical Sciences* 3 (1971), pp. 1–116.

French, Stanley, *The History of Downing College Cambridge* (Downing College Association, 1978).

Fuller, Steve, *Thomas Kuhn: A Philosophical History for Our Times* (University of Chicago Press, 2000).

Geertz, Clifford, "Deep Play: Notes on the Balinese Cockfight," *Daedalus* 100 (Winter 1971), pp. 1–38.

The Interpretation of Cultures: Selected Essays (New York: Basic Books, 1973).

Gilman, Nils, *Mandarins of the Future: Modernization Theory in Cold War America* (Baltimore: Johns Hopkins University Press, 2003).

Goldie, Mark, "Churchill College: Origins and Contexts," unpublished paper (2001).

Gould, Stephen Jay, *The Mismeasure of Man* (New York: Norton, 1981).

Graff, Gerald, *Professing Literature: An Institutional History* (University of Chicago Press, 1987).

Green, E. H. H., *Thatcher* (London: Hodder Arnold, 2006).

Gross, Jan, *Revolution from Abroad: The Soviet Conquest of Poland's Western Ukraine and Western Belorussia* (Princeton University Press, 2002).

Guillory, John, "The Sokal Affair and the History of Criticism," *Critical Inquiry* 28 (Winter 2002), pp. 470–508.

Gunnarsson, Bo, *The Novels of William Gerhardie* (Abo Akademi University Press, 1995).

Halperin, John, *C. P. Snow: An Oral Biography, Together with a Conversation with Lady Snow (Pamela Hansford Johnson)* (New York: St. Martin's Press, 1983).

Halsey, A. H., *Decline of Donnish Dominion: The British Academic Professions in the Twentieth Century* (Oxford: Clarendon, 1992).

Harvey, A. D., "Leavis, *Ulysses*, and the Home Office," *Cambridge Review*, October 1993, pp. 123–128.

Headrick, Daniel, *Tools of Empire: Technology and European Imperialism in the Nineteenth Century* (New York: Oxford University Press, 1981).

Heyck, T. W., "The Idea of a University in Britain, 1870–1970," *History of European Ideas* 8 (1987), pp. 205–219.

The Transformation of Intellectual Life in Victorian England (New York: St. Martin's Press, 1982).

Hobsbawm, E. J., *The Age of Extremes: A History of the World, 1914–1991* (New York: Pantheon, 1994).

"Democracy Can Be Bad for You," *New Statesman*, 5 March 2001, pp. 25–27.

"From Social History to the History of Society," *Daedalus* 100 (Winter 1971), pp. 20–45.

"Growth of an Audience," *Times Literary Supplement*, 7 April 1966, p. 283.

"The Historians' Group of the Communist Party," in *Rebels and Their Causes*, ed. Maurice Cornforth, pp. 21–47.

Interesting Times: A Twentieth-Century Life (London: Allen Lane, 2002).

Hodge, Joseph Morgan, *Triumph of the Expert: Agrarian Doctrines of Development and the Legacies of British Colonialism* (Athens: Ohio University Press, 2007).

Hodgson, Godfrey, *The World Turned Right Side Up: A History of the Conservative Ascendancy in America* (Boston: Houghton Mifflin, 1996).

Hogendorn, J. S. and Scott, K. M., "The East African Groundnut Scheme: Lessons of a Large Scale Agricultural Failure," *African Economic History* (1981), pp. 81–115.

Hogg, Quintin (Baron Hailsham of St. Marylebone), *A Sparrow's Flight* (London: Collins, 1990).

Hoggart, Richard, *A Measured Life: The Times and Places of an Orphaned Intellectual* (New Brunswick: Transaction, 1994).

Hollinger, David, "The Knower and the Artificer," *American Quarterly* 39 (Spring 1987), pp. 37–55.

"Science as a Weapon in *Kulturkämpfe* in the United States During and After World War II," *Isis* 86 (September 1995), pp. 440–454.

Holroyd, Michael, "Gerhardie, William Alexander (1895–1977)," *Oxford Dictionary of National Biography* (Oxford University Press, 2004).

Iggers, Georg G., *Historiography in the Twentieth Century: From Scientific Objectivity to the Postmodern Challenge* (Hanover, NH: Wesleyan University Press, 1997).

New Directions in European Historiography (Middletown, Conn.: Wesleyan University Press, 1975).

Inglis, Fred, *Raymond Williams* (London: Routledge, 1995).

Jacobson, Dan, *Time and Time Again* (New York: Atlantic Monthly Press, 1985).

James, Clive, *May Week Was in June* (London: Cape, 1990).

Jay, Martin, *The Dialectical Imagination: A History of the Frankfurt School and the Institute of Social Research, 1923–1950* (Boston: Little, Brown, 1973).

Jenkins, Roy, *A Life at the Center: Memoirs of a Radical Reformer* (New York: Random House, 1991).

Jones, Harriet, "The Impact of the Cold War," in *A Companion to Contemporary Britain, 1939–2000*, ed. Paul Addison and Harriet Jones, pp. 23–41.

Jones, Harriet and Kandiah, Michael, eds., *The Myth of Consensus: New Views on British History, 1945–1964* (New York: St. Martin's, 1996).

Judt, Tony, *Postwar* (New York: Penguin, 2005).

Kammen, Michael, ed., *The Past Before Us: Contemporary Historical Writing in the United States* (Ithaca: Cornell University Press, 1980).

Kellner, Peter and Lord Crowther-Hunt, *The Civil Servants* (London: Macmillan, 1980).

Kenny, Michael, *The First New Left: British Intellectuals after Stalin* (London: Lawrence and Wishart, 1995).

Kermode, Frank, *Romantic Image* (London: Routledge and Paul, 1957).

Kern, Stephen, *The Culture of Time and Space, 1880–1914* (Cambridge, Mass.: Harvard University Press, 1983).

Kernan, Alvin, *In Plato's Cave* (New Haven: Yale University Press, 1999).

Kershaw, Baz, "Oh for Unruly Audiences! Or, Patterns of Participation in Twentieth-Century Theatre," *Modern Drama* 44 (Summer 2001), pp. 133–154.

Kibble, T. W. B., "Salam, Muhammad Abdus (1926–1996)," *Oxford Dictionary of National Biography* (Oxford University Press, 2004).

Kinch, M. B., Baker, William and Kimber, John, *F. R. Leavis and Q. D. Leavis: An Annotated Bibliography* (New York: Garland, 1989).

King, Desmond and Nash, Victoria, "Continuity of Ideas and the Politics of Higher Education Expansion in Britain from Robbins to Dearing," *Twentieth Century British History* 12 (2001), pp. 185–207.

Knight, Christopher J., *Uncommon Readers: Denis Donoghue, Frank Kermode, George Steiner and the Tradition of the Common Reader* (University of Toronto Press, 2003).

Koeneke, Rodney, *Empires of the Mind: I. A. Richards and Basic English in China, 1929–1979* (Stanford University Press, 2004).

Kristol, Irving, *Neoconservatism: The Autobiography of an Idea* (New York: Free Press, 1995).

Kuhn, Thomas, *The Structure of Scientific Revolutions* (University of Chicago Press, 1962).

Kynaston, David, *Austerity Britain: 1945–1951* (London: Bloomsbury, 2007).

LaCapra, Dominick, *History and Criticism* (Ithaca: Cornell University Press, 1985).

Landes, David, *The Unbound Prometheus: Technological Change and Industrial Development in Western Europe from 1750 to the Present* (Cambridge University Press, 1969).

Latour, Bruno, *Pandora's Hope: Essays on the Reality of Science Studies* (Cambridge, Mass.: Harvard University Press, 1999).

Lepenies, Wolf, *Between Literature and Science: The Rise of Sociology* (Cambridge University Press, 1988).

Litz, A. Walton, Menand, Louis and Rainey, Lawrence, eds., *The Cambridge History of Literary Criticism, Vol. 7: Modernism and the New Criticism* (Cambridge University Press, 2000).

Louis, Wm. Roger, *The Ends of British Imperialism: The Scramble for Empire, Suez, and Decolonization* (London: I. B. Tauris, 2006).

ed., *Penultimate Adventures with Britannia: Personalities, Politics, and Culture in Britain* (London: I. B. Tauris, 2008).

ed., *Yet More Adventures with Britannia: Personalities, Politics, and Culture in Britain* (London: I. B. Tauris, 2005).

Lowe, Roy, "Education," in *A Companion to Contemporary Britain, 1939–2000*, ed. Paul Addison and Harriet Jones, pp. 281–296.

MacKay, Marina, "'Doing Business with Totalitaria': British Late Modernism and the Politics of Reputation," *ELH* 73 (2006), pp. 729–753.

Modernism and World War II (Cambridge University Press, 2007).

MacKenzie, Donald, *Statistics in Britain, 1865–1930: The Social Construction of Scientific Knowledge* (Edinburgh University Press, 1981).

MacKillop, Ian, *F. R. Leavis: A Life in Criticism* (London: Allen Lane, 1995).

We Were That Cambridge: F. R. Leavis and the 'Anthropologico-Literary' Group (Austin: University of Texas, 1993).

MacKillop, Ian and Storer, Richard, eds., *F. R. Leavis: Essays and Documents* (Sheffield Academic Press, 1995).

Maclean, Alan, "Johnson, Pamela Helen Hansford [*married name* Pamela Helen Hansford Snow, Lady Snow] (1912–1981)," *Oxford Dictionary of National Biography* (Oxford University Press, 2004).

Mandler, Peter, "Against 'Englishness': English Culture and the Limits to Rural Nostalgia, 1850–1940," *Transactions of the Royal Historical Society*, 6th series, 7 (1997), pp. 155–175.

"The Consciousness of Modernity? Liberalism and the English National Character, 1870–1940," in *Meanings of Modernity: Britain from the*

Late-Victorian Era to World War II, ed. Martin Daunton and Bernhard Rieger, pp. 119–144.

The English National Character: The History of an Idea from Edmund Burke to Tony Blair (New Haven: Yale University Press, 2006).

Marr, Andrew, *A History of Modern Britain* (London: Macmillan, 2007).

Marwick, Arthur, *The Sixties: Cultural Revolution in Britain, France, Italy, and the United States, c.1958–c.1974* (Oxford University Press, 1998).

May, Derwent, *Critical Times: The History of the Times Literary Supplement* (London: Harper Collins, 2001).

McCloskey, D. N., *If You're So Smart: The Narrative of Economic Expertise* (University of Chicago Press, 1990).

McGucken, William, *Scientists, Society, and State: The Social Relations of Science Movement in Great Britain, 1931–1947* (Columbus: Ohio State University Press, 1984).

McKibbin, Ross, *Classes and Cultures: England 1918–1951* (New York: Oxford University Press, 1998).

Metzger, Linda and Straub, Deborah H., eds., "Hoff, Harry S(ummerfield)," *Contemporary Authors*, New Revision Series (Detroit: Gale, 1987), vol. XX, pp. 231–232.

Morgan, Kenneth, *The People's Peace: British History, 1945–1989* (New York: Oxford University Press, 1990).

de la Mothe, John, *C. P. Snow and the Struggle of Modernity* (Austin: University of Texas, 1992).

Mount, Ferdinand, "Ration Book," *Times Literary Supplement*, 15 June 2007, pp. 7–8.

Mulhern, Francis, *The Moment of "Scrutiny"* (London: New Left Books, 1979).

Nash, George, *The Conservative Intellectual Movement in America, since 1945* (New York: Basic Books, 1976).

Nehring, Holger, "The Growth of Social Movements," in *A Companion to Contemporary Britain, 1939–2000*, ed. Paul Addison and Harriet Jones, pp. 389–406.

Nye, Mary Jo, *Blackett: Physics, War and Politics in the Twentieth Century* (Cambridge, Mass.: Harvard University Press, 2004).

"Michael Polanyi (1891–1976)," *HYLE* 8 (2002), pp. 123–127.

Obelkevich, Jim, "New Developments in History in the 1950s and 1960s," *Contemporary British History* 14 (Winter 2000), pp. 125–142.

Olendorf, Donna, "Gerhardie, William Alexander," in *Contemporary Authors*, ed. Linda Metzger and Deborah A. Straub, New Revision Series (Detroit: Gale, 1986), vol. XVIII, pp. 179–181.

Ortner, Sherry B., ed., "The Fate of 'Culture': Geertz and Beyond," *Representations* 59 (Summer 1997).

Ortolano, Guy, " 'Decline' as a Weapon in Cultural Politics," in *Penultimate Adventures with Britannia*, ed. Wm. Roger Louis, pp. 201–214.

"Human Science or a Human Face? Social History and the 'Two Cultures' Controversy," *Journal of British Studies* 43 (October 2004), pp. 482–505.

"The Literature and the Science of 'Two Cultures' Historiography," *Studies in History and Philosophy of Science* 39 (March 2008), pp. 143–150.

"Two Cultures, One University: The Institutional Origins of the 'Two Cultures' Controversy, *Albion* 34 (Winter 2002), pp. 606–624.

Pegg, Mark Gregory, *The Corruption of Angels: The Great Inquisition of 1245–1246* (Princeton University Press, 2001).

Perkin, Harold, *Key Profession: The History of the Association of University Teachers* (New York: A. M. Kelley, 1969).

The Origins of Modern English Society, 1780–1880 (London: Routledge, 1969).

The Rise of Professional Society: England since 1880 (London: Routledge, 1989).

The Third Revolution: Professional Elites in the Modern World (London: Routledge, 1996).

Pinch, Trevor, "Scientific Controversies," in *International Encyclopedia of the Social and Behavioral Sciences*, ed. N. J. Smelser and P. B. Baltes (Oxford: Elsevier, 2001), pp. 13719–13724.

Podhoretz, Norman, *The Bloody Crossroads: Where Literature and Politics Meet* (New York: Simon and Schuster, 1986).

Breaking Ranks (New York: Harper and Row, 1979).

Ex-Friends (New York: Free Press, 1999).

Making It (New York: Random House, 1967).

Pollard, Sidney, *The Wasting of the British Economy: British Economic Policy from 1945 to the Present* (London: Croom Helm, 1982).

Porter, Roy, "The Two Cultures Revisited," *Cambridge Review*, November 1994, pp. 74–80.

Porter, Theodore, *Trust in Numbers: The Pursuit of Objectivity in Science and Public Life* (Princeton University Press, 1995).

Rabinovitz, Rubin, *The Reaction against Experiment in the English Novel, 1950–1960* (New York: Columbia University Press, 1967).

Reading, Bill, *The University in Ruins* (Cambridge, Mass.: Harvard University Press, 1996).

Rebellato, Dan, *1956 and All That: The Making of Modern British Drama* (London: Routledge, 1999).

Reynolds, David, ed., *Christ's: A Cambridge College over Five Centuries* (London: Macmillan, 2005).

Ritschel, Daniel, *The Politics of Planning: The Debate on Economic Planning in Britain in the 1930s* (Oxford: Clarendon, 1997).

Roberts, Neil, " 'Leavisite' Cambridge in the 1960s," in *F. R. Leavis: Essays and Documents*, ed. Ian MacKillop and Richard Storer, pp. 264–279.

Rothblatt, Sheldon, *The Modern University and Its Discontents: The Fate of Newman's Legacies in Britain and America* (Cambridge University Press, 1997).

Rubinstein, W. D., *Capitalism, Culture, and Economic Decline in Britain, 1750–1990* (London: Routledge, 1993).

Rüegg, W., ed. *Meeting the Challenges of the Future: A Discussion between the "Two Cultures"* (Florence: Leo S. Olschki, 2003).

Russo, John Paul, *I. A. Richards: His Life and Work* (Baltimore: Johns Hopkins University Press, 1989).

Salingar, Leo, *Cambridge Quarterly* 25 (1996), pp. 399–404.

Samson, Anne, *F. R. Leavis* (University of Toronto Press, 1992).

Sandbrook, Dominic, *Never Had It So Good: A History of Britain from Suez to the Beatles* (London: Little, Brown, 2005).
  White Heat: A History of Britain in the Swinging Sixties (London: Little, Brown, 2006).
Satia, Priya, "Developing Iraq: Britain, India, and the Redemption of Empire and Technology in the First World War," *Past and Present* 197 (November 2007), pp. 211–255.
Saunders, Frances Stonor, *Who Paid the Piper? The CIA and the Cultural Cold War* (London: Granta Books, 1999).
Schaffer, Simon, "Godly Men and Mechanical Philosophers: Souls and Spirits in Restoration Natural Philosophy," *Science in Context* 1 (1987), pp. 55–85.
Schwarz, Bill, "The End of Empire," in *A Companion to Contemporary Britain, 1939–2000*, ed. Paul Addison and Harriet Jones, pp. 482–498.
Scott, Joan W. and Keates, Debra, eds., *Schools of Thought: Twenty-Five Years of Interpretive Social Science* (Princeton University Press, 2001).
Sedgemore, Brian, *The Secret Constitution* (London: Hodder and Stoughton, 1980).
Segerstrale, Ullica, ed., *Beyond the Science Wars: The Missing Discourse about Science and Society* (Albany: SUNY Press, 2000).
Sewell, Jr., William H., "Whatever Happened to the 'Social' in Social History?" in *Schools of Thought: Twenty-Five Years of Interpretive Social Science*, ed. Joan W. Scott and Debra Keates, pp. 209–226.
Shapin, Steven, "The House of Experiment in Seventeenth-Century England," *Isis* 79 (September 1988), pp. 373–404.
  " 'The Mind Is Its Own Place': Science and Solitude in Seventeenth-Century England," *Science in Context* 4 (1990), pp. 191–218.
  A Social History of Truth: Civility and Science in Seventeenth-Century England (University of Chicago Press, 1994).
Shapin, Steven and Schaffer, Simon, *Leviathan and the Air-Pump: Hobbes, Boyle, and the Experimental Life* (Princeton University Press, 1985).
Shusterman, David, "C. P. Snow," *Dictionary of Literary Biography, Vol. 15: British Novelists, 1930–1959; Part 2: M–Z*, ed. Bernard Oldsey (Detroit: Gale, 1983), pp. 472–490.
Singh, G., *F. R. Leavis: A Literary Biography* (London: Duckworth, 1995).
Snow, Philip A., *Stranger and Brother: A Portrait of C. P. Snow* (London: Macmillan, 1982).
  A Time of Renewal: Clusters of Characters, C. P. Snow, and Coups (London: Radcliffe Press, 1998).
Spiller, Elizabeth, *Science, Reading, and Renaissance Literature: The Art of Making Knowledge, 1580–1670* (Cambridge University Press, 2004).
Steedman, Carolyn, "State-Sponsored Autobiography," in *Moments of Modernity: Reconstructing Britain, 1945–1964*, ed. Becky Conekin, Frank Mort and Chris Waters, pp. 41–54.
Steiner, George, *Language and Silence: Essays on Language, Literature, and the Inhuman* (New York: Athenaeum, 1967).
Steinfels, Peter, *The Neoconservatives: The Men Who Are Changing American Politics* (New York: Simon and Schuster, 1979).

Stone, Lawrence, *The Past and the Present Revisited* (London: Routledge, 1987).

Storer, Richard, "The After-life of Leavis," paper delivered at Loughborough University, 20 April 2002.

"*Education and the University*: Structure and Sources," in *F. R. Leavis: Essays and Documents*, ed. Ian MacKillop and Richard Storer, pp. 129–146.

"F. R. Leavis and the Idea of a University," *Cambridge Review*, November 1995, p. 98.

"Richards, Ivor Armstrong (1893–1979)," *Oxford Dictionary of National Biography* (Oxford University Press, 2004).

Supple, Barry, "Fear of Failing: Economic History and the Decline of Britain," *Economic History Review* 47 (1994), pp. 441–458.

Taylor, Miles, "The Beginnings of Modern British Social History?" *History Workshop Journal* 43 (Spring 1997), pp. 155–176.

Thomas, Keith, "The Changing Shape of Historical Interpretation," in *Penultimate Adventures with Britannia: Personalities, Politics, and Culture in Britain*, ed. Wm. Roger Louis, pp. 43–51.

Thompson, Denys, ed., *The Leavises: Recollections and Impressions* (Cambridge University Press, 1984).

Tomlinson, Jim, "Conservative Modernisation, 1960–64: Too Little, Too Late?" *Contemporary British History* 11 (Autumn 1997), pp. 18–38.

"The Decline of the Empire and the Economic 'Decline' of Britain," *Twentieth Century British History* 14 (2003), pp. 201–221.

"Economic 'Decline' in Post-war Britain," in *A Companion to Contemporary Britain, 1939–2000*, ed. Paul Addison and Harriet Jones, pp. 164–179.

"Inventing 'Decline': The Falling Behind of the British Economy in the Postwar Years," *Economic History Review* 49 (1996), pp. 731–757.

The Politics of Decline: Understanding Post-war Britain (Harlow: Longman, 2001).

Toulmin, Stephen, *Cosmopolis: The Hidden Agenda of Modernity* (New York: Free Press, 1990).

Tribe, Keith, "Bauer, Peter Thomas, Baron Bauer (1915–2002)," *Oxford Dictionary of National Biography* (Oxford University Press, 2006).

Turner, Frank Miller, *Contesting Cultural Authority: Essays in Victorian Intellectual Life* (Cambridge University Press, 1993).

"Public Science in Britain, 1880–1919," *Isis* 71 (December 1980), pp. 589–608.

Veldman, Meredith, *Fantasy, the Bomb, and the Greening of Britain: Romantic Protest, 1945–1980* (Cambridge University Press, 1994).

Vernon, James, *Hunger: A Modern History* (Cambridge, Mass.: Harvard University Press, 2007).

Wang, Zouyue, "The First World War, Academic Science, and the 'Two Cultures': Educational Reforms at the University of Cambridge," *Minerva* 33 (1995), pp. 107–127.

Warwick, Andrew, *Masters of Theory: Cambridge and the Rise of Mathematical Physics* (University of Chicago Press, 2003).

Watson, Ivar Alastair, "'The Distance Runner's Perfect Heart': Dr. Leavis in Spain," *Cambridge Review*, November 1995.

Weart, Spencer, *Scientists in Power* (Cambridge, Mass.: Harvard University Press, 1979).

Weinstein, Barbara, "Developing Inequality," *American Historical Review* 113 (February 2008), pp. 1–18.

Weintraub, Stanley, "Snow, Charles Percy, Baron Snow (1905–1980)," *Oxford Dictionary of National Biography* (Oxford University Press, 2004).

Werskey, Gary, "The Marxist Critique of Capitalist Science: A History in Three Movements?" www.human-nature.com/science-as-culture/werskey.html.

The Visible College: The Collective Biography of British Scientific Socialists of the 1930s (London: Allen Lane, 1978).

White, Paul, *Thomas Huxley: Making the "Man of Science"* (Cambridge University Press, 2003).

Wiener, Martin, *English Culture and the Decline of the Industrial Spirit, 1850–1980* (Cambridge University Press, 1981; 2nd edn., 2004).

Williams, Raymond, "Seeing a Man Running," in *The Leavises: Recollections and Impressions*, ed. Denys Thompson, pp. 113–122.

Wilson, Adrian, ed., *Rethinking Social History: English Society 1570–1920* (Manchester University Press, 1993).

Winder, Simon, *The Man Who Saved Britain: A Personal Journey into the Disturbing World of James Bond* (New York: Farrar, Straus and Giroux, 2006).

Wolin, Sheldon, *Tocqueville between Two Worlds: The Making of a Political and Theoretical Life* (Princeton University Press, 2001).

Wood, James, "Don't Mess with the Don," *Guardian*, 21 July 1995.

Wootton, David, "Liberalism," in *The Oxford Companion to Twentieth-Century British Politics*, ed. John Ramsden (Oxford University Press, 2002), pp. 380–381.

Young, Robert and Teich, Mikulas eds., *Changing Perspectives in the History of Science: Essays in Honor of Joseph Needham* (London: Heinemann Educational, 1973).

Zaidi, S. Waqar H., "Barnes Wallis and the 'Strength of England'," *Technology and Culture* 49 (2008), pp. 62–88.

RADIO BROADCASTS

Briggs, Asa, "Matters of Moment: Art and Sciences in the Schools," October 22, 1959, BBC WAC: MF "MAT," T331.

Lythgoe, M., "The New Two Cultures," 18 April 2007, BBC Radio 4.

Snow, C. P., "The Imperatives of Educational Strategy," September 8, 1959, BBC WAC: MF T491.

"Ten O'clock News," March 1, 1962, BBC Home Service, BBC WAC: Microfilm "Ten": T539–540.

DOCUMENTARIES AND FILMS

Arguing the World, dir. Joseph Dorman, First Run/Icarus Films, 1997.

Europa, Europa, dir. Agnieszka Holland, Central Cinema Company Film, 1990.

GOVERNMENT PUBLICATIONS

Higher Education: Report of the Committee Appointed by the Prime Minister under the Chairmanship of Lord Robbins, 1961–1963 (London: HMSO, 1963; cmnd. 2154).

Higher Education: Evidence, Part I, Vol. A (London: HMSO, 1963; cmnd. 2154).

Higher Education: Evidence, Part I, Vol. B (London: HMSO, 1963; cmnd. 2154).

Higher Education, Appendix Two (A): Students and Their Education (London: HMSO, 1963; cmnd. 2154–II).

Parliamentary Debates, Lords, 5th ser., vol. 293, 11 June 1968–28 June 1968.

The Scientific Civil Service: Reorganisation and Recruitment during the Reconstruction Period (London: HMSO, 1945; cmnd. 6679).

Scientific Manpower: Report of a Committee Appointed by the Lord President of the Council (London: HMSO, 1946; cmnd. 6824).

DISSERTATIONS AND THESES

de Greiff, Alexis, "The International Centre for Theoretical Physics, 1960–1979: Ideology and Practice in a United Nations Institution for Scientific Cooperation and Third World Development," PhD thesis, University of London (2001).

Gryta, Caroline Nobile, "Selected Letters of C. P. Snow: A Critical Edition," PhD thesis, Pennsylvania State University (1988).

Leavis, F. R., "The Relationship of Journalism to Literature: Studied in the Rise and Earlier Development of the Press in England," PhD thesis, University of Cambridge (1924).

Perrin, Nicola M. R., "Discovery: A Monthly Journal of Popular Knowledge," MSc thesis, University of London (1999).

Plumb, J. H., "Elections to the House of Commons in the Reign of William III," PhD thesis, University of Cambridge (1936).

Reinisch, Jessica, "The Society for Freedom in Science, 1940–1963," MSc thesis, University of London (2000).

WORLD WIDE WEB RESOURCES

Oxford Dictionary of National Biography, online edition: http://www.oxforddnb.com.

Times Literary Supplement Centenary Archive: http://www.tls.psmedia.com.

Index